Economic Anthropology and Development

Economic
Anthropology and
Development

ESSAYS ON TRIBAL
AND PEASANT ECONOMIES

GEORGE DALTON

BASIC BOOKS, INC., PUBLISHERS
New York / London

TO KARL POLANYI AND PAUL BOHANNAN

ACKNOWLEDGMENTS

When I was a student at Columbia in 1950, I learned from Karl Polanyi what a wealth of information about economies there was in the literature of anthropology and the history of pre-industrial Europe. He was extremely generous and helpful in reading drafts of the early papers I wrote. After his death in 1964, I had the good fortune to come to know his widow, Ilona, who continues to be a source of encouragement. I met Paul Bohannan in 1958 at a series of seminars Polanyi held for his colleagues and former students. He suggested to me that the systematic analysis of tribal and peasant economies was only just beginning, and that Polanyi's ideas on economy and society were an excellent starting point for economic anthropology. His confidence in the work I was doing has meant a great deal to me over the years.

Almost all the essays in this book were written since I came to Northwestern University in 1961. Irma Adelman, Robert Clower, Robert Eisner, Jonathan Hughes, Stanley Reiter, and Robert Strotz, good friends and colleagues in the Department of Economics at Northwestern, have made my work easier in various ways, as have my friends Saul Benison, Katharine Ehle, Heyward Ehrlich, Corinne Klafter, and Morton Sternberg, to all of whom I am very grateful.

Irma Adelman and Paul Bohannan have kindly allowed me to reprint essays written in collaboration with them. I am grateful also to the editors and publishers listed at the beginning of each essay for permission to reprint essays which first appeared in their journals and books. I have made minor corrections and revisions throughout, and extensive revisions in essays 1, 2, 5, and 10.

GEORGE DALTON

CONTENTS

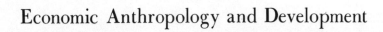

Economic Anthropology and Development

Introduction

Except for students of Melville Herskovits and Raymond Firth, I doubt that any anthropologist over thirty-five had any courses in economic anthropology in his university training. Economic anthropology is still a new subject and one whose theoretical structure is still malleable. It seems clear to me, however, that its general field of interest comprises the three sets of topics into which the essays in this book are grouped: (I) Scope and content—the subject's leading ideas and conceptual language, the kinds of questions raised and answered, and its relation to history, economics, and the other social sciences. (II) The traditional economic organization and performance of pre-colonial and pre-industrial bands, tribes, and peasantries, as economy relates to social and political organization, culture, technology, and ecology. (III) Colonial, post-colonial (and for Europe and Japan, post-feudal) change, development, and modernization.

The geographical scope of the subject is extraordinarily wide, its historical range is deep, and its analytical interests are many. The communities of interest to economic anthropology are on all the continents during all historical time periods. At one end they include the societies unearthed by archaeology and at the other today's developing areas studied by all the social sciences. Economic anthropology draws empirical information and theoretical ideas from European economic history and development, agricultural economics, and comparative economic systems.

Economic anthropology is a new, complex, and diverse subject. What I should like to impress on students—what, indeed, I hope these essays impress on them—is the enormous amount of valuable work yet to be done in all its branches. Malinowski, Firth, and Polanyi discovered gold and mined a few veins. Most of the digging remains to be done.

On the scope and content of the subject, the most useful concepts and theoretical ideas to use, we are still haggling over fundamentals. Even the elementary vocabulary of the subject, terms such as "tribal," "peasant," "economy," and "surplus," remains ambiguous. The dispute between the "formalists" and the Polanyi group (see essays 1–3) is another symptom that theory in economic anthropology is still in its infancy. No one has yet written a history of economic anthropology showing its theoretical origins, how the works of the eminent nineteenth- and early twentieth-century writers on economy and society—Marx, Weber, Durkheim, Maine, Tönnies —have shaped the theoretical approaches that have been forthcoming since Malinowski's pioneer work on the economy of the Trobriands. Nor is sufficient use made of the work of historians. From Maitland, Pirenne, and Bloch to M. I. Finley, historians have written brilliantly on early economies and societies. We are doomed to be unnecessarily original until factual knowledge about pre-industrial Europe and the analytical writings of its historians are incorporated into economic anthropology.

On the nature of aboriginal economies, we know enough theory now to be able to go back to old sources and draw from them new conclusions as Uberoi (1962) has done and I attempt to do in the essay on "Primitive Money." Little is understood about aboriginal systems of inheritance. We are only beginning to look at primitive technology and ecology in systematic fashion. We need to follow up Polanyi's work (1966) on the economic aspects of primitive state systems and on types of early external trade (1957:ch. 13; 1963). We also need more work on the nature and role of prestige sectors, particularly non-commercial primitive monies and the social transactions they enter. We are beginning to see how the pig-tusk, potlatch copper, and kula sorts of primitive money functioned indigenously as institutional devices that enabled those who acquired primitive valuables to control people and activities in communities without central government (Bohannan 1959; Douglas 1958; 1967; Polanyi 1968:essay 8; Dalton 1970). We now have something like a rudimentary theory of primitive money. It could be improved and extended by examining early literature, such as the German accounts of primitive money usage in the colonies they held on islands in the Pacific before World War I (see the bibliographies in Einzig 1948; Quiggin 1948).

On development and modernization from an anthropological perspective there is also much to be done. We have hardly gone beyond the stage of disentangling acculturation and applied anthropology from micro-development. Essays 10 and 11 in this volume give suggestions for further work.

Perhaps some indication of the future of economic anthropology can be found in the recent past. The growth of interest in the subject is not an isolated event. A growing number of economists (including some of great eminence) are now turning to unorthodox themes of political economy and society in capitalist, communist, and developing nations. John Hicks (1969) and Joan Robinson (1970), economic theorists of the highest rank, have just recently published books which range far into early economic history and anthropology. It has not always been so.

Up to 1930, *the* economy meant national industrial capitalism, the market economy of the United States, Britain, or France in the nineteenth and twentieth centuries. From David Ricardo to Maynard Keynes, these and only these were the economies economists invented economic theory to analyze. "In history, we learned of the growth and decay of economic systems; in theory, there was one set of principles that governed life on Robinson Crusoe's island, and among the mythical peasants who bartered cloth for wine, as much as in the City of London or in Chicago [Robinson 1962:79]."

From 1930 onward, when the Russians began their central planning and collectivized agriculture, the Soviet economy came into view; and a small band of American, British, and West European economists detached themselves to measure what the Russians were doing and explain to us their new organizations (not, in the early days, without grave theoretical qualms that the Russians were risking economic catastrophe in thinking they could supplant a market economy. See Hayek 1935).

With Keynes' *General Theory* of 1936 and the traumatic depression he taught us how to cure, with the success of central planning in Britain and America during World War II, with the New Deal and welfare state reforms of the 1930's and 1940's, and with the world-wide changes in economies and societies experienced since 1950, our deeply ingrained ideas about economics and economies have been changed continually. The Russians are becoming more like us. We are becoming more like the Russians. The Swedes are breaking new paths in welfare, the French in planning, and the Yugoslavians in factory organization. A dozen new communist economies (by no means uniformly organized) and sixty or more new national economies in Africa and Asia have come into being.

For two generations now, economics has been moving beyond its neoclassical preoccupation with static equilibrium at the margin, a sort of celestial mechanics which absorbed economists between the times of Darwin and Keynes. It is a painful wrench to old habits of mind to turn away from the neat precision of static equilibria to study the messy indeterminancy of a world in change—to study changing capitalist, communist, and developing economies buffeted by society, culture, politics, physical environment, and technology. But there are compensations in so doing. Some of us are learning, with Gunnar Myrdal, Everett Hagen, and J. K. Galbraith, that it is better to be vaguely useful than precisely useless; others, with Irma Adelman, that it is possible to be precise and useful at the same time.

I wrote most of the essays in this book with a double purpose in mind: to describe economic anthropology as a subject, and to draw from its literature theoretical insights into the nature of pre-industrial economies and their subsequent economic development and cultural modernization. The three essays in the first section—Economics, Anthropology, and Economic Anthropology—give an expository account of Karl Polanyi's work, and reasons why economic anthropology is best studied within the frameworks of comparative economic systems and historical time periods. These essays also sketch out a set of terms and leading ideas for the study of tribal and peasant economies, and try to resolve contentious issues concerning the applicability of conventional economics to the small economies anthropologists study.

Students new to economic anthropology have less difficulty with these matters than some of their teachers have. Those who grew up in the postcolonial period as aware of Africa and Asia as my generation was of England and France have less to unlearn—fewer preconceptions about economics and the economy. The Peace Corps prepares them to study economic anthropology rather better than Robbins' *Nature and Significance of Economic Science.*

Essays 4 through 7 in the second section—Tribal and Peasant Economies—describe the distinctive characteristics of subsistence and prestige sectors of one subset of economies of interest to anthropologists: the small agricultural communities of tribal Africa and Oceania before colonial incursion. They also describe how the early commercial and cultural impact of European incursion changed tribal economies in characteristic ways. The concluding essay, "Peasantries in Anthropology and History," shows how a study of European peasantries in historical sequence throws light on the traditional and modernizing peasantries in Asia and Latin America presently studied through field work by anthropologists.

Part III—Development and Modernization—contains two general and two specific essays on the economic and social transformation of village communities in the post-colonial context of national development, a complicated subject whose literature is now vast. "Economic Development and Social Change" surveys the subject, stressing what I believe to be the most fruitful theoretical guidelines and literature (I would now add the work of Guy Hunter [1967; 1969]). It also shows the relevance of the older concerns of economic anthropology to its newer ones of change and modernization. This essay, as well as essay 9 (on peasantries), touches on the differences between the subjects of acculturation, applied anthropology, and what I call micro-development; the first two are topic headings under which anthropologists usually consider socio-economic change.

The essay on factor analysis of 108 villages in India employs a statistical technique which allows one to use comparable empirical information drawn from a large number of village communities. It also permits one to include in the formal analysis information on several dimensions of village organization and performance—economic, technological, demographic, social, and cultural—and to express analytical conclusions in semi-quantitative form. To get at the forces generating economic development and cultural modernization, factor analysis differentiates between high- and low-performing villages by clustering characteristics most closely correlated with differential performance. It was my colleague Irma Adelman's idea that we attempt to analyze micro-development in India with a statistical technique that she and Cynthia Taft Morris used to analyze national development and modernization in seventy-four countries (Adelman and Morris 1967). We hope that the result is judged to be sufficiently promising to encourage departments of planning and statistics in Third World countries to emulate the Government of India in collecting hard data series on village communities.

"History, Politics, and Economic Development in Liberia" shows that the present structure and performance of a developing national economy is unintelligible without knowledge of historical events leading up to the present and without statistical information on national income and its composition. It also shows why development and modernization are properly subjects of inquiry for all the social sciences (as well as for history), particularly in countries like Liberia, at the very beginnings of development.

Finally, "Economic Development and Economic Anthropology" gives additional reasons why development and modernization of Third World countries requires a combined social science approach in order to understand and make policy for the several structural transformations underway. This essay, which ends the volume, also returns briefly to one of the themes of the first section: the reasons why formal economics is insufficient to analyze traditional tribal and peasant economies.

REFERENCES

ADELMAN, IRMA, and CYNTHIA TAFT MORRIS
    1967   *Society, politics, and economic development*. Baltimore: Johns Hopkins University Press.
BOHANNAN, PAUL
    1959   The impact of money on an African subsistence economy. *Journal of Economic History* 19:491–503.
DALTON, GEORGE
    1970   Currency, primitive. In *Encyclopaedia Britannica*.
DOUGLAS, MARY
    1958   Raffia cloth distribution in the Lele economy. *Africa,* 28:109–122.
    1967   Primitive rationing: a study in controlled exchange. In *Themes in economic anthropology*, R. Firth ed. London: Tavistock Publications.
EINZIG, PAUL
    1948   *Primitive money*. London: Eyre and Spottiswoode.
HAYEK, FREDERICH
    1935   *Collectivist economic planning*. London: Routledge and Kegan Paul.
HICKS, SIR JOHN
    1969   *A theory of economic history*. London: Oxford University Press.
HUNTER, GUY
    1967   *The best of both worlds*. London: Oxford University Press.
    1969   *Modernizing peasant societies*. New York: Oxford University Press.
POLANYI, KARL
    1957   The economy as instituted process. In *Trade and Market in the Early Empires*. Glencoe: The Free Press.

1963   Ports of trade in early societies. *Journal of Economic History* 23:30–45.

1966   *Dahomey and the slave trade.* Seattle: University of Washington Press.

1968   The semantics of money-uses. In *Primitive, archaic, and modern economies: essays of Karl Polanyi,* G. Dalton ed. New York: Anchor Books.

QUIGGIN, A. H.

1948   *A survey of primitive money.* London: Methuen.

ROBINSON, JOAN

1962   *Economic philosophy.* London: Watts.

1970   *Freedom and necessity.* London: Allen and Unwin.

SAHLINS, MARSHALL

1965   The sociology of primitive exchange. In *The relevance of models for social anthropology.* M. Banton ed. London: Tavistock.

UBEROI, J. P. SINGH

1962   *Politics of the kula ring.* Manchester: The University Press.

I

ECONOMICS, ANTHROPOLOGY, AND ECONOMIC ANTHROPOLOGY

The ideas which are here expressed so laboriously are extremely simple and should be obvious. The difficulty lies, not in the new ideas, but in escaping from the old ones, which ramify, for those brought up as most of us have been, into every corner of our minds.

JOHN MAYNARD KEYNES

1

Primitive, Archaic, and Modern Economies: Karl Polanyi's Contribution to Economic Anthropology and Comparative Economy[1]

It is only our Western societies that quite recently turned man into an economic animal.

MARCEL MAUSS

Karl Polanyi was a warm, generous, and committed man whose enormous range of interests spanned all the social sciences and beyond.[2] His was an original mind, although he never claimed excessive originality. In his lectures at Columbia and in print he emphasized his indebtedness to Marx, Maine, Bücher, Weber, Thurnwald, Pirenne, Menger, Malinowski, and others. His concept of "redistribution" as an integrative mode of economic organization, and much that he said about money, external trade, market places, ports of trade, operational devices, and the birth and reform of industrial capitalism, was, I believe, original with him. His forceful presentation and keen insight made us aware of economies of record in ways different from those of the distinguished writers from whom he learned much.

The qualities that made him a brilliant lecturer also made him a difficult writer. His passionate commitment and enormous learning drew large numbers of students to his lectures, several of whom made his research interests their own (Dalton 1959; Neale 1957; Pearson 1957). But what was forceful, lucid, and articulate in the lecture hall sometimes became hyper-

Reprinted, with revision, from "Primitive, Archaic, and Modern Economies: Karl Polanyi's Contribution to Economic Anthropology and Comparative Economy," in June Helm, ed., *Essays in Economic Anthropology* (Seattle: University of Washington Press, 1965). Reprinted by permission of the publisher.

11

bole and polemic in print. A friend sympathetic to his work describes Polanyi's writing style as a stiletto set in the far end of a battering ram. Aca-
demics do not always like to be lectured at in print (Rottenberg 1958;
Smelser 1959).

Polanyi's substance is also difficult. To discuss Ricardo's England, Malinowski's Trobriand Islands, and Hitler's Germany in the same book (*The
Great Transformation*) is to demand much of the reader; but to expect the
reader to follow him into Hammurabi's Babylonia, Aristotle's Greece, and
eighteenth-century Dahomey (*Trade and Market in the Early Empires*) is
to expect altogether too much.

In the very range of economies he analyzes and draws from, however,
lies one of his principal contributions: that economic anthropology becomes possible only as part of comparative economic systems. To understand what is special to the economies anthropologists deal with and what
they share with all other economies requires comparative analysis of the
kind Polanyi provides. In order for anthropologists to see what is analytically important in Trobriands economy, they must first understand the
structure of industrial capitalism (Dalton 1961; 1962); to understand the
special usage of pig tusk and cowrie money, they must first understand the
organization and usage of dollars and francs (Dalton 1965a). One reason
why theory in economic anthropology remains underdeveloped is that anthropologists have not brought to the economic branch of their subject the
same comparative grounding they bring to kinship, law, politics, and religion.

The message is reversible. The farther back one goes into European or
Asian history, the more closely do economies resemble those studied by
anthropologists (Oppenheim 1957; Sweet 1959; Goody 1963). The historians concerned with pre-industrial economies and the economists concerned
with comparative economic systems and development have much to learn
from economic anthropology. Firsthand accounts of primitive economy are
as close to a laboratory as economic historians and those concerned with
comparative economy can get (Malinowski 1921; 1922; 1935; Nadel
1942).

This should not come as a surprise. The economic historians today are
teaching us about African and Asian economic developments by pointing
out what was special to European and American development (Gerschenkron 1952; Rostow 1960). So, too, can we learn about modern communistic and welfare state economies by contrasting them with primitive,
peasant, archaic kingdoms and other pre-industrial systems. Polanyi's work
provides a corrective to one of the shortcomings in the field of comparative
economic systems: its almost exclusive concern with recent and contemporary industrial economies. The field is too narrowly confined to comparisons of industrial capitalism—the laissez faire, welfare state, and fascist
varieties—and industrial communism. The areas of fruitful comparison

can be widened. The facts and theories in economic anthropology and economic history should become part of comparative economic systems.

Any writer of consequence in the social sciences—Adam Smith, Karl Marx, J. M. Keynes—may be regarded as presenting a number of leading ideas and also an analytical system of concepts, causal analysis, and application of these to real-world processes and problems. Intelligent laymen come to know his leading ideas; the experts concentrate on his analytical system. In what follows, I shall describe Polanyi's leading ideas and the analytical system he designed to examine two broad problems that absorbed him: (1) the origin, growth, and transformation of nineteenth-century capitalism and (2) the relation of economy to society in pre-industrial systems.

LAISSEZ FAIRE CAPITALISM CONTRASTED WITH PRIMITIVE AND ARCHAIC ECONOMIES

The subject of *The Great Transformation* (1944) and "Our Obsolete Market Mentality" (1947) is the birth of laissez faire capitalism in England between 1750 and 1850 and its death in Europe and America during the 1930's and 1940's.[3] Polanyi's main concern is to show the uniqueness, historically, of uncontrolled market exchange as the integrating transactional mode of nineteenth-century national and international economy and to show why the organization and performance of market economy were socially divisive and inevitably led to extensive social control (the New Deal, the welfare state, fascism).

One of his themes is that the pursuit of material self-gain as the *institutionally enforced* incentive to participate in economic life eroded social and community life and induced protective measures throughout the nineteenth century.[4] Here Polanyi brings economic anthropology to bear to show that the attempt to create a self-regulating national market economy was a radical departure from the past.

His political economy of contrast shows that in traditional bands, tribes, and kingdoms, the institutions through which goods were produced and distributed were "embedded" in—an inseparable part of—social institutions: that the "economy" functioned as a by-product of kinship, political, and religious obligations and relationships. "We must rid ourselves of the ingrained notion that the economy is a field of experience of which human beings have necessarily always been conscious [Polanyi, Arensberg, and Pearson 1957:242]." Where markets existed, they were most frequently confined to a few produced items the sale of which did not contribute importantly to the livelihood of any but a few producers or sellers (Pirenne 1936). Markets were contained, and nowhere did they create an economy-wide network. Typically in traditional primitive and peasant economies, land and labor were allocated in accordance with kinship, political, or tribal rights and obligations, and not as commodities to be bought and sold.

In traditional economies subsistence livelihood in effect was guaranteed as a right of membership in a human community. It is the social right to receive land, labor, and products in ordinary times, and emergency support from kin, friends, leaders, and rulers, that Polanyi also meant by the "embeddedness" of economy in society. Fear of hunger—the "economic whip" of nineteenth-century capitalism (Carr 1951)—and the quest for material self-gain were not structured as incentives to participate in economic activity.[5] In short, Polanyi analyzes the institutional substance underlying Tönnies' point that primitive and archaic societies are *Gemeinschaften* rather than *Gesellschaften* and Maine's point that they are organized by status rather than contract. ". . . ranging over human societies we find hunger and gain not appealed to as incentives for production [Polanyi 1947:112]."

Table 1–1   *Modes of Transaction*

Transactional Mode	Reciprocity	Redistribution	Market Exchange
Underlying social relationship which is expressed by the transaction	Friendship, Kinship, Master/Client	Political or Religious Affiliation	None

Political, religious, and familial organizations arrange production and distribution in various ways (Sahlins 1965), but the specific institutions express variants of two broad transactional modes ("patterns of integration") that Polanyi called reciprocity (obligatory gift-giving between kin and friends) and redistribution (obligatory payments to central political or religious authority which uses the receipts for its own maintenance, to provide community services, and as an emergency stock in case of individual or community disaster).[6] Reciprocity and redistribution are best regarded as socio-economic transactional modes because they describe internal and external appropriations, allocations, exchanges and movements of goods, employment of craft services and ordinary labor, and the control and use of land—induced by specific social relationships and obligation. Market exchange transactions differ because they are not expressions of social relationships, which therefore makes them seem especially "economic" (Table 1–1).

Polanyi used economic anthropology and early economic history to jar us loose from ideas and generalizations about man and society implanted by the Industrial Revolution. (Classical economics and the ideology of laissez faire, as well as Marxian socialism, came out of the English Industrial Revolution [Keynes 1926]. He was particularly concerned to dislodge the notion—so widely and implicitly held—that markets are the ubiquitous and invariable form of economic organization and that any economy can be *translated* into market terms (Goodfellow 1939; Rottenberg 1958), and the further notion that economic organization in some strict sense determines social organization and culture. These he regarded as wrong generalizations from the one very special case of laissez faire capitalism for which they are true. He argued that these generalizations must be disproved and disbelieved if we are ever to make industrial technology serve the needs of human community (Fromm 1955) and, indeed, if we are to understand the nature of economic organization in early and primitive economies.

Man does not have an innate propensity to truck, barter, and exchange, if by this is meant to buy and sell:

> . . . Adam Smith's suggestions about the economic psychology of early man were as false as Rousseau's were on the political psychology of the savage. Division of labor, a phenomenon as old as society, springs from differences inherent in the facts of sex, geography, and individual endowment; and the alleged propensity of man to barter, truck, and exchange is almost entirely apocryphal [Polanyi 1944:44].

There is a semantic difficulty here. All communities institutionalize exchanges of material items and services and make systematic the allocation of rights to land and other natural resources (there are no Robinson Crusoe economies). But it is not a commercial gene that makes it so. Rather it is the need for all communities—whatever their size and technology—to organize material life so as to assure the sustained, repetitive provision of food, shelter, and the items necessary for community life. (This is what Polanyi meant by the "substantive" definition of economic, universally applicable to all societies.)

Exchanges, allocations, transfers, and appropriations of resources, labor, produce, and services occur in all economies not only because of the need to structure material provision but also because division of labor, if only according to sex and age, is universal, which itself necessitates "exchanges" of some sort. That one finds "exchanges" in U.S., Soviet, and Trobriands economy does not tell us very much: it is how resources are directed to specific uses, how production is organized, and how goods are disposed of—in short, how the economy is instituted—that gives us insight into similarities and differences among U.S., Soviet, and Trobriands economy.

Polanyi's use of economic anthropology and early economic history forces us to unlearn the simplistic notion of the economic determination of history and social change, so widely shared by the Left and the Right (Hayek 1944). "The market mechanism . . . created the delusion of economic determinism as a general law for all human society [Polanyi 1947:114]."

With regard to the primacy of economy in social structure, Polanyi argues that Marx was right for laissez faire industrial capitalism.

> A market economy can only exist in a market society . . . a market economy must comprise all the elements of industry, including labor, land, and money. . . . But labor and land are no other than the human beings themselves of which every society consists and the natural surroundings in which it exists. To include them in the market mechanism means to subordinate the substance of society itself to the laws of the market [Polanyi 1944:71].

But Marx was wrong in generalizing economic determination of social organization to early and primitive societies.[7] Indeed, the lesson of economic anthropology is the inextricable fusion of economic with social organization and culture in primitive societies. Kinship, tribal affiliation, political rule, and religious obligation permeate material transactions in those bands, tribes, and peasantries where market dependence is absent. Economy does not determine society; society does not determine economy. They are mutually dependent.

> The exchanges of archaic societies which he [Mauss] examines are total social movements or activities. They are at the same time economic, juridical, moral, aesthetic, religious, mythological, and socio-morphological phenomena. Their meaning can therefore only be grasped if they are viewed as a complex concrete reality [Evans-Pritchard 1954:vii].

Hayek's *Road to Serfdom* may be taken as a forward extrapolation of economic determinism. Published in the same year as Polanyi's *The Great Transformation,* it argues exactly that thesis which Polanyi's work was designed to disprove: that departures from the self-regulating market system must erode political democracy and personal freedom; that Hitler's Germany was the inevitable consequence of governmental regulation of the economy.[8]

THE SOCIAL CONSEQUENCES
OF THE INDUSTRIAL REVOLUTION

Polanyi's views on the social and cultural consequences of uncontrolled industrial capitalism in Great Britain during the first half of the nineteenth century (Polanyi 1944; 1947) are relevant to three issues: (1) the debate between the radical and the conservative economic historians who interpret in different ways the "impact" of early British industrial capitalism on the working classes; (2) the reasons for the growth of market controls and governmental regulation especially after 1860, culminating in the radical departures from the system in the 1930's and 1940's; (3) the present concern with social and cultural consequences of economic development in the former colonies in Africa and Asia.

From Toynbee's *Lectures on the Industrial Revolution in England* (1884) to Carr's *The New Society* (1951), radical writers have pictured the early phase of the Industrial Revolution in England in terms of misery and degradation heaped upon the mass of the populace. Conservative writers have challenged this view (Hayek 1954) by arguing two points: that even during the early period the real income of a substantial portion of the industrial labor force was rising (displaced handicraft workers and others in rural areas whose real income had fallen); and that the evil conditions, misery, and harshness of life depicted were vastly exaggerated because the radical writers had nostalgic and fanciful notions about the attractions of rural life in agricultural villages—Merrie England; also because harsh conditions of urban and rural working-class life which had long gone unremarked received publicity for the first time. They were made to appear as new consequences of the factory system due to a heightened sociological awareness. In brief, the growth of cities and factory employment exposed conditions of life which long had remained nasty and unnoticed.

Polanyi argues that the conservative position misses the point. Here, again, anthropological and historical comparisons are brought to bear. Rising real income for a portion of the working class no more mitigated the social and cultural consequences of the Industrial Revolution than a higher real income for slaves in the southern United States mitigated the social and cultural catastrophe of their forced migration from Africa. It is the tenacity of nineteenth-century materialism which makes some economic historians still regard real income as the sole criterion of "welfare." [9] It was the fabric of personal and community life that was torn by the industrial factory system and by reliance for livelihood on uncontrolled labor, land, and product markets. In Polanyi's terms it was socially divisive to make the fear of hunger and the quest for profits the *socially enforced* incentives to participate in economic activity. To make livelihood depend on the uncertain sale of labor, and profits the necessary condition for entrepreneurial survival, was to divorce economy from the expression of social relationships and social obligations.

> The general diffusion of manufactures throughout a country generates a new character in its inhabitants; and as this character is formed upon a principle quite unfavourable to individual or general happiness, it will produce the most lamentable and permanent evils, unless its tendency be counteracted by legislative interference and direction.
>   . . . the governing principle of trade, manufactures, and commerce is immediate pecuniary gain, to which on the great scale every other is made to give way [Owen 1815:121, 123].

Although real income for many industrial workers may have risen, material insecurity had also increased, because of the threat of industrial unemployment and the absence of subsistence guarantees for the unfortunate which characterize rural societies in which kinship and village ties remain in force (Arensberg 1937).

With his anthropological base, Polanyi was quick to see the similarity between the social consequences of the English Industrial Revolution and the disintegration of traditional societies when forced to change by colonial domination. *The Great Transformation* has things to say to those presently concerned with the social and cultural implications of economic and technological change in developing areas (Dalton 1964).

> Not economic exploitation, as often assumed, but the disintegration of the cultural environment of the victim is then the cause of degradation. The economic process may, naturally, supply the vehicle of destruction, and almost invariably economic inferiority will make the weaker yield, but the immediate cause of his undoing is not for that reason economic; it lies in the lethal injury to the institutions in which his social existence is embedded. The result is loss of self-respect and standards, whether the unit is a people or a class, whether the process springs from so-called "culture conflict" or from a change in the position of a class within the confines of a society [Polanyi 1944:157; see also 290–294]. . . .
>
> But if the organized states of Europe could protect themselves against the backwash of international free trade, the politically unorganized colonial peoples could not. The revolt against imperialism was mainly an attempt on the part of exotic peoples to achieve the political status necessary to shelter themselves from the social dislocations caused by European trade policies. The protection that the white man could easily secure for himself through the sovereign status of his communities was out of reach of the colored man as long as he lacked the prerequisite, political government [Polanyi 1944:182–183].

HUMANISTIC REFORM: SOCIALLY CONTROLLED INDUSTRIAL ECONOMIES

There are two main streams of modern socialism—Marxism and Democratic Socialism—and one small tributary, utopian socialism (such as Owen, Fourier, kibbutzim). All socialisms have two features in common. They are reactions against laissez faire industrial capitalism, movements and doctrines of criticism and protest. They are also movements of reform, blueprints for improvement, models claiming superiority over capitalism. And in their reforms, blueprints, and claims for superiority are interwoven two themes: the need for higher income and material security widely diffused, and something much different, the need to create a new society in which industrial technology and economic organization are made subordinate to the needs of human community—the economy to be embedded in society.[10] The idea of a new society expresses the ethical aspiration of socialisms: the family writ large, social communion and social responsibility expressed in everyday economic activities. Although the idea is part of all socialisms, its clearest example was the small-scale, face-to-face utopian communities created in the nineteenth and twentieth centuries (Dalton 1959; Bestor 1950; Bishop 1950; Noyes 1870; Spiro 1956).

The tragedy of contemporary socialism is that only the first theme is being realized. Both the welfare state and Soviet Communism are creating higher incomes and material security widely diffused. This is all to the good. But neither recognizes the need to create new social policy so that industrial technology is deliberately organized to express social relationships and ethical norms. Affluence and material security, lamentably, are compatible with materialism and individualism.[11] "I plead for the restoration of that unity of motives which should inform man in his everyday activity as a producer, for the reabsorption of the economic system in society, for the creative adaptation of our ways of life to an industrial environment [Polanyi 1947:115–116]."

Polanyi phrased these matters as "the place of economy in society." One could state some of his principal themes in these terms: typically, primitive and archaic economies were of small scale, with simple technology, and organized as an inseparable part of political and kinship structure.[12] The economy was socially controlled in the sense that resource and labor allocation, the organization of work within production processes, and the disposition of produce were expressions of kinship or political obligation or some other social relationships (Dalton 1964; Neale 1957). (In economies where reciprocity and redistribution are the dominant transactional modes, it is impossible to analyze economic transactions apart from the kinship, political, and religious institutions of which they form an inextricable part.[13] Therefore analysis of traditional band, tribal, peasant, and archaic economies is socio-economic or institutional analysis—political economy rather than economics.)

In England, the Industrial Revolution followed the expansion of commercial agriculture (through enclosures and the application of improved technology) and the expansion of external commercial trade with the New World and exotic continents (like Africa). The expansion of agricultural capitalism and foreign trade capitalism preceded industrial capitalism. So, too, did mercantilism, the extension of market controls to the entire nation-state.

The Industrial Revolution was also an institutional revolution. A condition for the profitable use of expensive, long-lasting machinery was that entrepreneurs be assured of uninterrupted supplies of labor and other resource inputs to work the machines as well as internal and external markets to effectively demand the outputs of the machines (Polanyi 1944:74–75). Laissez faire national capitalism was created in response to the needs of machine technology. By acts of government, national labor, land, and other resource markets were decontrolled, and financial markets (money and capital markets) were created or enlarged.

In Polanyi's terms, the institutional structure of laissez faire industrial capitalism separated out economy from society and polity by turning labor, land, and other natural resources into commodities—organizing their supply as though they were items produced for sale—and by allowing the price mechanism, working through interdependent national and international markets, to determine their allocation and the incomes of their owners. One consequence of this great institutional transformation was that classical and then neoclassical economics could be created: the analysis of this separate and autonomous sphere of uncontrolled resource and product market networks. With Adam Smith, political economy ended; with David Ricardo, economics began.

One of Polanyi's most perceptive and telling arguments concerning the social divisiveness of uncontrolled market economy emphasizes the spontaneity with which social control of labor, land, money, and some product markets was imposed in England and the Continent, especially after 1860 (Polanyi 1944:chapters 11, 12, 13). Not only were similar controls in different countries instituted to protect workers, farmers, businessmen, but the sponsors and supporters of the market controls varied radically in politics and ideology. "When men who think differently behave alike, is it not probable that they are both responding to forces that are stronger than their conscious beliefs? [Lippmann 1949:35]."

It was not only the stability or amount of specific groups that was protected, but community life also was protected, in response to conditions created by *industrialism* and *urbanism,* as well as uncontrolled markets. Governmental intervention was not solely in the form of protective tariffs but also in the form of laws prohibiting child labor, safety requirements for hazardous occupations, zoning laws, building codes, industrial accident insurance, and so on.[14]

> It is manifestly impracticable to separate the humane, the political, the economic, and the religious objectives of these interventions.
> . . . The one common characteristic is the consistent readiness of interested groups to use the state for collective ends [Brebner 1952:509; see also Robinson 1954].

Most of *The Great Transformation* is devoted to a detailed analysis of what Polanyi calls the double movement in the nineteenth century: the growth of free market transactions of produced goods throughout the world while market controls were imposed in Europe—and later America, on transactions of labor, land, and money in response to elementary needs of community stability, cohesion, and security. His analysis of unions and factory acts, agricultural tariffs, and central banking as devices to prevent free market forces from allocating labor and other factor resources in accordance with the model of pure competition is illuminating. So, too, is his analysis of the crises of the 1920's and 1930's in which German fascism and the American New Deal transformed market economies which failed to function. "In order to comprehend German fascism we must revert to Ricardian England [Polanyi 1944:30]."

The ideology of laissez faire outlived the structural reforms which changed uncontrolled market economy. Indeed, the discrepancy between what some think we ought to do—laissez faire—and what we in fact are doing—creating a welfare state—has not yet entirely disappeared in the United States. Balanced budgets and the gold standard are not yet regarded as costly anachronisms, even by all economists.

In Polanyi's terms, the welfare state is a movement toward "re-embedding" economy in society by controlling markets, assuring a minimum level of income to all as a matter of political right, and enlarging the redistributive sphere of the economy by allocating medical and some other important services on non-market criteria. (The Soviet system represents the first example of an industrial economy in which redistribution, as the dominant transactional mode, has displaced market exchange.)

THE REALITY OF SOCIETY

> But he who is unable to live in society, or who has no need, because he is
> sufficient for himself, must be either a beast or a god. . . .
>
> ARISTOTLE

Keynes' *General Theory* and Galbraith's *Affluent Society* contain a theme that Polanyi returned to repeatedly: that deeply ingrained beliefs about man, society, and economy, fashioned in the very special setting of early industrial capitalism, inhibit understanding and further reform of the changed economy of the present day. This is the theme of Polanyi's "Our Obsolete Market Mentality." But Polanyi goes further. He asserts that the conventional wisdom about economy and society we inherit from nineteenth-century capitalism and economic theory is also a barrier to the analysis of traditional band, tribal, and peasant economies studied by anthropologists and historians. Economic anthropology still suffers from the inability of anthropologists to perceive tribal economies in ways different from those instilled by Marshallian market theory and Marxian analysis. But the grand theoretical scheme of conventional economics created from David Ricardo to Maynard Keynes was designed to analyze national industrial capitalism of Western Europe and the United States. Marxian economics, the other grand theoretical scheme, was designed also to analyze the very same set of capitalist economies. (Until recently, when the underdeveloped world of tribal and peasant economies became a subject of analytical interest, we perceived all economies through one or the other of these theoretical frameworks. Rostow, Gerschenkron, Hagen, Lewis, Myrdal, and others are now creating a political economy of development, one by-product of which is to point up how very special were the economies and societies of nineteenth-century Europe and America.)

It is not with the success or failure of conventional or Marxian economic theory to analyze industrial capitalism that Polanyi takes issue, but rather with the leading ideas associated with these analytical systems—ideas that have become fossilized, as it were, as permanent and universal truths. The pursuit of material gain compelled by laissez faire market rules is still not seen as behavior forced on people as the only way to earn livelihood in a market system, but as an expression of their inner being; individualism is regarded as a norm, and society remains invisible as a cluster of individual persons who happen to live together without responsibility for anyone other than kin; economic improvement is assumed to be more important than any social dislocations that accompany it; *man* is seen as a utilitarian atom having an innate propensity to truck, barter, and exchange; material maximization and the primacy of material self-interest are assumed to be constants in all human societies.

> The general conception which Bentham had is one that is widely prevalent today. . . . The bulk of orthodox economic theory . . . rests upon a conception of *human nature* which is not very different from that which Jeremy Bentham drew up in such formal shape [Mitchell 1935:92, italics added].

> The elements of scarcity and choice, which are the outstanding factors in human experience that give economic science its reason for being, rest *psychologically* on firm ground. . . . Our primary concern in these pages is to understand the cross-cultural implications of the process of economizing [Herskovits 1952:3, 4, italics added].

> The aim of this book is to show that the concepts of economic theory must be taken as having universal validity. . . . The proposition that there should be more than one body of economic theory is absurd. If modern economic analysis with its instrumental concepts cannot cope equally with the Aborigine and with the Londoner, not only economic theory but the whole of the social sciences may be considerably discredited . . . if [economic theory] does not apply to the whole of humanity then it is meaningless [Goodfellow 1939:3, 4, 5].

But this makes conventional economic theory into a Holy Ghost: everywhere present but often unseen. It is gross ethnocentrism to assume that the monk, the feudal lord, the Inca priest-king, the commissar, and the Trobriander are directed in their material lives to abide by the same market rules that drive the London stockbroker and the Iowa wheat farmer.

The powerful engine of nineteenth-century industrial capitalism and the powerful theoretical analysis by economists of its market structure and performance so permeate our thinking as to make it extremely difficult for us to understand economies markedly different from our own. The leading ideas of economics improve our vision of our own economy, but become blinders when we look at primitive and archaic economies—economies which are neither industrialized nor organized by networks of market exchange. The differences between primitive and archaic economies and our own have been pointed to by many before Polanyi (and since). Maine's differentiation between status and contract societies, and Tönnies' between *Gemeinschaft* and *Gesellshaft,* underscore a fundamental distinction of the same sort that Polanyi makes in contrasting national market economies with the organic fusion of society and economy in traditional primitive communities. Indeed, the same point has been stated succinctly by anthropologists and economists recently.

> In primitive communities, the individual as an economic factor is personalized, not anonymous. He tends to hold his economic position in virtue of his social position. Hence to displace him economically means a social disturbance [Firth 1951:137].

> . . . the economist who studies the non-market economy has to abandon most of what he has learnt, and adopts the techniques of the anthropologist [Lewis 1962:vii].

Polanyi's work gives us more than an occasional insight into the organization of exotic economies. He attempts to create a system of analysis designed to show how social organization institutes labor, land, product, and service transactions in primitive and archaic economies. He created a theory of social and economic organization for economies without market integration which gives us new insights into a large number of societies studied by anthropologists and historians. His special concern was the way in which economy relates to social organization and culture. It is a strength of Polanyi's analyses that the concepts he uses—reciprocity, redistribution, administered trade, gift-trade, special-purpose money, ports of trade—are at the same time social and economic categories. "[We do not yet have] . . . those conceptual tools required to penetrate the maze of social relationships in which economy was embedded. This is the task of what we will here call institutional analysis [Polanyi, Arensberg, and Pearson 1957:242]."

The insights gained from examining exotic economies in systematic fashion are of more than antiquarian interest. Polanyi's analysis of the redistributive sphere of eighteenth-century Dahomey confers a perspective of use in understanding the redistributive spheres of Soviet Russia and welfare state Sweden. To see the exact ways in which economy is embedded in Trobriands society helps us understand those specific features of nineteenth-century industrial capitalism that Robert Owen and other socialists were reacting against in trying to create similarly embedded economies.

Several times Polanyi uses the phrase "the reality of society," by which he means the opposite of "man as a utilitarian atom." Rather, man is a social being whose arrangements for the production and distribution of goods in many societies are an indistinguishable part of congruent arrangements for family, political, and religious life. This leading idea—an idea abundantly illustrated by economic anthropology—should make us view our continuing departure from the model of laissez faire capitalism as an unremarkable occurrence. When contrasted with earlier and later economies, laissez faire capitalism can be seen to be a unique and transitory event. The attempt to approximate an automatically functioning economy whose autonomous market rules required the fracturing of community cohesion created an engine for material abundance at the expense of personal security and community protection. It was the "atomistic individualism" and the social disunity and insecurity engendered by the laissez faire rules of the game that Polanyi pointed up. That controlled markets are an efficient allocative mechanism (compared to any known alternative) is not in doubt, as is shown by the experience of Western Europe and the United States since World War II and by the continual enlargement of the controlled market sphere in the communist economies since the mid-1950's.

> . . . the end of [laissez faire] market society means in no way the absence of markets. These continue, in various fashions, to ensure the freedom of the consumer, to indicate the shifting of demand, to influence producers' income, and to serve as an instrument of accountancy, while ceasing altogether to be an organ of economic self-regulation [Polanyi 1944:252].

Those reforms of laissez faire capitalism that we call the welfare state are designed primarily to strengthen the economic performance of capitalism (to create full employment and higher growth rates) and, at the same time, to control markets by political decisions and politically decided compensators where the results of laissez faire were squalor, material insecurity, and abject poverty. Polanyi is not alone in applying insights from early and simple communities to reforms of our own day.

> Hence we should return to the old and elemental. Once again we shall discover those motives of action still remembered by many societies and classes: the joy of giving in public, the delight in generous artistic expenditure, the pleasure of hospitality in the public or private feast. Social insurance, solicitude in mutuality or co-operation, in the professional group and all those moral persons called Friendly Societies, are better than the mere personal security guaranteed by the nobleman to his tenant, better than the mean life afforded by the daily wage handed out by managements, and better even than the uncertainty of capitalist savings [Mauss 1954:67].

THE ECONOMY AS INSTITUTED PROCESS

In English, we used the word "economic" to mean "material" and also to mean "economizing." Polanyi's conceptual scheme insists on keeping these meanings separate. All societies must have some sort of economic organization in the first sense—structured arrangements for providing material goods and services—but whether or not the arrangements resemble the economizing rules of market exchange is a matter for empirical investigation. It is a further indicator of the deep penetration of the market model into our modes of thinking that the issue is a point of theoretical contention. We seem to accept readily the idea that people in Africa and New Guinea can have markedly different religious, political, and marriage arrangements from our own—but somehow not economic arrangements.

> Does this economistic postulate allow us to infer the generality of a market system in the realms of empirical fact? The claim of formal economics to an historically universal applicability answers in the affirmative. In effect this argues the virtual presence of a market system in every society, whether such a system is empirically present or not. All human economy might then be regarded as a potential supply-demand price mechanism, and the actual processes, whatever they are, explained in terms of this hypostatization [Polanyi 1957:240].

What some economists, anthropologists, and historians assume is either the universal presence of market institutions or the presence of functional equivalents which compel the same economizing actions as a market system, because it is further assumed that "scarcity" in the economist's sense is universally present. These writers simply translate whatever primitive and archaic economic institutions and activities they find into market terms (Rottenberg 1958; French 1964).

One may perhaps restate Polanyi's distinction between the "substantive" and "formal" definitions of "economic" in the following way: every society studied by anthropologists, historians, and economists has an economy of some sort because personal and community life require the structured provision of material goods and services. This is a minimal definition of economy which calls attention to similarities among economies otherwise as different as those of the Trobriand Islands, an Israeli kibbutz, a twelfth-century feudal manor, nineteenth-century Britain, and the present-day economy of the Soviet Union. These very different economies also have in common that they make use of natural resources, technology, division of labor—and, frequently, practices such as external trade with foreigners, the use of markets, and some form of money. But the specific institutionalization of these may vary radically among economies. Polanyi's substantive definition of "economy," "money," and "external trade" points up what is generally true for all economies regardless of size, technology, and so forth and what features money and external trade have in common regardless of which economy one examines. His formal definition relates to the special case of economy, money, foreign trade, as these are organized in a national economy integrated by market exchange.

If we are to investigate in systematic fashion the large number of economies without machines and markets studied by anthropologists and historians, we need a conceptual approach that does not commit us to the view that whatever we find may be regarded merely as some minor variant of our own market system. In a word, we have to approach pre-industrial economies in the same way that anthropologists approach religions and polities different from our own.

> . . . most anthropologists have ceased to take their bearings in the study of religion from any religion practiced in their own society [Lienhardt 1956:310].

> One important discovery made in . . . [*African Political Systems*] was that the institutions through which a society organized politically need not necessarily look like the kinds of political institutions with which we have long been familiar in the Western world, and in the great nations of Asia [Gluckman and Cunnison 1962:vi].

And so, too, for economies:

> . . . the anthropologist, the sociologist, or the historian each in his study of the place occupied by the economy in human society, was faced with a great variety of institutions other than markets, in which man's livelihood was embedded. Its problems could not be attacked with the help of an analytical method devised for a special form of the economy, which was dependent upon the presence of specific market elements [Polanyi 1957:245].

RECIPROCITY, REDISTRIBUTION, AND [MARKET] EXCHANGE: DOMINANCE AND INTEGRATION

In our own economy, market exchange is the *dominant* transactional mode because basic resources which enter many lines of production— labor and land—are organized for market sale, and most people depend on market sale as their primary source of income. Indeed, the income categories conventionally used to analyze our economy are chosen to indicate what item or service is being sold to provide the income: wage and salary, rent, interest, profits. Note that market exchange is the transactional mode used not only in the final disposition of products (such as the retailing of cars to final users) but also in production processes, because natural resources, machinery, and labor are also transacted through purchase at market price stated in money.

Market exchange *integrates* capitalist economy in a strictly economic sense. Labor and natural resources are brought together, moved, allocated to specific lines of production in response to profitability as measured by money cost and money price. The integrative function of markets remains basic to that reformed variety of capitalism we call the welfare state. What has changed is the extent of autonomy we allow to market forces alone.

Conventional economic theory—price, distribution, aggregate income, and growth theory—selectively analyzes those features of industrial capitalism that are relatively independent of kinship, politics, religion, and other aspects of society and culture. The same economic analysis is used in the United States, Sweden, Germany, and Japan. This systematic exclusion from their analyses of what economists call institutions does not mean that kinship, religion, and the like do not have economic consequences. A Japanese factory is different from an American factory in interesting ways attributable to cultural differences. But industrial sociologists, not economists, study such matters. The structural facts of market integration, the use of similar monetary systems, and machine technology allow economists to analyze an important range of matters—prices, incomes, growth, international trade, and so on—without reference to those many cultural matters that differentiate Sweden from Japan from the United States.

Not all transactions in capitalist economy are market exchanges. Following Polanyi, let us call those payments to and disbursements by central political authority "redistributive" transactions. Immediately a social dimension appears which is absent in market exchange transactions. Redistributive payments to government are an expression of politically defined obligation, and redistributive disbursements by government are determined by political decision. A third transactional mode is what Polanyi calls "reciprocity," a general category of socially obligatory gift-giving. Perhaps it is correct to say that in welfare state capitalist economies of the present day reciprocal and redistributive transactions are in some degree socially "integrative." Gift-giving is simply a material expression of those socially cohesive relationships that we call friendship and kinship. With us, however, the quantitative importance of gift-giving is small, and our prime sources of livelihood are not connected with gift receipts.

Polanyi's categories of reciprocity, redistribution, and market exchange and his analytical distinctions between kinds of money, markets, and foreign trade permit us to describe our own economy so as to make its important aspects directly comparable with economies studied by anthropologists and historians, thereby allowing a systematic comparison of similarities and differences using our own economy as a base. They enable us, moreover, to analyze the structural features of pre-industrial economies without perceiving them through the theoretical spectacles designed for our own economy. The value of the approach is shown, I believe, by what it is possible to say about forms of money, external trade, and markets in traditional bands, tribal, peasant, and archaic economies and by what one can point out about the structured relationships between economic, political, religious, and kinship and organization in all societies.

MONEY, EXTERNAL TRADE, AND MARKETS IN PRIMITIVE AND ARCHAIC ECONOMIES

When we say that market exchange is the dominant and integrative transactional mode (but not the exclusive mode) of modern capitalism, we are using the category of "market exchange" in a broad sense. For their purposes of analyzing price determination, economists differentiate between many types of market exchange (pure competition, oligopoly). So, too, with reciprocity and redistribution as broad categories to describe primitive and archaic economies. There are many varieties of socially obligatory gift and counter-gift-giving and of obligatory payments to central political and religious authority. Moreover, as with our own economy, more than one transactional mode typically is present in any traditional economy.

In the same sense that we can say that market exchange integrates capitalist economy, we can also say that reciprocity and redistribution integrate primitive and archaic economies: they are the transactional modes through which resource allocation, work organization, and product disposition are arranged. But one can go further here and say that reciprocity and redistribution are *socially* integrative, as well, and indicate in specific fashion for economies such as the Trobriands where exactly its *Gemeinschaft* aspects are located that link the economic to the social.

> . . . *the whole tribal life is permeated by a constant give and take;* that every ceremony, every legal and customary act is done to the accompaniment of material gift and counter-gift; that wealth, given and taken, is one of the main instruments of social organization, of the power of the chief, of the bonds of kinship, and of relationships is law [Malinowski 1922:167].

In primitive and archaic economies foreign trade, money, and markets are organized in ways different from those we are so familiar with in capitalism. (Even without further examination, one may say that the use of foreign trade, money, and markets in the Soviet economy indicates that devices and practices familiar to capitalism can be incorporated within economies differently organized.) As always, there are similarities and differences in the organization and functioning of, say, foreign trade, in the U.S.S.R. and the United States. But note that the differences are surface expressions of more fundamental differences in economic organization.

Anthropological and historical literature indicate that many kinds of external trade, money usages, and market places existed in primitive and archaic economies: kula gift trade, silent trade, slave trade, the use of cows to make status payments (bridewealth, bloodwealth), petty markets in ninth-century Europe, are a few among hundreds of ascertained practices. Polanyi's schema attempts to make analytical sense of these by suggesting that foreign trade, money, and markets took only a few characteristic organizational forms in these traditional economies, depending on which of the transactional modes ("patterns of integration") dominated.

ECONOMIC ANTHROPOLOGY AND COMPARATIVE ECONOMY

In *The Great Transformation* (chapter 4) and "Our Obsolete Market Mentality," Polanyi touched briefly on the economic organization of tribal and archaic economies simply to provide a contrast to nineteenth-century European market economy, which was his main concern. In his later writings (1957; 1960; 1963; 1964; 1966) he created a conceptual framework with which to analyze primitive and archaic economies. This system of socio-economic analysis is of interest to the subjects of economic anthropology, economic history, the history of economic thought,[15] and comparative economic systems.

Rather than give a more detailed account of his work on transactional modes, special-purpose money, external trade, ports of trade, markets, and operational devices, I shall indicate the kinds of questions and problems to which Polanyi's conceptual framework is designed to apply.

ECONOMIC ANTHROPOLOGY

One of the peculiarities of economic anthropology is that neither the facts nor the folk views of primitive economic life are in doubt. The ethnographic record is large and detailed. What is in doubt is the most useful theoretical approach to interpret analytically the many descriptive accounts and the most fruitful concepts to use in order to make statements of importance about economic life in band, tribal, and peasant [16] communities. The theoretical disputes seem to be various expressions of one unsettled problem: Should anthropologists use concepts and categories drawn from conventional economic theory and our own economy, or are special categories of analysis necessary? This question will remain unsettled as long as the similarities and the differences between industrial capitalism and band, tribal, and primitive economies are insufficiently described.

Polanyi believed the differences between traditional economies and industrial capitalism were more important than the similarities, and so he contrived conceptual categories to delineate these structural differences. To indicate why some of us find his approach useful requires some preliminary remarks about different approaches to economic anthropology.

A disturbing feature of anthropology is that some practitioners display a sort of nervous inferiority toward physical science and economics. Perhaps it is because more laymen can understand a book on anthropology than a book on physics or economics that some anthropologists seem to feel naked before their mathematically padded colleagues (Berliner 1962). They grab for fig leaves by using what they regard as scientific words, such as "hypothesis" or "behavior"—as though "behavior" meant something more than what people do. Others, believing that science is concerned exclusively with universal laws of Parsonian generality—and above all wanting to be scientists—search for similarities between traditional and modern societies, even where differences provide greater insight into social structure and process.

One way anthropologists think they find similarities between primitive economies and our own is by translating primitive economy into the categories of industrial capitalism and conventional economic theory. By describing the potlatch as an investment yielding 100 percent interest, and bridewealth as the price one pays for sexual and domestic services, primitive economies inevitably are made to appear merely as simpler and bizarre versions of our own—capitalism writ small (Pospisil 1963). But if it is true that the similarities between primitive economies and American capitalism are so striking and that primitive economies differ from our own only in degree, not in kind (Berg 1964; Schneider 1964; Herskovits 1952), why do economists have so much difficulty developing primitive economies (Moore 1955; Sadie 1960; Douglas 1962)? And if the similarities between small-scale subsistence economies without money, markets, or machines, and large-scale, industrial market economies are so striking, why can't anthropologists find use for that powerful corpus of pure and applied economics—price, distribution, aggregate income, and growth theory; national income accounting—invented for our own economy, to analyze traditional economies such as the Trobriands or the Nuer?

> The fact that the attention of economists has been focused so exclusively on just those aspects of our economy least likely to be found among non-literate folk has thus confused anthropologists who turned to economic treatises for clarification of problems and methods in the study of the economic systems of non-literate societies [Herskovits 1952:53].

> An attempt to examine the structure and problems of a primitive community in the light of the existing body of economic thought raises fundamental conceptual issues. Economic analysis and its framework of generalization are characteristically described in terms appropriate to the modern exchange economy. It is by no means certain that the existing tools of analysis can

usefully be applied to material other than that for which they have been developed. In particular it is not clear what light, if any, is thrown on subsistence economies by a science which seems to regard the use of money and specialization of labor as axiomatic. The jargon of the market place seems remote, on the face of it, from the problems of an African village where most individuals spend the greater part of their lives in satisfying their own or their families' needs and desires, where money and trade play a subordinate role in motivating productive activity [Deane 1953:115–116].

The differences between tribal economies and our own are of some importance in answering the questions anthropologists put to their data. Indeed, the fact that anthropologists put different questions to their economic data from those asked by economists for our own economy is itself an indicator of structural differences between primitive economies and our own (Dalton 1961). "Economic anthropology deals primarily with the economic aspects of the social relations of persons [Firth 1951:138]."

One must be clear about similarities and differences among economies. All economies—the United States, the Soviet Union, the Trobriands—share three basic features and in this sense are similar:

1. Whatever the human grouping is called, tribe, village, nation, society, it consists of people who must eat to stay alive and acquire or produce material items and specialist services to sustain social and community life (that is, goods and services for religion, defense, rites of passage, and the like). The acquisition or production of these material items and services necessary for physical and social existence is never left to chance because deprivation means death. All societies therefore have an "economy" of some sort, that is, structured arrangements and enforced rules for the acquisition or production of material items and services.

2. All economies make use of natural resources (land), human cooperation (division of labor), and technology (tools and knowledge). Again, this is true for the United States, Soviet, and Trobriands economies. What we call *economic* organization, or *economic* structure, or *economic* institutions are the rules in force through which natural resources, human cooperation, and technology are brought together to provide material items and services in sustained, repetitive fashion. (One need hardly point out that the rules are somewhat different in U.S., Soviet, and Trobriands economies.)

3. A third similarity—if not universal, then extremely frequent—is that superficially similar institutional practices are used: market places (peasant markets and retail stores in the U.S.S.R., retail stores in the United States, *gimwali* in the Trobriands); monetary objects (rubles, dollars, shell necklaces); accounting devices (double-entry bookkeeping, Inca *quipu* strings, pebble counts in Dahomey); and external trade (exports and imports in the United States, U.S.S.R., and kula and *wasi* in the Trobriands).

If it would be rash to conclude that because the United States and the U.S.S.R. both use money, market places, accounting devices, and foreign trade they have basically similar economic organization (rules, structure, transactional modes, institutions), I suggest it would be even more egregious to conclude that because the United States and Malinowski's Trobriands both use some form of money and foreign trade they have basically similar economic organization.

One of Polanyi's contributions to economic anthropology and comparative economy is to have shown how similar economic devices (money, external trade) play different economic and social roles where economies are organized differently. Economies differ not only with regard to structure (transactional modes) and economic devices but also with regard to technology, size, physical environment, and the range of items and services produced or acquired. And since economies function within societies and cultures, there are economic differences among them because there are differences in social relationships (kinship systems, political systems) and culture (literacy, religion).

It is a task of economic anthropology (and comparative economy) to show the distinguishing characteristics of different types of economy by considering similarities and differences and relating these to social organization and culture. To do so requires categories of analysis which are meaningful for economies markedly different from our own. The analytical categories of modern economies were designed exclusively for the special case of national, industrialized, market economy (Dalton 1961).

> English economists, from Ricardo to Keynes, have been accustomed to assume as a tacitly accepted background the institutions and problems of the England each of his own day; when their works are studied in other climes and other periods by readers who import other assumptions, a great deal of confusion and argument at cross-purposes arises in consequence [Robinson 1961:xvii].

If we are to understand economies which are neither industrialized nor integrated by resource and product networks of market exchange, special analytical categories are necessary to reveal their structural characteristics. Polanyi invented several such analytical concepts and used them to indicate the distinguishing characteristics of primitive and archaic economies.

Polanyi's analysis is designed to answer two sets of questions: For any economy of record, what is the place of the economy in the society? How are the arrangements for acquiring or producing goods related to kinship, politics, religion, and other aspects of social organization and culture? Since all human communities require the sustained provision of goods and services and all make use of natural resources, human cooperation, and technique, what are the structured rules for combining resources, cooperation, and technique to provide material items and services in repetitive fashion? What are the institutionally imposed incentives to participate in economic activity? [17]

The second set of questions Polanyi's analysis is designed to answer concerns the ways in which institutional devices function—money, market places, external trade, accounting devices, ports of trade, equivalency ratios—in traditional economies in which forms of reciprocity and redistribution are the dominant transactional modes (Dalton 1961; 1962; 1965*a*). His distinctions between gift trade, politically administered trade, and market trade, and between special-purpose money and our own kind, open up promising lines of investigation into systematic types of economic organization. And his work on ports of trade and sortings is an important addition to our scanty knowledge of economic devices of culture contact —devices like silent trade—used to facilitate material transactions between peoples in different cultures under pre-industrial conditions.

COMPARATIVE ECONOMIC SYSTEMS

These matters should be as much the concern of comparative economic systems as of economic anthropology. For example, there is not (to my knowledge) any work which systematically compares similarities and differences between the organization and usage of money in Soviet compared to capitalist economies and relates these similarities and differences to economic organization (transactional modes), as Polanyi's work allows us to do for money in primitive compared to capitalist economies (Dalton 1965*a*). Similarly, I do not know of any work which sets out to answer the question: What exactly is the relevance of conventional economic theory —invented for industrial capitalism—to the problems and processes of Soviet economy? [18] Obviously the similarities between the two systems allow the application of familiar measurement devices (suitably amended), such as national income accounting. Obviously the difference between the two systems does not allow the application of branches of price theory, because some Soviet prices are determined differently and perform some different functions from capitalist prices (Grossman 1959; Nove 1963). But how about other areas of relevance or non-relevance of formal economic theory to the Soviet system?

So, too, for comparisons relating to welfare states and the underdeveloped countries. Galbraith (1958) and Myrdal (1957; 1960) are right to raise new questions and create new socio-economic analysis to answer them. But they have not exhausted the field. The American welfare state has some special characteristics that seem to go unremarked. Philanthropic foundations (Ford, Rockefeller, Carnegie, Guggenheim), for example, have become a device of private redistribution (something like *leiturgy* in ancient Greece, when noble families were obliged to provide public services).

One final word. Economics at present is stretching at both of its method-ological extremes. Mathematics and statistics have opened whole new areas of fruitful application of economics to real problems and processes, to the benefit of the Russians as well as ourselves (Leontiev 1960). But those problems and processes wherein economics becomes intertwined with politics, sociology, anthropology, and history—areas traditionally swept under the rug of "institutionalism"—are also getting increased at-tention. The analysis of "meaningfulness in work" which Bell (1956; 1959), Galbraith (1958), and Crosland (1962) give us adds to the brilliant insights of Tawney (1920) two generations ago. The remarkable fact that socialist doctrines and policies designed for industrialized Europe are being embraced by underdeveloped Africa (Senghor 1964; Berg 1964; Friedland and Rosberg 1964) surely is worth investigation. These are im-portant matters. Polanyi's work has much to teach us in these areas of economy and society.

NOTES

1. This essay is an expanded and revised version of a paper given at the Annual Spring Meetings of the American Ethnological Society (Dalton 1965*b*). I am grateful to Joseph S. Berliner, Paul Bohannan, Edward Budd, Robert Campbell, Helen Codere, J. R. T. Hughes, Walter Neale, and Ilona Polanyi for their critical comments.

2. Karl Polanyi died in April, 1964.

3. For an expository account of Polanyi's leading ideas, see Heilbroner (1962). A detailed analysis of *The Great Transformation* is the subject of Siev-ers (1949).

4. For similar conclusions about the social and cultural implications of capitalism arrived at from a different analytical viewpoint, see the work of Erich Fromm (especially 1945, 1955).

5. To suggest that primitive economy and society provide material and psy-chological security is to risk being accused of ethnic nostalgia—the modern equivalent of belief in the noble savage. Frequently in primitive societies, mate-rial life is poor and physical life is nasty and short: poverty, disease, death, and pain are the common lot. But social life is meaningful, and social relationships immediate and crucial to one's well-being, livelihood, and emergency support. Undoubtedly, the facts of illiteracy and of isolation contribute to the intensity and inwardness of personal relations within community life, as does mutual de-pendence for livelihood being structured in the local community alone.

6. Polanyi calls reciprocity, redistribution, and [market] exchange "pat-terns of integration." Just as market exchange is integrative in U.S. economy be-cause land and labor are transacted through purchase and sale (that is, produc-tion entails purchasing factors and selling products), and because most people depend for their livelihood on income got from selling something, so, too, are forms of reciprocity and redistribution integrative in band, tribal, and tradeburial

peasant economies. In Malinowski's Trobriands, for example, the bulk of one's staple food (yams) comes through reciprocity—gifts from wife's brother expressed as an obligation of kinship; land also is allocated as a matter of lineage affiliation.

7. Some anthropologists seem to retain the general idea of economic determination of society and history. See the economic "surplus" controversy (Pearson 1957; Harris 1959; Dalton 1960; 1963).

8. Polanyi [1947:117] points out that even during World War II, the extensive governmental controls over economy in Great Britain and the United States did not abrogate essential freedoms. Nor should we forget that the fiscal policies and market controls used by fascist Germany, although geared to purposes of war preparation, are not inevitably so geared; with a few exceptions, such as governmental prohibitions of strikes and special foreign trade devices, they are the same fiscal techniques and market controls which the democracies have now institutionalized for purposes of providing welfare services, full employment, and growth. See Walker (1957).

This is not the place to consider Hayek's argument (see Finer 1945; Wootton 1945). However, in passing one might point out that in the generation since Hayek's book was published, the United States and Great Britain have become welfare states through the extension of market controls and the application of Keynesian fiscal policy. Great Britain, of course, has gone further in nationalization of industry and in the provision of some welfare services. Aside from Goldwater and his followers, there seems to be no serious concern in either country that the steady departure from the unregulated market system is destroying political democracy and personal freedoms. The evidence is to the contrary; for instance, civil rights for American Negroes and less inequality of job opportunities in Great Britain (because of educational reforms).

9. What economists call "psychic income" deserves much more analysis than it has ever been given.

10. For an extended treatment of these themes, see Dalton (1959); Fromm (1955); Myrdal (1960).

11. Sweden, perhaps, is an exception (see Myrdal 1960). Lewis (1955:68–69) may be right about the impossibility of infusing a sense of personal participation and enmeshment in large-scale organizations. The organization of factory work is constrained not only by the requirements of machine technology (for example, the pace of assembly lines) but also by market economy and efficiency constraints which compel the need to produce at minimum costs.

12. Large-scale archaic and primitive societies—the Inca, the Nupe, the eighteenth-century kingdom of Dahomey, the archaic empires of the Middle East—are described less frequently than the small-scale society (the Nuer, the Trobriands, the Tiv) with which the literature of economic anthropology abounds. Two good accounts of large-scale systems are Nadel (1942) and Polanyi (1966).

13. There is a kernel of truth in the wrong-headed notion of "primitive communism." Socialism and communism are meant to apply to large-scale, industrialized economies whose decentralized market organization is to be either controlled or superseded by central planning. Primitive economies are not

large-scale, industrialized, nor capitalist (integrated by market exchange). The local face-to-face communal ties of family, neighborhood, and common ancestry and language—together frequently with isolation from other groups—account for the organization of production and distribution being controlled by local social institutions. To those who define things in such a way that if a system is not capitalist, it must be "communist," primitive economies appear communistic. If so, they more nearly resemble the communalism of small utopian communities whose economic arrangements express a community ethos than the kinds of socialism we associate with modern Russia and the welfare states (see Nyerene 1964). It is better, however, not to use terms such as capitalism or communism to characterize pre-industrial systems.

14. I believe Polanyi overstates one of his important arguments. He asserts that the socially intolerable results of uncontrolled markets induced governmental controls and policy which, in preventing the equilibrating forces of markets from working, hampered the economic system fatally (Polanyi 1944:chapters 18, 19). But surely a decisive feature of laissez faire capitalism was its chronic inability to generate full employment for Keynesian reasons. Even without the pre-1930 market controls, the system would have created chronic depression and so induced fiscal intervention of the kind now used. Uncontrolled market economy was not viable because of its economic as well as its social consequences.

15. On three matters Polanyi's work should be of interest to those concerned with the history of economic thought: (1) His interpretation of early writers who were considering economic matters in preindustrial economies in which markets were not important; for example, "Aristotle Discovers the Economy" (1957), and Polanyi's remarks on "just price" in medieval economy. (2) Most important is Polanyi's analysis of the English transition period from mercantilism and the institutional structure which crucially influenced the classical economics of Bentham, Ricardo, and Malthus (Polanyi 1944). (3) His concern with the social and cultural consequences of economic organizations and performance along the institutionalist lines of Veblen and Galbraith.

16. Polanyi said little about the organization of peasant economies. He used the phrase "primitive economy" to mean one in which market exchange is absent or only of minor importance, such as the economy of the Trobriand Islands.

17. To summarize Polanyi's analytical answers to this first set of questions: three modes of transaction are employed widely in primitive and archaic economies, the socio-economic modes of reciprocity and redistribution and the economic mode of market exchange. These are not mutually exclusive, but typically, one mode is integrative, that is, it organizes basic production—it is the mode which allocates labor and land and through which the bulk of produce for livelihood is obtained. Reciprocity and redistribution take a variety of specific forms (Sahlins 1965) which have in common that underlying social relationships are the impetus for labor, land, and produce transactions. Reciprocity and redistribution express the ways in which social organization relates the economy to its contextual society. In nonindustrial economies studied by historians and anthropologists, forms of reciprocity and redistribution are more frequently dominant and integrative than is market exchange. Where they are

dominant (the Trobriands, the Tiv, the Nuer), the economy is "embedded" in society in the sense of having no separate existence apart from its controlling social integument: transactional dispositions of natural resources, labor, produce, and services are expressions of socially defined obligation and relationships.

18. Professor Berliner has kindly told me that specialists in Soviet economy have begun to consider these matters in recent years. See Berliner (1964) and his references cited.

REFERENCES

ARENSBERG, CONRAD M.
   1937   *The Irish countryman*. London: Macmillan.
BELL, DANIEL
   1956   *Work and its discontents*. Boston: Beacon.
   1959   Meaning in work. *Dissent,* summer issue.
BERG, ELLIOT J.
   1964   Socialism and economic development in tropical Africa. *Quarterly Journal of Economics* 78: 549–573.
BERLINER, JOSEPH S.
   1962   The feet of the natives are large: an essay on anthropology by an economist. *Current Anthropology* 3:47–76.
   1964   Marxism and the Soviet economy. *Problems of Communism,* issue of September–October.
BESTOR, A. E., JR.
   1950   *Backwoods utopias*. Philadelphia: University of Pennsylvania Press.
BISHOP, CLAIRE
   1950   *All things common*. New York: Harper.
BOHANNAN, PAUL
   1959   The impact of money on an African subsistence economy. *Journal of Economic History* 19:491–503.
BREBNER, J. B.
   1952   Laissez-faire and state intervention in nineteenth-century Britain. *The making of English history*, R. L. Schuyler and H. Ausubel ed. New York: Dryden.
CARR, E. H.
   1951   *The new society*. London: Macmillan.
CROSLAND, C. A. R.
   1962   Industrial democracy and workers' control. In *The conservative enemy*. London: Jonathan Cape.
DALTON, GEORGE
   1959   Robert Owen and Karl Polanyi as socioeconomic critics and reformers of industrial capitalism. Unpublished Ph.D. dissertation, University of Oregon.
   1960   A note of clarification on economic surplus. *American Anthropologist* 62:483–490.
   1961   Economic theory and primitive society. *American Anthropologist* 63:1–25.

1962   Traditional production in primitive African economies. *Quarterly Journal of Economics* 76:360–378.

1963   Economic surplus, once again. *American Anthropologist* 65:389–394.

1964   The development of subsistence and peasant economies in Africa. *International Social Science Journal* 16:378–389.

1965a Primitive money. *American Anthropologist* 67:44–65.

1965b Primitive, archaic, and modern economies: Karl Polanyi's contribution to economic anthropology and comparative economy. In *Essays in economic anthropology*, June Helm ed. Proceedings of the American Ethnological Society.

DEANE, PHYLLIS

1953   *Colonial social accounting.* Cambridge: Cambridge University Press.

DOUGLAS, MARY

1962   Lele economy compared with the Bushong: a study of economic backwardness. In *Markets in Africa*, Paul Bohannan and George Dalton ed. Evanston: Northwestern University Press.

EVANS-PRITCHARD, E. E.

1954   Introduction. In *The gift*, by Marcel Mauss. Glencoe: The Free Press.

FINER, HERMAN

1945   *The road to reaction.* New York: Little, Brown and Co.

FIRTH, RAYMOND

1951   *The elements of social organisation.* London: Watts.

FRENCH, A.

1964   *The growth of Athenian economy.* London: Routledge and Kegan Paul.

FRIEDLAND, W. H., and ROSBERG, C. G., JR., ed.

1964   *African socialism.* Stanford: Stanford University Press.

FROMM, ERICH

1941   *Escape from freedom.* New York: Rinehart.

1955   *The sane society.* New York: Rinehart.

GALBRAITH, JOHN KENNETH

1958   *The affluent society.* Boston: Houghton Mifflin.

GERSCHENKRON, ALEXANDER

1952   Economic backwardness in historical perspective. In *The progress of underdeveloped areas*, B. Hoselitz ed. Chicago: University of Chicago Press.

GLUCKMAN, MAX, and I. G. CUNNISON

1962   Foreword. In *Politics of the kula ring*, by J. P. Singh Uberoi. Manchester: The University Press.

GOODFELLOW, D. M.

1939   *Principles of economic sociology.* London: Routledge.

GOODY, JACK

1963   Feudalism in Africa? *Journal of African History* 4:1–18.

GROSSMAN, GREGORY

1959   Industrial prices in the U.S.S.R. *American Economic Review* 49:50–64.

HARRIS, MARVIN
    1959   The economy has no surplus? *American Anthropologist* 61:185–199.
HAYEK, F. A.
    1944   *The road to serfdom.* Chicago: University of Chicago Press.
    1954   *Capitalism and the historians.* Chicago: University of Chicago Press.
HEILBRONER, ROBERT L.
    1962   *The making of economic society.* Englewood Cliffs: Prentice-Hall.
HERSKOVITS, MELVILLE J.
    1952   *Economic anthropology,* revised ed. New York: Knopf.
KEYNES, JOHN MAYNARD
    1926   *The end of laissez-faire.* London: Hogarth.
LeCLAIR, EDWARD E., JR.
    1962   Economic theory and economic anthropology. *American Anthropologist* 64:1179–1203.
LEONTIEV, W.
    1960   The decline and rise of Soviet economic science. *Foreign Affairs* January: 261–272.
LEVITT, KARI
    1964   Karl Polanyi and co-existence. *Co-Existence* 1:113–121.
LEWIS, W. ARTHUR
    1955   *The theory of economic growth.* London: Allen and Unwin.
    1962   Foreword. In *Economic development and social change in South India,* by T. Scarlett Epstein. Manchester: Manchester University Press.
LIENHARDT, R. GODFREY
    1956   Religion. In *Man, culture, and society,* Harry L. Shapiro ed. New York: Oxford University Press.
LIPPMANN, WALTER
    1949   The permanent new deal. In *The new deal: revolution or evolution?* Department of American Studies, Amherst College, ed. Boston: D. C. Heath (Reprinted from the *Yale Review,* June, 1935).
MALINOWSKI, BRONISLAW
    1921   The primitive economics of the Trobriand Islanders. *Economic Journal* 31:1–15.
    1922   *Argonauts of the western Pacific.* London: Routledge.
    1935   *Coral gardens and their magic.* New York: American Book.
MAUSS, MARCEL
    1954   *The gift: forms and functions of exchange in archaic societies.* Glencoe: The Free Press. Translated by I. G. Cunnison from the French ed. of 1925.
MEILLASSOUX, CLAUDE
    1962   Social and economic factors affecting markets in Guro land. In *Markets in Africa,* Paul Bohannan and George Dalton ed. Evanston: Northwestern University Press.
MITCHELL, WESLEY C.
    1949   *Lecture notes on types of economic theory.* New York: Kelley.

MOORE, WILBERT E.
1955   Labor attitudes toward industrialization in underdeveloped countries. *American Economic Review* 45:156–165.

MYRDAL, GUNNAR
1957   *Rich lands and poor.* New York: Harper.
1960   *Beyond the welfare state.* New Haven: Yale University Press.

NADEL, S. F.
1942   *A black Byzantium: the Kingdom of Nupe in Nigeria.* London: Oxford University Press.

NASH, MANNING
1964   The organization of economic life. In *Horizons of anthropology,* Sol Tax ed. Chicago: Aldine.

NEALE, WALTER C.
1957   Reciprocity and redistribution in the Indian village. In *Trade and market in the early empires,* K. Polanyi, C. M. Arensberg, H. W. Pearson ed. Glencoe: The Free Press.

NOVE, ALEC
1963   The changing role of Soviet prices. *Economics of Planning* 3:185–195.

NOYES, JOHN HUMPHREY
1870   *American socialisms.* Philadelphia: Lippincott.

NYERERE, JULIUS
1964   Communitarian socialism. In *Seeds of liberation,* Paul Goodman ed. New York: Braziller.

OPPENHEIM, A. L.
1957   A bird's-eye view of Mesopotamian economic history. In *Trade and market in the early empires,* K. Polanyi, C. M. Arensberg, H. W. Pearson ed. Glencoe: The Free Press.

OWEN, ROBERT
1815   Observations on the effect of the manufacturing system. In *A new view of society and other writings.* New York: Dutton, Everyman ed., 1927.

PEARSON, HARRY W.
1957   The economy has no surplus: critique of a theory of development. In *Trade and market in the early empires,* K. Polanyi, C. M. Arensberg, H. W. Pearson ed. Glencoe: The Free Press.

PIRENNE, HENRI
1936   *Economic and social history of medieval Europe.* London: Routledge.

POLANYI, KARL
1944   *The great transformation.* New York: Rinehart.
1947   Our obsolete market mentality. *Commentary* 13:109–117.
1957   Marketless trading in Hammurabi's time. Aristotle discovers the economy. The economy as instituted process. In *Trade and market in the early empires,* K. Polanyi, C. M. Arensberg, H. W. Pearson ed. Glencoe: The Free Press.
1960   On the comparative treatment of economic institutions in antiquity with illustrations from Athens, Mycenae, and Alalakh. In *City invin-*

cible, C. H. Kraeling and R. M. Adams ed. Chicago: University of Chicago Press.

1963 Ports of trade in early societies. *Journal of Economic History* 23:30–45.

1964 Sortings and "ounce trade" in the west African slave trade. *Journal of African history* 5:381–393.

1966 *Dahomey and the slave trade*. American Ethnological Society series. Seattle: University of Washington Press.

POSPISIL, LEOPOLD

1963 *Kapauku Papuan economy*. Yale University Publications in Anthropology no. 67.

ROBINSON, JOAN

1954 The impossibility of competition. In *Monopoly and competition and their regulation*, E. H. Chamberlin ed. London: Macmillan.

1955 *Marx, Marshall, and Keynes*. Occasional paper no. 9, Delhi School of Economics, University of Delhi.

1961 *Exercises in economic analysis*. London: Macmillan.

1962 *Economic philosophy*. London: Watts.

ROSTOW, W. W.

1960 *The stages of economic growth*. Cambridge: Cambridge University Press.

ROTTENBERG, SIMON

1958 Review of *Trade and market in the early empires*. *American Economic Review* 48:675–678.

SADIE, J. L.

1960 The social anthropology of economic development. *Economic Journal* 70:294–303.

SAHLINS, MARSHALL

1965 On the sociology of primitive exchange. In *The relevance of models for social anthropology*, M. Banton ed. London: Tavistock.

SCHNEIDER, HAROLD K.

1964 Economics in east African aboriginal societies. In *Economic transition in Africa*, Melville J. Herskovits and Mitchell Harwitz ed. Evanston: Northwestern University Press.

SENGHOR, LEOPOLD S.

1964 *On African socialism*. New York: Praeger.

SIEVERS, ALLEN MORRIS

1949 *Has market capitalism collapsed? A critique of Karl Polanyi's new economics*. New York: Columbia University Press.

SMELSER, NEIL J.

1959 A comparative view of exchange systems. *Economic development and Cultural Change* 7:173–182.

SPIRO, M. E.

1956 *Kibbutz: venture in utopia*. Cambridge: Harvard University Press.

SWEET, R. F. G.

1959 On prices, moneys, and money-users in the Old Babylonian period. Unpublished Ph.D. dissertation, Oriental Institute, University of Chicago.

TAWNEY, R. H.

　1920　*The acquisitive society*. New York: Harcourt, Brace, and Howe.

TOYNBEE, A.

　1884　*Lectures on the industrial revolution in England*. Paper ed. Boston: Beacon, 1956.

WALKER, GILBERT

　1957　*Economic planning by program and control in Great Britain*. New York: Macmillan.

WOOTTON, BARBARA

　1945　*Freedom under planning*. Chapel Hill: University of North Carolina Press.

2

Economic Theory and
Primitive Society [1]

> Economics is the study of that broad aspect of human activity
> which is concerned with resources, their limitations and uses, and
> the organization whereby they are brought into relation with
> human wants. In modern industrial societies economists have
> worked out an elaborate technique for the study of this organiza-
> tion, and have produced a body of generalizations upon it. It is still
> a matter of argument as to how far this technique and these gener-
> alizations can be applied in the study of primitive communities [FIRTH
> 1958:63].

There is a lack of clarity in the literature of economic anthropology concerning the relevance of formal economic theory to the economic organization of primitive communities (Knight 1941; Herskovits 1940; 1941).
Anthropologists sometimes study the economics of their own society in the
hope of acquiring analytical categories and useful insights into primitive
economy. Such procedure seems especially reasonable because of the success formal economic theory has had in analyzing the developed, industrialized capitalist economies. It is not well understood, however, that much
economic theory is inapplicable to primitive economy. "The fact that the
attention of economists has been focused so exclusively on just those aspects of our economy least likely to be found among non-literate folk has
thus confused anthropologists who turned to economic treatises for clarification of problems and methods in the study of the economic systems of
non-literate societies [Herskovits 1952:53]."

Reprinted, with revision, from "Economic Theory and Primitive Society," *American
Anthropologist,* 63 (February 1961):1–25. Reprinted by permission of the publisher.

ECONOMIC THEORY AND MARKET ECONOMY

Both the method and content of economic theory were shaped by two central features of nineteenth-century Britain: factory industrialism and national market organization. Market exchange, as the principle of economy-wide integration, compels its participants to conform to very special rules. *Everyone derives his livelihood from selling something to the market.* Laborers must sell their labor; landowners must sell the use of their land and natural resources; farm and factory owners must sell end products. The same market network transacts factor ingredients of production —labor, land, natural resources, finance, transportation—as well as finished goods and services of all varieties.

Market exchange refers not only to the existence of market places (sites wherein buyers and sellers congregate) but, more importantly, to the organizational process of purchase and sale at money price which is the mechanism of transacting material products, labor, and natural resources. In Western Europe and America such transactions frequently take place outside of market places. For example, labor is not brought to a market place to sell, but its use is bought and sold through the same price-making process that transacts produced items at a market place. Land, too, becomes such a marketed commodity, whose ownership or use is something bought and sold for a money price determined by the same forces of market exchange which determine prices of labor and material items. The market forces of cost and demand which transact material items such as wheat are functionally linked with those that transact the labor and land resources producing wheat. A change in wheat price "feeds back" on the rent price of wheat land and the wage price of farm labor. Land and labor use become rearranged in response to such price changes because the landowners and laborers depend for their livelihood on the money price of their land and labor, which, in turn, depends on the sales price of the material product land and labor produce. This is what is meant by the market network, market mechanism, or market principle integrating—bringing together in mutually dependent fashion—the components of capitalist economy.

The distinguishing feature of a market-organized national economy, then, is the special nature of interdependence: all material livelihood is derived from selling something through market transactions; resource and labor ingredients of production are organized for purchase and sale, as are produced material items; market price changes rearrange labor and resource uses. Economists sum up the essential process in the shorthand expression that market-made prices allocate resources among alternative output uses, and wage, profit, rent, and interest incomes among the resource owners.

Market organization compels its participants to seek material self-gain: each *must* sell something of market value to acquire the material means of existence. The "economic man" of nineteenth-century economics was not a myth, but a succinct expression of this institutional fact: the necessity for each of the atomistic units in an impersonal market exchange system to acquire his livelihood through market sale.

Throughout the nineteenth century a body of formal economic analysis was developed primarily concerned with a single set of questions: What are the forces which determine labor, natural resource, and product prices in a national, market-organized, industrial economy? Such theoretical concentration on price mechanics was simply a reflection of the crucial integrative role of prices in determining outputs and incomes.

The market system, moreover, functioned in a self-regulating way. The "economy" was a cohesive entity apart from other subsystems in society. It is true that government protected property and enforced contracts, but neither government, family, nor religion controlled market organization or price results. Where social institutions did impinge on market forces, they did so only in an indirect way by affecting supply or demand conditions (such as the demand for fish in Catholic countries) and thereby prices, incomes, and production. The market process was self-regulating in the sense that it required the components of the system to move—land to change its use, labor to change its location or occupation—in response to price changes made in markets. Price changes induced buyers and sellers to "economize," that is, to seek monetary cost reduction, or monetary gain increase. Production methods as well as the choice of which items to produce were guided by market prices. A condition for undertaking production is that the producer must expect to make a profit, which is the money differential between two sets of prices: those that determine his costs of production and those that determine his sales revenue.

When market organization is economy-wide or national, it creates a "market society," in the sense that social organization has to adapt to market needs to allow the sustained provision of material goods and of money incomes with which to acquire goods.

A market economy can only exist in a market society . . . a market economy must comprise all the elements of industry, including labor, land, and money. . . . But labor and land are no other than the human beings themselves of which every society consists and the natural surroundings in which it exists. To include them in the market mechanism means to subordinate the substance of society itself to the laws of the market [Polanyi 1944:71].

For example, that laborers are compelled to sell their labor for a market-determined wage means that they must move to remunerative labor markets when their present employments and wages fall. The location of population thereby conforms to market-registered needs for labor.

Finally, a market economy is a highly decentralized network. It consists of a multitude of related but nonetheless individual purchase and sale transactions. The operational units are individual business firms buying resources and selling outputs and individual families buying household goods and selling labor and other resources. Such decentralization reinforces the atomistic view of society as simply an aggregate of self-interested individuals.

The question arises: Why is it believed that the body of economic theory derived from such a special institutional matrix has analytical relevance to all economies, including small, tribal, marketless economies? The reasons are several.

The English originators of formal economic theory grounded their analyses on postulates which seemed structured in the *physical* universe, and therefore universally applicable (Polanyi 1944: chapter 10). In addition, the repeal of mercantilistic economic controls and the consequent formation of nationwide markets allowed the later neo-classical economists to use an "economistic" approach—to focus on economy as separate from society. They regarded the economy as having such an inner consistency and autonomy as to allow the derivation of distinct economic laws which seemed to operate independently of social relationships and cultural institutions.

The classical economists delineated purely "economic" motivation (material self-gain) as being both necessary and sufficient to induce laborers to conform to market needs. For example, in urging repeal of Poor Laws which guaranteed subsistence as a traditional social right, William Townsend based his argument on the assertion that the "natural" force of fear of hunger was the most efficacious inducement to work.

> Hunger will tame the fiercest animals, it will teach decency and civility, obedience and subjection, to the most perverse. In general it is only hunger which can spur and goad them on to labour; yet our laws have said they shall never hunger. The laws, it must be confessed, have likewise said, they shall be compelled to work. But then legal constraint is attended with much troubles violence and noise; creates ill will, and never can be productive of good and acceptable service: whereas hunger is not only peaceable, silent, unremitting pressure, but as the most natural motive to industry and labour, it calls forth the most powerful exertions [Townsend 1786, quoted in Polanyi 1944:113–114].[2]

With Malthus, too, immutable biology was the starting point for deriving economic laws: that the natural fertility of humans made food scarce because of the pressure of population growth led him to deduce his subsistence theory of wages. The conclusions of biology—that the populations of all plant and animal life are limited only by their food supplies—were projected to the social world.

Ricardo's postulate, the "law" of diminishing returns, was also a physical phenomenon from which he deduced his income distribution theory: if one or more ingredients of production, such as land, is fixed in quantity, output growth will consist of diminishing increments. In a market economy, owners of the fixed ingredient (landlords) will gain at the expense of the others (laborers and entrepreneurs).

Utilitarianism provided the crowning sanction, again in the guise of universal law: self-interest as the wellspring of all human action. The quest for material self-gain need be the only regulator of an economic system based on the physical nature of man and the universe: "The general conception which Bentham had is one that is widely prevalent today. . . . I think we shall conclude before the course is over that the bulk of orthodox economic theory as we have it at the present time [1935] rests upon a conception of human nature which is not very different from that which Jeremy Bentham drew up in such formal shape [Mitchell 1949:92]."

The parametric assumptions of early economic analysis appeared as physical facts. The derived laws of market economy were thereby given the authority of nature. It seemed that economic processes had separate physical laws of their own, divorced from social convention (Polanyi 1944:115; 1968).

This economistic approach, which separated out economy from society and created a body of theoretical analysis of market industrialism, received more refined expression later in the nineteenth century in the works of Stanley Jevons, Carl Menger, John B. Clark, and Alfred Marshall. What is important for our purposes is that these neo-classicists made theoretical refinements also derived, it seemed, from universal truths: that the condition of "natural scarcity" (insufficiency of resources relative to unlimited material wants) necessitated economizing choice if maximum fulfillment of material wants was to be attained.

It is important to note how the condition of "scarcity"—so relevant for market economy—became regarded as universal fact and a further basis for assuming the universal relevance of economic theory.

The institutional necessity for individuals to sell something to get a living—pursue material self-gain—in market economy had ideological reflections in the form of generalizations about the nature of "man" in society. One such is the textbook homily that man's material wants are everywhere insatiable, a dictum that often implies the immutability of genetic impulse. If man's material wants are insatiable, then scarcity of enabling material means exists by definition in all societies, past, present, and future: regardless of the absolute quantity of resources, they are scarce, that is, insufficient relative to the unlimited desire for the material end products they produce. If "man" places great emphasis on fulfilling his insatiable material wants, economizing, rational calculation results so as to arrange some preferred ordering of resource uses. But if such is ever the case in an actual community, it is a *socially* determined result—a result which obtains only in a society which places great value on material acquisition relative to other goal attainments and therefore contains an institutional structure which impels its members to act accordingly (Mead 1937; Fusfeld 1957:343).

To the extent that the syllogistic chain—man's material wants are infinite, his material means are finite, maximum material acquisition therefore requires economizing calculation—is regarded as true for every economy, it is incorrect and misleading. It confuses the universally correct, *biologically* derived postulate—man's existence requires continual material sustenance—with a special type of *social* structure: man's social organization impels him always to want more material goods than he has at the moment and makes him value such material acquisition more than the fulfillment of other goals with which it might be in conflict. If it is once seen that the extent of importance attached to material acquisition is most definitely determined by social institutions and values, it immediately follows that the presence, absence, or existing degree of "scarcity" of enabling material means (in any society) also depends on social, not physical, circumstances.[3]

It is not so, as some literature of economic anthropology asserts, that the postulates of scarcity and economizing calculation are of universal relevance. "The elements of scarcity and choice, which are the outstanding factors in human experience that give economic science its reason for being, rest psychologically on firm ground. . . . Our primary concern in these pages is to understand the cross-cultural implications of the process of economizing [Herskovits 1952:3, 4]."

It is an erroneous linking together of two different meanings of the concept "economic" which is at the root of the misleading assumption of universal scarcity and the misleading conclusion that formal economic theory has relevance to all economies. Clarification of two points is necessary: what it is that all economic systems—industrial capitalist and primitive alike—have in common; and the nature of those structural differences between them which makes formal economic theory inapplicable in the analysis of non-market sectors of traditional economics.

TWO MEANINGS OF ECONOMIC [4]

The word "economic" has two distinct and independent meanings, both in common use, but differing essentially in the extent to which each can be fruitfully applied to real-world economies. In the substantive sense, economic refers to the provision of material goods which satisfy biological and social wants. The substantive meaning is perfectly general in applicability, because all communities, regardless of differences in natural environment, production techniques, or cultural traits, are composed of human beings whose physical and social existence depends on the sustained provision of material items. "The basic problem is universal: not only to have enough to eat to keep alive, but also to satisfy the demands of personal tastes, religious rules and a multitude of social obligations, all as important to the life of the group as mere subsistence is to the life of the organism [Herskovits 1952:294]."

The broad agencies of material-means provision are everywhere the same: physical environment and social organization. "We may move first of all, to those human and ecological factors that provide the goods and services which satisfy the demands of living, both biological and psychological, and that are at the core of any economic system. In some form, these factors are present everywhere; without their interaction life as we know it could not exist [Herskovits 1952:8]."

With unambiguous meaning, therefore, one can talk about the "economic" system of Imperial Rome, of the Kwakiutl Indians, of the Benedictine Order of Monks, of nineteenth-century England, or of Soviet Russia —meaning nothing more than the organization and processes through which material goods are provided; one need not assume anything beforehand about necessary techniques, motivations, or specific types of economic organization.

All societies have some type of *systematic* economic structure for the following reasons: the exploitation of natural resources requires the use of technique for the acquisition or creation of material goods (horticulture, farming, hunting, manufacture). The use of technique and of natural resources, together with the need for distributing material goods among all the inhabitants, requires definite institutional arrangements—structured rules of the game—to assure continuity of supply, that is, to assure repetition of performance. The participants are mutually dependent for other reasons as well: the use of technology, division of labor, natural environment, and the fact that economic processes take place within a social community—all make necessary recognized rights and obligations. *It is the rules which integrate the use of natural resources and technique and assure continual cooperation in the provision of material goods that we call an economic "system."* Mutual dependence among persons is structured in all economies, but, of course, may be structured very differently in different economies.

The substantive meaning of economic, however, is not analytically informative in the investigation of specific economies because of the diversity of technology and institutions which exists. But it does have the merit of pointing up and explaining the general existence of organizational requirements for the sustained provision of material goods which must be fulfilled in any society. It is, of course, what anthropologists usually mean when they refer to the "economic" aspects of primitive society.

The second meaning of economic is described by the terms "economical" and "economizing." It denotes a *special* set of rules designed to maximize the achievement of some end or to minimize the expenditure of some means. Four aspects of this formal meaning of economic deserve emphasis.

1. It has no necessary connection with the substantive meaning of economic. It would be prejudicial to assume that the organizational provision of material goods must be universally achieved through economizing calculation; whether such is the case for any specific economy can be established only by empirical investigation of actual institutions.

2. Economizing calculation by no means need be confined to the creation, distribution, or use of material goods. It derives rather from the general logic of rational action which is appropriate to a large number of theoretical and empirical situations; these have in common explicit ends, delimited means, and definite rules of alternative choice for the achievement of the ends with the scarce means. For example, economizing calculation unrelated to substantive economic organization appears in games such as chess, in military problems, and in preparing for academic examinations: each entails allocating scarce means to achieve goal maximization within a set of prescribed rules.

3. A primary field of economic analysis, price and distribution theory, is an application of the formal meaning of economic—economizing calculation—to a special set of real-world conditions and organizations for the provision of material goods: that the acquisition of material items is valued greatly relative to other goal attainments; that factor resources are therefore scarce (insufficient in quantity to achieve all ends), are multipurposed (capable of fulfilling more than one end); that the ends for which the material means shall be used are graded (of differential preferment); that the hierarchy of preferred ends is known; and that the rules for relating the scarce, multi-purposed resource means to the graded ends be that (*a*) any material end shall be fulfilled with no more than the minimum resource means necessary for its fulfillment; (*b*) no means shall be provided for lesser ends before provision for greater ends is made (Robbins 1932).

4. The fruitful application of micro-economic theory (derived from the formal meaning of economic) depends on the existence of a substantive, real-world economy so organized that at least some of the special postulates of the analysis are institutionally fulfilled. If the members of some society do not show an economizing predisposition in their use of means (they use more than the minimum necessary to achieve the end); if their rules of social organization dictate that some means may be used only for one purpose (such as religion proscribing all but one kind of crop grown on land); or if there is no condition of "scarcity" because extensive material acquisition is not culturally regarded as important as other goals, for-

mal economic analysis is not capable of yielding insights if applied to that economy (Knight 1941; Herskovits 1941; Fusfeld 1957; Neale 1957b).

NATIONAL MARKET INDUSTRIALISM
AND PRIMITIVE ECONOMY

A distinguishing characteristic of market-organized industrialism is that both meanings of economic are relevant. The institutionalized economic structure through which material want satisfaction is provided for consists of a special set of economizing practices applied to scarcity situations through a nationally-integrated market network. The participants need material goods to survive; the national market structure compels economizing performance for their acquisition and provides integrating unity and stability to such performance. The institutional complex which integrates the system—which links together the efforts of each and assures the sustained provision of material goods—is the supply-demand-price mechanism working through a national network of labor, resource, and product markets. Conformity to the market rules is assured through competition and by structured motivation: the institutionalized pursuit of material self-gain through market participation. One has to abide by the market rules to acquire material livelihood in a market-organized economy.

As with competitive market organization, the use of machine technology also imposes a need for economizing calculation. Regardless of who owns them, machines are expensive. In the American context of private ownership and market organization, economizing is enforced by potential market penalties in the form of money losses. The competitive striving for profits —the source of material livelihood for owners—requires efficient machine use to minimize costs. In the Soviet context of state ownership and central planning, economical use is required for fulfillment of priority goals: output maximization, rapid growth, and the production of crucial output components such as military and capital goods. Both the United States and Soviet Russia use structured mechanisms of economizing such as cost accounting, contract obligation to assure continual resource supply, hierarchical authority discipline within factory organization, and price and wage formation so as to economize on the use of most scarce factor resources.

That every society must have economic organization of some sort to provide material means of existence does not mean that each must have that special set of market exchange institutions for the analysis of which formal economic theory was uniquely designed. Indeed, there is increasing evidence that the market-integrated national economy is historically and anthropologically rare.

A considerable body of evidence runs contrary to the notions that human wants are unlimited, that financial incentives will transfer labor from nonindustrial to industrial pursuits and thus that the potential worker may be viewed as welcoming release from traditional restraints. Some of this evidence can be interpreted in terms of "rational conduct," but not in terms of economic maximization. The potential worker in underdeveloped areas is typically required to give up traditional forms of organization and reciprocal obligations that have combined to afford him security—both material and affective. The kinship system in any nonindustrial society is likely to provide a major barrier to individual mobility, because it is a social security system, because it is the focus of positive values and advantages, and because extended kin obligations are likely to reduce the effective appeal of individual rewards [Moore 1955:158–159].

Karl Polanyi and his associates (Polanyi, Arensberg, Pearson 1957) have shown that there exist at least two non-market principles of integrative economic organization for the analysis of which conventional economic theory is inappropriate. But such is the tenacity of belief that market theory is universally relevant—even to non-market and non-industrial structures—that one economist says the following:

> What are the qualities which, it is said, are possessed by the [primitive and archaic] economies for the study of which conventional analysis is not helpful? They are: inflexible or sluggish prices or exchange ratios; inelastic (sometimes absolutely inelastic) supply; inelastic (sometimes absolutely inelastic) demand.
>
> The specific instances enumerated by the authors—e.g., set rates, customary or statutory equivalencies, gift trade, administered trade, status-trading, trading partnerships, the influence of kinship, magic and etiquette on economic behavior, noncompeting groups—seem to fall into one or more of these boxes.
>
> . . . now, the conventional doctrine and techniques of formal economics have much to say about economies or markets in which inflexibilities and inelasticities occur. It is not true that economic analysis cannot perform useful predictive tasks in such economies [Rottenberg 1958:676].

The use of concepts such as "inelastic demand" to refer to primitive economies assumes that markets exist universally and that economic theory is universally relevant because scarcity situations are universal and everywhere compel materially self-gainful economizing, such as maximization of consumer utility and production at least cost. It is to translate *all* economies into market terms.

Economic theory has much to say about inelastic supply and demand conditions, but what is said concerns economic sectors so organized that resource ingredients and product outputs are bought and sold through the market mechanism. As Herskovits rightly points out, economic theory requires market-determined prices to be applicable. "The problem of how value flows from fluctuations in supply and demand, in its essentially mathematical character, needs the quantitative index of value contained in price as manifest in the market to permit its analysis [Herskovits 1952:49]."

Polanyi and his associates show that economy-wide market networks, materially self-gainful economizing, and monetized internal and external trade do not exist as integrative transactions in most band and tribal economies; rather, that production and distribution of material goods are organized by transactional principles essentially different from market exchange. "For in these societies, production and distribution involve little of the profit motive, and labor is only in special instances for hire [Herskovits 1952:11]. . . . The process of distribution, in many tribes, is thus set in a non-economic [non-economizing] matrix, which takes the form of gift and ceremonial exchange [Herskovits 1952:155]."

The integrative modes of transaction which do exist widely in traditional bands, tribes, and peasantries are (1) reciprocity, that is, material gift and counter gift-giving induced by social obligation derived, typically, from kinship, as is the case with the Trobriand Islanders; and (2) redistribution, the channeling upward of goods or services to socially determined allocative centers (usually king, chief, or priest), who then redistribute either to their subordinates at large by providing community services, or in specific allotments to individuals in accordance with their political, religious, or military status? Redistribution at the state level, often accompanied by reciprocity at the village level, was the dominant mode of transaction in ancient Egypt, Mexico, and Dahomey and in feudalistic societies generally (Malinowski 1922; Thurnwald 1932; Herskovits 1952: chapter 19; Mauss 1925; Firth 1958:65, 68–69). ". . . *the whole tribal life is permeated by a constant give and take;* . . . every ceremony, every legal and customary act is done to the accompaniment of material gift and counter gift; . . . wealth, given and taken, is one of the main instruments of social organization, of the power of the chief, of the bonds of kinship, and of relationships in law [Malinowski 1922:167]."

That all societies must have substantive economic organization means that there will be similarities even between two widely differing economies —say, the Trobriand Islands and present-day United States. Thus one could talk meaningfully about the creation, distribution, and use of material goods in each, as well as the roles of money and external trade and the organization of land tenure. However—and this is the point to be underscored—the fact that the United States has a national economy pervasively market-organized and industrialized (and thereby amenable to analysis by formal economic theory), while the Trobriands has neither, *makes the differences in economic organization and processes between the two more important than the similarities,* especially so on matters of interest to the anthropologist.[5]

There are three ways to clarify the issue and reinforce the point: (1) to contrast the questions of economic interest to the anthropologist with those the economist asks in his own field; (2) to show that economic mechanisms, practices, and processes such as market places and foreign trade, common to both primitive and Western economies, are institutionalized differently and often function in different ways and for different purposes; (3) to cite examples which show how misleading results follow from the non sequitur that because bands, tribes, and peasantries must have (substantive) economic organization of some sort their economies are amenable to analysis by formal economic theory.

The matters of interest to the anthropologist investigating the general aspects of primitive and peasant economy can be classified, perhaps, into some six overlapping categories.

1. *Technological processes and bases of subsistence.* Are they horticulturalists, fishermen, gardeners, hunters? Which technical devices are used? How are canoes and houses built, land tilled, fish-traps made?

2. *Material performance and fluctuations in output.* What is the level of material subsistence and how secure is it?

3. *Ecology.* What is the natural physical environment (climate, waterways, land acreage and fertility) from which livelihood is extracted?

4. *Economic organization and transactions.* Which economic devices and processes are used, and how do they work? Are there money uses? If so, for which types of transactions? Which goods are transacted without the use of money? Is there more than one kind of money used? Are there market places or external trade? If so, how are they organized and which items do they transact? Are there prices or equivalency ratios for goods which change hands? How are such determined?

5. *Economy and society.* What is the place of the "economy" in the society? How are production processes, material goods transactions, labor services, and land utilization organized? How are they related to kinship, religion, political authority, and other social institutions? On what principles do things and labor services change hands and location? What is the nature of economic interdependence which allows division of labor to be practiced? What are the socially sanctioned motives which induce conforming participation in substantive economic activity? How is continuity assured in the supply of material items? How are the inefficient, the unusually efficient, and the recalcitrant treated?

6. *Subsistence economy and prestige economy.* Are there distinct economic spheres with different goods, operational principles, and value norms in each (DuBois 1936; Steiner 1954; Polanyi 1957a; Bohannan 1959)? Is it meaningful in terms of the specific goods transacted, the processes and mechanisms which transact them, and the value judgments attached to such transactions by the participants, to distinguish between subsistence and prestige spheres? Are there treasure items or items of elite

circulation? Is external trade carried out on the same principles as internal transactions?

Economists are not concerned directly with social institutions or physical environment. Religion, law, and kinship are regarded as given, in the sense of existing as part of the total environment of market-organized industrialism, within which economic mechanism functions.

> It is *precisely* the separate class of variables which it employs which for the economist, at any rate, distinguishes economics from the other sciences. Economics studies prices; quantities of commodities exchanged, produced, consumed; interest rates, taxes, tariffs: its basic abstraction is that of the commodity. It seeks to find reasonably stable relationships among these variables, but it is the variables not the relationships, which delimit the subject matter of the science [Boulding 1957:318].

Physical environment and social institutions (and, indeed, technology) are studied only when they affect the economic variables in which the economist is interested. Two examples will illustrate the point.

For problems of aggregate output determination and national income growth in a market-industrial economy, an important quantity is the annual money expenditure by business firms in purchasing new plant and equipment. By changing the complex of costs, proportions used of resource ingredients, and profit expectations, an innovation in technique of producing will affect yearly investment outlays and so is of interest to the economist. But the anthropologist's interest in technology is both more direct and somewhat different. The economist is not interested in how the machine is built and operated (or in the social organization of the factory) as is the anthropologist in how the fish-trap is built, operated, shared, and inherited.

The same is true of cultural and social institutions. On the rare occasion when the economist considers kinship, religion, or government, he does so only when they have significant impact on economic quantities; for example, the impact of governmental price-support programs on agricultural prices and incomes. Because the organization of market economy is a cohesive entity in itself, the economist can describe and analyze that range of processes of interest to economics without reference to the social.[6] In contrast, the close integration of social and economic institutions in primitive society makes it impossible for the anthropologist to describe the economic, without at the same time showing its relation to the social.

> Basically, the anthropologist is not asking the same set of questions as the economist. The business of anthropology is not economics; it is rather something that we might call "ethno-economics" . . . a statement of the categories of thought and language, the ideas, the principle of action, in terms of

which a people institutionalize the business of getting a living. . . . For the anthropologist's task is to explain how people get a living, then to classify those modes . . . and theorize about the way they are linked with other cultural or social attributes [Bohannan 1958].

The exchanges of archaic societies which he [Mauss] examines are total social movements or activities. They are at the same time economic, juridical, moral, aesthetic, religious, mythological, and sociomorphological phenomena. Their meaning can therefore only be grasped if they are viewed as a complex concrete reality [Evans-Pritchard 1954:vii].

Neither the problems of interest nor the methods of analysis are the same for economics and that branch of economic anthropology which analyzes traditional economics before modernization begins.

ECONOMIC INSTITUTIONS

Economic mechanisms, practices, and processes such as the use of money, external trade, division of labor, market places, debt, prices are present in industrial capitalist and in primitive economies. But to conclude that because both use them, their organization, functioning, or purpose in primitive economy must be essentially the same as in ours, is not warranted.[7] Yet such is sometimes implied in the literature of economic anthropology. ". . . there can be no division of labor without a resulting economic exchange. The universality of the fact of division of labor, even if only on sex lines, underscores the essential soundness of the reasoning which has made of exchange and distribution basic factors in all economic theory [Herskovits 1952:13]."

Surely one could not conclude that because division of labor is practiced in the United States, in Soviet Russia, and in the Trobriand Islands, the same principles of "exchange" are operative in each. All one can infer from the universality of division of labor is the universality of structured interdependence. There must be some transactional modes for persons to acquire what they do not themselves produce.[8] The institutional means for such exchange in any economy can be discovered only by empirical investigation. "And as with the mechanisms of production, the distribution system, though a universal in human social life, takes on a vast number of forms [Herskovits 1952:12]."

Similarly, when we compare other economic institutions of industrial capitalism with what seem to be their counterparts in primitive economy, it becomes clear that the differences in their organization and functioning are more important than their similarities. The point is especially important for understanding the nature of money uses, external trade, and market places in primitive economy (Polanyi 1957a).

In national economies integrated by market exchange, money is all-purpose money, in the sense that commercial and non-commercial transactions of very different sorts are carried out with the same kind of money serving as medium of exchange, standard of value, store of value, and means of payment (for example, of debts). Few economic transactions take place without the use of money; and only one kind of money—conveniently interchangeable as check deposit, paper currency, and coin—is in general use. It is no accident that such is the case: the use of all-purpose money is a requisite for a market-organized economy because all labor and resource ingredients as well as finished outputs must bear price tags expressed in the same money in order for buyers and sellers to transact them through the market exchange network. The use of the same money instrument makes physically different items both "commensurable" and "commodities," that is, things to be bought and sold whose market values can be compared. (Indeed, money itself becomes a marketed commodity, the price of which is an interest rate.)

Where money is used in primitive economy, it is not all-purpose money; each kind can be used only for a special range of transactions, such as the use of cattle as a money object for acquiring a bride or paying blood-wealth, but not for acquiring food or craft products. In primitive economy a given money object sometimes serves one use only, as when debts are calculated in terms of brass rods but actually paid in strips of cloth (Bohannan 1959). What should be emphasized is that the differences in money usage between primitive economy and our national market system are indicators of underlying differences in transactional principles of economic integration (such as reciprocity, redistribution, and market exchange). The disposition of natural resources, material outputs, and labor is often compartmentalized separately in primitive economy. Frequently each is transacted without the use of money and neither enter market places nor are transacted by market purchase and sale. Rather, natural resources, labor, subsistence goods, and treasure items change hands and location in different economic spheres—in accordance with different sets of social rules, such as kinship obligation inducing gift exchange; political obligation inducing payment to central authority.

So, too, with other economic devices common to both primitive and Western economies such as external trade and markets. Usually they are not functional equivalents, but rather superficially similar practices not only organized differently but often with different social as well as economic purposes (Firth 1958:63).

For example, in American economy exports and imports are transacted by the same market principle which transacts internal exchanges, both economy-wide and local. In primitive economy, transactional mechanisms used in external trade are sometimes distinctly different from those used internally; moreover, external trade transactions of a non-market kind are frequently found. Some examples are the fish-yam and kula gift trade of the Trobriands (Malinowski 1922) and politically administered trade of elite items in traditional West African kingdoms (Arnold 1957). A further point of difference is that external trade in primitive economy is induced by the absence of the import items at home. Indeed, such seems invariably to be the rationale for primitive external trade (Herskovits 1952:36–37, 181; Polanyi 1957*a*, 1957*b*). In contrast, external trade among Western market economies takes place on the least-cost principle: things *are* imported which can be produced at home if such imports are cheaper than the domestic equivalents. The market principle of least-cost economizing, which pervades internal production and sale, characterizes external trade as well.

Of special importance is the fact that where markets do exist in traditional primitive economy, they almost invariably are restricted to produced material items: *rarely, if ever, does land or labor get transacted through the price-making mechanism of market exchange*. Prices made in local markets do not reallocate labor and other resource ingredients of production, as in modern market economy. Neither land usage nor labor location and occupation responds to market price changes, because subsistence livelihood does not depend on market sale. Before European colonial incursion, markets in primitive economies were local, specific, and contained market places whose price results did not "feed back" into non-market spheres of economy. A primitive community often had a market place, but not a market system, that is, an economy-wide network of resource and output markets through which most people acquired their livelihood.[9]

It is indicative that in economic anthropology the term "market" usually is used to mean "market place," an actual site wherein goods change hands by purchase and sale (Neale 1957*b*). In U.S. economy, the term "market" is applied not only to specific market-place sites such as a cluster of retail stores, and to sites where ownership changes hands but not the goods themselves (the New York Stock Exchange, the Chicago Wheat Pit), but also to the diffusive economic forces of market exchange: the pervasive supply-demand-price mechanism which systematically transacts resources, labor, and products regardless of what specific site—market bazaar, retail store, hiring firm—is the location of such transactions. Indeed, that where an economy-wide market network exists the market-place site is of little importance, is indicated by such concepts as the "market" for automobiles or for engineers' labor, meaning the mass of potential buyers or sellers of something, wherever they are located. A further indicator of the importance, complexity, and special role of the market mechanism in American and European national economy is that market forces are classified in many ways: controlled and uncontrolled markets; factor ingredient and output markets: local, economy-wide, and international markets; competitive and oligopolistic markets.

In summary, Western industrial economy is organized through markets, prices, and the use of all-purpose money: these are pervasive, interrelated, and they integrate all sectors of production and distribution. Market economy has been appropriately termed "uni-centric" because of the wide variety of material items and labor transacted in the sphere of market exchange (Bohannan 1959). In contrast, primitive economy is "multi-centric," and the dominant centers are organized through non-market modes of transaction, reciprocity, and redistribution which integrate the local economy; special-purpose monies are in use, and market-place exchange (where it exists at all) is subordinate and contained (Polanyi 1957a).

A MONEY ECONOMY IS A MARKET ECONOMY

Anthropologists use the term "money economy" as a shorthand expression for the type of economic organization prevalent in Europe and the United States. Thus Watson (*Tribal Cohesion in a Money Economy,* 1958) uses the term in describing how the Mambwe absent themselves temporarily from their villages to work for money wages in European industrial enterprises in Rhodesia; and Firth contrasts uni-centric Western "money economy" with primitive spheres of non-exchangeable goods:

> Another feature of such primitive transactions is the existence of what may be termed "spheres of exchange." There are various groups of goods and services, and exchange of one item can only take place with another item in the same group. In southeastern New Guinea, for instance, a very important series of exchanges takes place between the possessors of shell arm-rings and of necklaces of shell discs, while other important exchanges are of fish for vegetables. But the food items can only be exchanged against each other, and so also the shell valuables. It would be unthinkable for a man who wished a shell valuable to offer in return yams or fish or other property not of a shell kind. There is no free market, no final measure of the value of individual things, and no common medium whereby every type of goods and services can be translated into terms of every other. A primitive economy thus presents a strong contrast to our money economy [Firth 1958:69].

The term "money economy" emphasizes a derivative rather than the dominant feature of Western economic structure. The use of francs or sterling is not an independent trait, but rather a requirement for the functioning of a market exchange economy. Continuity in supply of material goods in market economy is assured through several practices, one of which is the use of all-purpose money. It is only when land and labor as well as fabricated goods are organized as available commodities to be bought and sold through market networks that a money economy exists. From the anthropologist's viewpoint, they enter the same transactional sphere of market exchange. Where all-purpose money is absent in primitive economy, it is because market exchange as the economy-wide principle of integration is absent. ". . . one cardinal feature of a primitive economic system is clearly the absence of money, of a price mechanism, and in many cases of a formal market [Firth 1958:70]."

What is a "money economy" to an anthropologist appears as a "market economy" to an economist.

ECONOMIC THEORY, MARKET CATEGORIES, AND PRIMITIVE ECONOMY

Those who attempt to analyze primitive economy with the economic theory and categories derived from Western market industrialism seem uniformly selective in their choice of specific theories to apply. Almost invariably, it is from one field of economic analysis—price theory—that they choose (Goodfellow 1939; Rottenberg 1958).

The question arises: If it is thought that concepts from price theory—supply, demand, elasticity, economizing—are relevant to primitive economy, why not other concepts of formal economic theory—say, Keynesian income and employment theory—as well? To apply Keynesian theory to small bands or tribes where markets are either absent or petty is to point up the structural differences between traditional and developed economies. In a word, it cannot be done.

The contribution of Keynes was to show why, *in national market economies* such as those of England and America in the early 1930's, the full employment rate of production is not automatically sustained, but rather that we experienced sharp and deep output fluctuations. The basic reason is institutional: in a market economy, all incomes are derived from the sale of end products to private households (consumption goods—C), business firms (investment goods—I), government (governmental purchases—G), and foreigners (export goods—E); but there exists no automatic mechanism to assure that the total amount of such market purchases (effective demand) by the millions of buyers of C, I, G, and E will be sufficient to keep the national labor and machine force fully employed. Moreover, the interdependence of the segments of market economy is such—each person acquires his livelihood by selling something to someone else—that a sharp reduction in one category of expenditure (say, business firm outlay on new machinery—I) inevitably induces spending cutbacks in other effective demand sectors (household consumption good purchases—C): those who earn their wage and profit incomes in producing machinery will be forced by income cuts to spend less on household goods.

One cannot apply such analysis to traditional bands and tribes because the basic institutional precondition is absent: the bulk of material income

is not derived from, and therefore does not depend on, market sales of
output. In tribal economies mutual dependence is not structured through
the market mechanism: the Trobriander does not depend for his material
livelihood on sale of his labor for a money wage which he then uses to buy
material items; "effective demand" for goods cannot shrink, as it does in
market economy, because the aggregate amount of money incomes received for market sale of labor and other resources shrinks.

In what surely must be the most vigorous attempt to apply economic
theory to primitive economy, it is asserted:

> The aim of this book is to show that the concepts of economic theory must
> be taken as having universal validity, and that, were this not so, the result
> would be not only scientific confusion but practical chaos [Goodfellow
> 1939:3].

Repeated assertion of the credo—faith means salvation, doubt means
chaos—is preliminary to exegesis.

> Actually, once it is baldly stated, the proposition that there should be more
> than one body of economic theory is absurd. If modern economic analysis
> with its instrumental concepts cannot cope equally with the Aborigine and
> with the Londoner, not only economic theory but the whole of the social sci-
> ences may be considerably discredited. For the phenomena of the social sci-
> ences are nothing if not universal. . . . When it is asked, indeed, whether
> modern economic theory can be taken as applying to primitive life, we can
> only answer that it if does not apply to the whole of humanity then it is
> meaningless. For there is no gulf between the civilized and the primitive;
> one cultural level shades imperceptibly into another, and more than one
> level is frequently found within a single community. If economic theory does
> not apply to all levels, then it must be so difficult to say where its usefulness
> ends that we might be driven to assert that it has no usefulness at all [Good-
> fellow 1939:4, 5].

But there is a gulf between industrial, developed, capitalist economies
and traditional bands and tribes; types of *economic organization* do not
shade imperceptibly one into another; and it is not impossible to say where
the usefulness of economic theory ends.

Economic theory was created to analyze and measure the special structures, processes, performance, and problems of national market-organized
industrialism, with its special features of all-purpose money, impersonal
contract obligation, atomistic individualism, and the institutional necessity
for individuals to acquire livelihood through market sale of labor, natural
resources, and outputs. It is these which create the gulf between primitive
and industrial capitalist economies. It would, indeed, be remarkable if economic theory *were* relevant to economies which differed from ours in markets, money, technology, and size.

Confusion is compounded by reiterating the credo while, at the same time, offering evidence for disbelief: the economizing concepts of economic theory are applicable to Bantu economy despite the absence of machines, market exchange, all-purpose money, rent, interest, wages, profit, and the private business firm.

> . . . the functions are always actively carried out, but often by organizations, of which the family or household is the most important. . . . The difficulty of discovering the *forms* of modern economic life may well lead to a mistaken belief that the *functions* of that life are not to be discoverable among our less advanced people. . . . Modern economic theory has supplied us with a technique which transcends those forms and has the great merit of being applicable to the economic aspect of life, simply as an aspect, and independently of the forms prevalent in any given culture [Goodfellow 1939:7, 8].

Here again the root of ambiguity lies in the erroneous identification of the two meanings of economic: because Bantu society must provide for a sustained flow of material goods (the substantive meaning of economic, universally relevant), it is erroneously concluded that Bantu economy must consist of *economizing structures* like those of market industrialism; and, therefore, that Bantu structures must also be amenable to analysis by market theory.

ECONOMIC ANTHROPOLOGY: DESCRIPTION AND ANALYSIS

The literature of economic anthropology often contains excellent description of economic organization, processes, values, and technology, together with inadequate theoretical analysis and generalization. Perhaps the dichotomy reflects the institutionalized preparation of anthropologists. Precise description of data in which the anthropologist immerses himself is a distinguishing feature of the profession (Evans-Pritchard 1954:viii). Theoretical analysis, however, is one step away from the data; and, as we have seen, the obfuscating preconceptions of the economics and economy of the anthropologist's own European or American culture make theoretical analysis of primitive economy yet more difficult and less successful.

> Admittedly, there is as yet no body of generalizations that treats "economic" behavior from the specifically anthropological point of view. . . . "Economic anthropology," to date, is not yet a reality. It is still freeing itself from the belief . . . that economic theory itself already has something to offer for an easy explanation of other economic systems than the market system of the recent West [Arensberg 1957:99, 100].

In conclusion, several points will be summarized in order to underscore those important differences between traditional bands and tribes and national market industrial economies which make formal economic theory incapable of yielding analytical insights when applied to traditional communities.

For economic anthropology, only the substantive meaning of economic is relevant. For any primitive community, one can only assume the existence of some kind of institutional apparatus through which material goods are acquired and distributed. One cannot assume as a universal the presence of any special economizing institutions such as those which distinguish market economies. It is not economizing calculation induced by "scarcity" which is universal, but rather the need for all societies to structure the provision of material goods and services (Arensberg 1957:110).

No economic "system" is of one piece. In any society—including our own, and most certainly the primitive—there exist spheres of economy with different principles of organization, different sanctions to induce conformity, different institutionalizations of economic mechanisms, indeed, different moral values for judging worth and performance (Bohannan 1959:492). Even in our own economy, which is unusual for the quantity and variety of resources, outputs, and services transacted at money price in the gigantic sphere of market exchange, there exist sectors such as family, government, and military organization, within which non-market principles operate (Smelser 1959:173).

Primitive economy is different from market industrialism not in degree but in kind. The absence of machine technology, national resource and product market organization, and all-purpose money, plus the fact that economic transactions cannot be understood apart from social obligation, create, as it were, a non-Euclidean universe to which formal economic theory cannot be fruitfully applied. The attempt to translate primitive economic processes into functional equivalents of our own inevitably obscures just those features of primitive economy which distinguish it from our own.

It is true that many economic mechanisms and practices are either universal or very frequently found in primitive, historical, and modern economies. But their presence is not prima facie evidence of organizational, operational, or functional similarity. Division of labor, money uses, external trade, and market places are best regarded as adaptable devices (like language and mathematics), capable of varied use for different purposes in a variety of organizational contexts. Here, the poverty of our terminology is a source of built-in ambiguity. Although categories such as land tenure and division of labor may be universals, their meanings are so colored by their special organization in our own economy that when used in reference to primitive economy they inadvertently impart the familiar, specialized meaning of our own. Conceptual categories are useful analytically only when they fit real-world structures; when diverse real-world structure is made to fit our specialized categories, distortion results. "The mistake of judging the men of other periods by the morality of our own day has its parallel in the mistake of supposing that every wheel and bolt in the modern social machine had its counterpart in more rudimentary societies [Maine, quoted in Bohannan 1957:iii]."

A matter of general theoretical significance to economic anthropology concerns the dominance and frequency of reciprocative and redistributive forms of economic integration. A distinguishing characteristic of primitive life is the fusion of social and economic institutions. Indeed, even the word "fusion" is distorting because it implies the bringing together of separate elements. It would be better to say that there is no awareness of the "economy" as a distinct set of practices apart from social institutions. Transactions of material goods in marketless economies are expressions of social obligation which have neither mechanism nor meaning of their own apart from the social ties, social obligations, and social situations they express. In the Western meaning of the word, there is no "economy" in traditional society; only socio-economic institutions, processes, and transactions.

Finally, these matters are no longer of interest to anthropologists alone. Understanding primitive economy has become a necessity for those economists concerned with development and modernization (Moore 1955; Myrdal 1957; Keyfitz 1959; Shea 1959; Neale 1959). The phrase "economic growth" joins together two different kinds of change which go on simultaneously in underdeveloped areas: institutional transformation from indigenous socio-economic forms, such as reciprocity and redistribution, to market-organized industrialism; and additions to real material output generated by the new economic organization and technical apparatus. Economists are concerned with inducing real output increases, anthropologists with reducing the social decimation inherent in rapid institutional departure from indigenous forms. Both must understand the nature of the primitive economies which are being dismantled as well as the economic and social characteristics of market industrialism. For the economist to assume that the problem is primarily quantitative—more machinery, more roads, more food—would be to blind himself to the social realities of economy as well as to the social miseries of culture disintegration. "In primitive communities, the individual as an economic factor is personalized, not anonymous. He tends to hold his economic position in virtue of his social position. Hence to displace him economically means a social disturbance [Firth 1951:137]."

Formal economic theory has proved a powerful tool for making industrialized market systems grow. But primitive economies are neither industrialized nor market systems. One must start from ethno-economic analysis —with Malinowski, not Ricardo—in order to choose those transformation paths to industrialization which entail only the unavoidable social costs.

NOTES

1. I am very grateful to Karl Polanyi of Columbia University and Paul Bohannan of Northwestern University for their helpful suggestions and criticisms. Much of this essay consists of an application of Polanyi's work (1944; 1947; 1957) to the special problems considered. Part of the essay is drawn from my doctoral dissertation (Dalton 1959a).

2. As Polanyi points out, hunger is natural in the biological sense, but it is not synonymous with an incentive to produce. It becomes such an incentive if society makes eating specifically dependent on that individual's producing, which early market economy in fact did. For views similar to those of Townsend, that only poverty and the fear of hunger could make the lower classes industrious, see Bendix (1956:63–82); on the origins of laissez faire market economy in England, see also Keynes (1926).

3. In the economist's sense, "scarcity" does not mean physical shortage, but a condition of *insufficiency relative to desire*. Any item in market economy which has a money price is regarded as scarce. Scarcity is, so to speak, a fraction: the numerator is resource ingredients available, and the denominator is desire for material outputs. The cultural emphasis on material acquisition in the United States, ironically, makes factor resources very "scarce" in the most affluent society in the world.

4. I am indebted to Karl Polanyi for his illuminating distinction between the two meanings of economic (Polanyi 1957a; 1959; Hopkins 1957).

5. Compare the following two statements: "Whether we consider the motivations underlying the economic activities of peoples without writing or a machine industry, or the institutions that are the framework of the economic systems of non-literate, non-industrialized societies, it is clear that these are directed toward the same ends and utilize substantially the same means to attain those ends, as do people who are equipped with writing, and with the superior technologies of the historic societies [Herskovits 1952:487]." "Whether one looks at undeveloped areas or the most highly industrialized ones, a fundamental theoretical point is evident. That point is the great complexity of human motivation. Men will work for as many reasons as there are values to be served by such activity and will refuse to work where that serves their values. The fact that industrial systems emphasize values that are commanded in a market and incentives that provide monetary claims on a market should not blind us to the diversity of ends or the diversity of means for their satisfaction [Moore 1955:162]."

6. The extent of autonomy of market processes has been drastically reduced in Anglo-American systems, especially in the last thirty years. The experiences of depression and war have induced extensive structural reforms, increasing the number and variety of social controls over market processes. Some examples are minimum wage legislation and agricultural price supports; also, increased governmental spending and taxing for welfare, full employment, and growth purposes. From the viewpoint of this essay, two results of increased market control in the West are that formal price theory is less usefully applicable to

present-day Western economy, and the areas of similarity between economic organization in the West and in traditional society have been enlarged (Dalton 1959a: chapter 6; 1959b).

7. One need only point out that both the Soviet and American systems employ money, division of labor, foreign trade, market places, and the like, to indicate that similar economic mechanisms can be adapted to dissimilar organizational structures and used for different purposes. The point was not obvious in the nineteenth century because all Western industrialized economies were integrated through the same pattern of market exchange (Neale 1957b; Pearson 1957).

8. Adam Smith's famous dictum—that division of labor is limited by the extent of the market—is, of course, true for market economy. It does *not* mean that the prior existence of market organization is a necessary condition for division of labor to be practiced. Division of labor based on sex seems to be universal.

9. Max Weber contrasted primitive and archaic economies with the modern by singling out two features of market-organized industrial capitalism as historically unique: that the provision for a wide range of daily material needs is organized through market purchase and sale; and "Persons must be present who are not only legally in the position, but are also economically compelled, to sell their labor on the market without restriction [Weber 1923:276–277]."

REFERENCES

ARENSBERG, CONRAD
    1957   Anthropology as history. In *Trade and market in the early empires,* K. Polanyi, C. M. Arensberg, H. W. Pearson ed. Glencoe: The Free Press.
ARNOLD, ROSEMARY
    1957   A port of trade: Whydah on the Guinea coast. In *Trade and market in the early empires,* K. Polanyi, C. M. Arensberg, H. W. Pearson ed. Glencoe: The Free Press.
BENDIX, R.
    1956   *Work and authority in industry.* New York: Wiley.
BOHANNAN, PAUL
    1957   *Justice and judgment among the Tiv.* New York: Oxford University Press.
    1958   Problems in studying primitive and changing economies. Paper read at the American Anthropological Association meetings.
    1959   The impact of money on an African subsistence economy. *Journal of Economic History* 19:491–503.
BOULDING, KENNETH
    1957   The Parsonian approach to economics. *Kyklos* 10:317–319.
DALTON, GEORGE
    1959a   Robert Owen and Karl Polanyi as socioeconomic critics and reformers of industrial capitalism. Unpublished Ph.D. dissertation, University of Oregon.

1959*b* Review of *Trade and market in the early empires. Boston University Graduate Journal* 7:156–159.

1960 A note of clarification on economic surplus. *American Anthropologist* 62:438–490.

DuBois, Cora

1936 The wealth concept as an integrative factor in Tolowa-Tututni culture. In *Essays in anthropology presented to A. L. Kroeber*, R. H. Lowie ed. Berkeley: University of California Press.

Evans-Pritchard, E. E.

1954 Introduction. In *The gift*, by Marcel Mauss. Glencoe: The Free Press.

Firth, Raymond

1951 *The elements of social organisation*. London: Watts.

1958 Work and wealth of primitive communities. In *Human types*, by Raymond Firth, revised ed. New York: Mentor Books.

Fusfeld, D. B.

1957 Economic theory misplaced: livelihood in primitive society. In *Trade and market in the early empires*, K. Polanyi, C. M. Arensberg, H. W. Pearson ed. Glencoe: The Free Press.

Goldman, Irving

1937 The Kwakiutl of Vancouver Island. In *Cooperation and competition among primitive peoples*, M. Mead ed. New York: McGraw-Hill.

Goodfellow, D. M.

1939 *Principles of economic sociology*. London: Routledge.

Herskovits, Melville J.

1940 Anthropology and economics. In *The economic life of primitive peoples*, by M. J. Herskovits. New York: Knopf.

1941 Economics and anthropology: a rejoinder. *Journal of Political Economy* 49:269–278.

1952 *Economic anthropology*, revised ed. New York: Knopf.

Hopkins, Terrence K.

1957 Sociology and the substantive view of the economy. In *Trade and market in the early empires*, K. Polanyi, C. M. Arensberg, H. W. Pearson ed. Glencoe: The Free Press.

Keyfitz, N.

1959 The interlocking of social and economic factors in Asian development. *Canadian Journal of Economics and Political Science* 25:34–46.

Keynes, John Maynard

1926 *The end of laissez-faire*. London: Hogarth Press.

Knight, Frank

1941 Anthropology and economics. *Journal of Political Economy* 49:247–268.

Malinowski, Bronislaw

1922 *Argonauts of the western Pacific*. London: Routledge.

Mauss, Marcel

1925 *The gift: forms and functions of exchange in archaic societies*. Glencoe: The Free Press, 1954.

MEAD, MARGARET
  1937   Interpretive statement. In *Cooperation and competition among primi-
         tive peoples,* M. Mead ed. New York: McGraw-Hill.
MITCHELL, WESLEY C.
  1949   *Lecture notes on types of economic theory.* New York: Kelley.
MOORE, W. E.
  1955   Labor attitudes toward industrialization in underdeveloped countries.
         American Economic Review 45:156–165.
MYRDAL, GUNNAR
  1957   *Rich lands and poor.* New York: Harper.
NEALE, WALTER C.
  1957a Reciprocity and redistribution in the Indian village. In *Trade and
         market in the early empires,* K. Polanyi, C. M. Arensberg, H. W.
         Pearson ed. Glencoe: The Free Press.
  1957b The market in theory and history. In *Trade and market in the early
         empires,* K. Polanyi, C. M. Arensberg, H. W. Pearson ed. Glencoe:
         The Free Press.
  1959   Discussion of problems of economic development in nonindus-
         trialized areas. *Journal of Economic History* 19:525–527.
PEARSON, HARRY W.
  1957   The secular debate on economic primitivism. In *Trade and market in
         the early empires,* K. Polanyi, C. M. Arensberg, H. W. Pearson ed.
         Glencoe: The Free Press.
POLANYI, KARL
  1944   *The great transformation.* New York: Rinehart.
  1947   Our obsolete market mentality. *Commentary* 13:109–117.
  1957a The economy as instituted process. In *Trade and market in the early
         empires,* K. Polanyi, C. M. Arensberg, H. W. Pearson ed. Glencoe:
         The Free Press.
  1957b Aristotle discovers the economy. In *Trade and market in the early
         empires,* K. Polanyi, C. M. Arensberg, H. W. Pearson ed. Glencoe:
         The Free Press.
  1959   Anthropology and economic theory. In *Readings in anthropology* II,
         Morton H. Fried ed. New York: Thomas Y. Crowell.
  1968   *Primitive, archaic, and modern economies.* New York: Anchor
         Books, Doubleday.
ROBBINS, LIONEL
  1932   The subject matter of economics. In *An essay on the nature and sig-
         nificance of economic science,* by Lionel Robbins. London: Macmil-
         lan.
ROTTENBERG, SIMON
  1958   Review of *Trade and market in the early empires. American Eco-
         nomic Review* 48:675–678.
SHEA, THOMAS W., JR.
  1959   Barriers to economic development in traditional societies: Malabar, a
         case study. *Journal of Economic History* 19:504–522.

SMELSER, NEIL J.
  1959 A comparative view of exchange systems. *Economic Development and Cultural Change* 7:173–182.
STEINER, FRANZ
  1954 Notes on comparative economics. *British Journal of Sociology* 5:118–129.
THURNWALD, RICHARD C.
  1932 *Economics in primitive communities*. London: Oxford University Press.
WATSON, WILLIAM
  1958 *Tribal cohesion in a money economy*. Manchester: The University Press.
WEBER, MAX
  1923 *General economic history*. Glencoe: The Free Press, 1950.

3

Theoretical Issues in
Economic Anthropology[1]

The publication of *Trade and Market in the Early Empires* (1957), and other work associated with Karl Polanyi's analytical schema, has intensified theoretical disputes in economic anthropology having their origins much earlier when the subject was of interest to many fewer anthropologists (Firth 1939:chapter 1; Herskovits 1940: chapter 2; 1941). These disputes are principally over which of several alternative sets of analytical concepts are best to interpret real-world processes and institutions, and what kinds of analytical questions should be put to primitive and peasant economies—those asked by economists about our own economy, or questions having to do with the connections between economic and social organization.

This essay is addressed to issues raised recently by anthropologists who have criticized the theoretical approach of Polanyi and myself (LeClair 1962; Burling 1962; Pospisil 1963; Cook 1966). Part I states the positions of Polanyi and his critics and explains why controversy persists. Part II suggests a theoretical framework for economic anthropology which takes account of both sets of ideas. Part III considers the recent extension of economic anthropology to processes of socio-economic change, growth, and development in communities undergoing "modernization."

THE CONTROVERSY

Whether one is collecting and analyzing fieldwork information (Salisbury 1962) or writing a general or comparative work drawing on the extensive ethnographic literature (Herskovits 1952; Belshaw 1965; Nash

Reprinted, with revision, from "Theoretical Issues in Economic Anthropology," *Current Anthropology*, 10 (February 1969):63–102. Reprinted by permission of the publisher. The author regrets that he cannot reprint here some twenty pages of comment that accompanied this article.

1966), one must choose a theoretical approach. Both fieldwork and synthesis in economic anthropology suffer from inadequate theory.

1. Anthropology has devoted less attention to economic organization and performance than to kinship or politics. Only two anthropologists, Bronislaw Malinowski and Raymond Firth, have a large corpus of writings in economic anthropology and relatively few—principally Cyril Belshaw, Paul Bohannan, Mary Douglas, Clifford Geertz, Maurice Godelier, Melville Herskovits, Sidney Mintz, Manning Nash, Marshall Sahlins, and Richard Salisbury—have written at length on its theoretical aspects.[2]

2. Anthropologists understand the economic organization and the economic theory of industrial capitalism much less well than they understand European and American politics, kinship, and religion and the theories which explain them. Some anthropologists seem not to understand that conventional economics—the most abstract and mathematical of the social sciences—does not deal with what anthropologists mean by human behavior and that the concepts of conventional economics relating to economic *organization* are not (with some minor qualifications) fruitfully applicable outside of market systems. What is a serious point of contention among anthropologists (LeClair 1962; Burling 1962; Cook 1966) is dismissed out of hand by a prominent development economist: ". . . the economist who studies the non-market economy has to abandon most of what he has learnt, and adopts the techniques of the anthropologist [Lewis 1962:viii]."

3. Economists have not been concerned with primitive and peasant societies and economies. Until recently they had been concerned exclusively with one type of economy, industrial capitalism. The concepts, leading ideas, and causal analyses of price theory, aggregate income theory, and growth theory—as well as fields such as international trade, and money— deal with the structure, performance, and problems of U.S. and West European economies in the nineteenth and twentieth centuries. Economists have had no reason to spell out the content and method of economics in such fashion as to make clear what in conventional economics is and what is not relevant to economic anthropology.

> The fact that the attention of economists has been focused so exclusively on just those aspects of our economy least likely to be found among non-literate folk has thus confused anthropologists who turned to economic treatises for clarification of problems and methods in the study of the economic systems of non-literate societies [Herskovits 1952:53].

Very few economists other than myself and those represented in *Trade and Market* (Polanyi, Neale, Pearson, and Fusfeld) have written on these issues. The few economists who have written on the relevance of economics to economic anthropology have done so principally in book reviews (Knight 1941; Rottenberg 1958; Boulding 1957).

The field of comparative economic systems came into being only in the

1930's and 1940's (with central planning in the Soviet Union, enlarged governmental spending, borrowing, taxing, and market controls in fascist Germany, the American New Deal, and welfare state reforms in England and Scandinavia). The field remains confined to the study of national industrialized economies. It compares the structure and performance of U.S. and Soviet-type economies and considers the literature of socialism (Gruchy 1966). "Comparative economic systems" has never included the economies studied by anthropologists or those described in the literature of pre-industrial economic history of Europe.

The field of economic development, which came into being after World War II with the achievement of political independence by former colonies in Africa and Asia, brought American and European economists for the first time into those areas of the world in which anthropologists have traditionally centered their interests. Most of the literature of economic development deals, however, with the same impersonal matters of investment and foreign trade relating to the *national* economy (for example, Nigeria, not the Tiv) that economists are concerned with in analyzing our own national economy. A small part of the development literature written by economists is concerned with social organization and culture (what economists call "institutional matters"), as these relate to national and local community development (Lewis 1955; Myrdal 1957; Hagen 1962; Yudelman 1964; Adelman and Morris 1965; 1967; Dalton 1965c).

With the minor and recent qualifications of comparative economic systems and economic development, conventional economics excludes entirely from its formal analyses matters relating to social organization and culture. Thus the relation of economic to social organization—a problem important in economic anthropology—does not arise in conventional economic theory. It is unfortunate that anthropologists have turned for guidance to post-industrial economic theory rather than to pre-industrial European economic and social history. Pirenne (1936), Bloch (1961; 1966), Bennett (1962), Weber (1950), and Polanyi (who was an economic historian) have more to teach anthropologists about the economies they study than do Marshall (1920), Knight (1941), or Robbins (1935).

4. Almost all the communities anthropologists study in the field are now experiencing some extent of economic, social, cultural, or technological change as parts of newly independent nation-states bent on "modernization" and economic development. The subject of socio-economic change within the context of developing nation-states is extremely complicated and, of course, very recent. We know more about "traditional" systems before European incursion and about the kinds of change that took place in the nineteenth century with colonialism. The scope of economic anthropology is now widening considerably. The older focus of interest was the organization and functioning of indigenous economy as it relates to social re-

lationships at one point in time, or under conditions of slow change (Malinowski 1922; 1935). The new focus of interest is modernization. The newly established political independence of Asian and African nation-states and their governments' explicit intention to create and develop national societies and economies make the context of present-day village community change sufficiently different from that of the early culture contact studies (for instance, on the depopulation of Melanesia or the introduction of the horse among the Plains Indians) to require new theoretical approaches and new policy concerns.

In the absence of adequate theory, controversy persists as to the merits of various alternative frames of reference for the analytical treatment of primitive and peasant societies. The main point of contention has aroused heated controversy: the extent to which anthropologists should adopt conventional economics as the conceptual language with which to analyze tribal and peasant economies (Firth 1958:63). Unlike Auden's academic warriors who "fight with smiles and Christian names," some of the participants in this dispute display the ferocity of those engaged in theological battle, a battle which has now become a thirty years' war (Goodfellow 1939: chapter 1; Firth 1939: chapter 1; Herskovits 1940: chapter 2; 1941; 1952; Knight 1941; Polanyi 1944: chapter 4; 1947; 1957; Rottenberg 1958; Sahlins 1960; Dalton 1961; 1962; 1965a; LeClair 1962; Burling 1962; Cook 1966).

The economic anthropologist finds two ready-made bodies of economic theory—concepts, leading ideas, terminology, and generalizations—both created to analyze industrial capitalist economies: conventional economic theory and Marxian theory.[3] The question that confronts him is whether to borrow concepts and leading ideas from these, or to invent a special set of concepts and leading ideas having no counterparts in conventional and Marxian economics—or, indeed, to use some combination of conventional economics, Marxian economics, and a special set of concepts designed for primitive and peasant economies.

The problem seems no longer to arise in other branches of anthropological inquiry. Anthropologists seem to agree that it is inappropriate to borrow concepts and leading ideas from Western religious theory (Christianity and Judaism) and political theory (democracy and dictatorship) to analyze religious and political organization:

Nothing is so misleading in ethnographic accounts as the description of facts of native civilizations in terms of our own [Malinowski 1922:176].

The mistake of judging the men of other periods by the morality of our own day has its parallel in the mistake of supposing that every wheel and bolt in the modern social machine has its counterpart in more rudimentary societies [Maine, quoted in Bohannan 1957:iii].

. . . most anthropologists have ceased to take their bearings in the study of religion from any religion practiced in their own society [Lienhardt 1956:310].

One important discovery made in . . . [*African Political Systems*] was that the institutions through which a society organized politically need not necessarily look like the kinds of political institutions with which we have long been familiar in the Western world, and in the great nations of Asia [Gluckman and Cunnison 1962:vi].

In economic anthropology, however, there are those who argue that the leading ideas, concepts, and terminology of conventional price theory (economizing, maximizing, elasticity, scarcity, supply, demand, capital, and so on) are applicable to primitive as well as peasant economies studied by anthropologists; that the basic similarities between tribal and peasant economies and industrial capitalism are sufficiently close so that some sort of universal economic theory—embracing the very large number of economies studied by anthropologists as well as our own—is achievable; and that anthropologists should learn more conventional economics so as to be able to put the same questions about economic *performance* to their data that economists put to theirs and (as economists do) to quantify their data when possible (Firth 1957; 1964a; 1965; Salisbury 1962: chapters 6–9).

With a few exceptions (Bohannan and Dalton 1965; Dalton 1964) Polanyi and the group associated with him have not concerned themselves with *peasant* economies. My own view is that conventional economics is relevant to the commercialized sectors of peasant economic *organization* (that is, where dependence on purchased land, wage-labor, and the market sale of produce is quantitatively important) and useful in quantifying economic *performance*—the amounts and composition of produce—for any economy, primitive, peasant, industrial capitalist, or industrial communist; but that the differences between traditional band and tribal economic organization (where market transactions of resources and produce are absent or present only in petty amounts) and our own are so great that a special set of concepts, leading ideas, and terms is necessary to analyze these subsistence economies. Special analytical concepts are necessary because social organization and culture—kinship, political organization, religion—affect economic organization and performance so directly and sensitively in non-market systems that only a socio-economic approach which considers explicitly the relationships between economy and society is capable of yielding insights and generalizations of importance (Sahlins 1968: chapter 5). A special set of questions should be put to primitive economies and the non-commercial sectors of peasant economies: questions about the social aspects of economic organization.

The ties between producers tend to reach out beyond this common interest in the act of production and its rewards alone. A production relationship is often only one facet of a social relationship. . . . Economic relations can be understood only as a part of a scheme of social relations. . . . Economic anthropology deals primarily with the economic aspects of the social relations of persons [Firth 1951:136–138].

Polanyi focuses on economy as a set of rules of social organization and on economic structure (organization) rather than quantifiable performance (levels of output; productivity). Moreover, he confines his analysis to primitive and archaic (state-organized, pre-industrial) economies.

The two groups agree that knowledge of economics and of our own economic system, industrial capitalism, should figure explicitly and importantly in economic anthropology. They disagree sharply, however, on the appropriate way to incorporate conventional economics and knowledge of our own economy. The "formalist" group take what they believe to be the universally applicable concepts of economic theory—scarcity, maximizing, surplus—as that which is to be incorporated in economic anthropology and analyze the empirical data of primitive and peasant economies in these terms (Pospisil 1963; Firth 1965). They use the leading ideas of elementary economics (Samuelson 1967: chapters 1–3) as a guide to analyzing all economies.

Polanyi (1944: chapter 4), Neale (1957*a*), Fusfeld (1957), and I (Dalton 1961; 1962) describe the salient characteristics of industrial capitalism and economic theory so as to provide a base of contrast with that subset of economies we call "primitive." We then show how variants of reciprocity and redistribution act as integrating organizational principles of land and labor allocation, work organization, and produce disposition (Polanyi 1957; Neale 1957*a*), and how external trade and money uses in such economies are derivative expressions of reciprocal and redistributive modes of transaction (Bohannan 1959; Dalton 1965*a*). Polanyi argues that the concepts of economic theory yield useful insights when applied to our own economy because the institutionalized rules of market exchange and the use of our kind of money and technology induce economizing and maximizing activities; but to employ these terms to analyze the non-market sectors of primitive and peasant economies is as distorting as it would be to use the concepts of Christianity to analyze primitive religions.

The "formalist" group confuse the *ability* to translate any socio-economic transaction or exchange (potlatch, kula, bridewealth) into market terms with the *usefulness* of doing so (Homans 1958; Pospisil 1963). Describing the potlatch as an investment which yields 100 percent interest (Boas 1897), bridewealth as the price one pays for sexual and domestic services (Gray 1960), and shell transactions on Rossel Island as cash payments for market purchases (Armstrong 1924; 1928) suggests they are basically similar to ordinary commercial transactions in our own economy. These are the analytical views of the anthropologist, his *interpretation* of real-world processes which remain the same regardless of what he calls them. Whether it is analytically revealing to interpret the potlatch, bride-wealth, and Rossel Island shells in such fashion depends on the folk views of these events and usages, as well as on an assessment of the differences between these and commercial transactions (Dalton 1961:10–14; 1966).

The Quest for a Universal Theory

There is a deep-seated yearning in social science to discover one general approach, one general law valid for all time and all climes. But these primitive attitudes must be outgrown [Gerschenkron 1954:254].

Those who insist on the applicability of conventional economics to primitive economies are really in quest of a universal theory—a single set of concepts which would yield fruitful insights for all economies, those studied by anthropologists as well as those studied by economists and historians.[4]

What is required . . . is a search for the general theory of economic process and structure of which contemporary economic theory is but a special case [LeClair 1962:1188].

What is required from economic anthropology is the analysis of material in such a way that it will be directly comparable with the material of modern economics, matching assumption with assumption and so allowing generalizations to be ultimately framed which will subsume the phenomena of both price and non-price communities into a body of principles about human behavior which will be truly universal [Firth 1966:14].

The difficulty with this approach is that economic anthropology deals with an extraordinary range of matters in an extraordinarily large set of economies: it is concerned with *organization and performance of band, tribal, and peasant economies under pre-colonial, colonial, and post-colonial conditions*. What Firth and LeClair suggest be treated under a single theory is assigned in economics (and sociology) to several subfields: price and distribution theory; aggregate income theory; growth theory; comparative economic systems; national income accounting; industrial sociology; and others. In economics we have one set of analytical concepts to answer the question, "What determines prices in U.S. type economies?" And we have a different set to answer the question, "What determines gross national product?"—and yet another to answer the question, "How do we measure national income?" In economic anthropology we also need several sets of analytical and measurement concepts because of the several kinds of economies we are dealing with and the different kinds of questions we put to the data.

In summary, those of the thousands of economies studied by anthropologists that are underdeveloped, small-scale market systems—peasant economies (Tax 1963; Firth 1946)—can be fruitfully analyzed with the concepts of conventional economics. Moreover, the quantifiable performance of all economies, primitive and peasant included, can be measured in simplified terms analogous to national income accounting terms. But to put interesting questions about the organization of traditional band and tribal economies, and primitive and peasant economies undergoing change, growth, and development, requires conceptual categories different from those used in conventional economics. This is especially the case in matters relating to the cultural and social consequences of economic change.

The Economy: Individual Behavior versus Rules of Social Organization

Another underlying difficulty is the existence of two rather different ways of perceiving an economy: one is to concentrate on economic "behavior" of individual persons and the motives that impel the individual behavers, so that the economy is seen as a cluster of individual actors and their motives.

Economics . . . has long been confidently felt to include a tolerably well-defined type of human behavior. . . . None of these definitions [of economics] covers exactly the same area of behavior as any other. . . . Even economists have long claimed to equate the material side of life with economic behavior. . . . Since this definition does not isolate any type of behavior from any other type. . . . If the unity of economics arises out of the fact that it deals with priced goods, then in some primitive societies it is silly to look for any behavior that can be called "economic.". . . Economics in this view focuses on a particular *aspect* of behavior and not on certain kinds of behavior [Burling 1962:802, 805, 808, 811].

The other approach is to perceive the economy as a set of rules of social organization (analogous to polity and political rules), so that each of us is born into a "system" whose rules we learn. It is from observing the activities and transactions of participants that we derive these systematic rules. This is how Polanyi regards an economy, and, indeed, it is the approach used in comparative economic systems in contrasting the organization (rules) of Soviet and U.S. economies.

Those who perceive an economy as a cluster of individual behavers frequently equate whatever economic activities the behavers undertake with explicit *choice* of those activities, and they believe that such choice affirms the economics textbook dictum that in all economies there must be choice of what to produce, how to produce it, and who is to get how much of what is produced. This way of introducing the topics of resource allocation, production functions, and income distribution in industrial capitalism to beginning students in economics is useful because the individual house-holds and firms in national market economies such as our own are con-fronted with many explicit choices: which of thousands of goods and services to buy; which of hundreds of job markets to enter; which of doz-ens of products to produce; which of several techniques to use to produce them. These alternative choices are subject to fine calculation because in-dustrial capitalism makes extensive use of money and pricing and because there are real alternatives among which economic choices can be made without calling down social opprobrium. For example, the American farmer, entirely depending on market sale for livelihood, must choose ex-plicitly how much of each kind of cash crop to grow. The relevant consid-erations are not personal taste, social obligation, or physical yield, but physical yield times expected money price compared to money costs of production. He makes explicit "economizing" decisions about costs rela-tive to expected market revenue for the several alternative crops he can grow and the several alternative combinations of resources he can *buy* to grow them. His livelihood depends on such choices. The constraints within which he must choose, the range of choice open to him, and his ability to make fine calculations in monetary terms, are all special to market-capital-ism.

In subsistence (non-market) economies, the question of choice among real alternatives does not arise in such explicit fashion. A Trobriand Is-lander learns and follows the rules of *economy* in his society almost as an American learns and follows the rules of *language* in his. An American is born into an English-speaking culture. In no sense does he "choose" to speak English, because no real alternative is presented to him. So, too, the Trobriander is born into a yam-growing economy. He does not "choose" to plant yams rather than broccoli. The question does not arise in this form, but rather in the form of how much of each of very few conventional crops to plant or how to apportion a given workday to several tasks.

In the Trobriand subsistence economy, labor, land, and other resources are not purchased, and produce is not destined for sale to others, so it is personal taste within the *ecological* constraints set by resource endowment, the *technological* constraints set by known techniques of production, and the *social* constraints set by the obligation to provide sister's husband with yams that dictate how much of each crop is to be planted.[5] So, too, for Ti-kopia:

> . . . in Tikopia on any given day a man has in theory a choice between working in his orchard and going out fishing, in a canoe or on the reef. It might be held that he will decide according to his preference at the time for an ultimate yield of crops or an immediate one of fish. But in practice his choice may be rigidly determined by social and ritual considerations. The re-cent death of a man of rank and the taboos associated with mourning may

bar him absolutely from any resort to canoe-fishing out at sea, although such may otherwise be his preference and would yield him a greater material return. . . . Moreover, the period of his abstention from canoe-fishing tends to vary directly in accordance with his propinquity of kinship to the dead [Firth 1966:12].

In traditional bands, tribes, and some peasantries—small economies without machines, markets, or commercial money—the constraints on individual choice of material goods and economic activities are extreme and are dictated not only by social obligation but also by primitive technology and by physical environment. There is simply no equivalent to the range of choice of goods and activities in industrial capitalism which makes meaningful such economic concepts as "maximizing" and "economizing." Nor is there the possibility of fine calculation in monetary terms which pricing allows.

As the literature of theoretical contention in economic anthropology grows, it becomes increasingly clear that those who argue that conventional economics is *applicable* to primitive economies—the Trobriand and Tiv type of economy—have three things in mind:

1. The first is the least difficult to unravel. It is to regard peasant economies as the typical cases to be analyzed in economic anthropology and to assume that what is true for peasant economies is also true for primitive economies because they are both within the universe of anthropological interest, and somehow a single set of concepts and generalizations should apply. Peasant economies are small-scale, underdeveloped market economies, in which production for market sale, the use of commercial money, the availability of purchased factors of production, and other features of market economies are present. The structure and performance of the commercialized sectors of peasant economies are amenable to analysis and measurement in conventional economic terms (precisely because money, prices, and markets are important). But this does not mean that the same is true for primitive band and tribal economies—the Trobriands, the Nuer —in which the crucial features of market organization which allow analysis in market concepts and measurement in money terms are absent.

2. The second reason some anthropologists think conventional economics is applicable to all economies is—to speak bluntly—due to their imperfect understanding of economic theory and its concepts. From Goodfellow (1939) and Herskovits (1952) to Burling (1962) and Cook (1966), there is misunderstanding of what economists mean by "scarcity," "economize," "maximize," and "rational choice." Given cost and demand schedules for a firm, there is one price-output combination at which a firm maximizes its profit. This can be shown unambiguously by reference to other price-output combinations for the firm. Anthropologists misuse—or better, mis-translate—this piece of analysis by erroneously equating all *purpose-*

ful activities with economizing or maximizing and then jumping to the conclusion that because purposeful choices are made in primitive economies, economic theory must apply.

> Our primary concern in these pages is to understand the cross-cultural implications of the process of economizing [Herskovits 1952:4].

> From this point of view, we are "economizing" in everything we do. We are always trying to maximize our satisfactions somehow, and so we are led back to the notion that economics deals not with a type but rather with an aspect of behavior. This economic view of society becomes . . . one model for looking at society. It is a model which sees the individuals of a society busily engaged in maximizing their own satisfactions—desire for power, sex, food, independence . . . [Burling 1962:817–818].

Such misinterpretations of economic concepts persist because economists who have had occasion to deal with anthropology or primitive societies— Irma Adelman, Joseph Berliner, Everett Hagen, Arthur Lewis—have not addressed themselves to these matters, and the economists who have are associated with Polanyi. Because a Tikopian chooses to fish today rather than to tend his garden does not mean that the economics of Tikopian fishing or gardening is usefully described by linear programming or oligopoly theory.

3. The third way in which it is thought that conventional economics applies to primitive economy is in the measurement of economic performance. Several branches of applied economics and statistics measure production flows (such as input-output analysis) and total output and its composition (national income accounting) for large-scale, nationally-integrated, industrialized economies of both the U.S. and Soviet types. Some kind of measurement of output is possible for any type of economy, no matter how primitive and small, because it is always possible to measure output and performance in terms of the resources used (labor days to build a hut), or in the real terms of the produce forthcoming (tons of yams produced).

Salisbury's book on a primitive economy in New Guinea before and after the introduction of purchased steel axes is cited by Firth (1965) and Cook (1966) as proof of the ability to "apply" conventional economics to a primitive economy because Salisbury does some rather elementary calculations such as the number of man-days of labor required to produce a variety of items (1962:147). Such calculations can be done for any economy —Robinson Crusoe's, a medieval monastery, an Israeli kibbutz, or Communist China.

If what anthropologists mean by "applying economic theory" is to count the number of yams produced and the number of labor days needed to build a hut, most certainly economic theory is applicable to all economies.

But this is a rather simplistic notion of what "applying economic theory" means.

A prominent national income economist at Cambridge says the following about her experience in measuring subsistence income in rural Rhodesia:

> An attempt to examine the structure and problems of a primitive community in the light of the existing body of economic thought raises fundamental conceptual issues. Economic analysis and its framework of generalizations are characteristically described in terms appropriate to the modern exchange economy. It is by no means certain that the existing tools of analysis can usefully be applied to material other than that for which they have been developed. In particular it is not clear what light, if any, is thrown on subsistence economies by a science which seems to regard the use of money and specialization of labor as axiomatic. The jargon of the market place seems remote, on the face of it, from the problems of an African village where most individuals spend the greater part of their lives in satisfying their own or their families' needs and desires, where money and trade play a subordinate role in motivating productive activity [Deane 1953:115–116].

It is true that in attempting to measure economic performance quantitatively, anthropologists put the same questions to small subsistence economies that economists put to our own and the Soviet national economy: What is the total output and its composition for the community? How is income divided? But the absence of cash and pricing means that only crude estimates of output can be indicated—nothing like the detailed components of national income and gross national product for developed economies; and the small number of goods and services produced, together with the absence of complicated processes of manufacture and fabrication (the absence of inter-firm and inter-industry transactions in developed economies), means that input-output analysis yields no useful information.

I would agree emphatically that output statistics for subsistence economies are worth having especially in the analysis of community change, growth, and development (Epstein 1962). They would give us additional information, along with knowledge of socio-economic organization, of the pre-modernization economy, as well as rough benchmarks from which to measure growth. I suggest, however, that for traditional, slow-changing, subsistence (and peasant) economies, it is the analysis of socio-economic organization rather than performance that yields insights of comparable interest and depth to those got in analyzing primitive religions, polity, kinship, and so forth.

Traditional, Subsistence Economies

Cook (1966) criticizes Polanyi and me for analyzing in detail the structure of traditional subsistence economies such as the Trobriand Islands in

Malinowski's time. At present, very few such economies exist intact, almost all of them undergoing various kinds and degrees of economic, social, cultural, and technological change.[6] This kind of complaint seems not to be made in other branches of anthropology: do anthropologists criticize each other for studying traditional political organization or traditional religion because—like traditional economy—they are now undergoing change? Indeed, why study history, then, since it is concerned with forms of social organization no longer in being?

Here we have an example of an odd double standard in anthropology. Anthropologists who would condemn out of hand a theoretical approach which regarded primitive religion or political organization as being simply variants of European religions and polities, to be analyzed in the conceptual language of Christianity and democracy, nevertheless approach primitive economy as though it were simply a variant of capitalism to be analyzed in the conceptual language of supply, demand, elasticity, capital, maximizing, (bride) price, and so on (LeClair 1962; Pospisil 1963).

To answer the question specifically: Anthropologists have both old and new reasons to study the organization of traditional, subsistence economies, even today when these are changing. One old reason is precisely the same that justifies their studying other aspects of traditional social organization and culture—religion, polity, kinship, language: to find out how these are (or were) organized in as many societies as we can, make analytical generalizations about them, and compare them to our own Western systems. But there are special reasons as well.

Writings in economic anthropology are either descriptive ethnographies or theoretical analyses. The theoretical portion of economic anthropology has been poorly done. I do not mean to suggest that theoretical light began to dawn only with the publication of *Trade and Market in the Early Empires*. Malinowski (1921; 1922; 1935), Mauss (1954), and Firth (1929; 1939; 1946)—to name only the outstanding—have made contributions of great importance. But much was not done, and much of what was done was done poorly. And it is Polanyi's work on modes of transaction, money, markets, external trade, and operational devices in primitive and archaic economies that has begun important new lines of analysis and, indeed, has allowed us to clear up some old muddles such as "primitive money" (Polanyi 1957; 1968; Dalton 1965) and economic "surplus" (Pearson 1957; Dalton 1960; 1963).

The peoples and communities of Africa, Asia, Latin America, and Oceania traditionally studied by anthropologists are experiencing the several kinds of change entailed in economic development, industrialization, urbanization, and the formation of nation-states. Anthropologists are increasingly concerned with the processes and problems of change. There is a rapidly growing literature of theory and case studies (Smelser 1963;

Douglas 1965; Brokensha 1966). Indeed, anthropologists have returned to places they did field work in twenty or more years earlier, to study social and economic change (Firth 1959; 1966).

I suggest that analytical insights and generalizations about change and development have to be based on firm understanding of traditional organization (Dalton 1964; 1965b). Change is always change of what is; and what is, depends on what has been: "Any planned growth is embedded in a set of institutions and attitudes which come from the past [Keyfitz 1959:34]."

One can illustrate the point from European and American experience. How is it possible to understand the causes and consequences of those New Deal, Fair Deal, or "Great Society" changes in the U.S. economy and their counterparts in the English and Scandinavian welfare states, except by knowing the structure and performance of nineteenth- and early twentieth-century capitalism in Europe and the United States? How is it possible to understand the impact of Western money on subsistence economies in Africa unless one first understands the nature of indigenous money and its uses, which, in turn, requires knowing how indigenous economy functioned before the monetary incursion (Bohannan 1959; Douglas 1958)? So, too, in order to understand why litigation over land rights sometimes occurs when land is first made subject to contractual purchase and sale, one has to know the nature of land tenure *before* land was made marketable (Biebuyck 1963).

Processes of modernization—industrialization, the expansion of commercial production—ramify into all segments of society and culture. Many of the anthropological studies being undertaken are addressed to two broad questions, both of which require knowledge of traditional, "premodernization" structures: (1) What are those features of traditional social organization, culture, polity, and economy that make for receptivity or resistance to technological, economic, and cultural innovations (Douglas 1965)? (2) What are the "impacts"—processes of sequential change—on traditional social organization and culture when a group undertakes enlarged production for sale, the use of Western money and technology, and incorporates other such innovations (Gulliver 1965; Epstein 1962; Firth and Yamey 1964)?

A THEORETICAL FRAMEWORK
FOR ECONOMIC ANTHROPOLOGY

A good theoretical framework for economic anthropology should be clear about the similarities and differences between our own economy and primitive and peasant economies and about the relevance of conventional economics to economic anthropology; and it should contain an explicit

Table 3–1   *Economic Anthropology*

---

1. Socio-economic Organization: Band and Tribal Economies, before modernization
   Peasant Economies, before modernization
2. Economic Performance: Band and Tribal Economies, before modernization
   Peasant Economies, before modernization
3. Socio-economic Organization and Economic Performance in Traditional Primitive and Peasant Economies Compared to Industrial Capitalism
4. Processes and Problems of Socio-economic Change, Growth, and Development in Primitive and Peasant Communities

---

statement of the matters to be analyzed in economic anthropology (Table 3–1).

I shall discuss some of the conceptual categories I think most useful in economic anthropology, indicating the questions they help answer and the leading ideas they are associated with (see Tables 3–2 and 3–3). In doing so I hope to make several points: to show how much at the beginnings of theoretical analysis we are in economic anthropology; to show what a wide variety of structures, processes, and problems are dealt with in the subject; and to suggest lines of analysis and conceptual categories that seem promising.

Economic Anthropology As Part of Comparative Economy

The economies of direct interest to anthropologists are the large set of subsistence and peasant communities in Africa, Asia, Latin America, Oceania, and the Middle East. The focus of analytical interest is either their traditional organization and performance before serious Western incursion (Malinowski 1922; 1935) or matters relating to socio-economic change and development (Epstein 1962; Firth 1966). In either case there is an important literature outside of anthropology. The fields in economics which provide complementary information are pre-industrial economic history (Postan 1966; Takizawa 1927), comparative economic systems (Grossman 1967; Myrdal 1960; Carr 1951), and the institutional literature of economic development (Lewis 1955; Myrdal 1957; Hagen 1962; Adelman and Morris 1967).

Economic anthropology is best done within a framework of comparative economic systems which draws on all economies of record. The analysis of pre-industrial, developed, and developing economies is now scattered in various branches of economics, history, sociology, and anthropology, all of which contribute factual information and theory of use to the broad range of topics considered in economic anthropology (see Table 3–2).

Table 3-2 *Economies of Record and Social Science Subfields*

	Economies of Record				
Small-Scale			*National*		
Band, Tribal, and Peasant, Before Modernization	*Band, Tribal, and Peasant, Change and Development*	*Utopian*[a]	*Nineteenth-Century Capitalism*	*Welfare State and Fascism*	*Communist*
Economic Anthropology	Economic Anthropology Applied Anthropology	European and American History	Economic History	Comparative Economic Systems	Soviet Economy[b]
Preindustrial Economic and Social History (e.g., Europe and Asia)	Economic Development		History of Economic Thought	Economic History	Comparative Economic Systems
	Economic History		Classical and Neoclassical Economic Theory	Modern Economic Theory	
			Industrial Sociology	Industrial Sociology	Industrial Sociology

[a] The important connections between the structure of traditional, primitive economies and utopian communities (Noyes 1870; Nordhoff 1961; Bestor 1950; Bishop 1950) have never been systematically analyzed. Both kinds are small-scale economies whose internal organization is of non-market sorts; where production processes—especially land tenure, work organization, and produce allocation—express social relationships. It is this feature which makes writers like Nyerere (1964) and Senghor (1964) assert that traditional African communities had a "socialist" ethos.

[b] Soviet economy has developed as a separate field of specialization within economics; see Nove (1962).

Table 3–3 *Analytical Categories and Relevant Questions in Economic Anthropology*

I. Traditional Economies

A. *Types*

1. Primitive bands and some tribes, all without centralized polity (Tiv).
2. Primitive tribes with centralized polity: chiefdoms, kingdoms, empires (Nupe, Bantu, Inca).
3. Peasant (Malay fishermen, Latin American peasantries).

B. *Analytical Distinctions*

1. Organization

   a. Size of economy; technology; natural resource endowment.

   b. Transactional modes (reciprocity, redistribution, market exchange; dominant-integrative modes distinguished from petty modes).

   c. Production processes: (1) allocation of resources (land acquisition, use, and transfer; labor acquisition and use; the acquisition, use, and transfer of tools and equipment); (2) work organization; (3) disposition of produce; (4) specialist services and their remuneration.

   d. Organization and role(s) of external trade (reciprocal gift trade; politically administered trade; market trade).

   e. Organization and role(s) of internal markets and market places (marketless economies, petty market places, small-scale market-integrated economies; resource markets and produce markets).

   f. Organization of money and money uses (general-purpose and special-purpose monies; commercial and non-commercial uses of money; relation of money uses to transactional modes).

   g. Operational devices: record-keeping, accounting, and measurement devices (quipu strings, pebble counts); devices of culture contact (silent trade, border markets, ports of trade).

   h. Prestige economy contrasted with subsistence economy (transactional spheres and conversions; bridewealth; ceremonial transfers; valuables and treasures as special-purpose monies).

   i. The relation of economic to social organization (the place of economy in society): social control of resource allocation, work organization, and produce disposition; social guarantee of livelihood through resource allocation and the provision of emergency subsistence.

2. Performance

   a. Number of goods and specialist services produced or acquired.

   b. Level of output; fluctuations in output; frequency of dearth or

Table 3–3 (*Continued*)

famine (emergency devices in dearth or famine: use of trade partners for emergency gifts; use of less-preferred foods; emergency conversions, such as sale of treasures and people for food).

    c. Distribution of real income: equal or unequal? Why?

    d. Distribution of subsistence goods contrasted with distribution of prestige goods (spheres of exchange; conversion between spheres).

C. *Special Problems Relating to Peasant Economies*

  1. The nature of markets in traditional peasantries contrasted with national, developed market economies; why "penny capitalism" is an appropriate description of traditional peasant economy.

  2. Peasant economy and culture before and after the Industrial Revolution.

  3. The mixture of traditional and market economy; of traditional and modern technology; of traditional social organization and culture and elements of modern culture. Traditional peasantries; early modernization; late modernization.

  4. Traditional peasant economy and society in contrast to traditional band and tribal economy and society and in contrast to industrial capitalist economy and society.

  5. Hybrid—Composite peasantries of recent settlement in Latin America different from European peasantries of long settlement.

II. Socio-Economic Change, Growth, and Development: Sequential Process Analysis

A. *Contexts of change and development: colonialism-culture contact; political independence with explicit national and village level modernization*

B. *Types of change*

  1. Degenerative: severe cultural disruption, loss of autonomy, and absence of substitute forms of organization.

  2. Cash income growth without development: primitive economies becoming peasant; adoption of cash-earning activities with little or no disruption of ordinary life and without concomitant technological and other innovations which diversify and sustain income growth.

  3. Development: sustained income growth for the local community through integration—economic, political, cultural—into the larger socio-economic nation of which it is a part, without loss of ethnic identity or group malaise. Continual diminution in differences between rural and urban life as micro-development proceeds.

What Is an Economic "System"?

One of the many semantic difficulties in economic anthropology is that the word "economy" (like the words "society" and "culture") has no size dimension attached to it. We speak of the economy of a hunting band comprising a few dozen persons or the economy of Communist China, comprising several hundred million.

Whatever the size of the economy, it will have several features in common, three of which are of special interest.

1. Whether the human group is called band, tribe, village, or nation, and whether its economy is called primitive, peasant, capitalist, or communist, it consists of people with recognized social and cultural affinities—kinship, religion, language, neighborhood—expressed in some sort of shared community or social life. This means that two kinds of goods and specialist services [7] must be provided for use within the community (however defined): food and other material requisites of *physical* existence, and goods and services for religion, defense, settlement of dispute, rites of passage, and other aspects of *social* and community life. The acquisition or production of material items and specialist services necessary for physical and social existence is never left to chance because neither individuals nor communities can survive without them. It is for this reason that it is useful to regard all communities or societies as having economic systems. The word "system" refers to structured arrangements and rules which assure that material goods and specialist services are provided in repetitive fashion. Economic anthropology has to spell out these rules and systematic arrangements for that set of societies of interest to anthropologists.

2. A second similarity among economies is that they all make use of some form(s) of natural resources (land, waterways, minerals), human cooperation (division of labor), and technology (tools, and knowledge of production or acquisition processes). Each of these features is structured: the use of tools, natural resources, and division of labor require social rules —specified rights and obligations. The rules for the acquisition, use, and transfer of rights to land we call "land tenure"; the rules specifying human cooperation in production processes we call "division of labor" or "work organization"; if tools and technical knowledge are important in any economy there will be rules for their acquisition, use, and transfer.

Two general points emerge. When the rules specifying rights of acquisition or usage of any of these components of an economy are expressions of kinship or political relationships, the economic component is inextricably related to the social, and we have a *socio-economic* practice, institution, or process. Aboriginal land tenure in parts of Africa is an obvious example, where land is acquired through kinship right or tribal affiliation (Bohannan 1954; Schapera and Goodwin 1937: 157). Second, what we call economic organization is the set of rules in force through which natural resources, human cooperation, and technology are brought together to provide material items and specialist services in sustained and repetitive fashion.

3. A third similarity is the incorporation of superficially similar devices and practices in economies differently organized. Economies as different as the United States, the U.S.S.R., and the Tiv make use of market places, foreign trade, monetary objects, and devices for measuring and record-keeping.

In summary, all societies of record—those studied by anthropologists, historians, and economists—have structured arrangements to provide the material means of individual and community life. It is these structured rules that we call an economic system. Economic anthropology delineates these rules of economy by describing activities and folk views and analyzing transactional processes and relationships in the small-scale, preindustrial communities of the underdeveloped world; and it makes comparisons between primitive, peasant, and industrialized developed economies. So, too, with comparing the components and sectors of economy: the allocation of land and labor, the organization of work, the disposition of produce, and the organization and usage of forms of money, markets, and external trade. There are very important differences among economies, however—differences in organization and in performance—and much valuable analysis lies in contrasting bands, tribes, and peasantries in different historical conditions: pre-colonial, colonial, and post-colonial.

Traditional, Primitive Economies: Structure and Performance [8]

The questions about traditional band and tribal economies of most interest to anthropologists relate to their organization (structure) and to comparisons of their organization with that of other types of economy (peasant, industrial capitalist). With regard to their performance, one can indicate the relatively narrow range of goods and specialist services produced or acquired. The level of output and fluctuations in output can be measured in terms of quantities produced (Deane 1953; Reynders 1963). Input measures can be devised (Salisbury 1962), indicating amounts of equipment used in production processes and workdays employed, and so arrive at some estimates of productivity. Dietary standards can be scrutinized (Richards 1939). Some impressions of the equality or inequality in real-income distribution can be conveyed. Given the absence of Western money and pricing and the relatively few resources used and goods produced, these measures of performance can only be rough indicators stated in terms of the resource and product units themselves.

The Scale of Primitive Economies

"It is this smallness of scale, so hard for a modern European to grasp imaginatively, which is the fundamental characteristic of primitive life . . . [Wilson 1941:10]."

There are some useful distinctions to be made among traditional economies. Much of the literature of primitive economies describes those without centralized polities—"tribes without rulers"—Malinowski's Trobriands being the most minutely described case in the literature. In saying that most primitive economies without centralized polity are small, one means several things: that the economy of the Tiv, the Nuer, or the Trobriand Islanders is small relative to modern, nationally-integrated economies of Europe and America; that most (but not all) resource, goods and service transactions take place within a small geographical area and within a community of persons numbered in the hundreds or thousands. It is true that external trade is common and, as with the Kula, sometimes is carried out over long distances. Typically, however, it is intermittent, petty in amount, or confined to very few goods. It is rare (except in peasant economies) for foreign trade transactions to be frequent, quantitatively important, or essential to livelihood.

There are two other ways in which band and tribal economies are small-scale. Frequently one or two staple items (yams in the Trobriands, cattle among the Nuer) comprise an unusually large proportion of total produce. It is common for these important staples to be produced within the small framework of village, tribe, or lineage. Finally, a relatively small number of goods and services is produced or acquired—dozens of items and specialist services rather than hundreds of thousands, as in developed, industrial economies.

There are mutually reinforcing connections between size and other aspects of the structure and performance of an economy. Two widely shared characteristics of the small economies anthropologists study are a simple technology (compared to the industrialized economies of the West) and geographical or cultural isolation (again, compared to those of Europe and North America). The absence of sophisticated machines and applied science, and of the extreme labor specialization characteristic of national economies numbering their participants in the millions, means a relatively low level of productivity. Two direct consequences for primitive economies of their simple technology and small size is that their peoples are sharply constrained in production activities by physical resource endowment (ecology) and that their peoples depend greatly on human cooperation for ordinary production [9] processes as well as emergencies such as famine and personal misfortune. Low-level technology, combined with small size and relative isolation, results in ingrained mutual dependence among people sharing many relationships: those with whom one is economically involved are the same as those with whom one is involved through neighborhood, religion, kinship, and polity. The primitive economy in that sense is "embedded" in other community relationships and is not composed of associations separate from these (Dalton 1962; 1964).

> Association is a group specifically organized for the purpose of an interest or group of interests which its members have in common. . . . Community is a circle of people who live together, who belong together, so that they share not this or that particular interest, but a whole set of interests wide enough and comprehensive enough to include their lives [MacIver 1933:9, 10, 12, quoted in Nadel 1942:xi].

Some points may here be underscored: (1) "Primitive" or "subsistence" economies require for the analysis of their *organization* conceptual categories which are socio-economic because material and service transactions are frequently part of kinship, religious, or political relationships. (2) Two general features of primitive or subsistence economies are the pervasive social control of production and distribution, and the assurance of subsistence livelihood to persons through the social determination of labor and land allocation and the social right to receive emergency material aid in time of need.

These points have frequently been made before: to Tönnies, primitive economies are *Gemeinschaft* rather than *Gesellschaft*; to Maine, they are characterized by status rather than contract; to Weber and MacIver, they are communities rather than associations; to Karl Polanyi (1944: chapter 4; 1957), the economy is "embedded" in the society; to Raymond Firth (1951:142), the formula is "From each according to his status obligations in the social system, to each according to his rights in that system."

Primitive economies are so organized that the allocation of labor and land, the organization of work in production processes (farming, herding, construction of buildings and equipment), and the disposition of produced goods and specialist services are expressions of underlying kinship obligation, tribal affiliation, and religious and moral duty. Unlike the economist, who can analyze important features of industrial capitalism (such as price and income determination) without considering kinship and religion, the economic anthropologist concerned with the *organization* of primitive economies finds there is no separate economic system that can be analyzed independently of social organization. He can, however, measure economic performance separately, for example, how much of each kind of item is produced yearly.

The ways in which tools and implements are acquired, used, and disposed of is another point of contrast between primitive, peasant, and industrial capitalist economies. Typically in primitive economies tools are either made by the user himself, acquired for a fee from a specialist craftsman, or, as is sometimes the case with dwellings, storehouses, and canoes, acquired from a construction group specifically organized for the task. The construction group providing ordinary labor as well as the services of craftsmen specialists is remunerated either by food provided by the host (Thurnwald's *Bittarbeit* and barn-raising in the American West), or with food and luxury tidbits (tobacco, betel), or with these as well as payments in valuables or special-purpose money to the craftsmen-spacialists (Dalton 1965a). Western cash is not paid. The making of tools, canoes, and dwellings is an occasional event rather than a continuous activity of specialist producers, and the construction workers do not derive the bulk of their livelihood from providing such services. The tools, canoes, and buildings, when put to use, do not yield their owners a cash income. Typically, the Implements are used until they are physically worn out, when they are either repaired or discarded. Unlike some peasant economies (Firth 1946), primitive economies have no second-hand markets for tools and buildings.

Polanyi's analytical distinctions between reciprocity, redistribution, and (market) exchange and their application to specific cases have been written up in detail (Polanyi 1944: chapter 4; 1947; 1957; 1966; Dalton 1961; 1962; 1965c). Unfortunately, they have been misconstrued as applying to transactions of produce only (Smelser 1958; Burling 1962; Nash 1966). These socio-economic categories apply to inanimate resource and labor allocation and to work organization as well as to produce disposition—to production as well as to distribution of goods and craft services (LeClair 1962). It is misleading to regard "systems of exchange" as something apart from production processes because exchange transactions enter into *each* of the three component processes of production (Dalton 1962: 1964).

Consider any production process: automobile manufacturing in the United States, yam-growing in the Trobriands, collective farming in the U.S.S.R., Malay peasant fishing, or cattle-raising among the Nuer. All these production lines require the allocation of land, labor, and other resource ingredients to the production process; the organization of work tasks within the production process; and the disposition of the items produced. Among the Tiv, acquiring farm land (in accordance with one's lineage affiliation) is as much a "reciprocal" transaction as yam-giving (in accordance with one's *urigubu* obligation) is in the Trobriands. For an excellent account of varieties of reciprocity, see Sahlins (1965).

Primitive States: Internal Redistribution and External Administered Trade

As in other branches of anthropology, the typical unit of analytical interest in economic anthropology is a relatively small group, the tribe, the lineage segment, the village community. There is a small, internal economy to be analyzed, whether our focus of interest is a primitive economy without centralized polity (such as the Tiv), a primitive economy within a centralized polity, such as the local farming communities in Nupe (Nadel 1942), or a peasant economy, such as the Malay fishermen (Firth 1946). To be sure, persons or groups in each of these small economies may carry out transactions with outsiders—external trade, tax and tribute payments to outside political authorities—but it is meaningful to distinguish between internal (local community) transactions and those external to the local group, however defined.

Primitive economies which are part of centralized political authority—what Polanyi called archaic societies and Fortes and Evans-Pritchard (1940) called primitive states—have socio-economic transactions in addition to those found within the local community and between local communities (see Figure 3–1). These are of two principal sorts: transactions

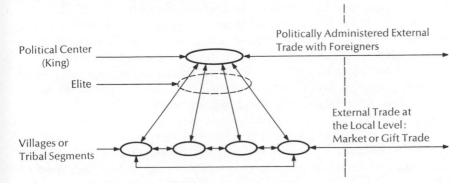

Figure 3–1 *Socio-Economic Transactions within a Centralized Political System*

between the political center and its local constituencies, and external trade transactions between the political center and foreigners (Arnold 1957*a*; 1957*b*; Polanyi 1963; 1966). The local constituents pay tribute to the political center—ordinary subsistence goods, luxuries reserved for elite usage, labor for construction projects and military service—and usually receive from the center military protection, juridical services, and emergency subsistence in time of local famine or disaster.

Where there is a centralized political authority, there is a redistributive sector which has no counterpart in primitive economies without a centralized polity (that is, that are not chiefdoms, kingdoms, or empires). Indeed, where there is an intermediary elite between the king (his royal household economy and his domain) and the villages or tribal segments which express their political subordination through tax and tribute payments and other upward transactions, there are socio-economic sectors that some writers call feudal (Nadel 1942; Maquet 1961), although others question the usefulness of so labeling them (Goody 1963; Beattie 1964).

Peasant Economy

Writers on peasantry (Redfield 1956; Wolf 1966) emphasize the special nature of peasant personality and culture as that which distinguishes peasant from primitive: the semi-isolation from urban culture with which it shares religion and (in Europe) language; that peasants and peasant communities are the rank and file, so to speak, of larger political groupings, so that in Latin America, Europe, and India there are political authorities externally located who exercise some formal political jurisdiction over the peasant villages.

It is important to note that if we confine ourselves to cultural aspects such as religion, language, and political subordination, we can point up what is common to an enormous number of peasantries and at the same time justify the use of the special category "peasant culture" by showing it is different in these ways from band and tribal culture. Trobriand Island culture has none of the characteristics so far enumerated for peasants.

To go further, however, requires some special distinctions because of the long periods of historical time over which groups called peasant by social analysts have existed intact and because there are other criteria used to differentiate peasant from primitive and modern.

One line of demarcation is the Industrial Revolution. Before the Industrial Revolution occurred in their regions, all peasantries used primitive technology, differing in no important way from the technologies used by groups (Tiv, Lele, Nuer) anthropologists identify as being primitive. Let us call peasant communities, as they existed before the Industrial Revolution in their regions, "traditional" peasantries. Then we can point out immediately that traditional peasantries, although differing from primitive societies in those cultural ways specified earlier, were like primitive communities in their use of simple (machineless) technology, their small units of production (principally but not exclusively agricultural), and the relatively few items produced in a peasant community. In traditional peasantries, as in primitive communities, there is the same reliance on one or two staple foodstuffs which comprise a large proportion of total output and the same unusually large reliance on local natural resources because of the simple technology used and the absence of complicated fabrication processes. With regard to the size of production units, technology, dependence on physical resource endowment, and the narrow range of items produced, traditional peasant communities resemble the primitive much more closely than they do with regard to culture. Moreover, material performance is roughly the same as in primitive communities, and for the same reasons.

The ethnographic record does not indicate that traditional peasantries were typically less poor materially than primitive societies. [10]

What anthropologists mean by peasant culture is clear; what they mean by peasant economy is sometimes not clear. "By a peasant economy one means a system of small-scale producers, with a simple technology and equipment often relying primarily for their subsistence on what they themselves produce. The primary means of livelihood of the peasant is cultivation of the soil [Firth 1951:87]." But this is a perfect description of the Lele (Douglas 1965), the Tiv (Bohannan and Bohannan, 1968), and the Trobriand Islanders in Malinowski's time: all have primitive economies. If we are to make analytical sense of the large literature of economic anthropology, we need some finer distinctions.

It is as useful to distinguish between traditional peasant and primitive economy as it is to distinguish between peasant and primitive culture. The *economic* organization of a peasant community has two sets of distinguishing characteristics: (1) Most people depend for the bulk of their livelihood on production for market sale or selling in markets; purchase and sale transactions with cash are frequent and quantitatively important; and, frequently, resource markets are present: significant quantities of labor, land, tools, and equipment are available for purchase, rent, or hire at money price. It is the relative importance of markets for resources and products and of cash transactions that is the principal difference between peasant and primitive *economies*. It is this feature which gives peasant economies their crude resemblance to the least productive of our own farming sectors and which justifies Tax's appropriate phrase, "penny capitalism." But in all other ways relating to productive activities, peasant economies— especially traditional peasantries—more closely resemble the primitive than they do the modern: small-scale, simple technology, a narrow range of output, a few staples comprising the bulk of output, unusual reliance on physical resource endowment because of the absence of applied science and the technology of extensive fabrication; low levels of output—poverty and material insecurity.

(2) What strikes the economist is that although the rudiments of capitalist (market) economy are present and important in peasant communities, they are *incomplete* and *underdeveloped* compared to market organization in a modern national economy. By incomplete is meant that in a given peasant community some markets may be absent or petty—land may be frequently purchased or rented, but labor is not (Chayanov 1966), or vice versa; and that subsistence production may still be quantitatively important in some households. By underdeveloped is meant the absence of facilitative institutions and social capital of advanced capitalist countries: on the one hand, banks, insurance companies, and stock markets; on the other, electricity, paved roads, and educational facilities beyond the elementary

school. In peasant communities the extent of economic, cultural, and technological integration with the province and nation is markedly less than is the case with hinterland communities in developed nations.

In summary, peasant society, like primitive society (and also feudalism, jajmam in village India, and slavery) is a socio-economic category (Firth 1964:17). If we include peasantries of all times and places in our analysis, it is fair to say that peasant culture is more homogeneous and distinctive than is peasant economy (Fallers 1961). The spectrum of peasantries is wide and contains varying mixtures of primitive and modern institutions. At one end are those in medieval Europe—the Russian mir, the feudal village (Bennett 1962), and some of present-day Latin America, which are peasant cultures (in religion, language, political subordination) with primitive economies (because of the absence of market dependence and cash transactions). There are also cases of peasant economy with a primitive culture, as in the early transition period of African groups enlarging their cash-earning production while retaining their tribal organization and culture (Fallers 1961; Gulliver 1965; Dalton 1964). [11]

COMMUNITY CHANGE AND DEVELOPMENT

The most promising area for fruitful interchange and collaboration between economics and anthropology is the field of economic development. Most development economists, however, are interested in processes and problems of *national* economic growth and development that have little in common with anthropologists' interests in village community social and economic change. But a growing number of economists are working on matters requiring anthropological insight: creating an industrial labor force, transforming subsistence agriculture (Yudelman 1964), devising policies for investment in educational facilities. Others are devising techniques of measurement and analysis to show the connections between socio-political organization and economic development (Adelman and Morris 1965; 1967). And yet other economists are making use of anthropology, sociology, and psychology to analyze—what is for economists—an unusual range of processes and problems entailed in economic growth and development (Hagen 1962; Myrdal 1957).

Matters relating to what I shall call socio-economic change, growth, and development at the village community level conventionally appear in anthropology under the headings of evolution, diffusion of innovations, social change, culture change, culture contact, acculturation, and applied anthropology. There are two points about this literature of change that I should like to emphasize.

The subject is extraordinarily diverse and complicated. It includes a wide range of complex processes: urbanization, industrialization, commercialization, national integration (cf. Southall 1961; UNESCO 1963). Moreover, these processes take place over much longer periods of time than anthropologists customarily remain in the field, and their analysis requires consideration of the policies of central government which impinge on the small group (village or tribal segment) that traditionally has been the focus of interest in anthropology.

The case studies of socio-economic change reach back to the early days of European colonization of Africa (Schapera 1934; Hunter 1961), Latin America (Chevalier 1963), and Asia (Bocke 1942), when neither political independence was a fact nor economic development of indigenous peoples an explicit intention. The recent case studies are of change taking place in villages which are now parts of independent nation-states whose central governments are initiating nation-wide development and modernization. The literature includes cases of piecemeal change, where a new cash crop or a new school or a new religion is introduced in an otherwise traditional community (Dalton 1964), and cases of comprehensive community development, such as the famous case of Vicos (Holmberg *et al.* 1965).

Given the complexity of the processes, the large number and diversity of case studies on record, and the changed political and economic national conditions under which local community development now proceeds, it is not surprising that relatively few theoretical insights and conceptual categories with which to analyze socio-economic change have been contrived. Some notable contributions are Myrdal (1957), Hagen (1962), Smelser (1963), and Adelman and Morris (1967).

Socio-economic change as an anthropological subject is unusual in another way, as well. Many of us who work on problems of development and modernization hope not only to come to understand these processes but also to use such knowledge to reduce the social costs of economic improvement. Therefore, this extension of the traditional concerns of economic anthropology into processes of change and development has policy implications to an extent that is unusual in anthropology (Erasmus 1961; Goodenough 1963; Arensberg and Niehoff 1964).

What is also true is that each of us—the anthropologist, the economist, the sociologist—comes to a novel situation such as change and development in an African village community with two kinds of professional knowledge: the theory of one's subject and an intimate knowledge of some portion(s) of the real world. The economist (typically) comes with price, income, growth, and development theory, plus his knowledge of the structure and performance of his own and perhaps several other economies. If he is a specialist in economic history or Soviet economy (Gerschenkron 1962), he brings with him knowledge of the sequential processes through which England, Japan, Russia, or the United States developed. When he comes to examine local development in an African community, he is struck by similarities to and differences from what he is already familiar with.

First, with the exception of agricultural economics, there is no counterpart in conventional economic analysis to the study of village community change and development. European and American villages and townships —the local community counterparts of the Tiv lineage segment or an Indian village—are never the focus of analytical concern. Economics is about national economies and the component activities of business firms and households thoroughly integrated with their national economy through purchase and sale transactions. Immediately we can feed back into our new concerns knowledge that we know is important from our old ones. Empirically, *how do small groups—the tribe, the village—become part of a regional or national economy?*

Similarly, local community change or development seems never to be a "natural" process of immanent expansion of the village or tribe, but rather the local community's response to incursion from outside itself. Whether it is the Conquistadores' invasion of Peru 400 years ago, or Cornell University's invasion of Vicos 15 years ago, or European colonial incursion into Africa, or the slave-raider, missionary, or merchant who comes, the process of community change starts with impingement from without. Therefore, a second question we can ask of the empirical case studies is, *What is the nature of the initial incursion which starts the processes of socio-economic change, and to what extent does the character of the initial incursion shape the sequential changes that follow?* [12]

Most of the ethnographic case studies fall into one of three broad categories that I shall designate (1) degenerative change; (2) cash income growth without development; and (3) socio-economic development. The three categories—which are really ideal types—are not stages of progression. Moreover, they are clearly overlapping. Some of the empirical literature fits neatly into these categories; some does not. My point is to make sharp analytical distinctions, and to do so I must oversimplify.

Degenerative Change

Much of the literature of early culture contact consists of European and American incursions which produced decimation, misery, and community degeneration among indigenous groups (Rivers 1922; Jaspan 1953). "Native [Fiji] society [in the 1880's] was severely disrupted by war, by catastrophic epidemics of European diseases, by the introduction of alcohol, by the devastations of generations of warfare, and by the depredations of labor recruiters [Worsley 1957b:19]."

By degenerative change I mean severe disruption of the traditional life of a community over several generations with accompanying indicators of novel sorts and frequencies of personal and social malaise. I do not postulate frictionless bliss in the traditional society; but whatever conflicts and malaise were generated by traditional society—warfare, vendetta, sorcery —were coped with by traditional institutions (Malinowski 1959), without prolonged disruption of ordinary life. Where degenerative change occurs, it is, obviously, because the situation is such that traditional institutions designed to deal with traditional sorts of stress and conflict are unable to deal with the novel change because it embodies forces which are at the same time without precedent, irreversible, and overwhelming to traditional organization.

The extreme cases are marked by military conquest and displacement of traditional political authority by conquerors who neither understand nor respect the culture of the society they now control. The indigenous people are unable to resist imposed changes, are prohibited from pursuing rituals or activities which are meaningful and integrative in their own traditional society, and are made to pursue new activities (such as forced labor in mines and plantations) which are not integrative—do not fulfill social obligation and so reinforce social relationships—in traditional society (Steiner 1957). "For the sting of change lies not in change itself but in change which is devoid of social meaning [Frankel 1955:27]."

Degenerative situations and the psychological processes of individual and group reaction to them have caught the attention of many writers, perhaps because the consequences are so dramatic. Having lost the primary ties of meaningful culture, social relationships, and activities (Fromm 1941), and having been forced into meaningless activities and degrading helplessness, individuals and groups react to the bewildering changes with fantasy, aggression, withdrawal, and escape (Hagen 1962: chapter 17; Smelser 1963). And so we have the ethnography of cultural disintegration, from the Pawnee Ghost Dance to Melanesian cargo cults [13] and Navaho alcoholism.

If one examines these cases of degenerative change from the viewpoint of community development, several features stand out:

1. *The nature of the initial incursion.* In cases of severe degenerative change, the initial incursion causes cultural decimation: military conquest, political subjugation, and severe disruption of usual activities. A by-product of the incursion may be material worsening, or, indeed, slight material improvement. But these economic consequences are really beside the point because the force of change is perceived and felt to be deprivation of valued activities and the community's subjugation to militarily superior foreigners with hostile intentions and contempt for indigenous ways. The foreigners may come with the intent to deprive the people of gold or land, but typically it is not the deprivation of gold or land which causes the deep disruption.

Not economic exploitation, as often assumed, but the disintegration of the cultural environment of the victim is then the cause of degradation. The economic process may, naturally, supply the vehicle of the destruction, and almost invariably economic inferiority will make the weaker yield, but the immediate cause of his undoing is not for that reason economic; *it lies in the lethal injury to the institutions in which his social existence is embodied.* The result is loss of self-respect and standards, whether the unit is a people or a class, whether the process springs from so-called "culture conflict" or from a change in the position of a class within the confines of a society [Polanyi 1944:157, italics added].

The nature of the initial incursion seems invariably important, not only to the generation experiencing the initial impact but also—in its shaping the sequence of socio-economic change—to successive generations (Hagen 1962). The group's cultural memory of what they regard as early injustice is long (Schapera 1928) and sometimes is nurtured several generations later (Colson 1949).

2. *The absence of new economic, technological, and cultural achievement.* The incursion prevents the society from functioning in customary ways without providing substitute ways which are meaningful to the people in terms of traditional culture (Steiner 1957; Frankel 1955). It is disintegrative to traditional organization without providing new forms of organization which reintegrate the society along new lines (Smelser 1963). These are useful ways to state the problem, but much detailed analysis of socio-economic change needs to be done: What are the sequential processes of disintegration and subsequent reintegration? Which specific features of traditional society are most vulnerable? How long do these processes take? Under what conditions has reintegration taken place? We are here concerned with historical processes to be analyzed in sociological terms. The problems require explicit concern with long stretches of calendar time and with sequential process analysis of old and new economy, technology, polity, social organization, and culture.

Degenerative change does not mean that some people believe themselves to be worse off materially or culturally under the new conditions. Some people are made worse off by any kind of social change. Rather, it means that the old society ceases to function in important ways, most people perceive the changes as worsenings, and in no important area of social or private life is there widespread absorption of new culture (like literacy), new technology and economy (such as new farming methods and enlarged production for sale), of the sorts which create social reintegration. Neither is degenerative change necessarily a permanent state of affairs. Worsley (1957b) argues that Melanesian cargo cults, despite their traumatic symptoms of malaise, misunderstanding of European economy, and distorted religiosity, contain the beginnings of wider political organization of an anticolonial sort which may possibly evolve into more orthodox and productive political activity (see also Hagen 1962).

Growth without Development

Most of the case studies of community change reported in the literature differ from the one described above in two principal ways. First, the incursion was not severely disruptive of traditional society. The Trobriands (during Malinowski's residence), the Tiv (at the time of Bohannan's field work), and many other groups carried on their traditional activities largely intact for generations after the foreign presence was felt. Second, the peoples became engaged in new cash-earning activities (principally growing cash crops and selling wage-labor), and this was the *only* innovation of importance widely adopted. Subsistence economies became peasant economies as cash earnings and dependence for livelihood on market sale of crops or wage-labor grew, while traditional culture and society remained largely intact (except for those changes induced by the enlarged commercial production or cash-earning).

Here we have the two salient features experienced by a large number of primitive societies: untraumatic incursion which allows ordinary activities, ceremony, and social relationships to continue on much as before; and enlarged cash-earning activities without the concomitant adoption of improved technology, literacy, or any of the other important accounterments of "modernization" (Gulliver 1965).

I call this situation "cash income growth without development." The community's cash income grows somewhat because of its enlarged sales of crops or labor, but the structural changes in economy, technology, and culture necessary for sustained income growth and the integration over time of the local community with the nation are not forthcoming. During the period when cash income grows while old culture, values, and folkviews remain initially unchanged (because literacy, new vocational skills, new lines of production, new technology, are not adopted), some characteristic responses are generated:

1. The use of new cash income for old status prerogatives (bridewealth, potlatch).

2. New conflict situations (land tenure litigation).

3. The undermining of traditional arrangements providing material security through social relationships (cash-earning and individualism).

Typically, cash income is earned by individual or household activities rather than lineage or large cooperative group activities (such as canoe-building and reciprocal land-clearing). Writers on peasant economy (Chayanov 1966; Yang 1945: chapter 7) stress the economic importance of the *family household* as a production unit for good reasons. The growth of de-

pendence on market sale of labor or crops for livelihood means the lessened dependence on political heads, extended kin, age-mates, friends, and
neighbors—in a word, lessened dependence on local social relationships
—to acquire labor, or land, and emergency support.

The new form of income, Western cash, is utterly different from anything known in traditional marketless economies. It is indefinitely storable
and so provides material security for its individual owner. It can be used
to purchase a variety of goods and discharge a variety of obligations which
no money-stuff or treasure item does in primitive economy. Not only a potentially enormous range of European imports—gin, tobacco, canned
foods, steel tools, crucifixes, transistor radios—school fees, and colonial
taxes, but also traditional subsistence goods (foodstuffs), traditional prestige sphere services, obligations, and positions (like bridewealth), and natural resources (land), and labor all become purchasable or payable with
cash. This is what is meant by Western cash being a "general-purpose"
money (Dalton 1965*a*). The process of earning as well as spending Western cash in formerly primitive economies breaks down the traditional separation between spheres of subsistence and prestige goods and services
(Firth 1958: chapter 3; Bohannan 1959).

The use of new cash income for old status prerogatives, new conflict situations, and the undermining of traditional arrangements providing material security are related consequences of earning cash income *within an
otherwise traditional setting*. For example, that bridewealth has come to be
paid in cash rather than, as formerly, in high prestige items such as cows
indicates the great importance placed on cash (and what it will buy and
pay for). The *social* consequences of such displacement are several. Consider the contrasting situations before and after cash has displaced traditional valuables as bridewealth. Indigenously, bridewealth in cows could
be got by a young man wanting to marry only by soliciting the required
cows from kin, friends, elders, chiefs, that is, by drawing on social
relationships and thus creating obligations to repay them (reciprocate)
in some form (such as labor service or clientship). After cash becomes
acceptable as bridewealth, young men can earn their own cash and pay
their own bridewealth, thus weakening their dependence on traditional
superiors.

Indigenously, where bridewealth required the payment of prestige
goods, the items (such as cows) could be disposed of by the bridewealth
recipients in very few ways. Cows (like kula bracelets) could only be exchanged or paid within the prestige sphere which was narrowly circum-
scribed. But cash received as bridewealth has no such limitations. It can be
used for traditional prestige or subsistence goods or any of the array of
new goods. Bohannan (1959) has pointed out the moral ambivalence
which results in the changed situation where bridewealth receipts in cash
can be spent on goods in a lower prestige sphere.

Socio-Economic Development

Economists can answer the question, "What constitutes successful development?" with little difficulty. Their unit of analysis is the nation-state, and their base of reference is the already developed nations of North America and Europe. The indicators of successful development from the viewpoint of economics are impersonal, having little to do with folk views, attitudes, social relationships, or culture. Development is characterized in terms of the country's yearly percentage rate of growth in gross national product, the size of per capita income and its distribution, and the use of advanced technology in major production lines.

If anthropologists are asked, "What constitutes successful development?" the answer is more difficult. The anthropologists' unit of analysis is the tribal or village community, not the nation-state;[14] anthropologists are concerned not only with economy and technology but also with folk views, attitudes, social relationships, and the rest of culture. And they do not use the already developed nations of Europe and North America as a base of reference for successful development. Moreover, anthropologists are analytically concerned with the wider social process of which economic development is a part, and sensitive to social and cultural costs of economic change.

There is no such thing as a small-scale community's development independent of the larger units of economy and society external to the tribe or village. The several kinds of change that constitute modernization all entail integration with external groupings, that is, increased dependence on external groups with whom new economic, political, and cultural transactions take place.

Sustained income growth for the local community requires enlarged production for sale to regional, national, or international markets and a return flow of consumption goods, producer's goods, and social services (health and education) purchased with the ever-increasing cash income. The community becomes economically integrated with (and dependent on) the regional, national, or international economy through a continual enlargement and diversification of purchase and sale transactions. These can be enlarged and made to grow only with the use of improved technology (tools and technical knowledge) acquired or purchased initially from outside the local community.

The experience of a significant growth in income seems frequently to be a necessary pump-priming condition if traditional groups are to become willing to take the risk of producing new kinds of crops and goods or old ones with new, expensive, and unfamiliar techniques of production. Primitive and peasant unwillingness to change production is frequently a sensible expression of their poverty and material insecurity. They cannot afford unsuccessful experiments. The old techniques are not very productive, but they keep the people alive. One of the important lessons of the unusual (and unusually quick) development progress in Vicos (Holmberg *et al.* 1965) was that the *Cornell group* assumed the financial risk of planting improved varieties of potatoes. The demonstration effect of the sharp increase in the value product of the new potatoes convinced the people of Vicos to follow suit. A legitimate role for any central government wanting to accelerate local community development is for it to bear some portion of the financial risk of economic and technological innovation.

The local community's integration politically is yet another aspect of community development. But when central government traditionally acted only as a tax-gatherer, the local community is likely to perceive any governmentally initiated project to expand community output as a device to increase taxes and therefore to be resisted. Here, too, there must be demonstration effects: that government can provide the local community with important economic and social services and confine itself to taxing only a portion of enlarged income forthcoming.

Finally, there is cultural integration with the larger society: learning new language, new vocational skills, literacy, private and public health practices, and acquiring a participant awareness of alternatives, events, and institutions of the larger world.[15]

What perhaps deserves emphasis is that successful development from the economist's viewpoint is compatible with successful development from the anthropologist's viewpoint. Anthropologists are concerned with minimizing the social costs of community transformation and with preserving the community's ethnic identity in the new society of income growth, machines, and literacy. But we know from examining the sub-cultures in already developed nations, such as Japan, England, the U.S.S.R., and especially the United States (with its unusual ethnic diversity), that the retention of identity in both new and old institutional forms is compatible with modern activities. The point surely is to work with those powerful levers of new achievement which the people themselves perceive as desirable and which induce other positive changes—higher income and material security through new economic and technological performance and wider alternatives through education. If such developmental achievements are in fact incorporated, features of traditional culture and social organization that are incompatible with the new are sloughed off without the personal and community malaise that characterize degenerative change and growth without development. "Social policy has . . . to assure that the individual in losing both the benefits and the burdens of the old society acquires no weightier burdens and at least as many benefits as he had in his previous station [Okigbo 1956]."

CONCLUSION

Karl Polanyi's analytical concepts, insights, and generalizations relate to the social and economic organization of primitive and archaic economies in which market organization is absent or confined to petty transactions. Here, the components of economy—labor and resource allocation, work organization, product disposition—are inseparable parts of kinship, polity, religion. His analysis is not general in three senses. (1) He did not analyze peasant economies, where market organization, market dependence for livelihood, and the use of Western money are important. (2) He was not concerned with the quantifiable performance of primitive economies, but only with their organization. (3) His analysis of socio-economic change and development was confined principally to Europe (Polanyi 1944: chapters 3, 6, 7, 8, 13).

Much of the criticism of his work (and mine) is due to a misunderstanding of the range of economies we are referring to. Several anthropologists who have done field work in peasant economies (Firth 1946), or in primitive economies at the beginnings of commercialization and use of Western money (Salisbury 1962; Pospisil 1963), look for a universal theory. They complain that Polanyi's categories and generalizations (designed for primitive, static economies) do not fit their peasant and changing economies, and so criticism of Polanyi's work ensues.

If, as with Polly Hill, the investigator is interested exclusively in peasant economy, cash crops, and economic growth, and particularly with measurable performance rather than socio-economic organization, he is being rather short-tempered when he criticizes those of us who are interested in economies different from those of Ghanaian cocoa-farming and with aspects of economy and society other than measurable performance.

If, as with Firth and Salisbury, anthropologists are interested in comparative economic performance—how much is produced, how much equipment and labor are used, how income is divided (questions economists put to our own economy)—then (in vastly simplified fashion) some of the measurement concepts of conventional economics are usefully applicable, and they fail to understand Polanyi's criticism of conventional economics as inappropriate for analyzing the *organization* of primitive economies.

Some, like Pospisil (1963) and Burling (1962), perceive an economy not as a set of rules of social organization, but as economic behavior of individuals and their subjective motivations; when they detect greed and self-aggrandizement they equate these with capitalism and assert that economic "behavior" in primitive societies is the same as in market societies and that Polanyi's conceptual categories are wrong and "romantic" (Cook 1966).

Finally, some anthropologists obliterate all distinctions between descriptive statements, analytical statements, and statements about folk views, by describing and analyzing the economy and stating folk views about it exclusively in market terminology (supply, demand, price, maximizing, capital), and thus quite understandably convince themselves that conventional economics provides all the concepts necessary for economic anthropology (Pospisil 1963).

What must be recognized is that economic anthropology deals with two different sorts of economies, primitive and peasant, under two different sets of conditions, static and dynamic, and with two very different aspects of economy, organization, and material performance. Polanyi's theoretical categories are addressed principally, but not exclusively, to the organization of primitive and archaic economies under static conditions. That he did not analyze peasant economies and small-scale economies undergoing change, growth, and development does not vitiate his important contributions to the analysis of non-market economies and the transformations of eighteenth- and nineteenth-century capitalism.[16]

To adduce an analogy that illustrates the point: in the Anglo-America of 1933, the topics handled with Marshallian price and distribution theory (Marshall 1920), and its extensions into the analysis of markets in imperfect competition (Robinson 1932; Chamberlin 1933), were the dominant concern of economic theory (the pricing of resources and products under static conditions in market-integrated national economies). In the Anglo-America of the 1970's, this remains a concern of economic theory, but has declined in relative importance as different questions became important and new theories and conceptual categories were invented to answer them: what determines aggregate national output (Keynes 1936)? What determines the rate of growth of aggregate output over time (Harrod 1952; Domar 1957)? Polanyi's system is akin to Marshall's in its traditional concerns.

Moreover, when Soviet economy began to take its present form, beginning in 1928, special concepts and analyses were invented to deal with what is special to Soviet economic organization and performance. So, too, with the economics of underdeveloped areas. Economists are used to living in several theoretical universes—price theory, income theory, growth theory, development theory, Soviet economy—which overlap only partially. They do not throw out Marshall because he did not answer Keynes' questions; they do not throw out Keynes because he did not answer Harrod's and Domar's questions; and they do not throw out any of these market economy theorists because they did not address themselves to issues of collectivization and central planning in Soviet economy. This lesson must be learned in economic anthropology if we are ever to progress beyond the stage where deaf men ceaselessly shout at one another. Like the economists, economic anthropologists are dealing with several aspects of several sorts of economies and need several sets of concepts to understand and measure them properly.

> . . . we have no doubt that the future of economic theory lies not in constructing a single universal theory of economic life but in conceiving a number of theoretical systems that would be adequate to the range of present or past economic orders and would disclose the forms of their co-existence and evolution [Chayanov 1966:28].

ABSTRACT

While interest in economic anthropology grows rapidly, the creation of a widely accepted theoretical framework is impeded by the persistence—indeed, intensification—of disputes over conceptual issues. Part I of this essay clarifies the issues and explains why controversy persists. Part II attempts to reconcile opposing views by showing how the several different topics that comprise economic anthropology require different sets of analytical and measurement concepts for their fruitful investigation. Part III considers the recent extension of economic anthropology to processes of socio-economic change, growth, and development in communities undergoing "modernization."

NOTES

1. I have been very fortunate in getting critical comments on earlier drafts of this essay from anthropologists, economists, and others whom it is a pleasure to thank here: Irma Adelman, Conrad Arensberg, Joseph Berliner, Paul Bohannan, David Brokensha, Heyward Ehrlich, Clifford Geertz, Everett Hagen, Thomas Harding, Peter McLoughlin, Sidney Mintz, Walter Neale, and Ilona Polanyi.

2. I do not mean to slight the contributions of others, living or dead (for example, Mauss 1954), but only to name those who have written at some length on the theoretical aspects of economic anthropology. See Godelier (1965) and Dalton (1967) for further references to theoretical writings.

3. Among anthropologists who write in English there is only an occasional borrowing of Marxian concepts (such as economic surplus), rather than a systematic attempt to apply Marxian analysis to primitive and peasant economies (Herskovits 1952: part V; Pearson 1957; Harris 1959; Dalton 1960; 1963).

4. Clifford Geertz quite rightly points out (in private correspondence) that people confuse the generality of a theory with its ability to be applied universally. Polanyi most certainly is not arguing against generalization or abstract conceptualization; rather, he argues against the position that conventional economics—designed to analyze nationally integrated, industrial, market economies—provides an adequate conceptual basis for a universally applicable theory of economic structure and process. Specifically, he shows that for econ-

omies lacking the salient organizational features of developed capitalism (market integration, machine technology, and the modern kind of money— primitive and archaic economies, in his terms), principles of socio-economic organization exist which require for their analysis conceptual categories different from those of conventional economics (Polanyi 1957; Dalton 1961).

5. Just as an American who somehow chose not to learn English would be severely penalized by the social system in finding jobs, in his ability to communicate with others, and the like, so would a Trobriander be penalized in his society by choosing not to grow yams.

6. Although there are very few pure subsistence economies (economies in which commercial transactions are entirely absent), there are a good many primitive economies (especially in Africa) in which half or more of total income comes from subsistence production, and peasant economies in which smaller, but significant, amounts of subsistence production are the rule. In the early 1950's, a UN agency reported that ". . . between 65 per cent and 75 per cent of the total cultivated land area of tropical Africa is devoted to subsistence production" (United Nations 1954:13). In the 1960's, the problem of transforming subsistence agriculture in Africa was still very much a matter of concern. See Yudelman (1964); Clower, Dalton, Harwitz, and Walters (1966); Adelman and Morris (1967).

7. The concept of "services" causes difficulty in economic anthropology (as do the concepts of "capital" and "market") because the term is used to cover a wide range of items or activities in our own economy, only a few of which are found in primitive economies. In our own economy, the term "services" is used to describe ordinary labor, mechanized utilities (telephone and electricity services), the services performed by craftsmen and professional specialists, such as dentists, TV repairmen, musicians; and also the functions performed by political and religious officeholders. In our own economy, all but the latter services are organized for purchase and sale. In relation to primitive and peasant economies, I prefer to use the term "specialist services" to refer to those provided by craftsmen, such as blacksmiths, woodcarvers, and dancers, and those provided by persons performing political, religious, and ritual roles.

8. The literature of primitive (subsistence) economies—traditional economies most different from our own—is richest for Africa and Oceania, for small-scale communities rather than kingdoms and empires, and for agriculturalists rather than hunters, gatherers, herders, and so on. Malinowski's work (1921; 1922; 1935; 1959; also, Uberoi 1962) is the best source. On the economies of kingdoms and other politically centralized societies, see Nadel (1942), Maquet (1961), Arnold (1957a), and Polanyi (1966).

9. The extraordinary dependence on immediate physical environment for livelihood made it seem reasonable for an older generation of anthropologists to use classifications such as gathering, hunting, fishing, pastoral, and agricultural "economies." These categories do not classify according to *economic organization*, but rather according to principal source of subsistence, physical environment, and technology. Note that if we used these categories for developed economies, the United States and the U.S.S.R. would appear in the same category, both being manufacturing and agricultural "economies."

10. For many traditional peasant economies (village communities), it is un-

doubtedly true that real income is no higher than in most primitive economies. But, aside from difficulties of measuring real output, there are complicating features of peasant society which make it difficult to say whether many peasantries had consistently higher levels of output than is typical in primitive communities. Peasant communities, for example, seem invariably to be subordinate units of larger political (and religious) groupings, which means that significant portions of peasant produce and labor are paid "upward" as taxes, tributes, rents, and tithes. The elite recipients of such taxes and tributes channeled portions of them into the creation of churches, palaces, pyramids, armies, and the like, some of the services of which were received back by the local peasant communities. Again, the slow growth of improvement in agricultural and marketing techniques in some European peasant communities for several hundred years before the Industrial Revolution may have given some European peasant communities of, say, the eighteenth century higher incomes than is typical of other peasant and most primitive economies.

11. In this essay I can only call attention to how little work has been done on the economic aspects of peasantry (in the anthropological literature) and suggest that similar cultural features accompany dissimilar economic arrangements in the broad spectrum of peasant societies. There is a great deal more to be said about peasant economy. I am preparing an essay which classifies peasant societies into three sorts. Type I consists of peasant communities which have dependent (nonmarket) land tenure (such as those under European feudalism) in which land is acquired by clients from patrons as part of a long-run social and political relationship. Clients reciprocate with obligatory payments of material goods or labor services (farm labor, military labor, road repair, and so on), as well as with more diffuse social and political "payments"—loyalty, respect, homage, ceremonial services. Type II consists of peasant communities of a post-French Revolution sort, in which land tenure is strictly a matter of market purchase (or rental at money price) with no social or political obligations attached to land acquisition or usage. Types I and II refer to communities of long settlement. Type III is a hybrid sort, referring to communities of persons resettled in relatively recent historical times, frequently, as the aftermath of slavery in the Caribbean and the Spanish conquest of Latin America. Kroeber and Redfield, understandably, seized upon cultural attributes to differentiate "peasant" from "primitive" cultures. What remains to be done is socio-economic analysis of peasant groups from an anthropological perspective which takes account of the rich historical literature of European peasantries (for example, Chayanov 1966) as well as the more recent ethnographies.

The essay referred to in this note appears in this volume: "Peasantries in Anthropology and History."

12. A third general point of significance I believe to be the time rate of change which is experienced (Polanyi 1944: chapter 3). This is not, however, independent of the other features of the transformation process.

It should also be emphasized that the kind of incursion from outside differed in two ways: The kinds of outside *persons* who came—colonial conquerors, slave traders, merchants, missionaries, and so on; with each kind of intruder somewhat different sets of changes were introduced, each with a train of consequences leading up to the present. But much change currently underway in the

Third World, change that is now called "modernization," has not been introduced into villages by specific persons, but impersonally: regional irrigation facilities, new roads and vehicles, new schools, new credit facilities. An excellent case study of such impersonally induced change is Epstein (1962), which traces out the economic, social, and cultural consequences in two villages in India of irrigation facilities introduced in the region, twenty-five years earlier. "Acculturation," "Applied Anthropology," and "Modernization" are actually different subjects because the kinds of change, the kinds of persons introducing the change, the extent of regional or national change going on at the same time, the historical circumstances, and the political conditions under which the changes are introduced, are different in each of the three. See the essays in this volume entitled, "Peasantries in Anthropology and History," and "Economic Development and Social Change."

13. Cargo cults complicated movements expressing several aspects of fission and fusion. Here, I simply want to emphasize that among other things they are symptoms of malaise that indicate deep misunderstanding of the processes of modernization through which Western goods are acquired.

14. Clifford Geertz's work is a notable exception.

15. Gunnar Myrdal's point about the mutually reinforcing nature of developmental activities is indispensable for understanding the processes of sequential change, whether they be degenerative, cash income growth, or the structural changes entailed in successful development (Myrdal 1957:chapters 1–3).

16. Much that Polanyi said in *The Great Transformation* (1944) about the social and cultural consequences of the British Industrial Revolution is relevant to current socio-economic change in underdeveloped areas.

REFERENCES

ADELMAN, IRMA, and CYNTHIA TAFT MORRIS
    1965   Factor analysis of the interrelationship between social and political variables and per capita gross national product. *Quarterly Journal of Economics* 89:555–578.
    1967   *Society, politics, and economic development.* Baltimore: Johns Hopkins Press.
ARENSBERG, CONRAD M., and ARTHUR H. NIEHOFF
    1964   *Introducing social change.* Chicago: Aldine.
ARMSTRONG, W. E.
    1924   Rossel Island money: a unique monetary system. *Economic Journal* 34:423–429.
    1928   *Rossel Island.* Cambridge: University Press.
ARNOLD, ROSEMARY
    1957a A port of trade: Whydah on the Guinea coast. In *Trade and market in the early empires,* K. Polanyi, C. M. Arensberg, H. W. Pearson ed. Glencoe: The Free Press.
    1957b Separation of trade and market: great market of Whydah. In *Trade and market in the early empires,* K. Polanyi, C. M. Arensberg, H. W. Pearson ed. Glencoe: The Free Press.

BEATTIE, J. H. M.
1964   Bunyoro: an African feudality? *Journal of African History* 5:25–36.
BELSHAW, C. S.
1965   *Traditional exchange and modern markets.* Englewood Cliffs: Prentice-Hall.
BENNETT, H. S.
1962   *Life on the English manor, 1150–1400.* Cambridge: University Press.
BESTOR, A. E., JR.
1950   *Backwoods utopias.* Philadelphia: University of Pennsylvania Press.
BIEBUYCK, DANIEL, ed.
1963   *African agrarian systems.* London: Oxford University Press.
BISHOP, CLAIRE
1950   *All things common.* New York: Harper.
BLOCH, MARC
1961   *Feudal society.* London: Routledge and Kegan Paul.
1966   *French rural history.* London: Routledge and Kegan Paul.
BOAS, FRANZ
1897   The social organization and the secret societies of the Kwakiutl Indians. In *Report of the U. S. National Museum for 1895.* Washington, D. C.
BOEKE, J. H.
1942   *The structure of Netherlands Indian economy.* New York: Institute of Pacific Relations.
BOHANNAN, PAUL
1954   *Tiv farm and settlement.* London: H.M.S.O.
1957   *Justice and judgment among the Tiv.* New York: Oxford University Press.
1959   The impact of money on an African subsistence economy. *Journal of Economic History* 19:491–503.
BOHANNAN, PAUL, and LAURA BOHANNAN
1968   *Tiv economy.* Evanston: Northwestern University Press.
BOHANNAN, PAUL, and GEORGE DALTON
1965   Introduction. In *Markets in Africa,* Paul Bohannan and George Dalton ed. New York: Natural History Press.
BOULDING, KENNETH
1957   The Parsonian approach to economics, *Kyklos* 10:317–319.
BROKENSHA, DAVID W.
1966   *Social change at Larteh, Ghana.* Oxford: Clarendon Press.
BURLING, ROBBINS
1962   Maximization theories and the study of economic anthropology. *American Anthropologist* 64:802–821.
CARR, E. H.
1951   *The new society.* London: Macmillan.
CHAMBERLIN, E. H.
1933   *The theory of monopolistic competition.* Cambridge: Harvard University Press.

CHAYANOV, A. V.
  1966   The theory of peasant economy. Homewood: Irwin. (First published in Russian, in 1925.)
CHEVALIER, FRANÇOIS
  1963   Land and society in colonial Mexico. Berkeley: University of California Press.
CLOWER, R., G. DALTON, M. HARWITZ, and A. A. WALTERS
  1966   Growth without development: an economic survey of Liberia. Evanston: Northwestern University Press.
COLSON, ELIZABETH
  1949   Assimilation of an American Indian group. Human Problems in British Central Africa (Rhodes-Livingstone Journal) 5:1–13.
COOK, SCOTT
  1966   The obsolete "antimarket" mentality: a critique of the substantive approach to economic anthropology. American Anthropologist 68:323–345.
DALTON, GEORGE
  1960   A note of clarification on economic surplus. American Anthropologist 62:483–490.
  1961   Economic theory and primitive society. American Anthropologist 63:1–25.
  1962   Traditional production in primitive African economies. Quarterly Journal of Economics 76:360–378.
  1963   Economic surplus, once again. American Anthropologist 65:389–394.
  1964   The development of subsistence and peasant economies in Africa. International Social Science Journal 16:378–389.
  1965a   Primitive money. American Anthropologist 67:44–65.
  1965b   Primitive, archaic, and modern economies: Karl Polanyi's contribution to economic anthropology and comparative economy. Proceedings of the 1965 Annual Spring Symposium of the American Ethnological Society. In Essays in Economic Anthropology, June Helm ed. Seattle: University of Washington Press.
  1965c   History, politics, and economic development in Liberia. Journal of Economic History 25:568–591.
  1966   Bridewealth versus brideprice. American Anthropologist 68:732–737.
  1967   Bibliographical essay. In Tribal and peasant economies: readings in economic anthropology, George Dalton ed. New York: Natural History Press.
  1968a   Ed. Primitive, archaic, and modern economies: essays of Karl Polanyi. New York: Anchor Books.
  1968b   Review of Primitive and peasant economic systems, by Manning Nash (San Francisco: Chandler, 1966). American Anthropologist 70:368–369.
  1968c   Economics, economic development, and economic anthropology. Journal of Economic Issues. June.
  1969a   Economics, anthropology, and economic anthropology. In Anthropology and related disciplines, Otto von Mering ed. Pittsburgh: University of Pittsburgh Press.

1969*b* Traditional economic systems. In *The African experience,* John Paden and Edward Soja ed. Evanston: Northwestern University Press.

1969*c* The economic system. In *A handbook of method in cultural anthropology,* R. Naroll and R. Cohen ed. New York: Doubleday.

DEANE, PHYLLIS

1953 *Colonial social accounting.* Cambridge: University Press.

DOMAR, EVSEY D.

1957 *Essays in the theory of economic growth.* New York: Oxford University Press.

DOUGLAS, MARY

1958 Raffia cloth distribution in the Lele economy. *Africa* 28:109–122.

1962 Lele economy compared with the Bushong. In *Markets in Africa,* P. J. Bohannan and G. Dalton ed. Evanston: Northwestern University Press.

1965 The Lele—resistance to change. In *Markets in Africa,* P. J. Bohannan and G. Dalton ed. New York: Natural History Press.

EPSTEIN, T. SCARLETT

1962 *Economic development and social change in South India.* Manchester: Manchester University Press.

ERASMUS, CHARLES J.

1961 *Man takes control.* Minneapolis: University of Minnesota Press.

EVANS-PRITCHARD, E. E.

1954 Introduction. In *The gift,* by Marcel Mauss. Glencoe: The Free Press.

FALLERS, LLOYD A.

1961 Are African cultivators to be called "peasants"? *Current Anthropology* 2:108–110.

FALS BORDA, ORLANDO

1965 Violence and the break-up of tradition in Colombia. In *Obstacles to change in Latin America,* C. Veliz ed. London: Oxford University Press.

FANON, FRANTZ

1959 *L'an V de la révolution algérienne.* Paris: Maspero.

1961 *Les damnés de la terre.* Paris: Maspero.

1965 *The wretched of the earth.* London: MacGibbon and Kee.

FIRTH, RAYMOND

1929 *Primitive economics of the New Zealand Maori.* Wellington: R. E. Owen, Government Printer.

1939 *Primitive Polynesian economy.* London: Routledge and Kegan Paul.

1946 *Malay fishermen: their peasant economy.* London: Routledge and Kegan Paul.

1951 *The elements of social organization.* London: Watts.

1957 The place of Malinowski in the history of economic anthropology. In *Man and culture: an evaluation of the work of Bronislaw Malinowski,* R. Firth ed. New York: Harper Torchbooks.

1958 Work and wealth of primitive communities. In *Human types,* Raymond Firth, revised ed. New York: Mentor Books.

1959   *Social change in Tikopia*. London: George Allen and Unwin.
1964a   Capital, saving, and credit in peasant societies: a viewpoint from economic anthropology. In *Capital, saving, and credit in peasant societies*, R. Firth and B. Yamey ed. Chicago: Aldine.
1965   Review of *Kapauku Papuan economy*, by L. Pospisil (Yale Publication in Anthropology no. V). *American Anthropologist* 67:122–125.
1966   *Primitive Polynesian economy*, revised ed. London: Routledge and Kegan Paul.
1967   Ed. *Themes in economic anthropology*. A.S.A. Monograph no. 6. London: Tavistock.
FIRTH, RAYMOND, and BASIL YAMEY ed.
1964   *Capital, saving, and credit in peasant societies*. Chicago: Aldine.
FORTES, M., and E. E. EVANS-PRITCHARD
1940   *African political systems*. London: Oxford University Press.
FRANKEL, S. H.
1955   *The economic impact on under-developed societies*. Cambridge: Harvard University Press.
FROMM, ERICH
1941   *Escape from freedom*. New York: Rinehart.
FUSFELD, DANIEL B.
1957   Economic theory misplaced: livelihood in primitive society. In *Trade and market in the early empires*, K. Polanyi, C. M. Arensberg, H. W. Pearson ed. Glencoe: The Free Press.
GEERTZ, CLIFFORD
1962   Social change and economic modernization in two Indonesian towns: a case in point. In *On the theory of social change*, Everett E. Hagen ed. Homewood: Dorsey.
GERSCHENKRON, ALEXANDER
1954   Social attitudes, entrepreneurship, and economic development. *International Social Science Journal* 6:252–258.
1962   *Economic backwardness in historical perspective*. Cambridge: The Belknap Press of Harvard University Press.
GLUCKMAN, MAX, and I. G. CUNNISON
1962   Foreword. In *Politics of the kula ring*, by J. P. Singh Uberoi. Manchester: Manchester University Press.
GODELIER, MAURICE
1965   Objet et méthode de l'anthropologie économique. *L'Homme* 5(2).
GOODENOUGH, WARD HUNT
1963   *Co-operation in change*. New York: Russell Sage Foundation.
GOODFELLOW, D. M.
1939   *Principles of economic sociology*. London: Routledge.
GOODY, JACK
1963   Feudalism in Africa? *Journal of African History* 4:1–18.
GRAY, ROBERT F.
1960   Sonjo bride-price and the question of African "wife purchase." *American Anthropologist* 62:34–57.
GROSSMAN, GREGORY
1967   *Economic systems*. Englewood Cliffs: Prentice-Hall.

GRUCHY, ALLAN G.
1966 *Comparative economic systems.* Boston: Houghton Mifflin.
GULLIVER, P. H.
1965 The Arusha—economic and social change. In *Markets in Africa,* P. J. Bohannan and G. Dalton ed. New York: Natural History Press.
HAGEN, EVERETT E. ed.
1962 *On the theory of social change: how economic growth begins.* Homewood: Dorsey.
HARRIS, MARVIN
1959 The economy has no surplus? *American Anthropologist* 61:185–199.
HARROD, R. F.
1952 An essay in dynamic theory. In *Economic essays.* New York: Harcourt, Brace.
HERSKOVITS, MELVILLE J.
1940 Anthropology and economics. In *The economic life of primitive peoples.* New York: Knopf.
1941 Economics and anthropology: a rejoinder. *Journal of Political Economy* 49:269–278. (Reprinted in *Economic anthropology,* by M. J. Herskovits [New York: Knopf, 1952].)
1952 *Economic anthropology,* revised ed. New York: Knopf.
HILL, POLLY
1963 *Migrant cocoa-farmers of southern Ghana.* Cambridge: Cambridge University Press.
1966 A plea for indigenous economics. *Economic Development and Cultural Change* 15:10–20.
HOLMBERG, ALLAN R., *et al.*
1965 The changing values and institutions of Vicos in the context of national development. *American Behavioral Scientist* 18:3–8.
HOMANS, GEORGE C.
1958 Social behaviour as exchange. *American Journal of Sociology* 62:597–606.
HUNTER, MONICA
1961 *Reaction to conquest,* 2d. ed. London: Oxford University Press.
JASPAN, M. A.
1953 A sociological case study: communal hostility to imposed social changes in South Africa. In *Approaches to community development,* Phillips Ruopp ed. The Hague: W. Van Hoeve.
KEYFITZ, NATHAN
1959 The interlocking of social and economic factors in Asian development. *Canadian Journal of Economics and Political Science* 25:34–46.
KEYNES, JOHN MAYNARD
1936 *The general theory of employment, interest, and money.* New York: Harcourt, Brace.
KNIGHT, FRANK
1941 Anthropology and economics. *Journal of Political Economy* 49:247–268. (Reprinted in *Economic anthropology,* by M. J. Herskovits [New York: Knopf, 1952].)

LeClair, Edward E.
1962 Economic theory and economic anthropology. *American Anthropologist* 64:1179–1203.

Lewis, W. Arthur
1955 *The theory of economic growth*. London: Allen and Unwin.
1962 Foreword. In *Economic development and social change in South India*, by T. Scarlett Epstein. Manchester: Manchester University Press.

Lienhardt, R. Godfrey
1956 Religion. In *Man, culture, and society*, Harry L. Shapiro ed. New York: Oxford University Press.

MacIver, R. M.
1933 *Society, its structure and changes*. New York: R. Long and R. R. Smith.

Malinowski, Bronislaw
1921 The primitive economics of the Trobriand Islanders. *Economic Journal* 31:1–15.
1922 *Argonauts of the western Pacific*. London: Routledge.
1935 *Coral gardens and their magic*, vol. 1. New York: American Book.
1959 *Crime and custom in savage society*. Paterson: Littlefield, Adams. (First published in 1926.)

Maquet, Jacques
1961 *The premise of inequality in Ruanda*. London: Oxford University Press.

Marshall, Alfred
1920 *Principles of economics*. London: Macmillan.

Martin, Kurt, and John Knapp ed.
1967 *The teaching of development economics*. Chicago: Aldine.

Mauss, Marcel
1954 *The gift: forms and functions of exchange in archaic societies*. Glencoe: The Free Press.

Myrdal, Gunnar
1957 *Rich lands and poor*. New York: Harper.
1960 *Beyond the welfare state*. New Haven: Yale University Press.

Nadel, S. F.
1942 *A black Byzantium: the kingdom of Nupe in Nigeria*. London: Oxford University Press.

Nash, Manning
1966 *Primitive and peasant economic systems*. San Francisco: Chandler.
1967 Reply to reviews of *Primitive and peasant economic systems*. *Current Anthropology* 8:249–250.

Neale, Walter C.
1957a Reciprocity and redistribution in the Indian village. In *Trade and market in the early empires*, K. Polanyi, C. M. Arensberg, H. W. Pearson ed. Glencoe: The Free Press.
1957b The market in theory and history. In *Trade and market in the early empires*, K. Polanyi, C. M. Arensberg, H. W. Pearson ed. Glencoe: The Free Press.

NORDHOFF, CHARLES
 1961   *The communistic societies of the United States.* New York: Hillary House. (First published in 1875.)
NOVE, ALEC
 1962   *The Soviet economy.* New York: Praeger.
NOYES, JOHN HUMPHREY
 1870   *American socialisms.* Philadelphia: Lippincott.
NYERERE, JULIUS K.
 1964   Ujamua. In *African socialism,* William H. Friedland and Carl G. Rosberg, Jr. ed. Stanford: Stanford University Press.
OKIGBO, PIUS
 1956   Social consequences of economic development in West Africa. *Annals of the American Academy of Political Science* 125–133.
PEARSON, HARRY W.
 1957   The economy has no surplus: critique of a theory of development. In *Trade and market in the early empires,* K. Polanyi, C. M. Arensberg, H. W. Pearson ed. Glencoe: The Free Press.
PIRENNE, HENRI
 1936   *Economic and social history of medieval Europe.* London: Routledge and Kegan Paul.
POLANYI, KARL
 1944   *The great transformation.* New York: Rinehart.
 1947   Our obsolete market mentality. *Commentary* 13:109–117.
 1957   The economy as instituted process. In *Trade and market in the early empires,* K. Polanyi, C. M. Arensberg, H. W. Pearson ed. Glencoe: The Free Press.
 1960   On the comparative treatment of institutions in antiquity, with illustrations from Athens, Mycenae, and Alalakh. In *City invincible,* C. H. Kraeling and R. M. Adams ed. Chicago: University of Chicago Press.
 1963   Ports of trade in early societies. *Journal of Economic History* 23:30–45.
 1966   *Dahomey and the slave trade.* Seattle: University of Washington Press.
 1968   The semantics of money uses. In *Primitive, archaic, and modern economies: essays of Karl Polanyi,* G. Dalton ed. New York: Doubleday Anchor Books.
POSPISIL, LEOPOLD
 1963   *Kapauku Papuan economy.* Yale University Publications in Anthropology no. 67.
POSTAN, M. M.
 1966   *The agrarian life of the Middle Ages.* Volume 1 of The Cambridge Economic History of Europe, 2d ed. Cambridge: Cambridge University Press.
REDFIELD, ROBERT
 1956   *Peasant society and culture.* Chicago: University of Chicago Press.
REYNDERS, H. J. J.
 1963   The geographical income of the Bantu areas in South Africa. In *Afri-*

can studies in income and wealth, L. H. Samuels ed. Chicago: Quadrangle Books.

RICHARDS, AUDREY I.
  1939   *Land, labor and diet in Northern Rhodesia.* London: Oxford University Press.

RIVERS, W. H. R.
  1922   *Essays on the depopulation of Melanesia.* Cambridge: University Press.

ROBBINS, LIONEL
  1935   *An essay on the nature and significance of economic science.* London: Macmillan.

ROBINSON, JOAN
  1932   *The economics of imperfect competition.* London: Macmillan.

ROSTOW, W. W. ed.
  1963   *The economics of take-off into sustained growth.* London: Macmillan.

ROTTENBERG, SIMON
  1958   Review of *Trade and market in the early empires,* K. Polanyi, C. M. Arensberg, H. W. Pearson ed. (Glencoe: The Free Press, 1957). *American Economic Review* 48:675–678.

  1960   Political power and the economy in primitive society. In *Essays in the science of culture in honor of Leslie White,* G. Dole and R. Carneiro ed. New York: Crowell.

  1968   Tribal economics. In *Tribesmen.* Englewood Cliffs: Prentice-Hall.

SALISBURY, R. F.
  1962   *From stone to steel.* London and New York: Cambridge University Press.

SAWYER, JOHN E.
  1951   Social structure and economic progress. *American Economic Review* 41:321–329.

SCHAPERA, I.
  1928   Economic changes in South African native life. *Africa* 1:170–188.

  1934   *Western civilization and the natives of South Africa.* London: Routledge and Kegan Paul.

SCHAPERA, I., and A. J. H. GOODWIN
  1937   Work and wealth. In *The Bantu-speaking tribes of South Africa,* I. Schapera ed. London: Routledge and Kegan Paul.

SENGHOR, LEOPOLD S.
  1964   *On African socialism.* New York: Praeger.

SINGER, HANS
  1950   The distribution of gains between borrowing and lending countries. *American Economic Review, Papers and Proceedings,* May, 1950.

SMELSER, NEIL J.
  1958   *Social change in the industrial revolution.* London: Routledge and Kegan Paul.

  1963   Mechanisms of change and adjustment to change. In *Industrialization and society,* B. F. Hoselitz and W. E. Moore ed. The Hague: UNESCO-Mouton.

SOUTHALL, AIDAN
  1961 *Social change in modern Africa.* London: Oxford University Press.
STEINER, FRANZ
  1957 Towards a classification of labor. *Sociologus* 7:112–129.
TAKIZAWA, MATSUYO
  1927 *The penetration of money economy in Japan and its effects upon social and political institutions.* New York: Columbia University Press.
TAX, SOL
  1963 *Penny capitalism.* Chicago: University of Chicago Press. (First published in 1953.)
UBEROI, J. P. SINGH
  1962 *The politics of the kularing.* Manchester: Manchester University Press.
UNESCO
  1963 *Social aspects of economic development in Latin America.* New York.
UNITED NATIONS
  1954 *Enlargement of the exchange in tropical Africa.* New York: United Nations.
WEBER, MAX
  1950 *General economic history.* Glencoe: The Free Press.
WILSON, GODFREY
  1941 *An essay on the economics of detribalization in Northern Rhodesia.* The Rhodes-Livingstone Papers no. 5.
WOLF, ERIC R.
  1966 *Peasants.* Englewood Cliffs: Prentice-Hall.
WORSLEY, PETER
  1957a *The trumpet shall sound: a study of "cargo" cults in Melanesia.* London: MacGibbon and Kee.
  1957b Millenarian movements in Melanesia. *Rhodes-Livingstone Institute Journal,* pp. 18–31.
YANG, MARTIN C.
  1945 The family as a primary economic group. In *A Chinese village.* New York: Columbia University Press.
YUDELMAN, MONTAGUE
  1964 *Africans on the land.* Cambridge: Harvard University Press.

II

TRIBAL AND PEASANT ECONOMIES

Give all thou canst; high Heaven
rejects the lore
of nicely-calculated less or more
                WILLIAM WORDSWORTH

4

Traditional Production in
Primitive African Economies [1]

Economic historians often stress the role played by the traditional institutions of pre-industrial European countries in shaping their sequential patterns of development: that the costs, speed, and specific lines of development were influenced by what existed before industrialization (Gerschenkron 1952; Rostow 1960). However, we seem not to apply the lesson to exotic areas such as Africa. Economists rarely show interest in the voluminous anthropological literature concerned with the economic organization and performance of primitive societies before and during European colonial incursion. Yet it is these same primitive and peasant societies in Africa, Asia, and Latin America which are now so much the concern of the economics of development.

Although wage employment and dependence on cash cropping have become widespread in Africa, it is probably still true (as it was in the early 1950's) that most Africans get the bulk of their livelihood from traditional modes of production within the framework of tribal societies.[2] It is with such relatively unchanged, primitive economies in Africa that this essay is concerned.

There are at least two kinds of development problems for the solution of which knowledge of traditional economic structure is useful: (1) What accounts for the marked difference in receptivity to economic and technological change among primitive societies? Why do some adopt modern institutions and techniques with ease and alacrity while others resist the changes necessary to generate growth? (2) Why is economic development often accompanied by traumatic social change? Is it possible to reduce the

Reprinted, with revision, from "Traditional Production in Primitive African Economies," *Quarterly Journal of Economics*, 76 (August 1962):360–378. Reprinted by permission of the publisher.

social costs, conflicts, and dislocations by building compensators into the new economic forms? [3]

The point of this essay is to show how traditional primitive economies in Africa differ structurally from developed economies in the West. Our concern is not so much with technological differences as with differences in the organization of production. And for either the U.S. or tribal Africa it is convenient to regard production of any kind as consisting of three component subprocesses: the allocation of labor and other factors; the work process of arranging and transforming resources into products; the disposition of what is produced.

THE ABSENCE OF MARKET DEPENDENCE

At the outset, we may summarize our main theme as follows. The absence of market exchange as the *dominant* [4] economic organization allows indigenous African production to take forms different from those in Western economy. These forms invariably entail social control of production by kinship, religion, and political heads. Therefore, change in primitive economic processes means inevitable change in social relationships. "In primitive communities, the individual as an economic factor is personalized, not anonymous. He tends to hold his economic position in virtue of his social position. Hence to displace him economically means a social disturbance [Firth 1951:137]."

It is necessary to emphasize the economic importance of indigenous social organization because production in tribal Africa is most frequently a community activity in MacIver's sense, and only rarely associational:

> Association is a group specifically organized for the purpose of an interest or group of interests which its members have in common. . . . Community is a circle of people who live together, who belong together, so that they share not this or that particular interest, but a whole set of interests wide enough and comprehensive enough to include their lives [MacIver 1933:9, 10, 12].[5]

We are used to thinking in terms of "production units" because the Western firm is an association, not importantly affected by kinship, religious, or political affiliation of participants. In Africa, however, production is often undertaken by intimate communities of persons sharing a multitude of social ties and functions, one of which happens to be the production of material goods. If we are not to prejudge the nature of production organization in African economy, it must be understood that none of those special characteristics of Western production due to the use of machines and reliance on factor and output markets need be found. The component processes exist: the allocation of factors, the arrangement of work, and the disposition of produce. How they are organized in the absence of market integration must be a matter for investigation. In a word, every society has production processes, but not necessarily production "units."

Indigenously, the most important production lines in Africa are agricultural, carried on without machine technology, and for subsistence purposes rather than primarily for market sale (United Nations 1954).[6] Unlike his counterpart in the American Midwest, the African farmer typically is not enmeshed in that kind of larger economy from which he extracts his livelihood as a specialist producer of cash crops, the money proceeds of which are used to recoup his costs of production, and the residual (his income proper) used to buy daily-used material items and services.

The absence of machines and of market dependence are related: as with hired labor or any other *purchased* factor, a machine represents a money cost which can be incurred only if the purchaser uses the machine to enlarge his money sales revenue from which he recovers its cost. The analytical point to be stressed is that without purchased ingredients of production, and without reliance on market disposition of output, the input and output decisions of producers cannot be based on factor and output prices as guiding parameters. That neither factor nor product prices exist to constrain the indigenous African agriculturalist (as they do the American) is crucial to understanding why it is that Africans can organize production in such seemingly bizarre "social" ways.

The absence of Western technological and market constraints means also the absence of the Western kind of material insecurity. It is not technological unemployment and depression which are the threats to the continuity of production and income, but rather physical environment—bad weather, plant disease. That there is no counterpart to depression-born unemployment is simply a reflection of the absence of dependence on market sale.

A related point of contrast is that unlike the Western worker, the African is rarely a full-time specialist in one occupation or in one production group (Schapera and Goodwin 1937:153; Herskovits 1952:94, 106). Not only is it typical for him to produce for himself a wide range of the items he uses—his own house and tools as well as his food—but during the course of a year he is frequently a part-time participant in several production activities: he may join sporadic work parties to do specific tasks such as clearing fields for friends, kin, and chief; he may be of an age-set which is obliged to perform community services such as repairing roads (Nadel 1942:xi; Herskovits 1952b:113; Kluckhohn 1962); he may go on seasonal expeditions to extract ore for metals (Cline 1937:56). In sum, it is frequently the case that during the year an African will work in several production groups, no one of which is crucial to his own livelihood. It is also common for an African to receive substantial amounts of factors, goods, and services as gifts, or in forms other than remuneration for work performed.

PRODUCTION AND SOCIAL ORGANIZATION

The negative point stressed above, that the absence of machines and market dependence means the absence of those kinds of constraints on production organization in the West, clears the way to examine two positive points stressed repeatedly in the literature of traditional Africa: (1) that neighboring societies sharing the same physical environment often produce markedly different ranges of output (Winter 1962), with different technologies (Douglas 1962) used within differently organized production groups (Mead 1927; Udy 1959); (2) that such economic and technological differences are largely attributable to differences in social organization: that kinship, political, and religious institutions constrain and direct all phases of production, in the same sense that market structure and machine technology constrain and direct production in Western economy.

The connections between indigenous African production and social organization may be described in three ways.

1. In terms of the MacIver-Nadel distinction, production groups typically are not separate associations, but rather are integral parts of a set of community relationships and activities:

> . . . obligations to participate tend to be obligations to associate with the group involved rather than specifically engage in production [Udy 1959:104].

> The ties between producers tend to reach out beyond this common interest in the act of production and its rewards alone. A production relationship is often only one facet of a social relationship. . . . economic relations can be understood only as a part of a scheme of social relations. . . . Economic anthropology deals primarily with the economic aspects of the social relations of persons [Firth 1951:136–138].

> . . . special organizations to carry out cultivation or manufacture need not be expected among the Bantu; the functions are always actively carried out, but often by organizations of which the family or household is the most important, which exist to carry out almost all necessary functions including the religious, the legal, the political, and the educational, and which conduct manufacture and agriculture alongside of these other activities [Goodfellow 1939:7–8].

2. The same point is generalized by Karl Polanyi in saying that primitive economy is "embedded" in society, in the sense that the economic system functions as an inseparable part of non-economic institutions: that economy as a cohesive entity, a separate set of practices and relationships

apart from social organization, does not exist in primitive life (Polanyi 1944:chapter 4; 1947; 1957).

3. If the organization of production in African economies is, indeed, an inextricable part of social community, it should be possible to show how *each* component process of production—the allocation of factor resources, the arrangement of work, and the disposition of produce—is related to social structure.

ALLOCATION OF FACTORS OF PRODUCTION

Production in all economies requires organizational rules to direct labor, land, and other resources to specific uses. Resource allocation is never unstructured because continuity in the production of basic goods is never unimportant. One may gain insight into the special rules which mark off types of economy—say, the United States compared with the Soviet Union compared with the Bantu of South Africa—by asking which transactional procedures channel resources to production lines: how are land, labor, and other resources allocated; how do they change hands or usage?

In our own economy, labor and land as well as products are marketable commodities. In tribal Africa, products are frequently marketed, but factors—before European colonial incursion—very rarely. A distinguishing characteristic of such economies is that labor and natural resources have no separate "economic" organization: factor movements and appropriations are expressions of social obligation, social affiliation, and social right. A second characteristic is that, typically, land utilization is organized differently from labor utilization. Unlike Western market economy, *each* of the factor ingredients may enter production lines through *different* institutional channels, the channels being structured social relationships. Both points are illustrated by the following examples.

In much of agricultural Africa, land for homesteads and farms is acquired through tribal affiliation or kinship right. One receives land as a matter of status prerogative; only rarely is land acquired or disposed of through purchase and sale (Bohannan 1960; Herskovits 1952*b*:364–365). The Bantu are typical in this regard:

Every household-head has an exclusive right to land for building his home and for cultivation. Generally he can take up such land for himself within the area controlled by his sub-chief or headman, provided that he does not encroach upon land already occupied or cultivated by others. Failing this, it is the duty of his headman to provide him gratuitously with as much land as he needs. . . . He also has the right, subject to the approval of his headman, to give away part of it to a relative or friend, or to lend it to someone else. But he can never sell it or dispose of it in any other way in return for material considerations. Should he finally abandon the spot, his land reverts to the tribe as a whole and can subsequently be assigned to someone else. The only other way in which he can lose his right to the land is by confiscation, if he is found guilty of some serious crime [Schapera and Goodwin 1937:157].[7]

So, too, with the Tiv (Bohannan 1954), the Dahomeans (Herskovits 1938), the Nupe (Nadel 1942), and the Kikuyu.[8]

What makes the African social integument so important for factor allocation (and therefore production) is that land may be acquired through one set of social relationships, while labor to work the land is acquired through others. In the same Bantu societies in which land is acquired from chiefs by all family heads as a matter of tribal affiliation, labor to work the land is acquired by marriage rights (wives do the sustained cultivation) and by kinship and friendship reciprocity (work parties to do specific tasks such as clearing fields and harvesting). Put another way, the "labor" to perform different tasks in growing the same crop—clearing the field, planting, harvesting—may be acquired through different social relationships (Schapera and Goodwin 1937:149, 151–152).

The extent to which various community relationships allocate factors to production lines is even greater than indicated above. Each separate production line—farming, cattle-raising, house construction, road construction—may use somewhat differently institutionalized procedures for recruiting the labor and acquiring the land and material resources used in each; that is to say, labor for agriculture may be acquired in several ways, each different from labor used in producing other goods.

As will be pointed out below, such diversity in the allocation of land and labor in accordance with multiple social relationships and obligations is also the case with the disposition of the goods produced. African economies are "multicentric" (Bohannan and Dalton 1962: introduction) in the allocation of both resources and produce. This multicentricity is expressed in two ways, both extremely common in primitive economy: (1) Resources and products are arranged in groups, the items in one group exchangeable with each other, but not with items in other groups (Firth 1958:69); indeed, there may be items which are not exchangeable at all. Typically, "subsistence" items form one or more exchangeable groups, and "prestige" items, others. (2) Each commensurable group of factors and products may be transacted by an essentially different socio-economic procedure (reciprocity or redistribution); each procedure expressing the special social obligation which induces the material transaction and, where relevant, dictating the permissible ratios at which commensurable goods may change hands (Polanyi 1957; Dalton 1961).

Market exchange is also a common transactional procedure in tribal Africa, but differs sharply from reciprocity and redistribution in the permissible range of goods transacted in markets, in the forces which determine exchange ratios, and in the absence of a social imperative connected with market transactions.

In summary, an African's role in each production process is usually defined by some aspect of his social status—tribal member, husband, cousin, friend, elder. The question "What forces, institutions, or rules direct labor, land, and other resources to specific lines of production?" can be answered only with reference to community social organization.

WORK ARRANGEMENT

The specific arrangement of work in any production line in any economy is the combined result of physical environment, technology, economic structure, and social organization. But the relative importance of each may differ between different production lines and between different types of economy. Here we shall be concerned with one primary point of difference between Western and primitive economies: in our own system, the constraints imposed by economy-wide market integration and by machine technology are far more important in determining work organization than those imposed by physical environment and social relationships. In tribal Africa just the opposite is the case: physical environment and social structure are all-important because of the absence of machine technology and of a larger market economy to enforce economizing decisions on local producers.

That physical environment imposes sharp constraints on African work organization is due to the great reliance by the Africans on production lines entailing little fabrication, such as agriculture and herding. Compared with their Western counterparts, the African agriculturalist and herder lack those devices of applied science (irrigation equipment, disease-resistant seeds, scientific stock-breeding) which reduce ecological risks in the West (Forde and Douglas 1956:337). Indeed, technology and science have allowed some Western farmers to organize farm work on something like a factory basis. However, the economic as distinct from the technological differences between Western and primitive production deserve emphasis. Dependence on market sale for income, together with reliance on purchased factors, forces Western farmers into the same economizing choices of weighing costs against sales revenues that typify manufacturing processes. With us, farm production, too, is sensitive to market prices, which of necessity serve as guiding parameters for production decisions, including efficient work organization as measured by least cost.

Where African producers do not use purchased factors and do not depend on market sale, economizing least-cost choices in work arrangement are not enforced by technological or economic necessity, as in the West.

We are told frequently that in primitive economy social relationships and values are important determinants of work organization (Lloyd 1953:31; also Mead 1927; Udy 1959), that sexual division of labor is maintained, that magic and religion impinge on work schedules, that there are often a festive aspect to work parties, and that it is not uncommon for more labor to be lavished on a task than is strictly necessary. It is because of the absence of Western market and technological constraints that work *can be* arranged to express social relationships. The tribal producer does not have a payroll to meet. It is *not* that he is indifferent to material abundance or efficiency; rather, unlike the West, the larger economy neither compels producers to seek cost minimization nor provides them with economic directives (factor and output prices) to make economizing decisions in work arrangement. It is important to understand this point in order to understand why economic development or Western commercial "impact" induces such deep and wide social dislocation. When Western market economy comes to dominate some area of Africa—typically, through a land shortage forcing changeover to production of cash crops—there are socioeconomic repercussions because of the need to reorganize land and labor allocation, work arrangement, and the range of items to be produced, in accordance with market criteria (Gulliver 1962).

DISPOSITION OF PRODUCTS

The apportionment of outputs is a concept familiar to Westerners. We are used to tracing through the yearly flow of goods to their final recipients as is done in national income accounting and input-output analysis. But as one economist who tried to measure product and income flows in primitive African economy points out, our Western categories of analysis are derived from our own very special market-integrated structure.

> An attempt to examine the structure and problems of a primitive community in the light of the existing body of economic thought raises fundamental conceptual issues. Economic analysis and its framework of generalizations are characteristically described in terms appropriate to the modern exchange economy. It is by no means certain that the existing tools of analysis can usefully be applied to material other than that for which they have been developed. In particular it is not clear what light, if any, is thrown on subsistence economies by a science which seems to regard the use of money and specialization of labor as axiomatic. The jargon of the market place seems remote, on the face of it, from the problems of an African village where most individuals spend the greater part of their lives in satisfying their own or their families' needs and desires, where money and trade play a subordinate role in motivating productive activity [Deane 1953:115–116].[9]

The absence of purchased factors (including machinery) and the lack of dependence on market sale for livelihood, together with the pervasive influence of the social integument, are reflected in the disposition of produce as well as in the allocation of factors and the organization of work: "The income-creating process is itself part and parcel of the income it yields, and the results of the process cannot be abstracted from the process itself [Frankel 1955:41]."

If the categories we use to describe output disposition are to be analytically revealing, they must be derived from the special structural characteristics of indigenous African economies. We follow therefore the African emphasis on the social obligations to pay and to give, and the rights to receive labor, land, ordinary and emergency goods and services, built into social situations. In the succinct statement of Firth, "From each according to his status obligations in the social system, to each according to his rights in that system [1951:142]."

In primitive economy, transactions of products are like those of labor and natural resources in four ways: (1) Factors and products both may be transacted by different rules or mechanisms in the same economy. (2) Both may enter different transactional spheres, in the sense that the items in each sphere are commensurable and exchangeable only with other items in the same sphere, and not with items in different spheres. (3) The dispositions of factors and products cannot be understood outside the social situations which provide the impetus for their movement; that is, transactions of both express underlying social relationships. (4) What might be called "socially guaranteed subsistence" is arranged through both factor resource and product disposition. Illustration of each point is given below.

RECIPROCITY

Labor, natural resources, and products are transacted by any of three socio-economic rules or principles: reciprocity, redistribution, and market exchange (Polanyi 1957). Reciprocity is obligatory gift- and counter-gift-giving between persons who stand in some socially defined relationship to each other. Indigenously, gifts of produced items and factors are regarded simply as one form—material, or economic—of expressing such social relationships. (In our own society, a birthday gift from father to son is just one among many ways of expressing their kinship relation.)

Reciprocity plays a much more important part in primitive African economies than in our own: the frequency and relative amount of such gifts are greater; the number of different people with whom one person may engage in gift exchange is larger; the social obligations (and sanctions) to do so are stronger; and, above all, such gift reciprocity may play an important part in production (especially in labor allocation), which is rarely the case in our own economy outside the family farm.

After describing the network of obligatory gift transfers of labor and material products among kin and friends, at ordinary times as well as during festive occasions, Schapera and Goodwin explain the importance of reciprocal flows in Bantu societies:

> The main incentive to conformity with these obligations is reciprocity. In the relative absence of industrial specialization and consequent economic interdependence, kinship serves to establish greater social cohesion within the community, and to integrate its activities into a wider co-operation than obtains within the restricted limits of the household. The so-called "communal system" of the Bantu is largely a manifestation of this close bond of solidarity and reciprocity arising out of kinship and affecting well-nigh every aspect of daily life [1937:166].

The great variety of items and services transacted reciprocally with the same set of persons helps to explain why "production" is not a distinct activity (as it is with us) separate from other activities, in primitive economies: from the viewpoint of the participants, the movement of resources and products is one of many social activities. There are gifts of labor to help a kinsman clear his land (part of production), gifts of cattle to help him acquire a bride, gifts of a song or a name, and reciprocal gifts to be expected from him when the need arises. The pivotal matter is the social relationship between the persons which induces gifts of labor, cattle, songs, and names. When the source of the gift obligation is the same, there is no reason for the participants to mark off the labor gift as part of production. *It is only when production activities become divorced from activities expressing social relationships and obligations* that production becomes marked off as a peculiarly *economic* activity, apart from other activities (as, of course, occurs in market economy). With us, the place of production (factory, office) and the set of people we work with in production activities are usually different from the place where and the people with whom we live our family, religious, political, and social lives. Few of us live over the store in a family enterprise.

REDISTRIBUTION

Redistribution entails obligatory payments of material items, money objects, or labor services to some socially recognized center, usually king, chief, or priest, who reallocates portions of what he receives to provide community services (such as defense or feasts) and to reward specific persons. Typically, but not invariably, the central figure is also endowed with the right to distribute unused land or hunting sites; these allocation rights are vested in him in the name of the community by virtue of his high political, juridical, military, or religious authority. As with reciprocity between friends or kin, the obligations are multiple, economic and non-economic. One pays in labor, to farm the chief's garden or build his new house, and one pays in respect, homage, and political followership. Indeed, what appear to us as economic transactions of resources and products need not be distinguished indigenously from such as express the obligation to perform military service.

Among the Bantu the chief receives payments of specific goods and services from all his people and payments of fines and bloodwealth. Such tribute payments are partly in recognition of his position as the steward of tribal landholdings and of his juridical authority. The word "tribute" is important here in both its economic and social meanings: the goods and labor paid over are tribute, and the social recognition of authority signified by the payment is a tribute:

> By virtue of his official status as head of the tribe he also played an important part in the economic organization. . . . He received tribute from his people, both in kind and in labor. He was given a portion of every animal slaughtered or killed in the chase; the *lobola* [bridewealth] for his chief wife was paid by the members of his tribe; he had the right to call upon his subjects to perform certain tasks for him, such as building his huts or clearing the land for his wives' gardens; above all, he received fees for hearing cases and fines for misdemeanors, and, in cases of homicide the culprit paid compensation not to the relatives of the deceased but to him [Schapera 1928:175].[10]

His material receipts cannot be regarded apart from the chief's material obligations to his people. He uses the payments and fines for his own maintenance, but also to provide community services and to reward special service of his subjects; he also gives hospitality and provides emergency support to the afflicted.

> . . . all this accumulation of wealth by the chief was really made on behalf of the tribe. One quality which was always required of the chief was that he should be generous. He had to provide for the members of his tribe in times of necessity. If a man's crops failed he would look to the chief for assistance; the chief gave out his cattle to the poorer members of his tribe to herd for him, and allowed them to use the milk; he rewarded the services of his warriors by gifts of cattle; his subjects frequently visited him in his kraal and during their stay he fed and entertained them [Schapera 1928:175].[11]

Just as an individual receives land from his chief and labor from his wives, kin, and friends as a matter of right, so, too, does he receive material aid in time of need as a matter of social right. Rarely in African societies are there special institutions to care for the disabled or the destitute (Sadie 1960:297). Subsistence is guaranteed among the Bantu—as is the case widely in primitive Africa—in two ways: through socially structured rights to receive land and labor, and through emergency allotments of food from the chief and gifts from kin. It is these socially assured rights to labor, land, and emergency subsistence which have sometimes been mistaken for "primitive communism." [12]

MARKET EXCHANGE

As with reciprocity and redistribution, market exchange is a common transactional procedure, especially in West Africa. However, indigenous market transactions differ sharply from those labeled reciprocity and redistribution and differ also in important respects from market transactions in developed economies. [13]

Purchase and sale seem to us peculiarly *economic*—permeated by utility and material gain—precisely because market transactions are neither induced by nor express social obligations or relationships. Unlike the partners to reciprocal and redistributive transactions, buyers and sellers in the market share no social tie which *obliges* them to engage in the market transactions. Therefore terms of trade may be haggled out without social disruption, both parties to the exchange being socially free to seek their own maximum material advantage.

Indigenous market exchange in Africa might better be called marketplace exchange to point up the absence or infrequency of labor and land markets. In traditional Africa, market exchange is usually confined to a limited range of produced items transacted by face-to-face buyers and sellers in market places. Moreover, the market exchanges are usually petty, in the sense that most sellers do not acquire the bulk of their livelihood, and buyers the bulk of their daily-used goods and services, via the marketplace sales and purchases. Although the market prices are determined by familiar supply and demand forces, there is absent that crucial feedback effect which links change in market price to production decisions. Unlike the price mechanism in a market-integrated economy like the United States, prices formed in traditional African market places do not serve to reallocate factors among production lines, because labor and land do not enter the market and basic livelihood is acquired in non-market spheres. Market-place exchange is found widely in Africa as a peripheral pattern in the same societies in which all important output and factor flows are carried on via reciprocity and redistribution. [14]

COLONIAL IMPACT AND THE
NEW NATIONAL ECONOMIES

It is necessary to consider the impact of colonialism to understand the present situation in much of Africa. Two points especially must be made clear.

The destructive aspect of colonialism was not *economic* exploitation of Africans in the conventional Marxist sense; it could hardly be so, considering that material poverty was already the common lot before the Europeans arrived. It is, perhaps, our own cultural emphasis which makes us focus on the real-income component of welfare and regard it as the sole component. Typically, colonialism did not make Africans worse off *materially;* it destroyed culture and society of which the indigenous economy was an inextricable part.[15] It destroyed materially poor but unusually integrated ways of life, wherein economic and social processes were mutually dependent and reinforcing. This is something on a different plane from simple material betterment or worsening. The destructive colonial impact consisted in forcing socio-economic change which was not meaningful to Africans in terms of their traditional societies: "For the sting of change lies not in change itself but in change which is devoid of social meaning [Frankel 1955:27]."

Despite any real-income increases which may have resulted, European enterprise was devoid of social meaning for Africans because it required work which was not part of social obligation to kin, friends, or rulers. Work for Europeans was not done as a by-product of traditional social relationships, and work for Europeans meant not working at those traditional tasks which were expressive of social rights and obligations, and the source of material security in sickness and old age.

> Of [indigenous] labor itself, we can say . . . that it is a socially integrative activity. . . . Nor must we forget that wherever European and other more complex societies have encouraged primitive man, the carrot has been a bribe (and a pitiful indemnity) for those who must willingly neglect the performance of what are to them socially important functions so that they can perform during that time activities which are not integrative in their own society [Steiner 1957:118–119].

Material income is important to Africans not only because it sustains life but also—in Steiner's phrase—because the work processes which yield income and the transactional disposition of the labor, resources, and products are so organized as to express and strengthen social relationships and purpose: kinship, tribal affiliation, friendship, and religious duty. It is noteworthy that in the few cases in which Africans have been able to work for

Europeans without giving up most of their usual activities, traditional social life has remained intact (Watson 1958). Most frequently however, entering the newly created market economy as wage laborer, specialist producer of cash crops, or commercial trader buying for resale has meant enlarged material income at the sacrifice of work activities which were necessary to traditional social organization, and so the latter deteriorated.

What has been called the "demonstration effect"—increased willingness to enter commercial activities in order to acquire Western material items —works in the same direction. In traditional society material wealth acquisition was largely a by-product of social status (Douglas 1962; Herskovits 1938:73). Typically, only those of higher social rank were permitted to acquire certain wealth items or an unusual amount of wealth. In the kingdom of Dahomey, for example, "The accumulation of wealth, except by those whose status entitled them to wealth, was deemed treason to the state [Polanyi 1966]." A socially divisive impact of commercial economy in Africa has been the democratization of wealth. Neither market organization nor industrialism imposes status criteria on wealth acquisition. Rather the opposite is the case (as Sir Henry Maine has long since told us).

It should be added that the force of socio-economic change in Africa cannot be explained in the simple terms of changed ownership of property. To the extent that Africans sell their labor to European firms (and other Africans), they become proletarians. What strikes the Marxists is that the wage laborers engage in production processes the capital instruments of which they do not own. This is true, of course; but the crucial point is not that the workers do not own the buildings and machines, but that they come to depend for their livelihood on the impersonal market sale of their labor. Material income thereby depends on forces, people, and institutions outside of and not controlled by the indigenous social community. Work becomes a thing apart from the other aspects of life, organized as a separate association, and not merely one facet of community life.

What is important for our purpose is that the same is true where Africans do *not* become proletarians, but enter market economy by producing cash crops on their own land. Here they own the instruments of production, but like the wage laborers also come to depend for their livelihood on market sale for a money income. The latter mode of entering the exchange economy can be as disruptive to indigenous social and economic organization as wage labor, and for the same reasons. It is not alienation from the means of production which is socially divisive, but rather the dependence on impersonal market forces unrelated to indigenous social control; the separating of economy from society by divorcing resource allocation, work arrangement, and product disposition from expressions of social obligation —and, to be sure, the consequent loss of socially guaranteed subsistence, as well.

In advocating policy measures for developing African economies one must avoid the vice of utopianism: to create a blueprint of what ought to be which bears no relation to what is, and so is unachievable. However, to retain indigenous social organization in the new economies of markets and machines is obviously impossible. What is not impossible is to frame local economic organization and national policies which allow the expression of traditional values of reciprocity and redistribution within the new economic and technological context. As we are learning from our own welfare state experience, even within efficiency constraints, economic organization is capable of contrived flexibility to accommodate social values (Myrdal 1960). The extent of diversity among the already developed nations indicates the possibility of creating distinctive African forms viable economically and socially. "The real task is not to force change but to induce it in a manner which will be meaningful to the members of the societies it affects [Frankel 1955:78–79]." [16]

The institutions being fashioned in the newly-independent countries of Africa may appear somewhat suspect in the West. They include strong central controls, unions, producers' and consumers' cooperatives, and much else of the paraphernalia of welfare and socialist states, even at the very beginnings of development; indeed, even in countries without industrialization.

What deserves emphasis is that political and economic structures transplanted to Africa from the West are being adopted with major changes to suit African needs and traditions. Neither democracy nor the welfare state means to Africans what it does to Westerners because Africans did not share those Western political and economic experiences in reaction to which democracy and the welfare state came into being in the West.[17] To us, the welfare state is a reaction against the social and economic experiences of squalor, depression, and war resulting from industrialism in the economic context of the relatively uncontrolled market system. The Africans neither shared our experiences of the pre-1930 system nor committed themselves to our laissez faire ideology (which we so painfully had to unlearn).

We should not be eager to create in Africa an uncontrolled market idyll the blessings of which we so insistently deny ourselves. To Africans, the welfare state and policies of strong central control mean techniques for rapid economic development and political unification, which, at the same time, express social responsibility in accord with traditional usages. It would be unseemly to deny the Africans material aid or sympathy because —like us—they insist on having institutions shaped by historical [18] experience and current needs.

NOTES

1. This study was supported by the National Academy of Sciences— National Research Council, under Contract No. DA–19–129–AM 1309, with the Quartermaster Research and Engineering Command, U.S. Army. I am grateful to Karl Polanyi and Paul Bohannan for their comments on an earlier draft.

2. ". . . between 65 per cent and 75 per cent of the total cultivated land area of tropical Africa is devoted to subsistence production [United Nations 1954:13]." See also Wharton (1969).

3. On social aspects of economic development, see Bohannan (1959:491– 503); Keyfitz (1959:34–46); Douglas (1962); Moore (1955:156–165).

4. By dominant is meant that source which provides the bulk of material livelihood. Market-place exchange occurs frequently in indigenous Africa, but typically provides sellers with only a minor portion of their income, and labor and land are not subject to purchase, hire, or rental. The point is considered at length later. It should be emphasized that market-place exchange does *not* refer to long-distance trade, usually in prestige goods (gold, cattle, ivory), sometimes carried on by professional traders, sometimes under government commission. On such trade, see the writings of Karl Polanyi referred to throughout the essay.

5. The distinction goes back to Tönnies' *Gemeinschaft und Gesellschaft* and to Weber (1947:136–137). Association and community are not to be regarded as mutually exclusive, but as opposite ends of a range describing degrees of emphasis. What is here meant by community is characterized in a recent work as diffuse, ascription-centered, and socially recruited. See Udy (1959:39, 53).

6. The literature on indigenous nonagricultural production in Africa is fragmentary. A good study of handicraft production is contained in Nadel (1942).

7. See also Sadie (1960:297).

8. The Kikuyu came closest to Western concepts of land tenure, and land was sold on rare occasions. See Kenyatta (1938); Bohannan (1960).

9. The same point is made by Firth (1951:121).

10. See also Herskovits (1938:78–80).

11. See also Fortes and Evans-Pritchard (1940:8–9).

12. See Polanyi (1947:112); also Firth (1951:145–146). It should be added that the material insecurity which results from dependence on favorable weather and other aspects of physical environment, together with low productivity techniques and the lack of storage and processing facilities, also works in the direction of mutual aid and sharing. See Forde and Douglas (1956:337).

13. For an extended treatment of markets in primitive compared with developed economies, see Bohannan and Dalton (1962: introduction).

14. Soviet economy provides an analogy: peasant market-place exchange of a few food and craft items which are sold at freely fluctuating prices is a pe-

ripheral pattern compared with the dominant central planning complex through which most goods are produced and almost all factors allocated.

15. There is a familiar parallel situation worth mentioning. Some literature of the British Industrial Revolution addresses itself to the question, "Did the English workers get better off or worse off during the period of rapid industrialization?" The writers then attempt to measure real-income changes to find an answer. The ambiguity lies in implicitly defining better or worse off solely in terms of real income, despite the massive social dislocations involved in movement from a rural peasant to an urban commercial way of life, and the loss of material security in moving from agricultural to wage-earning industrial employment. See Ashton (1949).

16. Herskovits points out that the successful transition to market-oriented production in Ghana is characterized by ". . . inner developments based on pre-existing patterns rather than development induced by the direct application of forces impinging from outside and cast in terms foreign to native practices. Here there is no lack of incentive to expand production." Hoselitz (1952:102). See also Moore (1955:164); also Kenyatta (1938:317–318).

17. In much of Africa, creating conditions necessary for the success of democratic political institutions is likely to be even more difficult than creating the economic and technological bases for growth. Tribal instead of national identification, widespread illiteracy, and the initial power assumed by the single parties and leaders who brought political independence all militate against democracy as it is known in the West. Moreover, unlike economic development, political democracy must be fashioned almost wholly from within; there are really no equivalents in the political sphere to the massive economic aid and technical assistance to be had from abroad. However, the existence of single political parties should not be taken as *ipso facto* evidence of dictatorship. Diversity, and dissenting views in unified political and juridical structures are not uncommon African traditions. One must hope for the substance of democracy, but not for the familiar forms.

18. Africa has two kinds of history: the conventional kind to be studied through European accounts of exploration, settlement, and colonial rule, and an unconventional kind to be studied through anthropological accounts of indigenous economic and social organization.

REFERENCES

ASHTON, T. S.
  1949 The standard of life of the workers in England, 1790–1830. *Journal of Economic History* Sup. 9.
BOHANNAN, PAUL
  1954 *Tiv farm and settlement,* Colonial Office, Colonial Research Studies 15. London: H.M.S.O.
  1959 The impact of money on an African subsistence economy. *Journal of Economic History* 19:491–503.
  1960 Africa's land. *Centennial Review* vol. 4.
BOHANNAN, PAUL, and GEORGE DALTON ed.
  1962 *Markets in Africa.* Evanston: Northwestern University Press.

CLINE, WALTER
   1937   *Mining and metallurgy in Negro Africa*. Menasha, Wisc.: George
          Banta.
DALTON, GEORGE
   1961   Economic theory and primitive society. *American Anthropologist*
          63:1–25.
DEANE, PHYLLIS
   1953   *Colonial social accounting*. Cambridge: Cambridge University Press.
DOUGLAS, MARY
   1962   Lele economy compared with the Bushong: a study of economic
          backwardness. In *Markets in Africa,* Paul Bohannan and George Dal-
          ton ed. Evanston: Northwestern University Press.
FIRTH, RAYMOND
   1951   *The elements of social organization*. London: Watts.
   1958   *Human types*. New York: T. Nelson and Sons.
FORDE, DARYLL, and MARY DOUGLAS
   1956   Primitive economics. In *Man, culture, and society,* Harry L. Shapiro
          ed. New York: Oxford University Press.
FORTES, M., and E. E. EVANS-PRITCHARD
   1940   *African political systems*. London: Oxford University Press.
FRANKEL, S. H.
   1955   *The economic impact on underdeveloped societies*. Cambridge: Har-
          vard University Press.
GERSCHENKRON, ALEXANDER
   1952   Economic backwardness in historical perspective. In *The progress of
          underdeveloped areas,* B. F. Hoselitz ed. Chicago: University of Chi-
          cago Press.
GOODFELLOW, D. M.
   1939   *Principles of economic sociology*. London: G. Routledge.
GULLIVER, P. H.
   1962   The evolution of Arusha trade. In *Markets in Africa,* Paul Bohannan
          and George Dalton ed. Evanston: Northwestern University Press.
HERSKOVITS, M. J.
   1938   *Dahomey, an ancient West African kingdom*. New York: J. J. Augus-
          tin.
   1952a *Economic anthropology,* revised ed. New York: Knopf.
   1952b The problem of adapting societies to new tasks. In *The progress of
          underdeveloped areas,* B. F. Hoselitz ed. Chicago: University of Chi-
          cago Press.
HOSELITZ, B. F. ed.
   1952   *The progress of underdeveloped areas*. Chicago: University of Chi-
          cago Press.
KENYATTA, JOMO
   1938   *Facing Mount Kenya*. London: Seeker and Warburg.
KEYFITZ, N.
   1959   The interlocking of social and economic factors in Asian develop-
          ment. *Canadian Journal of Economics and Political Science* 25:34–
          46.

KLUCKHOHN, RICHARD
    1962   The Konso economy of Southern Ethiopia. In *Markets in Africa,* Paul Bohannan and George Dalton ed. Evanston: Northwestern University Press.

LLOYD, PETER
    1953   Craft organizations in Yoruba towns. *Africa* 23:31.

MACIVER, R. M.
    1933   *Society, its structure and changes.* New York: R. Long and R. R. Smith.

MEAD, MARGARET
    1927   Interpretive statement. In *Cooperation and competition among primitive peoples,* M. Mead ed. New York: McGraw-Hill.

MOORE, W. E.
    1955   Labor attitudes toward industrialization in underdeveloped countries. *American Economic Review* 45:156–165.

MYRDAL, GUNNAR
    1960   *Beyond the welfare state.* New Haven: Yale University Press.

NADEL, S. F.
    1942   *A black Byzantium: the kingdom of Nupe in Nigeria.* London: Oxford University Press.

POLANYI, KARL
    1966   *Dahomey and the slave trade.* Seattle: University of Washington Press.
    1944   *The great transformation.* New York: Rinehart.
    1947   Our obsolete market mentality. *Commentary* 13:109–117.
    1957   The economy as instituted process. In *Trade and market in the early empires,* K. Polanyi, C. M. Arensberg, H. W. Pearson ed. Glencoe: The Free Press.

ROSTOW, W. W.
    1960   *The stages of economic growth.* Cambridge: Cambridge University Press.

SADIE, J. L.
    1960   The social anthropology of economic development. *Economic Journal* 70:294–303.

SCHAPERA, I.
    1928   Economic changes in South African native life. *Africa* 1:170–188.

SCHAPERA, I., and A. J. H. GOODWIN
    1937   Work and wealth. In *The Bantu-speaking tribes of South Africa,* I. Schapera London: Routledge.

STEINER, FRANZ
    1957   Towards a classification of labor. *Sociologus* 7:112–129.

UDY, STANLEY H.
    1959   *Organization of work.* New Haven: Human Relations Area Files Press.

UNITED NATIONS
    1954   *Enlargement of the exchange economy in tropical Africa.* New York: United Nations.

WATSON, WILLIAM
    1958   *Tribal cohesion in a money economy*. Manchester: Manchester University Press.
WEBER, MAX
    1947   *The theory of social and economic organization*. Glencoe: The Free Press.
WHARTON, CLIFTON R., JR.
    1969   *Subsistence agriculture and economic development*, Clifton Wharton ed. Chicago: Aldine Press.
WINTER, E. H.
    1962   Livestock markets among the Iraqw of Northern Tanganyika. In *Markets in Africa*, Paul Bohannan and George Dalton ed. Evanston: Northwestern University Press.

5

Markets in Africa:
Introduction

Paul Bohannan and George Dalton

Most of the essays in *Markets in Africa* describe the technology, social and economic organization, and culture of small-scale African communities. They are of interest to two fields of social science: economic anthropology and economic development. Anthropologists are concerned with structural connections between economic transactions and the rest of culture and social organization. In marketless communities and those with petty markets only (the Lele and the Sonjo are examples) it is kinship or tribal affiliation—within constraints imposed by technology and physical environment—that dictate how land, labor, and products are produced and allocated. Therefore material, service, and resource transactions are invariably accompanied by a description of social and cultural matters which may appear bizarre, indeed even whimsical, to economists (Berliner 1962). The important feature of such communities is that they have no economic organization that can be analyzed apart from social organization.

Economists are concerned with inducing successful economic development in nations which contain many low-income communities of the types described here; with integrating local communities into regional and urban groupings through economic, technological, and cultural innovations necessary to generate continual increases in per capita income over time.

To consider those matters of interest to economic anthropology and development illuminated by the essays in *Markets in Africa,* this Introduction will focus on three topics: one section examines the economic aspects of African markets, one underscores the non-economic purposes of Afri-

Reprinted, with revision, from the Introduction in Paul Bohannan and George Dalton eds., *Markets in Africa* (Evanston: Northwestern University Press, 1962). Reprinted by permission of the publisher.

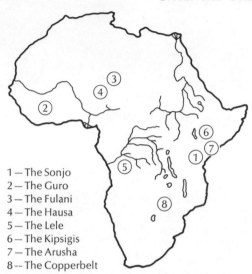

1 — The Sonjo
2 — The Guro
3 — The Fulani
4 — The Hausa
5 — The Lele
6 — The Kipsigis
7 — The Arusha
8 -- The Copperbelt

Figure 5–1 *Location of Tribes and Areas Represented in the Abridged Edition of* Markets *in Africa*

can market places, and finally one deals with current changes in Africa as they affect markets.

THE MARKET IN AFRICAN COMMUNITIES

To study markets in Africa, it is necessary to point out clearly the distinction between the institution of the market place and the transactional mode of market exchange. The market place is a specific site where a group of buyers and a group of sellers meet. The market mechanism, network, or market principle, on the other hand, entails the determination of prices of labor, resources, and outputs by the forces of supply and demand, regardless of the site of transactions. The market principle often operates outside the market place, as when a business firm hires labor, land is sold in the real estate market, or grain is sold on the "world market." When most anthropologists use the term "markets," they mean market places, and not the diffuse interaction of suppliers and demanders through a network of integrated resource and product markets such as in U.S. economy. The two, of course, overlap in many, but by no means all, instances.

The communities represented here can be classified either on the basis of the presence or absence of market places and the many functions that market places fulfill, or on the basis of the transactional mode of market exchange and its means of institutionalization. For the purposes in hand, we have used two criteria and have arrived at three classes.

First of all, we have distinguished communities with market places from those without (Figure 5–2).

Second, we have distinguished communities in which the market principle is the dominant transactional mode from those in which it is peripheral, that is, of small importance.

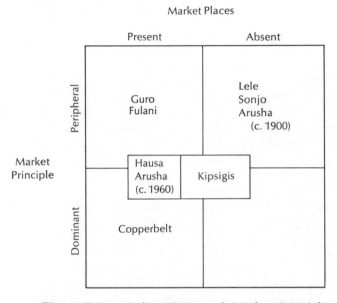

Figure 5–2 *Market Places and Market Principle*

The resulting three groups of communities are, first, one in which there are no market places and in which the market principle is present in only a few casual transactions. Traditionally, such "marketless" societies have been the concern solely of anthropologists, and it is the analytical categories of Malinowski, Thurnwald, Mead, Herskovits, Firth, and Polanyi (only the latter not an anthropologist) that explain their organization and functioning.

There are, in the second place, societies in which market places exist and the market principle operates, but only peripherally; that is to say, the subsistence requirements of the members of the community are not acquired, to any appreciable extent, in the market place or through other purchase and sale transactions. As in marketless societies, the test is a simple one: land and labor are not transacted by market purchase and sale, and if the market—in either sense—were to disappear from such a community, inconvenience would result, but no major hardship would necessarily follow because the basic necessities of life are acquired otherwise than by sale to or purchase from the market.

Finally, there are communities (or social agglomerations such as modern cities) in which market places may be (and usually are) present, but in which the primary source of subsistence goods for buyers and of income for sellers and producers is the market in the sense of transactional principle. In such a society, livelihood is acquired by first selling something, which means that not only products but the factors of production as well (particularly land and labor) come to be subject to purchase and sale. It is in such societies that the price mechanism functions as an integrative device to allocate resources, incomes, and products through a network of connected markets.

In Africa, two different situations characterize this market-dominated society. There is, in rural economies, dependence on the sale of a cash crop which makes the market of extreme importance to the producers; with the cash income they receive, they buy on the market not only the imported and luxury goods that they have come to demand but also a substantial portion of their daily subsistence requirements. There is also a situation that we have come to associate with modern industrial societies, in which most people sell their labor "to the market" and buy their subsistence on the market. Both types of market dependence may occur together, as is, indeed, the case in the United States and in some African communities. In others, only cash crop or wage-labor may appear.

The three typical situations can be summarized thus: (1) communities which lack market places, and in which the market principle is but weakly represented; (2) communities with petty markets—that is, the institution of the market place is present, but the market principle does not determine acquisition of subsistence or the allocation of land and labor resources; (3) communities dominated by labor, resource, and product markets and the price mechanism, but usually retaining simple technology and traditional culture (that is, underdeveloped peasant economies).

The main questions that we are asking in the subsequent discussion are: Do transactions in market places or by the market principle provide sellers and producers with the bulk of their material livelihood, or do they not? And what is the role of the market in each case?

Communities without Market Places

Small-scale societies without market places are marked by a multicentric economy, a characteristic they share with societies having petty markets. A multicentric economy is one in which there are several distinct transactional spheres. Each sphere is distinguished by different material items and services and may be distinguished by different modes of exchange. As an example, the conventional classification of material items into subsistence goods and prestige goods usually indicates separate spheres (DuBois 1936; Herskovits 1938; Bohannan 1955; 1959). The Trobriands case, although the limiting one, is also the most widely known. One transactional sphere

—the kula—contains treasure items (arm bands and necklaces) and the principle on which they are exchanged is the principle of reciprocity: socially obligatory gift exchange. Another sphere of exchange, gimwali, contains some subsistence items—food, utensils, and the like—and the mode of exchange is the market. However, the bulk of subsistence in the Trobriands is not acquired by purchase and sale, but rather through gift-giving reciprocity based on kinship obligations—that is to say, gimwali is peripheral or petty.

There is a further mode of transaction to be found especially in marketless societies and those with peripheral markets—the mode that Polanyi (1957) has called redistribution, entailing socially obligatory payments (tribute, corvée, tithe, tax, first fruits) of goods and services to an allocative center. The center—usually a king, chief, or priest—distributes material items, feasts, or military defense to the community at large or else makes allotments to groups or individuals in accordance with their status. It may be, of course, that within a single community one economic sphere utilizes the market mode, another the reciprocal, and still another the redistributive. It is common for several spheres to be present simultaneously in a single society, as, indeed, is so clearly the case in the Trobriands.

Firth (1958) has postulated that in many primitive economies, goods and services form separate spheres, and Thurnwald (1932) recognized the situation, but said little about it. Malinowski (1922), who so clearly described separate transactional spheres, did not recognize that there are certain institutionalized means by which items are disengaged (Steiner 1954) from the kula cycle. That is to say, a man must give his sister's son a treasure at certain times in his life; treasures change hands on a non-kula basis at the time of marriage and, indeed, are used for fines in some situations. In other words, even in the multicentric economy with its separate spheres there are prescribed means of transacting goods between the spheres under special circumstances. We have called such transactions "conversion," and they will be discussed below.

The movement of material goods in reciprocal and redistributive transactions cannot be fully understood outside the context of the social situations of which they form an integral part. The yams that change hands in the Trobriand Islands are material and therefore "economic" items. But one cannot understand why they change hands in recurrent transactions without considering the structure of kinship and political obligations. Market transactions in highly developed capitalist economies are institutionally distinguished from the kinship and political structures; hence the market sector can be analyzed, as it is by the economist, as a self-contained unit, separate from the rest of the "social" situation.

In traditional bands, tribes, and peasantries, the social integument structures the material flows and accounts for the moral attributes, whether strong or weak, of any transaction, including market transactions. The moral attitudes toward redistributive and reciprocal movements seem to be stronger than those toward market transactions precisely because non-market moral attitudes are brought to bear on exchanges between socially related persons. It is for this reason that, in marketless economies and those with peripheral markets only, the analyst cannot ignore the social setting which provides the impetus for transactions of resources, goods, and services.

These moral—indeed, emotional—aspects of material transactions deserve emphasis for two additional reasons. Anthropologists concerned with indigenous economic organization sometimes attach exaggerated importance to subsistence goods despite the abundant evidence that transactions of prestige items in marketless economies (and those with peripheral markets only) are often regarded as vital, focal activities. We have long known that potlatch coppers and kula arm bracelets are treasure items and that their transaction is an absorbing concern of primary social importance. It is not only the things involved which cause excitement but also the preparation and organization for their exchange. The transactional process through which the things change hands is itself an activity of prime importance. In a word, transactions of goods necessary for biological survival need not on that account be regarded socially as important as prestige-item transactions, especially so in traditional bands and tribes without centralized government where success in the prestige sphere is the path to power.

Conversions

Multicentric economies are, as we have seen, organized into independent spheres, each transacting different items or services; moreover, each sphere may (but may not) be characterized by a different transactional mode. The importance of separate spheres of economy, their relation to social organization, and their permeation by moral values are all illustrated by the inter-sphere transactions we have called "conversions." To distinguish conversions from ordinary transactions within any sphere, we call the latter "conveyances."

It seems to be universal in multicentric economies that the various spheres are hierarchically ranked on the basis of moral and status evaluations. It further appears that in all such communities, especially those in which the market principle is not dominant, there are institutionalized situations in which the spheres are overridden—situations in which items are "converted" from one sphere to another. Conversions are regarded as morally good or bad, rather than as skillful or unskillful. The concept of conversion, like that of price mechanism, may or may not be overtly recognized by the society that practices it, but because of the moral aspect of the hierarchy in which spheres are ranked, conversion always excites moral judgments.

In conversion, such as that found among the Sonjo and the Lele, the man who manages to obtain more highly ranked items for lower is regarded as successful, while he who obtains low-ranked items must rationalize his action by emphasizing high-value motives. On the other hand, in emergencies like war, drought, epidemic, or epizootic, additional food must be obtained in order to survive. Therefore highly ranked items must be sold off. In such situations treasures are sold, slaves are exchanged for food, children are pawned, and voluntary debt bondage may be incurred.

Conversion can be carried out by any of the three transactional modes (market, reciprocity, or redistribution). Institutionalized conversion within a community may be a socially approved form of wealth-getting (with adequate high-status reasons supplied for those who must "convert down"); emergency conversion is usually with outsiders and is carried on by the market principle. Such emergency conversion is always a last resort, a desperate expedient used only when sufficient aid can be obtained in no other way. Therefore it is done externally, with outsiders who have no kinship or social obligations to help the disaster-stricken group. Since it is done between comparative strangers, there is little moral reaction.

Another characteristic of a multicentric economy with accompanying conversion should be noted. One or more treasure items—highly ranked objects such as raffia cloths, cows, or brass rods—may take on roles as special-purpose money in non-commercial transactions (reciprocity and redistribution). With the growth of market transactions and production for sale, general-purpose money (francs, sterling, dollars) comes to displace the traditional kinds, as when bridewealth is paid in francs. Spheres of exchange formerly kept separate are now linked by the ability to use money earned commercially (in selling crops or labor) for bridewealth or entrance into secret societies. Such upward conversions are very common in African communities in the process of enlarging their commercial activities.

Peripheral Markets

Communities with peripheral markets differ from those without markets only in the sense that small produce markets are present. An excellent description of peripheral markets is provided by Pirenne for Europe in the ninth century:

The large number of markets might seem at first sight to contradict the commercial paralysis of the age, for from the beginning of the ninth century they increased rapidly and new ones were continually being founded. But their number is itself proof of their insignificance . . . there were only innumerable small weekly markets, where the peasants of the district offered for sale a few eggs, chickens, pounds of wool, or ells of coarse cloth woven at home. The nature of the business transacted appears quite clearly from the fact that

people sold *per deneratas,* that is to say, by quantities not exceeding a few
pence in value. In short, the utility of these small assemblies was limited to
satisfying that instinct of sociability which is inherent in all men. They constituted the sole distraction offered by a society settled in work on the land.
Charlemagne's order to the serfs on his estates not to "run about to markets"
shows that they were attracted much more by the desire to enjoy themselves
than by considerations of trade [Pirenne 1936:10–11].

Some distinguishing characteristics of the local economies with peripheral markets are: (1) From the viewpoint of the community, market sales
are not the dominant source of material livelihood. Either most people are
not engaged in producing for the market or selling in the market, or those
who are so engaged are only part-time marketers. Their livelihood comes
largely from non-market sectors of the economy. A common indicator of a
peripheral market is the small quantities transacted—it is on a pin-money
level. (2) Participants in peripheral markets are sometimes "target" marketers. This concept, first expressed with regard to "target labor," applies
equally well to other ways of obtaining cash income in situations in which
basic subsistence is acquired in non-market sectors. These "target marketers" engage in marketing sporadically to acquire a specific amount of cash
income for a specific expenditure. Typically, buyers in petty markets buy
only a small proportion of their daily-used material items; they, too, acquire the bulk of subsistence goods in other ways. However, it is common
in petty markets for buyers to regard the market place as economically important because it is the only place to obtain some special item or import.
There may also be present in petty markets foreign traders for whom the
market is not peripheral, however much it may be so for the local attendants.

Two aspects of petty markets of special interest to economists concern
the process of price formation and the role of market-made prices in the
local economy. With regard to price formation, supply and demand forces
are operative, but are affected by a variety of social and cultural factors
which impinge on price-making: kinship, clanship, religion or other status
indicators of buyers, traditional norms of just price, eagerness of market
women not to sell out quickly because the market place is a source of en-
tertainment and social intercourse. In such markets one finds seasonal fluctuations in price and predictable price changes, but within ranges not
wholly determined by cost and demand; local institutional peculiarities impinge on price formation in varying degree. Moreover, sellers of home-
produced items in peripheral markets frequently are unable to calculate
money costs of production because they have bought no factor ingredients,
and many have no alternative way of earning cash.

A unique aspect of local economies in which peripheral markets appear
is that prices made in the market place do not perform the function of al-

locating factor resources among alternative outputs. Here we come to the essential difference between markets in so-called primitive or subsistence economies and in Western economy: the peripheral market place is not integrated with production decisions. Although those products which enter the market are, indeed, apportioned by prices determined by supply and demand, there is absent that feedback effect on resource allocation which makes the interdependent formation of market prices—the market system —so crucially important in national capitalist economy and the price mechanism a central concern of formal economic theory. In this respect, prices in peripheral markets are like prices in antique auctions in our own economy. In both cases the prices do not affect future production of the things priced, although supply and demand forces determine the price in each market place. In a word, prices made in peripheral markets do not perform the economy-wide integrative function of the price mechanism in Western economy.

Where the market mode of transaction is dominant rather than peripheral, market prices integrate all sectors of the economy because all incomes are derived from the market price of output and all production decisions are guided by market cost of resource ingredients and the sales price of products. It is this fact that makes us emphasize as crucial the non-integrative role of prices in petty markets as compared to markets in national, developed, capitalist economies.

Market Economies: Peasant, Urban, and National

We reserve the term "market economy" for those rural communities, cities, or—as in Europe and America—nations in which purchase and sale of labor, other resources, products, and services are of prime importance to the livelihood of most people.

In rural Africa, where communities have come to depend for livelihood on producing cash crops, and land and labor have entered the market (as with the Kipsigis), one usually finds a peasant economy: the market mode of transaction and Western money dominate, but backward technology and traditional culture are retained in large measure. In neither economy nor culture are peasant communities fully integrated with cities or the nation.

In a city or a nationally-integrated economy in which market exchange is dominant, the "market place" takes on varied physical as well as organizational forms: a place where products are sold, such as a bazaar, a retail store, or a cluster of retail stores; a place where resource ingredients of production are sold or hired, such as a "labor market"; the "money market" in which loans are contracted; the "capital market" where titles to income-yielding property are bought and sold, as well as finance for new ventures transacted. What these diverse markets have in common is decidedly not similarity in the institutional place of sale involved—the market place—but rather that the goods, services, and resources are bought and sold in a market-dominated economy: (*a*) sale at a money price is determined by impersonal supply and demand forces; (*b*) the buyers and sellers depend on such market exchange for livelihood; (*c*) the market prices for resources and finished goods crucially influence production decisions and therefore the allocation of resources, including labor, into different lines of production.

What we have called "peripheral" or "petty" markets in Africa function differently and are much less important in the local economy. They refer to the institution of the market-place site where buyers and sellers meet to exchange a narrow range of products. When an anthropologist says that some African market operates like a Western market, he usually means simply that there are seasonal price fluctuations caused by changes in supply and demand; he does not mean that an interrelated set of market prices is formed which guides production decisions or that the populace derives its livelihood through selling something to the market.

A related point also requires careful distinction between the market place as a physical site and market exchange as a transactional mode. As with our own economy, when market exchange comes to dominate an African community, the traditional market place need not be the locus of the expanded market activity (United Nations 1954). For example, it is frequently the case that important cash crops such as cocoa and palm kernels by-pass the market place, which remains a pin-money affair for women. In Central Africa it is cooperatives and not local market places that have expanded as more goods are transacted by the market principle. In sum, the dominance of the market principle is indicated by dependence for livelihood on sale for money at prices determined by diffuse suppliers and demanders, whether the commodity sold is labor, cattle, or agricultural produce, regardless of the physical site of the sale.

Money and Money Uses

A similar point must be made about money and money uses in each of the market situations we have discerned. In considering the role of money in marketless economies and those with peripheral markets only, there are two pitfalls to be avoided: the assumption that the most useful distinction is that between transactions with and those without money, and the assumption that money plays the same role in these as it does in market-dominated economies.

The familiar dichotomy of barter versus money transactions does not reveal the mode of transaction involved in goods changing hands. The point is that moneyless transactions take a variety of forms, depending on the transactional principle involved. In the Trobriands both kula and gimwali are barter—that is, carried out without the use of Western money. But the goods which enter each sphere of exchange, the transactional mode, and the moral reactions—all are radically different. Kula prestige items are transacted as reciprocal gift exchanges; they are not random, impersonal transactions at bargained rates, but are carefully structured through gift partners, who exchange at traditional rates (all aspects of the transactions carried out within a code of etiquette). Gimwali, also moneyless, entails subsistence goods transacted in accordance with the market principle: random buyers and sellers sharing no social relationship haggle over price in the pursuit of material gain and utility. To call both kula and gimwali "barter" is correct but not analytically informative; to state that money is used in neither is not so important as to point out that each represents a different transactional sphere—that items transacted in one cannot normally be transacted in the other, that the terms of exchange are determined by a different principle, and that the social and the economic importance of each to the participants is entirely different.

The second difficulty in understanding the role of money in primitive economy is the assumption that the distinguishing characteristic of money in all economies is the same as in market-dominated Western economy: its role as a means of (commercial) exchange. In modern Western economy, the use of money as a means of (commercial) exchange with which to acquire labor, raw materials, and finished products of all kinds is undoubtedly its most important use, but not its only use. Even in modern economy money has subordinate uses, such as means of non-commercial payment (fines and taxes) and as a standard of value for transactions in which no "money" changes hands. A second distinguishing characteristic of money usage in national economies integrated by market exchange is that only one all-purpose money—dollars, francs—is used to carry out all money functions. It should be emphasized that these two prime characteristics of Western money are functionally related: because market exchange at money price is the dominant transactional mode, one kind of money must be used to make all material items, labor, and services available on the market. All-purpose money is a prerequisite for an economy in which market exchange dominates: it makes labor, material resources, and products "commensurable" and "commodities"; it allows all items to be purchased and sold and their market values to be compared. Because all material items enter market exchange, all must be purchasable with the same money. In sum, it is the dominance of the market exchange principle in Western economy which necessitates that one kind of money be used. Conversely, the use of all-purpose money can lead to the spread of the market principle to other spheres in which cash newly enters, even when market exchange is traditionally restricted to just one sphere.

In economies in which the market principle is either absent or peripheral, a single all-purpose money is necessarily absent. The absence of all-purpose money is an indicator of a multicentric economy in which markets are absent or unimportant—that is, labor, resources, goods, and services change hands in accordance with different principles. In such economies one may find one or more moneys (or valuables) in use, performing non-commercial money functions of payment and standard in reciprocal and redistributive spheres—the prestige sphere of bridewealth, bloodwealth, and such.

Trade, Market, and Surplus

There are some useful distinctions to be made between marketing and trading and between marketers and traders. The word "trade" is commonly used to mean several activities: (1) any commercial transaction, (2) activities of professional specialists, and (3) any external transaction (foreign trade).

The first two uses of the word "trade" distinguish two kinds of action. There is, on the one hand, selling one's own produce and buying one's needs, which we shall call "marketing." On the other hand, there is buying in order to resell. The French term *commercer* expresses precisely this latter meaning—that of professional trading. Most anthropologists express the same idea by the term "middleman." To market and to "commercize" are not the same thing, and in Africa they are sometimes institutionally separated. Selling a minor portion of produce can be an integral part of subsistence farming. Buying for resale, however, is not. It is an additional activity.

External trade has special aspects that distinguish it from marketing and professional trading. In precontact Africa, much external trade was an activity of state—"administered trade," to use Polanyi's term—primarily in prestige or treasure items of elite circulation. The market principle was not the mode of transacting nor, typically, was the market place the site of such transactions. In post-contact Africa, the enlargement of the market economy has affected all types of trade.

It has frequently been said that marketing, buying for resale, or external trade arises from surpluses. Several of the essays in *Markets in Africa* provide evidence for different views: external trade occurs among groups of people at all levels of material life, including those who by no stretch of terminology can be regarded as having a surplus of anything, including the items they trade. Too often the term "surplus" is used to mean simply that which is sold or exchanged, on the simplistic assumption that if something were needed it would not be sold or exchanged.

A special kind of external trade was induced by the exact opposite of surplus, namely an emergency shortage in which prestige items (including slaves, children, and women) were traded off for subsistence goods. Examples of such emergency conversions are found among the Guro, Kipsigis, and in the Copperbelt.

Markets in Africa also describes several instances in which neither external trade nor local marketing arose, despite their potential material advantages. The reasons that materially advantageous trade failed to arise among complementary producers are illuminating. Despite the relative abundance of cattle and the scarcity of vegetable foods, the Masai did not seek to trade off cattle for food. That was unthinkable because cattle were the essence of wealth—indeed, from the Masai point of view, there could be no such thing as a surplus of cattle. Moreover, when the Masai raided their neighbors, it was for more cattle, not for vegetables. Similarly, Dupire tells us that the commercially-minded Hausa regard the Fulani as foolish for not taking advantage of seasonal fluctuations in cattle prices and timing their sales to obtain the best price for cattle. But the Fulani do not regard cattle as a regular cash crop, so to speak, with which to acquire other goods. Other considerations override market price. The point is that material gain is sometimes not considered as important as other social ends, and therefore "surpluses" (meaning relative abundances of one item) are often not exchanged, even when it would seem to be materially advantageous to do so.

Finally, there can be trade without material gain. Meillassoux points out in *Markets in Africa:*

> Toward affines or kinsmen . . . Guro trading behavior was greatly affected by social considerations, as it was by the nature of the exchanged goods (guns, powder, woven cloth, cattle, *sombe*—used as matrimonial compensation) which involved prestige and not subsistence. Frequently, according to informants from this area, the terms of trade with the Baule were exactly repeated with the next Guro tribe, leaving absolutely no profit for the intermediary. All in all, trade was not what we would call in modern terms a "profitable business." It was, rather, that goods moved between people of pre-eminent status, on customary terms, until they reached the upper part of the country, whereupon they were traded at terms of exchange which profited the upper Guro.

The various characteristics that we have noted about market places and the market principle in the three typical situations are summed up in Table 5–1.

NON-ECONOMIC ASPECTS OF MARKET PLACES

"Demand crowds" and "supply crowds" when they *do* meet in market places provide another sort of crowd—a sort that may do many things besides buy and sell. Attendants at market usually represent cross sections of the population, although there are some places in Africa for which such a statement needs emending: in south Dahomey and Western Nigeria, men

Table 5–1   *Characteristics of Three Types of Local
African Communities*

	Subsistence Economies		Peasant Economies
	Marketless	*Petty Markets Only*	*Market-dominated*
Principal Source of Subsistence Livelihood	Self-production and use; reciprocity; redistribution	Self-production and use; reciprocity; redistribution	Production for sale; factor resources for sale; marketing and trading as occupations
Price Formation for Goods and Services Changing Hands	Equivalency ratios; gift exchange	Supply and demand forces qualified by idiosyncratic social influences and controls; absence of labor and land markets	Supply and demand forces; market principle transacts labor and land as well as outputs
Money and Money Uses	Non-commercial transactions use special-purpose monies for bridewealth, bloodwealth, etc. (e.g., means of reciprocal payment); moneyless transactions may be present	Non-commercial transactions use special-purpose monies for bridewealth, bloodwealth, etc. If medium of market exchange is used in marketplace transactions, its use is restricted outside of markets; moneyless transactions may be present	One, all-purpose money (i.e., European cash) is used for commercial and non-commercial transactions
External Trade	Reciprocity; administered trade (redistribution)	Reciprocity; administered trade (redistribution); market haggling (e.g., gimwali)	Market trade dominates; if gift or administered trade is present, it is peripheral
Technology	Traditional	Traditional	Mostly traditional (or mixed traditional and machine-using)
Cultural Practices	Traditional	Traditional	Mostly traditional (beginnings of literacy, etc.)

attend markets seldom and then almost entirely as buyers; women seldom attend cattle markets anywhere; market places are, in some communities, considered unwholesome places for children. It is, however, to be expected —and it is certainly borne out by the evidence in *Markets in Africa*—that market places are utilized for purposes far beyond the economic. In fact, they can be utilized for almost every conceivable purpose that requires a large number of people brought together in a controlled situation.

Probably the most important non-economic function of market places is their role as nodes in the network of communication. Undoubtedly one of the most important points for the dissemination of information is the market place, and that dissemination can take place either in an informal, more or less unrecognized manner or on a formal basis. Chiefs, priests, administrative officers, and many others make announcements in the market. In most areas, to make an announcement requires the permission of the market authorities, and it may even require that the announcement be made by one of them to signify his approval.

Market places also provide a place to meet one's friends and kinsmen and exchange news and gossip. Women in particular (most of Africa is virilocal even when it is matrilineal) meet their kinsmen at markets and keep in remarkably close touch with their natal villages by this means. Although it would be difficult to do, a study of markets (and perhaps other institutions) in their role of communications nodes would be extremely interesting.

The people at market provide not only listeners and gossipmongers but also an already gathered audience. It is not surprising that performances of dancers or of entertainers take place in the market places. The festival aspect of markets is also pointed up by its frequent use as the place to drink beer. The market day—especially in West Africa—tails off into a beer drink.

Like any large collection of people, the gathering in a market place is often used to recruit sexual partners. Several of the writers in *Markets in Africa* speak of the market as the place par excellence to form liaisons.

In a more organized fashion, market places can be of political relevance: it can be politically advantageous to control the market place itself, and hence to some degree the people in it. On the other hand, it can be politically advantageous to control, in whatever degree, the produce which goes through the market place. We thus find throughout Africa (as in thirteenth-century England) that control of market places is in the hands of the political authorities. In those parts of East and Central Africa where markets were introduced by the colonial administration, it continued to control them: the size and shape of the market place, the type and arrangement of buildings, the conditions for selling and the composition of the sales force and the selection of goods—all are to a greater or lesser degree dictated by political authority. On the other hand, in West Africa or anywhere else that the markets antedated European control, the market places remained in the hands of indigenous authorities. Control of a market put a man at the hub of communications where he could have immediate contact with people. It also gave him a recognized and approved *raison d'être* behind which he could hide any political chicanery which it was to his advantage to hide.

In return, the authorities that control markets provide a "market peace," to use the old English term. The markets were policed, and the safety of traders and customers was assured. It may even be that the market place, or a portion of it, is used as a point of political asylum.

Obviously it is also necessary, if the economic functions of a market are to be performed, for the market peace to be observed; this point has been made many times with reference to old European market places. Successful trade demands some degree of political stability. The man who is responsible for the market peace thus must have a police force of some description at his disposal, and he must control sufficient power to maintain the peace. To police their markets, West African market officials can call on either their families, clans, or other social groups or on the police force of the government.

An extremely important political consideration is the fact that the market is often used as the center of juridical activities. In some areas the chiefs or other judges actually establish themselves as courts in or near the market place; in others their presence assures that when one finds one's adversary (easier at a market than any other place), the case can be laid before the officials informally. No African chief can refuse to hear a case brought to his attention at market (though he may postpone it until a regular court hearing). These courts may be the same as—but are often different from—the arbitrating facilities for settling disputes which arise among sellers and customers in the market place itself.

Markets are also often accompanied by religious activities, some of which may be connected with the market peace. The peace of many West African markets is kept primarily in the name of, and with the sanction of, certain shrines and the forces that they symbolize. Some African market places—particularly in areas in which the market is indigenous—are founded with a religious ceremonial. European markets of the Middle Ages were similarly associated with the church and were often held in the shadows of cathedrals.

In summary, market places—particularly where the market is economically peripheral—fulfill many social and cultural needs of the population. Indeed, some markets are not regarded as primarily "economic" institutions by the people. They provide a meeting place where at least a certain minimum of security is assured, and hence they can be used for political, religious, social, and personal purposes. In a land in which collections of people on non-kinship bases or non-age-set bases may prove difficult, the market provides a facility for a very wide range of social usages.

A few words should be said also about the way in which markets fit together: in some parts of West Africa they form "rings," in other parts they do not. A market ring is a series of differently located markets meeting on successive days. Among the Ibo there are four-day cycles; among Yoruba, Dahomey, and Guro there are five-day cycles. In other areas there are seven-day cycles. In parts of East Africa, where the ring phenomenon is less highly developed, the "ring" is little more than the series of markets attended by a group of traders. In areas of West Africa where rings are important, each market in the ring may develop an economic or even a non-economic specialty, and the ring may be of very great local importance for the flow of goods, the settlement of disputes, or some other social activity.

Non-economic activities may also be influenced by market rings, if for no other reason than that the movements of a large number of people follow along (and hence create) the rings and that social activities follow (and are created by) people and their movements.

EUROPEAN IMPACT ON AFRICAN ECONOMY

Village Economies in Transition

Europe has long been a factor in African economy. Cowrie shells and gunpowder, gold and slaves, have gone in or out of Africa for thousands of years. But the role of Europe in Africa has undergone several climactic changes. In the middle decades of the fifteenth century, contact between Europe and sub-Saharan Africa became direct; trading ventures were established along the coasts, and in a few places there was an initial penetration of European ideas and, indeed, of Europeans themselves. Another drastic change occurred in the late nineteenth century, when European countries took over political control of most African areas. Again in the mid-twentieth century, with the emergence of independent African national states, the institutional impact of commercialization and European investment on African economy have undergone pervasive change.

It seems clear that the economic changes occurring in Africa today are of two sorts that must be analytically separated, even though they occur together. There are, on one level, extensive changes in institutions. On another level, those economic activities organized on the market principle are expanding, with a concomitant attenuation of indigenous redistribution and reciprocity. Obviously, these three modes of transaction may be present simultaneously in any society.[1] However, the "mixture" of the organizing principles of African economic life is in flux.

African economies are becoming like our own in the sense that the sectors dominated by the market principle are being enlarged. It does not follow that the institutions of our society need be duplicated exactly in Africa. Some, but not all, products and factors of production have entered the market; more, but not all, people get their basic livelihood in producing for or selling in markets; multicentric economies are in the process of becoming unicentric. Cash increasingly permeates non-market spheres of economy; external trade as well as internal becomes almost exclusively transacted on the market principle and (as with us) modified by such devices as marketing brands and redistributive taxation; technological innovations are adopted, and local communities become integrated into the national and world economies.

The questions, therefore, that we consider of greatest significance are these: What sequential patterns of entrance into a more inclusively market-dominated economy can be discerned? What accounts for the marked differences in receptivity to organizational and technological change which accompanies the increased importance of markets? What changes have market penetration and cash created in the rest of the institutions of the societies?

Community Entrance into Market Economy

Entrance into market economy is usually stated by anthropologists as "getting a cash income" or "entering the cash economy." However, getting a cash income always involves selling something on the market. Broadly, there are three things that Africans have to sell. First, they can sell agricultural or pastoral produce—cash cropping. Such produce may be destined for local, regional, or foreign consumption (United Nations 1954). Second, an African in search of cash can sell wage-labor—industrial or agricultural. The third course by which a person can secure cash is to enter into commerce—usually petty commerce—as a market-place seller, long-distance trader, transporter, itinerant hawker, or shopkeeper.

In short, (1) marketing of produce may increase, with direct repercussions on production, (2) labor may enter the market, and (3) buying for resale (as contrasted to marketing one's own product) may develop as a specialty. The greatest social changes have come where labor, entering the market, has moved geographically and occupationally in response to market demands, thus having repercussions in the rest of society. Almost as great a change occurs in the situation in which marketing and buying for resale have overlapped in a significant way, therefore increasing volumes of output and, concomitantly, changing work and consumption patterns.

Each African group makes a typical adjustment to its cash needs (United Nations 1954). That is to say, in the early stages of community change resulting from colonial incursion there is a greater or lesser specialization in one of these commercial activities. Each pattern of market entrance has, of course, different effects on traditional social organization.

The pattern of entrance into market economy experienced by the Arusha is an especially good illustration because of the absence of internal markets. Traditionally the Arusha were self-sufficient agriculturalists. They entered into market exchange in order to buy food and to earn cash with which to pay taxes. The need to buy food was traceable to a land shortage induced by population growth, colonial peace, and land occupation by European farmers. The ready accessibility of an urban market allowed the Arusha to continue their agricultural ways by producing cash crops. Two important results followed the reluctant entrance of the Arusha into commercial production. At first they sold to the market just that minimum of traditionally grown crops that would fetch them sufficient cash to buy extra food and pay taxes. The Arusha did not at first rearrange production lines to suit market demand or, indeed, even seek to specialize in the most profitable crops. However, production for the market increased in volume because the increasing shortage of land did not permit most Arusha to cultivate sufficient food crops any longer under the traditional economy. It was only after the reluctant acceptance of this necessity that the Arusha entered a market economy more fully by changing production to take advantage of market demands and prices. Moreover, all areas of Arusha culture then felt the impact of the market. Goats, beer, and craft items became objects of market exchange among the Arusha themselves. Second —and of especial interest to the anthropologist—is that the Arusha, in making this change, found it necessary to denigrate Masai culture, which formerly they had venerated as ideal.

It is, in fact, no accident that governments have had to do more than establish market places to create a market-dominated economy—in many instances production for the market has been made mandatory by separate and special legal means with heavy sanctions.

The Kipsigis have had an even more dramatic entry into market economy; indeed, their eagerness to produce for sale is only the most striking of many examples which belie the view that Africans were always forced to change. Traditionally a people whose values were pastoral in spite of their small patches of millet, Kipsigis have become farmers and marketers with alacrity and success. Perhaps their most striking achievement is the aplomb with which they have handled the situation of land entering the market. Their success may be explained by the fact that "land tenure" did not really exist in their old system, so that when they settled and changed their way of life, they had no traditional form of institutionalization for distribution of land or of labor which was relevant to the new situation. They had nothing basic to unlearn.

Receptivity to Economic Change

At the opposite pole from the Kipsigis, who have accepted economic and other social change, are the Lele who, in spite of contact with the Bushong economy which they admit to be superior, have consistently chosen to safeguard traditional social institutions at the sacrifice of economic improvement. The question of receptivity to economic change is a more general form of the commonly asked question, What "social" factors impede economic growth (Higgins 1956; Sadie 1960)?

This question actually harbors two problem areas that have commonly been confused. In economists' terms, they are: (1) Given the social, economic, ecological, and technological framework of some African community, why are continual increases in per capita output ("growth") not forthcoming within the indigenous system? (2) Given the indigenous framework above, why has European impact failed to induce greater development—organizational and technological change toward market industrialism —which would increase per capita output? Basic to both problems is the specific question of what constitutes "wealth," and the social importance and means of wealth-getting in indigenous African communities. On closer examination, it may be discovered that some indigenous economies do indeed "grow," but because the enlarged outputs need not pass through the market place or be transacted via the market principle, the growth is either unperceived by Western observers or considered beside the point.

In Western market economy, wealth means income-yielding property: an acre of agricultural land, a coal mine, a herd of cattle, an apartment-house building, and a steel mill all have in common that they produce goods or services salable at a market price which yield their owners a property income (variously split up as profit, rent, or interest). Moreover, the wealth items—the acre of land, the buildings—are themselves salable for a money price on markets. Wealth, in our own economy, then, is material, income-yielding, quantifiable in money terms, and salable. These characteristics are dependently linked to the dominating organizational principle of market exchange.

Where indigenous wealth concepts and socially structured principles of wealth-getting in African societies are radically different from those in market society, there is likely to be the most difficulty ("major obstacles") in transforming reciprocal and redistributive to market exchange institutions. Two examples are the following.

Wealth in some African societies is composed of items that do not contribute to enlarging material output, but whose possession does yield material returns in the form of gift transfers. Among the Lele, rights in women and children are considered the highest form of wealth, and the path to material security (and honorific status) is not material accumulation, but the creation of affinal dependencies which yield obligatory material gifts. Douglas, in *Markets in Africa,* contrasts the Lele path to high status with that of the Bushong:

> He [a Lele man] will eventually marry several wives, beget children, and so enter the Begetter's cult. His infant daughters will be asked in marriage by suitors bearing gifts and ready to work for him. Later, when his cult membership is bringing in a revenue of raffia cloth, from fees of new initiates, his newborn daughter's daughters can be promised in marriage to junior clansmen, who will strengthen his following in the village. His wives will look after him in his declining years. He will have stores of raffia cloths to lend or give, but he will possess this wealth because, in the natural course of events, he reached the proper status for his age. He would not be able to achieve this status through wealth.

For the Bushong, work is the means to wealth, and wealth the means to status. They strongly emphasize the value of individual effort and achievement, and they are also prepared to collaborate in numbers, over a sustained period, when this is necessary to raise output. Nothing in Lele culture corresponds to the Bushong striving for riches.

The pursuit of more highly ranked wealth items in Lele society is reinforced by technological considerations, such as the absence of storage facilities for perishables, as well as by the social obligation to share. The absence of monetary arrangements and capital markets also constrains the disposition of products. Currently produced items can either be self-consumed, given away, consumed in feasts, or used to obtain "superior" items or prerogatives via conversion. It seems clear, then, that one point of difference among traditional African societies is that the structured means to high status have markedly different effects on indigenous output growth as well as on receptivity to organizational and technological change. In the Bushong (as in market society), individual material accumulation is the path to status. This is not so with the Lele, for whom status is the means to individual material affluence.

Wealth concepts differ in African societies in another way. There are some wealth items physically identical with those in Western society, but regarded as wealth for reasons which make the African items primarily of social rather than of economic significance. For example, cattle in parts of East Africa are wealth to their owners, for reasons in addition to the material yield of the herds. They are rarely slaughtered and eaten by their owners, who part with them only in emergency or to make important status payments, such as bridewealth.

Dual Economy and Multicentric Economy

The idea of "dual economy" indicates the sharp differences in economy, technology, society, and culture between European colonial sectors of market economy and non-market communities in the African hinterland. However, the notion of a dual economy requires qualification.

It implies that the traditional portion of the economy is of one piece—a homogeneous sector or sphere. We find, rather, that several transactional spheres may be present in the traditional sector, each with a different mode for transacting goods and services. Indeed, as noted above, the conventional labels of anthropology (subsistence goods, prestige goods) make this point clearly. Even in the traditional economy some items may be transacted by the market principle. In brief, the traditional economy itself may be multicentric—have several distinct sectors. Moreover, it is rarely the case that some people in such a society are economically engaged wholly within the market sphere while others are wholly engaged within traditional spheres.

Subsistence, Peasant, and Developed Economies: Conclusion

As we have proceeded with this analysis, we have come upon what at first appeared to be a paradox. With a few exceptions in West Africa, the market place is a characteristic of economies in which the market principle is peripheral. The more pervasive the market principle, the less the economic importance of the market place.

Most African communities were marked by subsistence economies, with or without the presence of the peripheral market. The establishment of colonial status led in most areas to the enlargement or founding of market places. Items of petty trade, of European manufacture, entered these markets; produce entered these markets in newly large amounts. But as commercialization deepened and market transactions increased, there were instances in which the market place was by-passed, as was the case with the export crops from parts of East Africa and the Copperbelt that have been marketed through cooperative societies or specialist firms. As the market sphere expanded, labor and finally land entered the market, but not, of course, the market place. The market principle has affected more and more institutions and has outgrown the market place because the essential ingredients of production—labor, land, machines—cannot be transacted in a market place. Where the market mode comes to integrate a national economy, as in Europe and America, it is transactions between firms which are all-important, and not the petty transactions that occur in the market-place setting. Indeed, the very meaning of the market place changes from a bazaar to a group of buyers of something, wherever they may be located. The "market" for automobiles in the United States is everywhere, and the market for enamel basins becomes the collectivity of African housewives.

The market place and its institutional arrangement have undergone other, non-economic changes. Just as the economic importance of the market place lapses with the "development of the national economy," and it becomes merely a place of final sale, so its political importance lapses with the development of the polity, its religious significance with the acceptance of world religions, and its social significance with the adoption of the guitar, the radio, the "hoteli," and high life.

NOTE

1. In our own society, basic livelihood is acquired through the market; the services associated with education, welfare, military defense, and taxation employ the principle of redistribution; and we have a peripheral sphere of reciprocity—gift exchange and the like. In all developed capitalist economies, the market principle and the allocative price mechanism have been institutionally controlled by both governmental and private measures: labor legislation, unions, price supports, zoning laws, and oligopolization have reduced the range of price formation by purely competitive supply and demand forces. However, factor resources, including labor, as well as most goods and service outputs are still transacted by market purchase and sale; and the prices of such factors and outputs constitute the main source of income (livelihood) to the population. In a word, the United States is a controlled market economy. See Robinson (1954) and Galbraith (1955).

REFERENCES

BERLINER, J. S.
    1962   The feet of the natives are large: an essay on anthropology by an economist. *Current Anthropology* 3:47–76.
BOEKE, J. H.
    1953   *Economics and economic policy in dual societies.* New York: Institute of Pacific Relations.
BOHANNAN, PAUL
    1955   Some principles of exchange and investment among the Tiv. *American Anthropologist* 57:60–69.
    1959   The impact of money on an African subsistence economy. *Journal of Economic History* 19:491–503.
DuBOIS, CORA
    1936   The wealth concept as an integrative factor in Tolowa-Tututni culture. In *Essays in anthropology presented to A. L. Kroeber,* R. H. Lowie ed. Berkeley: University of California Press.
EVANS-PRITCHARD, E. E.
    1954   Introduction. In *The Gift,* by Marcel Mauss. Glencoe: The Free Press.
FIRTH, RAYMOND
    1958   *Human Types,* revised ed. New York: Mentor Books.

FURNIVALL, J. S.
   1939   *Netherlands India, a study of plural economy*. Cambridge: Cambridge University Press. (Edition used—New York: Macmillan, 1944.)
GALBRAITH, J. K.
   1955   *Economics and the art of controversy*. New Brunswick: Rutgers University Press.
HERSKOVITS, MELVILLE J.
   1938   *Dahomey*. New York: J. J. Augustin.
HIGGINS, B.
   1956   The "dualistic theory" of underdeveloped areas. *Economic Development and Cultural Change,* January, pp. 99–115.
MALINOWSKI, BRONISLAW
   1922   *Argonauts of the western Pacific*. London: Routledge and Kegan Paul.
PIRENNE, HENRI
   1936   *Economic and social history of medieval Europe*. New York: Harcourt, Brace, and World.
POLANYI, KARL
   1957   The economy as instituted process. In *Trade and market in the early empires*, K. Polanyi, C. M. Arensberg, H. W. Pearson ed. Glencoe: The Free Press.
ROBINSON, JOAN
   1954   The impossibility of competition. In *Monopoly and competition and their regulation*, E. H. Chamberlin ed. London: Macmillan.
SADIE, J. L.
   1960   The social anthropology of economic development. *Economic Journal* 70:294–303.
STEINER, FRANZ
   1954   Notes on comparative economics. *British Journal of Sociology* 5:118–129.
THURNWALD, RICHARD
   1932   *Economics in primitive communities*. London: Oxford University Press.
UNITED NATIONS
   1954   *Enlargement of the exchange economy in tropical Africa*. New York: UN, Department of Economic Affairs (E/2557 ST/ECA/23. Sales No.:1954, II.C.4).

6

Primitive Money [1]

In a subject where there is no agreed procedure for knocking out errors, doctrines have a long life.

JOAN ROBINSON

Primitive money is a complicated subject for several reasons. There is not in common use a set of analytical categories designed to reveal distinguishing characteristics of markedly different systems: economies without markets and machines still tend to be viewed through the theoretical spectacles designed for industrial capitalism (Arensberg 1957:99). Second, francs, sterling, and dollars are only the most recent of a long series of foreign monies introduced into band and tribal economies. Earlier, Arabs, Portuguese, Dutch, English, and others introduced cowrie, manillas, beads, and so on with varying permeation and varying disruption of indigenous monetary systems. Only rarely do anthropologists succeed in disentangling the foreign from the indigenous in a way which reveals the nature of the old money and the consequences of the new.

Moreover, if one asks what is "primitive" about a particular money, one may come away with two answers: the money-*stuff*—woodpecker scalps, sea shells, goats, dogs' teeth—is primitive (different from our own); and the *uses* to which the money-stuff is sometimes put—mortuary payments, bloodwealth, bridewealth—are primitive (different from our own).

Primitive money performs some of the functions of our own money, but rarely all; the conditions under which supplies are forthcoming are usually different; primitive money is used in some ways ours is not; our money is impersonal and commercial, while primitive money frequently has pedigree and personality, sacred uses, or moral and emotional connotations. Our governmental authorities control the quantity of money, but rarely is this so in primitive economies.

Failure to understand the implications of such differences leads to dis-

Reprinted, with revision, from "Primitive Money," *American Anthropologist,* 67 (February 1965):44–65. Reprinted by permission of the publisher.

putes about bridewealth versus brideprice, to arguments about whether cows, pig tusks, and potlatch coppers are "really" money, to the assumption that modern coinage merely "replaces" indigenous forms of money, and to disagreement of authorities over minimal definitions of money. In these disputes the characteristics of American or European money are invariably used as a model.

Some of the most respected comparisons between primitive and European money fail to go deeply enough into comparative economic and social structure. Even Malinowski and Firth do not explain that it is nationally-integrated market organization which accounts for those Western monetary traits they use as a model of "real" money:

> The tokens of wealth [*vaygua:* ceremonial axe blades, necklaces of red shell discs, and arm bracelets of shells] have often been called "money." It is at first sight evident that "money" in our sense cannot exist among the Trobrianders. . . . Any article which can be classed as "money" or "currency" must fulfill certain essential conditions; it must function as a medium of exchange and as a common measure of value, it must be the instrument of condensing wealth, the means by which value can be accumulated. Money also, as a rule, serves as the standard of deferred payments. . . . We cannot think of *vaygua* in terms of "money" [Malinowski 1921:13–14].

Firth registers his agreement:

> But according to precise terminology, such objects [strings of shell discs] can hardly be correctly described as currency or money. In any economic system, however primitive, an article can only be regarded as true money when it acts as a definite and common medium of exchange, as a convenient stepping stone in obtaining one type of goods for another. Moreover in so doing it serves as a measure of values. . . . Again, it is a standard of value . . . [Firth 1929:881].

Malinowski and Firth use the bundle of attributes money has in industrialized market economy to comprise a model of *true* money. They then judge whether or not money-like stuff in primitive economies is really money by how closely the uses of the primitive stuff resemble our own—a strange procedure for anthropologists who would never use the bundle of attributes of English or American family, religious, or political organization in such a way. Quoting from Lienhardt, ". . . most anthropologists have ceased to take their bearings in the study of religion from any religion practiced in their own society [1956:310]." And Gluckman and Cunnison write, concerning political organizations: "One important discovery made in . . . [*African Political Systems*] was that the institutions through which a society organized politically need not necessarily look like the kinds of political institutions with which we have long been familiar in the Western world, and in the great nations of Asia [1962:vi]."

Dollars have that set of uses called medium of exchange, means of payment, standard of value, and so on, precisely because our economy is commercially organized. Where economies are organized differently, non-commercial uses of monetary objects become important, and "money" takes on different characteristics. The question is not—as it is conventionally put—Are shells, woodpecker scalps, cattle, goats, dogs' teeth, or kula valuables "really" "money"? It is, rather, How are the similarities and the differences between such items and dollars related to similarities and differences in socio-economic organization?

We shall show the connections between Western money and economy, then go on to make some points about primitive money and economy, and finally, examine the case of Rossel Island money in detail.

CAPITALISM: NATIONAL MARKET INTEGRATION DETERMINES ALL MONEY USES

In the economies for which the English monetary vocabulary was created there is one dominant transactional mode, market exchange, to which *all* money uses relate. By contrast, in many primitive economies before colonial incursion, market exchange transactions are either absent (as with Nuer) or petty (as in the Trobriands), but non-commercial uses of money do exist. Seeing non-commercial uses of money through the blinders of commercial money causes difficulty in understanding primitive monies. We must first be made aware of the blinders.

U.S. dollars may be called general-purpose money (Polanyi 1957*a;* 1957*b*). They are a single monetary instrument to perform all the money uses. Moreover, the same dollars enter modes of transaction to be called redistribution and reciprocity as enter into market exchange. These features of U.S. money are direct consequences of economy-wide market integration and require explanation in an anthropological context. The essential point is that the characteristics of money in any economy, including our own, express the basic organization of that economy. Where the characteristics of money (or money-like valuables) are different from dollars, it is because that economy is different from our market economy. Money is linked to specific modes of transaction.

That U.S. economy is integrated by market exchange is explained by the wide range of natural resources, labor, goods, and services transacted by purchase and sale at market-determined prices, and by the extent to which people in our national economy depend for livelihood on wage, profit, interest, and rental income got from market sale. Natural resources and capital goods (land, labor, machines and buildings of all varieties), consumption goods (food, automobiles), personal and impersonal services (dentistry, electricity), are all purchasable "on the market." Goods and services which are ceremonial and religious, or which serve as prestige indicators—bibles, wedding rings, Cadillacs—are purchasable in the same way and with the same money as subsistence goods. In market-integrated economy very different items and services are directly comparable, because all are available at prices stated in the same money. The subject of price determination of products and resources under varying conditions of supply and demand (price and distribution theory) is an important field of economics because market exchange is our dominant and integrative transactional mode.[2]

Commercial Uses of Money in a Market-Integrated National Economy

Except for economic historians, most economists and all economic theory were (until recently) concerned exclusively with European and American economy since industrialization in the nineteenth century. Economists do not find it necessary to distinguish among the transactional modes of market exchange, reciprocity, and redistribution, because market exchange is so overwhelmingly important. For the same reason economists do not find it necessary to describe at length the different uses of money in our own economy: with only a few exceptions they all express market exchange transactions.

To make this point clear I shall attach to each of the money uses an adjective describing the transactional mode, thereby pointing up how they all serve market or commercial transactions: medium of (commercial) exchange; means of (commercial) payment; unit of (commercial) account; standard for deferred (commercial) payment.

The medium of (commercial) exchange function of money in our economy is its dominant function, and all other commercial uses of money are dependently linked—derived from—the use of dollars as media of (commercial) exchange. For example, dollars are also used as a means of (commercial) payment of debt *arising from* market transactions. It is purchase and sale of resources, goods, and services which *create* the money functions of means of (commercial) payment and standard for deferred (commercial) payment.[3] All the commercial uses of money are consequences of market integration, simply reflecting the highly organized credit and accounting arrangements that facilitate nation-wide market purchases. This is why economists in writing about our economy need not attach the qualifier "commercial" to the money uses. Indeed, we in our market-integrated national economy sometimes regard the terms "money" and "medium of exchange" as interchangeable. But for band and tribal communities where market transactions are absent or infrequent, it would be distorting to equate money with medium of (commercial) exchange, as Einzig warns us: "Since, however, money has also other functions and since in many instances [of money used in primitive economies] those functions are more important than that of the medium of exchange, it seems to be unjustified to use the term as a mere synonym for 'medium of exchange' [1948:321]."

Non-Commercial Uses of Money

Dollars are also used as a means of non-commercial payment: traffic fines paid to local government and taxes to all levels of government. A structural characteristic of U.S. economy is that redistributive transactions—obligatory payments to political authority which uses the receipts to provide community services—are made with the same money used as medium of (commercial) exchange in private transactions. The consequences are important and far-reaching.

In all societies having specialized political authority there must be some institutionalized arrangement for the governing authorities to acquire goods and services for their own maintenance and to provide social services (defense, justice) to the community. In this sense, we may regard the redistributive function (acquiring and disbursing such public goods and services) as an "economic" component of political organization. Exactly how the arrangements vary for political authority to acquire and disburse goods and services is one way of differentiating between the organization of Soviet, American, and (say) Bantu economies.

In U.S. economy the government makes use of the market in the process of redistribution: medium of (commercial) exchange money earned as private income is used by households and firms as means of (redistributive) payment of politically incurred obligation (taxes). The government then buys on the market the services and products it requires—civil servants, guns, roads—to provide community services.

In our system, the same can be said for another mode of transaction, reciprocity, or gift-giving between kin and friends. The same money serves the different transactional modes: in purchasing a gift, the money paid is used as medium of (commercial) exchange; giving the gift is part of a reciprocal transaction (a material or service transfer induced by social obligation between the gift partners). If cash is given as a gift, it is a means of (reciprocal) payment of the social obligation discharged by the gift-giving.

Here is yet another reason why economists, in dealing with our own economy, need not distinguish between transactional modes: with us redistribution and reciprocity make use of market exchange and make use of the same money used in market exchange. In American economy, therefore, tax and gift transactions appear as simple variations from the private market norm—special types of expenditure or outlay—which present no theoretical difficulties.

American reliance on market sale for livelihood and on the price mechanism for allocating resources to production lines does the following: it makes the medium of (commercial) exchange use of money its dominant attribute, it makes other money uses serve market transactions, and it confers that peculiar *bundle* of traits on our general-purpose money which mark off dollars from non-monetary objects. It is our national market integration which makes it necessary to institutionalize all uses of money in the same money instrument. As with Malinowski and Firth, we thereby come to think of "money-ness" as this *set* of uses conferred on the single monetary object. And because ours is a market economy, we come to think of medium of (commercial) exchange as the single most important attribute of "money-ness."

Limited-Purpose Monies

In primitive economies—that is, small-scale band and tribal economies not integrated by market exchange—different uses of money may be institutionalized separately in different monetary objects to carry out reciprocal and redistributive transactions. These money objects used in non-commercial ways are usually distinct from any that enter market-place transactions. And the items which perform non-commercial money uses need not be full-time money, so to speak; they have uses and characteristics apart from their ability to serve as a special kind of money.

In U.S. economy, objects such as jewelry, stocks, and bonds are not regarded as money because (like cattle among the Bantu) these come into existence for reasons other than their "money-ness." Each is capable of one or two money uses, but not the full range which distinguishes dollars, and particularly not the medium of (commercial) exchange use of dollars. It is worth examining these because, we shall argue, primitive monies or valuables used in reciprocal and redistributive transactions are the counterparts of these limited or special-purpose monies, and not of dollars as media of (commercial) exchange; they resemble dollars only in non-commercial uses (paying taxes and fines, and in gift-giving).

Dollars serve as a store of (commercial and non-commercial) value because dollars can be held idle for future use. But this is true also for jewelry, stocks and bonds, and other marketable assets. However, in U.S. economy jewelry is not a medium of (commercial) exchange because one cannot spend it directly, and it is not a means of (commercial or non-commercial) payment because it is not acceptable in payment of debt or taxes.[4]

As a measuring device (rather than as tangible objects) dollars are used as unit of account and standard for deferred payment of debts. Now, consider the accounting and payment procedures used by a baby-sitting cooperative in which a number of households club together to draw on each other for hours of baby-sitting time. Family A uses four hours of sitting time supplied by family B. Family A thereby incurs a debt of four hours it owes the co-op; family B acquires a credit of four hours that it may draw upon in future from some member of the co-op. Here, baby-sitting labor time is a unit of (reciprocal) account and a standard for deferred (reciprocal) payments—a limited-purpose money in the sense that it performs two of the subsidiary uses of dollars. Other examples (such as trading stamps) could be given. The point is that even where dollars perform all the money uses for all modes of transaction, there are situations in which a few money uses are performed by objects not thought of as money. These limited-purpose monies become important in small-scale communities without market integration and, therefore, without a general-purpose money, like dollars, used in both commercial and non-commercial transactions.

Control over the Quantity of Money; Absence of Status Requisites

In national market economies, governments deliberately control the quantity of general-purpose money because dollars (francs, sterling) carry out market sales which the populace depends on for livelihood. Roughly speaking, if the authorities allow too much money to come into use as medium of (market) purchase, the result is inflation. If the authorities allow too little money to come into use, the result is deflation and unemployment (a contraction in the rate of market purchasing below the full employment capacity rate of production). The need to deliberately vary the quantity of money is a direct result of economy-wide market integration.

It has often been noted (for example, Herskovits 1952:238) that in tribal societies there is seldom any conscious control by political authority over money objects. Such is not merely a difference between primitive *monetary* systems and our own but one that reflects differences between their *economic* systems and ours. In economies not integrated by market exchange, non-commercial monetary transactions are only occasional events (such as, bloodwealth, bridewealth), and non-commercial money is not usually connected with production and daily livelihood. That the non-commercial money-stuff may be fixed in quantity for all time (Yap stones), or increase in quantity only through natural growth (cows, pig tusks), does not affect production and daily livelihood (as would be the case with us if dollars were fixed in quantity).

What is also true of our market economy based on contract, rather than status, is that having the money prices is a sufficient condition for buying most goods. Not only is Western money anonymous, so to speak, but money users are also anonymous: the market sells to whoever has the purchase price and only rarely imposes status prerequisites on the use of money as medium of (commercial) exchange.[5] In contrast, there are usually status prerequisites in non-commercial uses of primitive money. For example, in the use of cattle as means of (reciprocal) payment of bridewealth, status requisites such as lineage, age, rank of the persons, must be complied with. The money users are not anonymous, and a special kind of limited-purpose money is necessary to the transaction.

PRIMITIVE MONEY AND SOCIO-ECONOMIC ORGANIZATION

Einzig points out:

> The overwhelming importance of unilateral non-commercial payments in primitive life as compared with payments arising from [commercial] trade is altogether overlooked by practically all definitions [of primitive money]. It is assumed that money must be essentially commercial in character and that any object which serves the purposes of non-commercial payments may safely be disregarded even if its use is of first-rate importance in the economic, political, and social life of primitive communities [1948:323].

When anthropologists employ commercial monetary terms to describe uses of money-stuff in non-commercial transactions, a crucial misunderstanding may result: when cattle or sea shells perform some money uses in ways unrelated to market purchase and sale, they are not media of (commercial) exchange or means of (commercial) payment.

The uncritical use of our general-purpose dollars or francs as the model of true money obscures the point that special-purpose monies used for non-commercial transactions express salient features of underlying socio-economic structure. When we consider money or valuables in communities not integrated by market exchange—the Nuer, the Trobriands, the Tiv—it becomes essential to distinguish among the several transactional modes and among the several money uses: *primitive money-stuff does not have that bundle of related uses which in our economy is conferred on dollars by market integration and by the use of dollars in both commercial and non-commercial transactions*. The differences between cattle-money or shell-money and dollars are traceable to the differences in the transactional modes which call forth money uses. When Malinowski says that kula valuables are different from English currency, he is really pointing out that reciprocal gift-giving is different from market purchase and sale (1922). Indeed, anthropologists use Western monetary terms ambiguously whenever they fail to distinguish between the market and the non-commercial modes of transaction. Reining, for example, states: "There seems to have been little exchange among households although iron tools and spears made from locally smelted ore had a limited application as a medium of exchange, being used primarily for marriage payments [1959:39]."

If Western monetary terms are to be used by anthropologists in the meanings they convey for our own economy, the unqualified phrase "medium of exchange" must mean medium of market (or commercial) exchange. Since brides are not acquired through impersonal market transactions by random buyers and sellers, the iron tools are not used as media of (market) exchange, but as media of (reciprocal) exchange: as part of non-commercial transaction in which a man acquires a bundle of rights in a woman and her children in return for iron tools and other indemnification payments to her kin.

It seems useful to regard the bridewealth valuables as special-purpose "money" because the iron tools and spears—or in other societies, cows or goats—are the *required* items and because they carry out money uses which do have counterparts in our own society. Whether one calls them special-purpose monies or highly ranked treasure items necessary to the transaction for which one may not substitute other items matters only when the subject of money uses in tribal compared to capitalist economies is raised. Then we can show that cows and armbands of shells do perform some of the uses of dollars, but in non-commercial situations. The goal is always to state the role of bridewealth or kula items, or other limited-purpose money, from the viewpoint of the analyst concerned with comparative economy, but without distorting the folk-meaning of the items and the transactions they enter. In short, the kind of exchange or payment—commercial or non-commercial—determines the kind of money or valuable to be used to make the exchange or payment.

Money Uses in Primitive and Peasant Economies

Because money and money uses in market-dominated economies differ sharply from money in other economies, it is useful to classify economies in accordance with the importance of market exchange transactions (Bohannan and Dalton 1962) (see Table 6–1).

Type I: Marketless

In marketless communities, land and labor are not transacted by purchase and sale, but are allocated in accordance with kinship right or tribal affiliation. There are no formal market-place sites where indigenously produced items are bought and sold. These are "subsistence" economies in the sense that livelihood does not depend on production for sale. The transactional modes to allocate resources and labor as well as produced items and services are variants of reciprocity and redistribution (Polanyi 1944: chapter 4; 1957b; Dalton 1962). In marketless economies, then, transactions of labor, resources, material goods, and services are of non-commercial sorts—obligatory gifts to kin and friends, obligatory payments to chiefs and priests, bridewealth, bloodwealth, fees for entering secret societies, corvée labor, mortuary payments, and so on—which immediately marks off as different from our own any money-stuff used. Valuables such as cattle, goats, spears, Yap stones, and pig tusks take on roles as special-

purpose money in non-commercial transactions within the prestige sphere:
they become means of (reciprocal or redistributive) payment, as is the case
with bloodwealth and mortuary payments; or media of (reciprocal) exchange, as is the case with bridewealth.

Table 6–1 *Underdeveloped Communities*

Primitive (or Subsistence) Economies		Peasant Economies
Type I	Type II	Type III
Marketless	*Peripheral or Petty Markets Only*	*Market-Dominated*
Sonjo	Trobriand Islanders	Malay Fishermen
Nuer	Tiv	Jamaica
Lele	Rossel Islanders	Haiti
Arnhemlanders		Kipsigis
Bemba		Cantel ⎫
Kwakiutl (1840)		Panajachel ⎬ Guatemala
		Kwakiutl (1890)

Type II: Peripheral or Petty Markets Only

Everything said above about marketless economies holds true for those
with only petty or peripheral markets, with one exception: market-place
sites exist in which a narrow range of produce is bought and sold, either
with some money-stuff used as medium of (commercial) exchange or via
barter in the economist's sense (moneyless market exchange). We call these
market exchanges "peripheral" because land and labor are not bought and
sold and because most people do not get the bulk of their income from
such petty market sales. In such small-scale subsistence economies market-place prices do not function—as they do in our national economy—as
an integrative mechanism to allocate resources to production lines: labor
and land use do not respond to changes in the prices of the small quantity
and range of products transacted in peripheral market places. Malinowski's gimwali are peripheral market transactions of an occasional sort without the formal trappings found in African market places.

Type III: Market-Dominated (Peasant) Economies

Small-scale market-dominated communities share with our own nationally-integrated market economy the following features: (1) a large
proportion of land and labor as well as goods and services are transacted
by market purchase and sale; (2) most people depend on market sale of
labor or products for the bulk of their livelihood; (3) market prices integrate production. Labor and land move into and out of different production lines in response to profit (and other income) alternatives, as indicated
by market prices. In such economies, the medium of (commercial) exchange function of money is the most important; the other commercial

uses of money facilitate market transactions, and the same money is used for non-commercial transactions (such as taxes and fines).

Peasant economies (Firth 1946) differ from primitive (subsistence) economies in that peasant producers depend on production for sale. However, both peasant and primitive communities differ from large-scale, developed, nationally-integrated American and West European economies on two counts: modern machine technology is largely absent, and traditional social organization and cultural practices are largely retained (Dalton 1964).[6]

ROSSEL ISLAND MONEY

Rossel Island money is an enigma in anthropological literature because of its monetary peculiarities. Although it was reported at an early date, and by an economist (Armstrong 1924; 1928) who was in the field for only two months, reanalysis in the light of points made earlier in this essay allows a different interpretation of Rossel Island money and economy.

Armstrong's Theoretical Presentation

Armstrong asserts that Rossel Island money is a rough equivalent of our own (1924:429): that it is a medium of exchange used to purchase a wide range of goods and services and that it is a standard of value for stating prices. He uses commercial monetary and economic terms throughout to describe the Rossel system—medium of exchange, standard of value, buy, sell, price (1928:59).

The Rossel Islanders use two types of shell money, *ndap* and *nko*.[7] Ndap money consists of individual shells (Armstrong calls them coins), each of which belongs to one of 22 named classes or denominations, which Armstrong ranks from 1 to 22, a higher-numbered class indicating a higher-valued shell (Table 6–2).

Armstrong could not determine the number of ndap shells in each class below 13, but he guesses there are fewer than 1,000 in all (1928:63), which would mean 800 or so in classes 1–12.

Armstrong's theoretical concern is with the value relationships among the ranked shells. He tells us that (as in capitalist economy) all goods and services on Rossel bear a money price stated as a piece (coin) of a specific class (1–22) of ndap, so that a big house costs a No. 20 ndap shell, and a pig a No. 18 (1928:88). But the shells are not quite like dollar bills numbered 1–22 with a No. 20 (say) bearing twice the value of a No. 10, or an item priced at No. 20 purchasable with two shells of No. 10 variety. In Armstrong's view it is merely an aberration due to custom, and, perhaps, to unsystematic thinking (1924:426) that the Rossel Islanders insist that something priced at No. 20 must be paid for with a No. 20 shell, rather than with lower-denomination pieces adding up to 20. He sees this as an inefficiency in their system as compared to ours—in which all bills and coins are directly convertible into each other. He therefore explains that the Rossel system requires elaborate borrowing to allow a person who

Table 6–2

Armstrong's numbering system for classes of ndap shell money (1928:62)	Number of individual ndap shells in each class
22	7
21	10
20	10
19	10
18	20
17	7
16	7
15	10
14	30
13	30–40

Total in classes 13–22 ≅ 146

does not happen to own a piece of No. 20 money to acquire an item "priced" at 20, and he argues that it is the borrowing system that reveals the value relationships among the ranked coins (1924:425, 423). This is a cumbersome equivalent of our own system—a Model T, so to speak— which does the same job as our own media of exchange, but with more work and fuss because one cannot substitute two $10 bills for something priced at $20. Armstrong writes:

> . . . the necessity for continual loans is largely the result of the peculiar na-
> ture of the system. The same "amount" of money, where the values are sim-
> ply related and "change" can always be given, could perform the same
> amount of real service (i.e., effect the same number of purchases) with per-
> haps a tenth or less of the amount of lending necessitated by the Rossel sys-
> tem [1928:65].

If one borrows a No. 12 for a short time, he will have to repay a No. 13; but for a longer time he will have to repay a No. 14, 15, and so on. Therefore, he says, the value relationships among the denominations 1–22 conform roughly to compound interest, which shows the relationship of an initial sum lent to its repayment equivalent, depending on the rate of inter- est and the time the initial sum is outstanding. Theoretically, a No. 1 shell is related to any other number, 2–22, by the length of time a No. 1 loan is outstanding before repayment must be made in any higher number (Armstrong 1928:63, 64).

Armstrong's analytical interpretation may be summarized: ndap shell money functions like dollars in that it is a medium of exchange, standard of value, standard for deferred payments, and the like. Debts are calculated and goods and services priced in shells of stated denomination. The peculiar (different from our own) feature of the system is that the shell denominations are not freely convertible into one another, which makes necessary frequent borrowing at interest to acquire the exact denomination shell needed for a given purchase.

Contradictory Evidence

There are two faults in Armstrong's analysis from which stem the subsidiary difficulties in his interpretation of the Rossel shell money system.

1. He assumes all ndap shells function as media of (commercial) exchange. He does not distinguish among modes of transaction (reciprocity, redistribution, market exchange), but regards all transactions as commercial purchases (1924:427); brides cost a No. 18 shell, just as baskets cost a No. 4 shell. He writes: ". . . any commodity or service may be more or less directly priced in terms of them [ndap shells] [1928:59]." Armstrong never doubts that Rossel Island money is essentially like our own media of (commercial) exchange. One could sum up his ethnocentric theorizing in a syllogism: ndap shells are "money"; money is a commercial instrument; therefore Rossel Island is a market economy.

2. This market preconception leads him to do what the Rossel Islanders do *not* do: to number the ndap classes 1–22. By so doing he can assume that convertibility of any numbered shell for any other via borrowing and repayment is practiced throughout the *entire* range, so that one could start by lending a No. 1 shell and, by continual loans at interest, wind up eventually with a No. 22 shell. For example, "Any [ndap shell] value can thus be regarded as any lower value plus compound interest for the number of time units equal to the number of values by which the two are separated, so that No. 22, for example, is No. 1 plus compound interest for 21 units of time [Armstrong 1928:64]."

By numbering them 1–22, Armstrong implies that the differences between ndap shell classes are cardinal differences: that a No. 22 is 22 times more *valuable* than a No. 1, in the sense that a $20 bill is 20 times more valuable than a $1 bill. There are no such cardinal differences among ndap shells. To number them 1–22 is to give a false impression of similarity between ndap shell classes and dollar, franc, or sterling denominations and a false impression about the commensurability or the "purchasing power" relationship between lower- and higher-numbered ndap shells.

The characteristics of monetary transactions on Rossel that lead us to doubt Armstrong's analytical interpretation may be set out with the following provisos kept in mind: Rossel Island economy is not integrated by market exchange; ndap shells (except for the lowest few classes) are not media of (commercial) exchange; and convertibility throughout the entire range could not be practiced.

There are (on the basis of Armstrong's own data) at least three groups of ndap shells, the shells in each group being necessary for a different range of transactions, and convertibility via borrowing and repayment being possible *within* the lowest two groups, but not *within* the highest group, and not between groups.

The shells Armstrong classes 1–8 or 9 are the only ones capable of increase in quantity (1924:424; 1928:60). The individual shells in each of these classes do not bear separate names, and some of them, at least, enter low-echelon transactions, casual market exchange between individuals. In one of the rare descriptions of how shells below class No. 18 are actually used, Armstrong tells us that one may buy a basket, a lime stick, or a lime pot with a No. 4 shell (1928:85).[8] However, the question, "What goods and services will *each* shell class 1, 2, 3, . . . 22 'buy,' or what transactions does each enter?" is not answered except for ndap shells Nos. 4, 18, 20, and 21. What is clear, however, is that shell classes 18–22 are used for a very special range of important transactions which mark them off sharply from lower-echelon shells and that shells below No. 18 are not convertible into shells 18–22 by borrowing and repayment. One cannot start with a No. 1 or 17 and, by lending, work it up to a No. 18–22.

Armstrong writes: "Nos. 18–22 seem to be in a somewhat different position from the lower values and one would imagine that they are not related to each other and the lower values in the precise manner set out in generalized form above [that is, according to the compound interest formula linking the entire series 1–22] [1928:68]." Convertibility via borrowing and repaying a higher-class shell most certainly breaks down between Nos. 17 and 18. I suspect, but cannot so readily document from the data, that it does so between Nos. 10 and 11 as well. If such is the case, convertibility is possible among Nos. 1–10 and among Nos. 11–17, but not between the two sets and not among Nos. 18–22. It is very clear that the entire series is not linked because the uses to which shells 18–22 are put are of an entirely different order from the uses of lower shells. "As a matter of fact, a peculiarity enters as soon as we reach No. 18, which is not, as a rule [when borrowed] repaid by a coin of higher value [Armstrong 1928:66]."

Numbers 18–22 (of which there are fewer than 60 shells in all) are obviously treasure items like especially venerated kula bracelets and potlatch coppers, items with individual names and histories, which must be used to validate important social events and transactions in the same sense that bridewealth items validate a marriage. The folk view toward these shells

helps to explain their role as limited-purpose money in reciprocal and redistributive transactions.

> Nos. 18–22 are peculiar in one other respect. They have a certain sacred
> character. No. 18, as it passes from person to person, is handled with great
> apparent reverence, and a crouching attitude is maintained. Nos. 19 to 22
> are proportionately more sacred, are almost always kept enclosed, and are
> not supposed to see the light of day, and particularly the sun . . . I am in-
> clined to think that there may be a real gap [in sacredness and prestige]
> . . . between Nos. 17 and 18 . . . [No. 22 shells] are said to be inherited in
> the male line and to be owned by the most powerful chiefs on the island
> [Armstrong 1928:68].

To have regarded Nos. 18–22 as especially valuable media of (commercial) exchange—high-denomination bills—with which to buy especially
high-priced merchandise is the most telling error Armstrong makes. Numbers 18–22 cannot be acquired by any amount of lower-class shells, and
there is no way of gauging how many times more valuable a No. 18 is
compared to a No. 6 because they enter entirely different transactions.

Without exception, Nos. 18–22 enter non-commercial transactions exclusively: they are used as means of (reciprocal or redistributive) payment
or exchange in transactions induced by social obligation. Payments of a
No. 18 are a necessary part of ordinary bridewealth, as well as necessary
payment for shared wives and for sponsoring a pig or dog feast or a feast
initiating the use of a special kind of canoe. Number 20 is a necessary indemnity payment to the relatives of a man ritually murdered and eaten, a
transaction which is part of mortuary rites for the death of a chief (Armstrong 1928:67; 1924:428). Moreover, there is a connection between shells
18–22 and lineage affiliation which Armstrong notes but makes nothing
of: ". . . Nos. 18 to 22 are regarded as property peculiar to chiefs, though
continually lent by the latter to their subjects [1928:66]."

The implication throughout is that there exists (as with us) an impersonal money market in which anyone may borrow from anyone else at the
going interest rate (1924:426). This is doubtful. Unfortunately, Armstrong
is silent on the question, "Who may borrow from whom, and with what
penalties for failure to repay?"

As with special-purpose money for non-commercial transactions elsewhere, there are status requisites involved in the acquisition and use of the
high-echelon shells on Rossel. Just as marriage is not a market purchase of
a wife by anyone who acquires a No. 18 ndap, but rather a reciprocal
transaction between two lineage groups (the ndap payment being one of
the several necessary conditions in the social situation), so, too, with pig
feasts on Rossel. Only persons of correct status may sponsor the feast and
pay the ndap shell. In this case Armstrong notes that social requisites determine who may use upper ndap shells; but he does not see this as a

symptomatic difference between Rossel and Western money, that is, between non-commercial means of (redistributive) payment and our cash media of impersonal (commercial) exchange. What Armstrong says of pig feasts is equally true of marriage and all the other *social events* which require payment of high-echelon ndap shells:

> There are . . . complex social factors determining who shall have a pig to sell [*sic*], and who shall be in a position to buy [*sic*], and the buying and selling is not a simple economic occurrence, but a much more significant and complex social occurrence. We must suppose a complexity of social facts, which I am not in a position to define, that determine most of the general relations of a particular pig feast. . . . A particular individual provides a particular *ndap*. . . . A certain readjustment of social relations thus results from the holding of the feast . . . though we abandon the view that the monetary operations at a feast of this nature are to be regarded merely as a collective buying from a collective seller, it still remains that this is a useful way of describing these operations [1928:82, 83].

It is about as accurate to describe a pig feast on Rossel as buying a pig with a No. 18 ndap as it is to describe marriage in America as buying a wife with a wedding ring. To describe the pig feast as a market purchase, one must ignore the social requirements of the transaction and the folk view of the event, both of which differentiate this redistributive transaction from market exchange. Armstrong is forced to use market terms, purchase and sale, to describe pig feasts and bridewealth, because he regards ndap shells as media of (commercial) exchange in a market system.

One bizarre feature of the Rossel system—that a transaction requires a single shell of a specifically named class, and neither a shell from a higher class nor several from lower classes would do—may be examined in the light of what has been said above. "A man may have to borrow, even though he has money of a higher value in his possession than he requires at the moment. He may have Nos. 11 and 13, but not No. 12 which he requires at the moment. He cannot get change as a rule, for No. 13 is not a simple product of any lower value [Armstrong 1928:64–65]."

The higher values have nothing to do with commercial purchase and sale. One could not use five petty shells, like No. 4 (which buys a pot), to perform a transaction such as bloodwealth (which requires that special treasure Armstrong numbers 20), for much the same reasons that in the Trobriands, one cannot "buy" a renowned kula valuable with the pots bought from hawkers in a gimwali.

One final point. In comparing primitive money with our own, it is important that the writer describe the frequency of different kinds of monetary transactions. Only so can one gauge what role, if any, the money item(s) play in the production system. Armstrong concerns himself with social and ritual events—marriage, death, redistributive feasts, fines—and says almost nothing about production, subsistence goods, natural resource and labor transactions, and all the other ordinary concerns of money and pricing in our own economy. That he nevertheless asserts that Rossel money is much like our own should make one wary. Einzig is properly suspicious: "It is a pity that there is not enough evidence to show to what extent, if at all, *ndap* and *nko* are used as a medium of exchange in everyday transactions, apart from the purchase [*sic*] of pigs [Einzig 1948:75]."

If all the ndap shell transactions which Armstrong describes were abolished, subsistence livelihood of Rossel Islanders would remain unimpaired. It is a pity he did not hit upon that distinction which is useful to analyze economies not integrated by market exchange. DuBois writes concerning this:

> . . . I should like to make a distinction between subsistence and prestige economy. By subsistence economy is meant the exploitation of the . . . natural resources available to any industrious individual. By prestige economy, on the other hand, is meant a series of social prerogatives and status values. They include a large range of phenomena from wives to formulae for supernatural compulsion [1936:50].

The upper values of ndap shells (and probably the middle values as well —Armstrong is silent here) enter prestige spheres in non-commercial uses. These transactions are outside the production system and subsistence livelihood. Despite Armstrong's assertion to the contrary, there is no evidence that one could opt out of the social and ritual games (through which upper ndap shells are paid and received) by converting upper shells into land, labor, or products, except perhaps as occasional events in emergency situations (Bohannan and Dalton 1962), or as status prerogatives of big men as with Malinowski's "Chief"—the senior male in the highest ranked lineage.

Rossel Island Money: A Case of Red Herrings [9]

"The study of economics in simple communities should properly speaking be a job for economists. But so far few economists have tackled it, and most of the investigation has perforce been done by anthropologists [Royal Anthropological Institute 1949:158]."

All social scientists are either Sherlock or Mycroft Holmes. Anthropologists are Sherlock: they go to the scene, observe minutely, gather their threads of evidence from what they observe, and—like Sherlock—sometimes reach Paddington before reaching conclusions. Economic theorists are Mycroft: they do not go to the scene to observe minutely. They have no equivalent to field work because economists are not concerned with social organization or human behavior, but rather with the behavior of prices, income determinants, capital-output ratios, and other impersonal matters relating to the performance of nationally-integrated, industrialized, market economies (for which field work is unnecessary). Institutional matters, personal roles, and the social implications of economic organization have long since been consigned to the limbo of sociology. Neither the problems of interest nor the methods of analysis are the same in economics and that branch of economic anthropology which analyzes traditional non-market systems.

Armstrong is an economist who played at anthropology. His mistake was to bring Mycroft's tools to Sherlock's subject (and without realizing he was doing so). The result—to mix my metaphors—was to create a sort of Piltdown Economic Man, Melanesians with monetary denominations which fit the formula for compound interest. Armstrong's pioneer work is not a hoax, but a red herring; and the lesson to be learned is not analytical —what primitive money is all about—but methodological: how not to do anthropology.

CONCLUSIONS

The distinctions spelled out in this essay may be used to answer questions of interest to economic anthropology, comparative economy, and economic development.

1. Anthropologists do not hesitate to contrive special terms for special actions and institutions when to use terms from their own society would be misleading. They do not talk about *the* family, but about nuclear, extended, and matrilineal families. The same should be done with economic matters.

Those aspects of primitive economy which are unrelated to market exchange can only be understood by employing socio-economic terms: ceremonial-prestige and subsistence goods; reciprocity and redistribution; spheres and conversions; limited-purpose money. Such terms contain a social dimension and so allow us to relate economic matters to social organization and to express the folk view toward the items, services, persons, and situations involved. The economist dealing with monetary transactions in U.S. economy need not concern himself with personal roles and social situations because of the peculiarly impersonal nature of market exchange. The anthropologist dealing with reciprocal and redistributive transactions cannot ignore personal roles and social situations and still make sense of what transpires.

Kula armbands, potlatch coppers, cows, pig tusks, Yap stones, and the like are variously described as money of renown, treasure items, wealth, valuables, and heirlooms. Malinowski says kula valuables are regarded like crown jewels or sports trophies in Western societies. Writers on East Africa say that cows are regarded like revered pets. Such treasures take on special roles as non-commercial money. Their acquisition and disposition are carefully structured and regarded as extremely important events; they change hands in specified ways, in transactions which have strong moral implications and which rearrange status rights and obligations. They are used to create social relationships (marriage; entrance into secret societies), to prevent a break in social relationships (bloodwealth, mortuary payments), or to keep or elevate one's social position (potlatch). Their "money-ness" consists in their being required means of (reciprocal or redistributive) payment.

2. Subsidiary characteristics of Western money-stuff, such as portability and divisibility, are actually requirements for media of (commercial) exchange. In peasant and national economies integrated by market exchange, purchases of goods and services are a daily occurrence, and so money must be portable; market purchases are carried out at widely varying price, so the medium of (commercial) exchange must be finely divisible.

Yap stones, cows, kula armbands, and Rossel Island shells are not divisible, and some are not conveniently portable. But neither are they media of (commercial) exchange; they are not used for daily purchases of varying amount. Their use as non-commercial money makes their lack of divisibility and portability unimportant. Here we see one way primitive money-*stuff* is related to primitive money *usage*. As means of (reciprocal or redistributive) payment used infrequently to discharge social obligations, it does not matter that the money-stuff lacks those characteristics required of a medium of (commercial) exchange.

3. Economics textbooks (such as Samuelson 1961:54; Reynolds 1963:475) err in citing primitive monies *indiscriminately* as equivalents of American media of (commercial) exchange, for the same reason that Armstrong errs in treating Rossel Island monies as a single type and as a crude equivalent of our own. By giving the impression that *all* primitive monies perform the same primary function as dollars, they quite wrongly imply that all primitive economies may be regarded as crude market systems.

Economists are correct in saying that some unusual money-stuffs have functioned as media of (commercial) exchange. They have in mind situations such as colonial America (Quiggin 1949:316ff.) where "primitive money-stuffs" (commodity money such as tobacco and cotton) functioned just as dollars do today, or prisoner of war camps where cigarettes (primitive money-stuff) became used as media of (market) exchange.

But to conclude that because some primitive money-*stuffs* do perform the primary function of dollars, *all* primitive monies may be regarded as crude media of (commercial) exchange, is an important error. As we have seen in the case of Rossel Island, this market preconception impedes our understanding of marketless economies and those with peripheral markets only. It implies that market exchange is the only transactional mode ever to exist, and so—as economists do in our own economy—one may ignore the social situations in which monetary transactions occur and the folk

view toward the persons, events, and items involved. It is precisely this
sort of ethnocentrism that regards all "exchanges" as commercial transactions and equates all money payments with market purchases, with the result that brides and murder are said to have a price, just as pots and yams
in the market place have a price.

4. A situation of special interest is one where cowrie (in times past), or
sterling or francs (in recent times), acquired initially in external market
exchange, became used internally for commercial and non-commercial
transactions.[10] Such cases of monetary incursion deserve examination for
reasons which are of interest to students of community economic development as well as economic anthropology.

Cowrie inflation, wampum inflation, and bridewealth inflation are related cases. Cowrie and wampum became used as media of (commercial)
exchange through external trade with Europeans in situations where the
quantity of money-stuff was uncontrolled and increased rapidly in supply.
Similarly, where bridewealth comes to be paid in sterling or francs, the
sum increases when earnings of Western cash through market sale of labor
or produce increase faster than the number of marriageable females (Bohannan 1959; Mayer 1951:22). What might be called "potlatch copper inflation" is a similar case: when the Kwakiutl became increasingly enmeshed in Canadian market economy, they used their cash earnings to
increase the stakes in the potlatch. The limited number of coppers (like the
limited number of brides elsewhere) fetched a larger bundle of market-
purchased goods. All such cases may be described as "upward conversions": newly expanded cash earnings are used to acquire treasure items
and brides which indigenously were not transacted through market exchange.[11]

Western cash does much more than merely displace primitive monies
where the latter were not media of (commercial) exchange indigenously. It
allows non-commercial payments and obligations of traditional sorts (such
as bridewealth) to be discharged with general-purpose money earned in
market transactions—instead of with traditional items of special-purpose
money. In economies which formerly were marketless or had peripheral
markets only, a structural link—Western cash—now exists between
spheres of exchange which formerly were separate. Western money therefore has inevitable repercussions on traditional social organization and cultural practices (Schapera 1928; Bohannan 1959; Gulliver 1962; Dalton
1964). Patrons, elders, lineage heads, big men, and chiefs lose their control over clients, junior clansmen, and subjects once these junior persons
can earn their own livelihood and their own cash income with which to
pay their own bridewealth. In brief, market earnings can now be used for
reciprocal and redistributive payments (just as in Western economy goods
purchased on the market enter gift-giving, and money earnings are used to
pay taxes and tithes).

5. One source of ambiguity in the literature is the quest for a single, universal definition of money that would include our own kind (and presumably Soviet money), as well as the welter of types in use in primitive and peasant economies differing widely in organization. Einzig writes: "It must be the ultimate goal of the study of primitive money to try to find the common denominator—insofar as it exists—in terms of which both the well-established rules of modern money and the apparently conflicting conclusions on primitive money can be explained [1948:19]."

To concentrate attention on what all monies have in common is to discard those clues—how monies differ—which are surface expressions of different social and economic organization. Money is not an isolated case. Much the same can be said for external trade and market places, which (like money) also are made use of in economies differing markedly in organization (say, the U.S., the Soviet, and the Tiv economies). Money traits differ where social and economic organization differs. To concentrate attention on money traits independently of underlying organization leads writers to use the traits of Western economy as a model of the real thing (while ignoring the structure of Western economy which accounts for the money traits). Then any primitive money which does not have all the traits of the Western model money is simply ruled out by definition—it is not money. This does not get us very far toward understanding primitive and peasant economies.

Two distinctions which allow us to contrast primitive and Western money are the distinctions between commercial and non-commercial uses of money and between marketless economies, those with petty markets only, and market-integrated economies. In short, money has no definable essence *apart from* the uses money objects serve, and these depend on the transactional modes that characterize each economy: as tangible item as well as abstract measure, "money is what money does [Reynolds 1963:474]."

NOTES

1. M. L. Burstein, Robert Clower, Ronald Cohen, George Delehanty, Mitchell Harwitz, Sidney Mintz, and A. A. Walters made critical comments on an earlier draft. I am grateful to these anthropologists and economists, and to Heyward Ehrlich who suggested changes in style and presentation. I must acknowledge separately the kindness of Paul Bohannan and Karl Polanyi, both of whom read several drafts and insisted on improvement. Much of the essay is an elaboration of ideas contained in Polanyi's lectures and writings.

2. For purposes of this essay we simply characterize the dominant transactional mode of Western economy as "market exchange." Price and distribution theory distinguish among many kinds of market exchange: pure competition, monopolistic competition, pure and differentiated oligopoly, and so on. These

distinctions do not concern us. Similarly, for our purposes we regard U.S. dollars as a single kind of money. For monetary problems in our own economy it is necessary to distinguish among currency, check deposits, and savings deposits, and sometimes between legal tender and money which is not legal tender; but for the matters of contrast that concern us, it is not necessary to make these distinctions. For a discussion of the fine points of money variations within Western economy, see Burstein (1963:chapter 1).

3. We can generalize the point by showing how all the commercial uses of money are brought into play as the result of a single purchase: I buy a house for $20,000, paying $5,000 down and borrowing $15,000 from a bank to be repaid in future installments:

i. I acquire rights to a house; the former owner acquires $20,000. The money is used as a medium of (commercial) exchange.

ii. Dollars here are used also as a measure or standard of (commercial) value, that is, as a measuring device to compare the house with any other commodity priced in dollars.

iii. The bank uses dollars as a unit of (commercial) account in recording my indebtedness to it.

iv. My debt to the bank also means that dollars are used as a standard for deferred (commercial) payments, that is, as a device to measure commercial debt.

v. If I save money currently in anticipation of repaying debt, dollars are used as a store of (commercial) value or wealth.

vi. When I begin to repay the bank, dollars are then used as a means of (commercial) payment of indebtedness incurred by the past market purchase.

4. Common stocks may be used as a medium of (commercial) exchange or payment, as when a company is purchased for stock, but it is nevertheless dollars that are used as the (commercial) standard of value.

5. The qualifications necessary are not due to the structure of market economy, but to cultural practices which differ among market societies: in U.S. society (but not, say, in French) Negroes cannot buy housing at will (but they can buy automobiles); people under eighteen cannot legally buy liquor; sale of some firearms is controlled by license. But for most people and for most goods and services, there are no status requisites imposed.

6. Marketless economies and those with peripheral markets only refer to descriptions in the literature of situations before serious European incursion. The term "primitive economy" is downright misleading when it is used to include all three types. I prefer to use it to mean only Types I and II (Dalton 1964). In Type III, where market exchange dominates, economic structure differs markedly, and so, too, do the uses of money. Firth (1946) is right to call the market-dominated Malayan economies "peasant" rather than "primitive" to indicate that a distinction should be made. A useful distinction between peasant and primitive economies is the following: by a peasant economy we mean one in which, (1) most people depend on market sale of resources or products for livelihood; (2) modern machine technology is largely absent; (3) traditional social organization and cultural practices are retained in significant degree. A primitive economy differs primarily on the first point: most people do not depend on market sale of resources or products for livelihood. One might also say

that the organizational component of community economic development consists in transforming economies of Types I and II into Type III.

Failure to distinguish among the three types is responsible for needless dispute in the literature, as when writers generalize from what is true in market-integrated economy to all economies. Jones (1960) and Miracle (1962) argue the case for "economic man" in Africa: that Africans respond to material incentives and choose among economic alternatives just as we do. But note that *all* their examples come from Type III economies, where Africans—like us—have come to depend for livelihood on market sale (of labor or cash crops). What is true for a Rhodesian copper miner is one thing; what is true for a Nuer or a Lele is another. On types of peasant economy, see essay 9 in this volume.

7. Following Armstrong, our treatment will concern ndap shells only. He said too little about strings of nko shells to allow anything more than guesses about how they functioned.

8. Armstrong says that No. 4 ndap is the commonest on the island, there being at least 200 of them (1928:63). Note also that each ndap shell in classes 12–22, some 150 shells in all, had individual names, as did some, at least, in classes 8–11 (1928:62).

9. Armstrong's short stay on Rossel, his inability to speak the language, his dependence on informants rather than direct observation, together with his preconception that Rossel money must be essentially like our own media of (commercial) exchange, prevented him from relating those aspects of Rossel money which differed from our own to their different socio-economic structure. Armstrong does not give enough information to make complete sense of the system.

The unresolved problems are many. To understand the system fully, we should have to know about the following: What transactions does each kind of ndap shell enter? What is the nko system all about: Why do certain transactions require a sorting of both ndap and nko? Armstrong tells us that there are really more than 22 classes of ndap shells because some of them are subdivided and given separate names, making about 40 distinctions in all; what are the shells in these subdivided classes used for? Who may borrow from whom, and with what penalties for failure to repay? How do rank and lineage affect borrowing and repayment? Are the high-echelon ndap shells related to kinship or political organization in some such fashion as potlatch coppers are? Who are the "brokers" who act as intermediaries between borrowers and lenders, and for what kinds of transactions and between whom do they intermediate? Specific ndap values are identified with specific parts of pigs and men (Armstrong 1928:79), a matter the people regard as important, but which remains unexplained. So, too, with the number ten, which appears repeatedly: several transactions require payment of a linked series of ten shells, for instance, one each of the ten ndap classes 20–11 is paid as compensation for ritual murder.

10. In Africa, at least, the impact of cowrie on indigenous economies and indigenous money varied widely. In some instances, as with sterling and francs, cowrie came to be general-purpose money which linked spheres of goods and services formerly kept separate and which serviced several transactional modes within one society (see Vansina 1962:198); such was the case where cowrie came to be used in market-place exchanges as well as bridewealth. In other

cases cowrie was incorporated as just another special-purpose money with limited usage within the indigenous system (see Quiggin 1949: chapter IV).

11. The very early date at which Canadian market exchange permeated Kwakiutl life is important to understand how and why potlatches changed over time: before serious Canadian market incursion, potlatches were given infrequently, were the prerogative of nobles, and were necessary to affirm one's rank (Codere 1951). Having the traditional potlatch goods was not a sufficient condition for giving a potlatch because one had to have the rank as well. (As in many primitive societies, only those of high rank could accumulate the necessary goods.)

The nature of the potlatch changed radically with (1) the population decimation around 1840—the population fell from an estimated 23,000 in 1840 to fewer than 3,000 in 1880, and under 2,000 in 1890 (Codere 1951:52). Note that the 600 rank positions remained fixed. (2) The second important change was the increasing use in the potlatch of items purchased on the Canadian market. Now the opportunity for upward conversions—the use of Canadian goods bought with cash to acquire internal rank and prestige positions—became unlimited. With a shrunken population, practically everyone had one of the 600 rank positions, which was not the case earlier, and everyone had access to Canadian goods (by simply earning cash), which certainly was not the case earlier. Potlatches then came to be given frequently, by anyone (even women and children), and for all kinds of reasons; and, no doubt, even a commercial element entered.

The trouble with the literature is that even the early anthropologists (Boas first wrote in 1887) were describing Western market incursion well under way, without fully appreciating the radical difference it made to the potlatch when everyone had rank positions and access to purchased goods. Any generalization made about the nature of the potlatch should bear a date. See Drucker (1939:56 footnote 3, 63 footnote 22).

REFERENCES

ARENSBERG, CONRAD
    1957   Anthropology as history. In *Trade and market in the early empires,* K. Polanyi, C. M. Arensberg, H. W. Pearson ed. Glencoe: The Free Press.
ARMSTRONG, W. E.
    1924   Rossel Island money: a unique monetary system. *Economic Journal* 34:423–429.
    1928   *Rossel Island.* Cambridge: Cambridge University Press.
BOHANNAN, PAUL
    1959   The impact of money on an African subsistence economy. *Journal of Economic History* 19:491–503.
BOHANNAN, PAUL, and GEORGE DALTON
    1962   Introduction. In *Markets in Africa,* Paul Bohannan and George Dalton ed. Evanston: Northwestern University Press.
BURSTEIN, M. L.
    1963   *Money.* Cambridge: Shenkman.

CODERE, HELEN
   1951   *Fighting with property*. New York: J. J. Augustin.
DALTON, GEORGE
   1962   Traditional production in primitive African economies. *Quarterly Journal of Economics* 76:360–378.
   1964   The development of subsistence and peasant economies in Africa. *International Social Science Journal* 16:378–389.
DRUCKER, PHILIP
   1939   Rank, wealth, and kinship in Northwest coast society. *American Anthropologist* 41:55–65.
DUBOIS, CORA
   1936   The wealth concept as an integrative factor in Tolowa-Tututni culture. In *Essays in anthropology presented to A. L. Kroeber*, R. H. Lowie ed. Berkeley: University of California Press.
EINZIG, PAUL
   1948   *Primitive money*. London: Eyre and Spottiswoode.
FIRTH, RAYMOND
   1929   Currency, primitive. In *Encyclopaedia Britannica*, 14th ed.
   1946   *Malay fishermen: their peasant economy*. London: Kegan, Paul Trench, Trubner and Co. Revised ed. 1966.
GLUCKMAN, MAX, and I. G. CUNNISON
   1962   Foreword. In *Politics of the kula ring*, by J. P. Singh Uberoi. Manchester: Manchester University Press.
GULLIVER, P. H.
   1962   The evolution of Arusha trade. In *Markets in Africa*, P. J. Bohannan and G. Dalton ed. Evanston: Northwestern University Press.
HERSKOVITS, MELVILLE J.
   1952   *Economic anthropology*, revised ed. New York: Knopf.
JONES, WILLIAM O.
   1960   Economic man in Africa. *Food Research Institute Studies* 1:107–134.
LIENHARDT, R. GODFREY
   1956   Religion. In *Man, culture, and society*, Harry L. Shapiro ed. New York: Oxford University Press.
MALINOWSKI, BRONISLAW
   1921   The primitive economics of the Trobriand Islanders. *Economic Journal* 31:1–15.
   1922   *Argonauts of the western Pacific*. London: Routledge.
MAYER, PHILIP
   1951   *Two studies in applied anthropology in Kenya*. London: H.M.S.O.
MIRACLE, MARVIN P.
   1962   African markets and trade in the Copperbelt. In *Markets in Africa*, P. J. Bohannan and G. Dalton ed. Evanston: Northwestern University Press.
POLANYI, KARL
   1944   *The great transformation*. New York: Rinehart.
   1957a   Notes on the place occupied by economies in societies. In *Selected memoranda on economic aspects of institutional growth* (mimeo.). New York: Reprinted in *Primitive, archaic, and modern economies:*

essays of Karl Polanyi, G. Dalton ed. New York: Anchor Books, 1968. 116–138.

1957*b* The economy as instituted process. In *Trade and market in the early empires*, K. Polanyi, C. M. Arensberg, H. W. Pearson ed. Glencoe: The Free Press.

QUIGGIN, A. H.

1949   *A survey of primitive money*. London: Methuen.

REINING, CONRAD C.

1959   The role of money in the Zande economy. *American Anthropologist* 61:39–43.

REYNOLDS, LLOYD G.

1963   *Economics, a general introduction*. Homewood: Irwin.

ROYAL ANTHROPOLOGICAL INSTITUTE OF GREAT BRITAIN AND IRELAND

1949   *Notes and queries on anthropology*, 6th ed. London: Routledge and Kegal Paul.

SAMUELSON, PAUL ANTHONY

1961   *Economics, an introductory analysis*, 5th ed. New York: McGraw-Hill.

SCHAPERA, I.

1928   Economic changes in South African native life. *Africa* 1:170–188.

VANSINA, JAN

1962   Trade and markets among the Kuba. In *Markets in Africa*, P. J. Bohannan and G. Dalton ed. Evanston: Northwestern University Press.

7

Bridewealth versus Brideprice [1]

The controversy over "bridewealth" versus "brideprice" (Gray 1960; Gulliver 1961; Gibson 1962) is a symptom of theoretical malaise that afflicts economic anthropology. Like controversies over whether sea shells and dogs' teeth are really money (Dalton 1965), the issue comes down to this: On what grounds is it useful to employ a term with a very special meaning in developed capitalist economy—price—to describe a transaction in primitive economy that in some ways resembles the price transaction in our own and in some ways does not? The issue is not merely terminological. To use the term "brideprice" is to imply that payment at marriage is a market or commercial transaction and therefore that marriage entails a commercial purchase of rights or services.

EVANS-PRITCHARD'S POSITION

The term "brideprice" is misleading because "price" has an inseparable association with the commercial transactions of market purchase in European economy. The material goods and the services that form a necessary payment at marriage—bridewealth—are not the same as the dollar price of a commodity: (1) the participants do not regard the payment of bridewealth as a commercial transaction (although it does have an "economic" component in the sense that material goods and services enter); and (2) from the viewpoint of the anthropologist, the social situation of which bridewealth is a part marks off the transaction sharply from impersonal market purchase. The events and circumstances of bridewealth are different in important ways from those of a commercial exchange.

There are very good reasons for cutting the term [brideprice] out of ethnological literature since at best it emphasizes only one of the functions of this wealth, an economic one, to the exclusion of other important social func-

Reprinted, with revision, from "Bridewealth versus Brideprice," *American Anthropologist,* 68 (June 1966): 732–738. Reprinted by permission of the publisher.

tions; and since, at worst, it encourages the layman to think that "price" used in this context is synonymous with "purchase" in common English parlance. Hence we find people believing that wives are bought and sold in Africa in much the same manner as commodities are bought and sold in European markets [Evans-Pritchard 1931:36].

Bridewealth paid at marriage has different functions in different societies and may have several in the same society: to indemnify the girl's family for the loss of her services, as an earnest of good intentions on the part of the groom and his family, to solidify the new affinal bonds created by marriage, and to legitimize children born to the union and affiliate them in the socially approved manner. It is better, therefore, to use a neutral term, one that does not single out one of these functions, the "economic," as *the* most important.

> I do not myself see the necessity of using a symbol which refers to any one particular function of this wealth as is the case with "price," "earnest," and "indemnity," but propose instead the term . . . "bride-wealth" . . . [because] it does not attempt to define what are the many aspects of this transference of wealth in the situation of marriage. . . . the term bride-wealth stresses very definitely the economic value of all the different things which are handed over by the group of a man to the group of a woman as one of the concrete obligations of the union. For, whatever else they may be, cattle, spears, goats, arrows, pots, labor, etc., have an economic value. But while the economic value of these things is suggested in the term "bride-wealth" there is no expressed indication that the wealth has any one particular economic function such as is implied in the word "price," a function which is, as a matter of fact, very little developed among African peoples out of contact with Europeans [Evans-Pritchard 1931:38].

GRAY'S POSITION

Among the Sonjo, transactions involving marriage payments are much like other transactions (such as those involving rights to irrigation water) because the same item—goats—is used to make payment. Therefore it is useful to emphasize the similarity between payments at marriage and other transactions by treating brideprice also as an economic transaction (just as we regard the exchange of irrigation rights for goats as economic). Indeed, the economic terms "purchase," "sale," and "price," *if properly redefined,* can be applied to point up the similarity between brideprice payments and other transactions in the Sonjo community.

> The real question at issue is not, as Evans-Pritchard's statement suggests, whether African wives are bought and sold in the same manner as commodities are bought and sold in European markets: it is whether women in some

African societies are transferred as wives in a manner that has a basic resemblance to the manner in which other economic commodities are transferred in the same societies. Where this resemblance is found, then if economic terms are applied to dealings in other commodities, I shall argue that it is legitimate to apply them to dealings in wives as well [Gray 1960:35].

CRITIQUE

The ambiguity in Gray's argument is due to his implicit use of the word "economic" to mean "commercial," so that all exchanges of "economic commodities" in Sonjoland are transmogrified into market exchanges. If goats paid for irrigation rights are economic (commercial), then goats paid for brides are economic (commercial), too. Therefore, we may call marriage payments "bride-*price*." But markets do not exist in Sonjoland, so he must redefine *market* terms (purchase, sale, price) to make them include any kind of exchange, whether it be reciprocal gift-giving, redistributive payments to central authority, or commercial purchase.

By *purchase* I mean the acquisition of property by giving goods in exchange for it. *Selling* is the action of the person who delivers the property in exchange for other goods. *Price* is the amount of goods asked or given for the property. . . . In thus defining these words I have simply removed those implications relating to a money [that is, a market] economy that inhere in their usual dictionary definitions or their use in "common English parlance." This is necessary if they are to be adapted to the economic systems of societies which lack money [that is, market exchange] [Gray 1960:35].

But this is precisely what one should not do if there are essential differences between market and Sonjo exchanges. To redefine familiar words in order to homogenize transactions does not solve the problem as long as the Sonjo exchanges are essentially different from the *market* exchanges in our own economy to which these terms apply. To call a cat a quadruped, and then to say that because cats and dogs are both quadrupeds I shall call them all cats, does not change the nature of cats. Neither does it confuse dogs; it merely confuses the reader. To say that Sonjo women are commodities purchased and sold at a price *is* to say that they are transacted like Cadillacs and shoe polish in our own economy. They are not. It is confusing to use the same words for different types of transactions; and by so doing, some points of analytical interest about Sonjo economy are obscured. If one redefined Soviet central planning transactions to make them the same as American market transactions, one thereby—by playing with definitions—obscures the differences between Soviet and American economic organization.

It is, indeed, true in Sonjoland that rights in women are transacted with goat payments, as are some other services (rights to irrigation water) and some goods (honey). But this is not the same as saying that they are commercial transactions properly described by the words "buy," "sell," "commodity," and "price."

One must be clear about this. Sonjo economy is not organized by market exchange. Aside from the absence of market places in Sonjo villages (Gray 1962:470), almost all the transactions in which goat payments enter are apart from subsistence livelihood. Bridewealth payments, as well as the other goat transactions, are relatively infrequent, and no one depends for his daily living on goat revenue from girls, honey, or irrigation rights. Gray tells us that occasionally land may be leased for a goat payment, but apparently there are no labor markets in Sonjoland. It is necessary to point all this out to understand the transactional modes employed. We are dealing here with the occasional use of goats as special-purpose money in *non-commercial* transactions.

Moreover, in our economy one can buy Cadillacs and shoe polish if one has the cash; religion, sex, ancestry, lineage, and political affiliation do not enter. There are few status barriers to commercial transactions. In bridewealth and irrigation-water transactions there are status constraints. Neither brides nor irrigation rights are bartered to the highest bidder. Payment of goats is a necessary but insufficient condition for acquiring wives and irrigation rights. In both, social relationships enter importantly.

In sum, what led Gray to prefer the term "brideprice" is that the items comprising the marriage payment—goats—are also used in other Sonjo exchanges. And if these other transactions are "economic," so, too, is the marriage transaction. In Gray's context, "economic" should mean simply "that which involves resources or goods and services"; it should not mean a commercial or market exchange (Dalton 1961:5–7). In American society, too, marriage has an "economic" component—material goods such as wedding rings and presents are involved—but this does not mean that we interpret marriage as the groom buying the bride with a wedding ring or gifts to her parents. Gray errs in using the word "economic" to mean "commercial" instead of simply "goods and services."

Our problem is to use Gray's important point and yet preserve the distinction that led Evans-Pritchard to prefer the term "bridewealth."

MONEY USES AND TRANSACTIONAL MODES IN SONJOLAND

Gray's important point is that in Western capitalist economy, rights in wives are transacted in a different manner than goods and services, but not so in Sonjoland. Here is one difference between Sonjo and U.S. economies —and between Sonjo and U.S. family arrangements—that must be accounted for. Indeed, it is this similarity between marriage transactions and some others that shaped Radcliffe-Brown's views on bridewealth.

> The payment of cattle for a wife is functionally parallel to the payment of cattle for a man who has been intentionally or accidentally killed: In both cases the payment is an "indemnity" payment of compensation to a group (family or clan) that loses a member [Radcliffe-Brown 1929, quoted in Evans-Pritchard 1931:37].

What makes the Sonjo case unusual is not that the bridewealth item—goats—enters other prestige transactions, but that goats are also used occasionally to acquire low-echelon goods as well.

> An individual who produces a crop of gourds exchanges them for goats with other Sonjo and also Masai. The prevailing rate of exchange was eight gourds for one goat. The Masai also exchange goats for Sonjo women and children. . . . Sonjo smiths formerly obtained iron from Masai smiths in exchange for goats. . . . [Beehives] represent a useful reserve of goods which can be mobilized and exchanged for other goods, usually goats, when the special need arises. . . . Owners sometimes wish to dispose of land because they are not able to utilize it or because they are in urgent need of goats. . . . water theft is a common offense. . . . it is punished with a fine of one goat . . . a common way to build up a goat herd is to exchange honey for goats [Gray 1962:469, 473, 478, 480, 485].

But goats are not the only item capable of performing one or more money uses.

> These transactions usually involved the exchange of grain for irrigation rights and sometimes for honey. A certain measure of grain . . . was regarded as equivalent to the standard jar of honey (about two gallons), and exchanges were based on these equivalences. Payments for irrigation water were usually evaluated in terms of honey—one-third of a jar was a common amount for this payment—and if it was agreed to make the payment in grain, the honey equivalent was calculated and paid [Gray 1962:484].

The unusual thing about goats in Sonjoland is that aside from being an important subsistence source for direct consumption, they perform several money uses in transacting both low- and high-echelon goods and services in reciprocal and redistributive exchanges. They also appear to be used occasionally in transactions that resemble market exchange, but at fixed-price or set-rate equivalences (for instance, in leasing land for goats).

Goats are more nearly like general-purpose dollars or francs than is commonly the case in subsistence economies. Still, we think it more useful to use non-market terminology to describe the role of goats as special money in Sonjoland: goats are used primarily as means of (reciprocal) exchange in bridewealth and other reciprocal transactions. Goats are also used as means of (redistributive) payment when set-rate fees (depending on one's status) are paid for irrigation rights.

> . . . a class of men, called *wakiama* . . . are required as individuals to pay substantial tribute in goats to the *wenamiji* [hereditary council of elders] as a group [for irrigation rights]. . . . The goats which are paid to them as water tax by the *wakiama* are all supposed to be used in communal sacrifices for the general spiritual benefit of the village, but much of this meat ends up in their own family pots. Some of these goats are turned over to the priests, again with the understanding that they will be offered to God on behalf of the whole village [Gray 1962:479].

In many subsistence economies there are ranked spheres of goods and services. Goods *within* any sphere may be exchanged (via reciprocity, redistribution, or the market), but not goods in different spheres (Firth 1958:69; Bohannan 1959). What is important in Sonjoland is that goats provide an institutionalized means of conversion between spheres:

> . . . fathers with more daughters than sons tend to accumulate goats which they can exchange for subsistence or luxury goods, land or superior irrigation rights [Gray 1962:489].

This is also true in emergency situations, in which the Sonjo convert downward to get goats for pressing purposes or, when subsistence livelihood is threatened, to get grain for goats.

> The Masai also exchange goats for Sonjo women and children. . . . in years of grain scarcity . . . goats are then readily exchanged for grain. . . . The decision to exchange [bee] hives for goats is only made when there is sudden and pressing need for a number of goats, as often happens, for instance when the deadline for paying a brideprice draws near. . . . a landowner . . . is willing to give up part of his land . . . temporarily because of a more pressing need for goats, perhaps as brideprice for a son's wife [Gray 1962:469, 484, 485, 478].

When we consider a community like that of the Sonjo, where market exchanges are absent or infrequent, we cannot expect any money-like objects to resemble dollars closely because the bundle of money attributes that characterize dollars is conferred by the nationally integrated market organization within which they are used (Dalton 1965). If in this community there exist quantifiable objects that perform one or more money uses— payment, standard, exchange, and so on—it is useful to regard them as limited- or special-purpose monies that express the special (non-commercial) transactional modes employed in that economy.

Because of the exchange use of money under our market organization of economic life we are apt to think of money in too narrow terms. No object is money *per se,* and any object in an appropriate field can function as money. In truth, money is a system of symbols similar to language, writing, or weights and measures. These differ from one another mainly in the purpose serviced, the symbols employed, and the degree to which they display a single unified purpose [Polanyi 1957].

It is not the intrinsic characteristics of the money-stuff that mark off money from other things, but rather the uses or purposes that the money-stuff serves. That dollars perform all the commercial and non-commercial money uses, service all transactional modes, and are a "full-time" money with no uses apart from the performance of money functions is due to our national economy's market integration. We should not be surprised to find money-stuff, money uses, and the folk view toward indigenous money and its uses differing from ours where market organization is absent (just as we are not surprised to find kinship obligations differing from ours where family organization is different).

CONCLUSION

As with controversies over primitive money and whether the potlatch is really investment, the bridewealth versus brideprice controversy is about the kinds of transactional modes that exist in primitive economies. The controversy indicates the need to establish unambiguous categories for classifying types of exchanges, appropriations, and transactions in small-scale economies that are neither industrialized nor integrated by markets for labor, land, or produce. Bridewealth, bloodwealth, potlatch, kula, silent trade, debt bondage, and the like are transactions that superficially resemble familiar commercial transactions in market economies—something is paid over in return for something else—but are different in objective ways from commercial exchanges and are regarded by the participants as different.

One must resort to analogy. In the United States, marriage and prostitution are superficially similar in that both entail an exchange of sexual services for material payments. I assume we would all agree, however, that the underlying differences between marriage and prostitution are more important than the similarities: the length of the relationship, the folk view of the relationship, the extent of the kinship connections established, the question of children, and so forth. Despite the similarity that both involve an exchange of sexual services and material goods or money, once the different folk views and social circumstances of each are taken into account, marriage and its material components are clearly seen as a reciprocal transaction, while prostitution is a market purchase.

What is needed in economic anthropology is analytical classifications that allow us to assess the relative importance of similarities and differences between commercial and non-commercial transactions. Implicitly or explicitly, anthropologists use their own market economy (capitalism) as their base of comparison in describing primitive economies. Many ambiguities—and therefore controversies—are created by an unjustified *translation* of primitive economy into market language due to the failure to appreciate the importance of differences between subsistence economy and our own (Dalton 1961; 1962). Where markets and Western cash are absent, digging sticks are tools, not capital, and in no society are brides priced in the sense that Cadillacs are in our own.

NOTE

1. I am grateful to Paul Bohannan and John Middleton for their critical comments. It is important to note that the controversy refers to the nature of bridewealth payments of traditional indigenous items—for example, cows, goats, and the like. Francs or sterling paid as bridewealth create a different situation (see Dalton 1964; 1965).

REFERENCES

BOHANNAN, PAUL
    1959   The impact of money on an African subsistence economy. *Journal of Economic History* 19:491–503.
DALTON, GEORGE
    1961   Economic theory and primitive society. *American Anthropologist* 63:1–25.
    1962   Traditional production in primitive African economies. *Quarterly Journal of Economics* 76:360–378.
    1964   The development of subsistence and peasant economies in Africa. *International Social Science Journal* 16:378–389.
    1965   Primitive money. *American Anthropologist* 67:44–65.
EVANS-PRITCHARD, E. E.
    1931   An alternative term for "bride-price." *Man* 31:36–39.
FIRTH, RAYMOND
    1958   Work and wealth of primitive communities. In *Human types*, revised ed. New York: Mentor Books.
GIBSON, GORDON D.
    1962   Bridewealth and other forms of exchange among the Herero. In *Markets in Africa*, P. Bohannan and G. Dalton ed. Evanston: Northwestern University Press.

GRAY, ROBERT F.
  1960 Sonjo bride-price and the question of African "wife purchase." *American Anthropologist* 62:34–57.
  1962 Economic exchange in a Sonjo village. In *Markets in Africa,* P. Bohannan and G. Dalton ed. Evanston: Northwestern University Press.
GULLIVER, P. H.
  1961 Bridewealth: the economic vs. the noneconomic interpretation. *American Anthropologist* 63:1098–1099.
POLANYI, KARL
  1957 Notes on the place occupied by economies in societies. In *Selected memoranda on economic aspects of institutional growth* (mimeo.). New York: Columbia University.
RADCLIFFE-BROWN, A. R.
  1929 Bride-price, earnest or indemnity? *Man* 29:131–132.

8

Two Notes on
Economic Surplus[1]

A NOTE OF CLARIFICATION ON ECONOMIC SURPLUS

In a recent controversy (Harris 1959; Pearson 1957:320–341), it is made clear that the term "surplus" is used by anthropologists in several meanings and for several purposes. Because of the important roles which have been assigned to material surpluses, especially in causing institutional change and development, clarity concerning such a "treacherous" (see Knight 1941) term seems particularly necessary.

This essay will argue three points. (1) Even when the term "surplus" is used in an unambiguous sense, meaning an actual increase in output, the role of a material surplus as inducer of socio-economic change is not at all certain. (2) When the term is used in ex post facto analysis of some unobserved change, or to explain some complex social structure, surplus becomes a definitional identity and its role as inducer of socio-economic change is incapable of empirical proof or refutation: it is a logical construct which need not have any connection with actual real-world events. (3) Finally, as it is used in a market-organized economy, the term surplus has special meaning wholly unlike its meaning in non-market economies.

Surplus as Empirical Fact

If it is explicitly recognized in any society that "this season" there is a growth in output—an unusually large amount of one or more material goods compared to the experienced norm of the past—we will call the extra output a factual surplus. As empirical fact, a surplus simply means that more of something is currently available than previously, and the so-

Reprinted, with revision, from "A Note of Clarification on Economic Surplus," *American Anthropologist*, 62 (June 1960):483–490; and from "Economic Surplus, Once Again," *American Anthropologist*, 65 (April 1963):389–394. Reprinted by permission of the publisher.

ciety recognizes that such is the case. The importance of such a surplus can vary greatly, depending on the society's institutions and values and the specific conditions under which the surplus arose.

1. The amount of such surplus must be specified, as well as the form it takes. If this season's larger output is only slightly larger than usual (indeed, even if it is much larger), the society may not recognize the existence of a surplus, in which case nothing may be changed by its appearance and conventional distribution. Actually, it would be meaningful to say that despite the increase in output no surplus has arisen, because none is recognized. Further, it will make a difference if the surplus represents a net increase in total output, or whether it consists of an expansion of one *component* of output while others are contracting (as usually occurs in war situations). A third possibility is that while there has been no change in the amounts and varieties of goods compared to last season, there has been a change in their appropriation (distribution), so that some groups of people have acquired *what is to them* "surplus," but what is not surplus to the society at large, because total output and its composition have not changed, but only its distribution.

2. Was the experienced surplus accidental (an unexpected windfall)? If so, was it unprecedented? If accidental surpluses have appeared occasionally in the past, it is likely that the society already possesses some mechanism(s) for dealing with them. Further, if the accidental surplus is regarded as a highly irregular occurrence—a gift of the gods—there need not be any change induced by its sporadic appearance.

3. Was the surplus deliberately contrived? If so, the "surplus" probably was regarded as both necessary and important because it had been created for a specific purpose, such as war or an unusual trading expedition. But here again should be underscored the possibility that the extra output for some special use was derived not from a growth in the total—a factual surplus—but rather via a diversion from its normal use, for example, the Norman conquerors imposing a special tax on the English.

4. Was the purposefully contrived surplus the result of an unusual intensity of conventionally applied effort, or did it result from some technological or organizational innovation, or from a military venture (war booty)?

5. Did the extra output consist of a new type of foodstuff or other material item? If so, our concept of surplus—an experienced increase in material output—becomes ambiguous unless it is further refined. If a new type of good was produced in place of some of the old, there can be no clear-cut surplus because new and old types of goods are not *directly* comparable in quantity. Whatever the quantity of the new good, it cannot (without redefining surplus) be measured against last season's quantity of old types of output. In general, when goods are measured in their natural units (hundreds of yams) rather than by money prices or by some measure

of effectiveness in specific use, there is no way of comparing two aggregates of differently composed items and saying that one is definitely larger than the other.[2] Of course, in the special case where this season the normal output of the usual goods is produced, plus some amount of the new good, the latter represents extra output and unambiguously can be called surplus.

6. Was the purposefully contrived surplus acquired this season the recognized beginning of a permanently higher level of available material goods; or was it regarded as temporary, the surplus disappearing with the fulfillment of the purpose for which it was originally contrived?

In summary, even in its simplest meaning—as the experienced fact of enlarged output—surplus can be of widely varying importance, depending on the society's specific institutions and on the special conditions which created the surplus: whether there was a growth in the total or a different allocation from an unchanged total; whether the extra output was recognized or not; whether it consisted of one type of good or several; whether it was temporary or permanent, accidental or deliberately created, induced by conventional means or by an innovation.

It should be pointed out that when the term "surplus" is meant, as it is above, to denote an experienced growth of output, it would be better to avoid using the term altogether. "Surplus" bears the (market-derived) connotation of redundancy, an amount over and above what is really useful or necessary, an excess of something. A deliberately contrived surplus (excess) would not make sense. It would be a contradiction in terms because the extra output would be deliberately sought only if it were, so to speak, earmarked prenatally for some special use. Whether or not an accidental increase in output would be in fact regarded as redundant (unnecessary) would depend wholly on the social apparatus of the community, that is, its structured mechanism for dealing with windfall increases in output and the conventional attitude toward the disposition of the specific good(s) which had increased in quantity.

Surplus as an Analytical Construct

It becomes clear from the Pearson-Harris controversy and the literature cited therein (Pearson 1957:339–341; Harris 1959:198, 199) that the importance attributed to material surplus stems from uncritical use of the concept as an analytical device, rather than as a term to describe a recognized growth in actual output. As an analytical device, surplus is a definitional identity—a logical construct—and is used as a deus ex machina which allegedly explains complex social structure or some unobserved socio-economic development.

Surplus is a definitional identity when it is equated with the existence of non-food producers; and it is an ex post facto rational construct when it is asserted as a necessary and/or sufficient precondition for social stratification or division of labor to come about. In the extreme case it is further asserted that the very appearance of a material surplus induces (causes) social stratification.

A syllogistic chain of deduction underlies surplus as a rational construct: every man must eat; if a man does not produce food for himself, he must acquire food from other men; let us call this acquired food "surplus"; therefore, by definition, every society which has non-food producers must be producing a food surplus to support them. An example is the following by Gordon Childe:

> The stone axe, the tool distinctive of part at least of the Stone Age, is the home-made product that could be fashioned and used by anybody in a self-contained group of hunters or peasants. It implies neither specialization of labour nor trade beyond the group. The bronze axe which replaces it is not only a superior implement, it also presupposes a more complex economic and social structure. The casting of bronze is too difficult a process to be carried out by anyone in the intervals of growing or catching his food or minding her babies. It is a specialist's job, and these specialists must rely for such primary necessities as food upon a surplus produced by other specialists. Again, the copper and tin of which the bronze axe is composed are comparatively rare, and very seldom occur together. One or both constituents will almost certainly have to be imported. Such importation is possible only if some sort of communications and trade have been established and if there is a surplus of some local product to barter for the metals (Quoted by Kluckhohn 1949:52).

There are ambiguities in the meaning of surplus as a definitional identity and as an ex post facto rational construct.

1. In the quotation above from Childe, two different bundles of goods are defined as surplus: the food acquired by the makers of bronze axes who are assumed to be non-food producers, and the locally produced stuff which is (by assumption) traded off in order to import the copper and tin to make bronze. Such usage is wholly non-empirical. If the people themselves do not regard the two kinds of produce as "surplus"—as things apart from other material goods—an artificial dichotomy is read into the data. Such distinction between surplus and non-surplus goods is justifiable only *if it serves some analytical purpose capable of empirical proof or refutation.* As a definition, surplus cannot by itself be assigned a causal role without empirical proof. For example, a key passage in the quote above is the following: "The bronze axe which replaces it [the stone axe] . . . presupposes a more complex economic and social structure. . . . these [bronze-axe-making] specialists must rely for such primary necessities as food upon a surplus produced by other specialists." What are the real-world implications of such deduction? That societies using the bronze axe must be more complex than those using the stone axe? That technological change is the most frequent (or most probable) inducer of socio-economic

organizational change? That a prior increase in foodstuffs is a necessary condition for making use of bronze implements? None by any means is necessary. Division of labor based on sex is found at relatively low as well as high levels of material subsistence. Bronze is an amalgam the proportions of whose components may vary considerably. Therefore, some bronze implements may require little more work than do stone implements. In a word, one cannot prove a theory of real-world social change with definitions.

2. An unproved social primacy is attached to food compared to other goods and services. In one deus ex machina use of surplus, an initial situation is assumed in which every person is himself a food producer (food being a biological necessity). Then a food surplus arises which allows the support of non-food producers, for example, priests. The implication is that because religion is not necessary for biological survival, it is a second-class sort of service, a luxury, which must have come later in time than did food production: ". . . mankind must first of all eat and drink, have shelter and clothing, before it can pursue politics, science, religion, art, etc. [Engels 1883:16]." This assumes that because food is necessary for biological survival, it must be socially valued more than goods not necessary for biological survival. But such is frequently not the case. The social importance attached to a good or service (such as kula armbands) may have little to do with its need for physical survival. Indeed, an outstanding characteristic of primitive prestige economy is the all-abiding concern for goods necessary, so to speak, for *social* survival, social position, social power.

Surplus, when analytically so used, serves as the basis for an empirically unwarranted exploitation theory: if only the material goods necessary for biological survival are important, it follows that the services of priests and political heads are, by definition, of lesser importance. The question then is raised, How does the rank and file become seduced into accepting this scheme of things in which they surrender material goods (by definition) of primary importance, to receive back (by definition) only less important services?

> . . . the almost universal inequities which seem to mark the distribution of surplus economic goods is striking. This surplus wealth, it is apparent, goes to two groups, those who govern, and those who command techniques for placating and manipulating the supernatural forces of the universe. The members of these groups are, therefore, to be regarded as belonging to a leisure class in that they, like their families and their retainers, profit from the social leisure which this economic surplus represents. They are . . . members of a leisure class . . . only in the sense that the goods they deal in consist of intangibles whose production does not require the exercise of the manual labor their less privileged fellows give to the production of the essentials to life they produce. . . . Having attempted to sketch the conditions

which make for the production of an economic surplus and the social leisure it represents, two further points must be considered. The first concerns the manner in which non-producers of subsistence goods obtain the support of their fellows and entails a description and analysis of the devices employed to ensure them command of the surplus they must have in order to live and function. The second point bears on the measures taken by those who benefit from the economic surplus to ensure that those who do not so benefit remain content with their lot [Herskovits 1952:414].[3]

Surely it is the definitions and values of the analyst, not those of the society being analyzed, which make the posed questions seem important.[4]

3. Not only is it true that surplus as a definitional identity is incapable of empirical proof or refutation, but when surplus is equated with the presence of non-food producers, the term loses empirical selectivity because it is a rare society which does not have non-food producers. What may be an empirically unimportant uniformity among societies (the presence of non-food producers) is elevated to a position of theoretical primacy.

4. In its analytical use as an ex post facto rational construct to explain social change, surplus implies a one-way causational sequence: material surpluses somehow arise which then induce (or make possible) more complex social organization. But the reverse could also be the case: a change in social organization inducing an increase in output, or a rearrangement of its uses so that (even without any growth in output total) one group gets more, or more of one particular good gets produced. The Incas' (or the Normans') imposing of tribute payments on conquered peoples is one example.

Surplus in a Market-Organized Economy

In an economy in which the participants derive most of their livelihood from market sales—both the sale of "factor inputs," such as labor or the use of land, and commodity outputs (finished goods and services), as do profit-receiving entrepreneurs—the term "surplus" commonly has been used in three different meanings.

In Marx's formal analysis of industrialized market capitalism, surplus value was a definitional identity expressed in terms of money price: the difference between the money labor cost of producing a commodity and its final sales price. In the aggregate, it was the sum of all market-derived non-labor incomes: rent, profit, and interest. The material output equivalent of aggregate surplus value consisted of all the consumer goods purchased by non-laboring classes, plus additions to capital equipment purchased by entrepreneurs. For our purposes it is sufficient to point out that Marx's definition, like that implicitly used by Childe and Herskovits, is not empirically derived. It proves or disproves nothing; it merely defines from the point of view of the definer, not from the point of view of the social participants. The same chain of deduction underlies Marxian surplus: only labor can produce value, if the laborer receives less value (market-determined wage) than he produces (product price on the market), we will call the money differential "surplus value."

Another analytical use of a surplus concept in market economy appears in formal economic theory derived from Ricardo. Here the concept relies on the important distinction between resources used in production which are variable in marketable supply and those which are inelastic—temporarily or permanently fixed in quantity and therefore unresponsive in supply to price changes. In the case of a fixed factor supply, a Ricardian "rent" arises which is regarded by economists as "surplus" in a special sense: it is a payment made for the use of something (say, land) which, if not made, would not reduce the quantity forthcoming. Pure economic rent is different from other factor payments in that it is not a necessary "supply price." The same quantity would be supplied even at a lower market price. That there is a price at all is due to competitive demand for something relatively scarce. In the same sense, the price of a Rembrandt painting is a "surplus" or economic rent, the exact amount of which is determined by competitive demand. The quantity of Rembrandt paintings is fixed; if the price fell, the quantity would remain unchanged. Ricardo first developed the concept in regard to land, but later market theorists have shown that land is just one of a family of such cases of fixed factor supply. As a contrast with the previously discussed concepts of surplus as an analytical device, the Ricardian rent concept is illustrative. Because it is grounded in empirical fact—the actual and recognized conditions of factor supply in a market-organized economy—it is an analytical device with direct application to empirical processes, problems, and policies.[5]

A third meaning of surplus in a market-organized economy is that associated with the farm commodities bought by the U.S. government in its price-support program. Here the meaning of surplus is both empirical and unambiguous, but significantly different from our previously considered meanings. Surplus consists of that amount of any commodity which, during a given period of time, cannot be sold on the market at some specified (parity support) price. The characteristics of such surpluses are worth describing.

1. The surplus exists because of very special institutional rules. If the rules were changed so as to remove parity support prices, the surpluses would disappear as uncontrolled market price fell to that level at which the entire quantities forthcoming could be sold. Alternatively, if the rules were changed so that much less was produced, the surpluses would disappear because the uncontrolled market price would rise to that level at which the quantities forthcoming could be sold at parity price on the private market (that is, without the government's buying any).

2. The surplus is socially recognized as being in excess—an amount over and above what is regarded as desirable.

3. A unique aspect of market-determined surplus stems from the fact that whether or not a surplus exists depends entirely on institutional criteria (market prices), rather than on a physical increase in absolute quantities of produce. The special result follows that in market economy it is possible to have surpluses even if the total quantity produced this season is less than it was last season. If market price falls below parity price for any reason (such as a shrinkage in demand), there is a recognized surplus, no matter how the total quantity this season compares to that of last season.

Summary

In general, there are two basic meanings that can be attached to economic surplus. In an empirical sense it can refer to some specified portion of material output which is recognized as being in some way different from the socially defined norm. The importance of such experienced surpluses can be very different. What difference, if any, the surplus makes depends on how it came into being and the special institutional apparatus and values of the society experiencing it. With regard to the meaning and usage of surplus as empirical fact, three points especially should be underscored if ambiguity is to be avoided: in each context it should be made clear whether the term is meant to describe an experienced increase in total output of usual material goods, an increase in one component of usual goods while the total has declined, an increase acquired by one social group out of an unchanged total, or the production of a new type of good qualitatively different from the old. Second, if it is believed that for some specific society experienced surpluses have been important, it is necessary to establish how the surpluses arose. Deliberately contrived surpluses can be created by social policy (such as taxation) as well as by technological innovation. Finally, only in a market-organized economy is it clear that empirical surpluses are recognized as being functionless and superfluous, surpluses being institutionally defined in market terms as those quantities of commodities which cannot be sold at some specified price.

The second general meaning of surplus derives from non-empirical definitions and is employed analytically. In two of the cases cited, surplus was defined as material goods acquired by non-food producers (Childe and Herskovits) and as the money differential between labor cost and product price, or, what is the same thing, the incomes and outputs acquired by non-wage-receivers in a market economy (Marx). Such usage is not empirical in the sense that the social participants do not recognize the defined surpluses as being apart from non-surplus outputs (or incomes). It is important to realize that surpluses so defined are rational constructs, which —in themselves—do not prove or disprove anything concerning the role or importance of the defined surplus in the process of institutional change or in accounting for social stratification in real-world societies. To build an elaborate superstructure on definitional foundations, as is sometimes done in evolution theory, entails oversimplification and unwarranted certainty about complex processes. Indeed, such theorizing contains a methodological act of faith in the relevance of definitional categories to real-world structures, which is unseemly in the social sciences, and, at the least, should not remain implicit.

ECONOMIC SURPLUS, ONCE AGAIN

"A Note of Clarification on Economic Surplus" pointed out how misleading it is to use the concept of economic surplus uncritically, especially as a causal mechanism to explain social change. Looking back at the Inca or some smaller stratified society (say, Malinowski's Trobriands), one sees rulers, priests, and other non-food producers. One does not know how they got there, but one does know that they eat food (and acquire other goods and services) that they do not themselves produce. When the tantalizing question is raised—"How did they get to be priests and rulers?"—it is sometimes answered by saying a food surplus must have arisen; because if no food surplus arose in the pre-stratified society, the potential priests and rulers would have had to produce food for themselves and hence could not become priests and rulers.

To attribute the existence of non-food producers to a food surplus—in the sense that a growth in food supply actively caused the priests and rulers to arise—is, to put it bluntly, silly. Without evidence, all one can assert for sure is a tautology based on the unesoteric fact that all men must eat: for non-food producers to exist in any society, there must be food producers who produce more than they themselves eat; and somehow, those persons who do not themselves produce food must get hold of the food they eat from the producers. One knows this from looking at an *already* stratified society. How it got this way may have nothing to do with a growth in the food supply. One cannot explain the *transformation sequence* to stratification by·knowing one of the functional characteristics of an already stratified society.

I should like to add two examples to give additional force to the ones given earlier.

I

In an otherwise brilliant paper, the author describes three historical stages of Asian civilization and says the following:

Around the irrigated rice fields of the second stage were formed stable communities, and a surplus of food *was possible*—where land and water are plentiful *today* a family using the simplest tools can grow three times as much food as it eats. On such a surplus have been *based* all the royal courts and armies, the art and philosophy and meditative religion of the East. Tax collectors and invading armies collected all they could of the food surplus. A hundred generations of holy men have begged for their share [Keyfitz 1959:35, italics added].[6]

I call attention to the word "based" in the quote, which links the food surplus to the existence of non-food producers in some unspecified way. (1) Either that means that the rulers, armies, priests, and other non-food producers were caused by surplus food (they came into being in direct response to a growth in the food supply above the needs of food producers); (2) or it means something very much more modest and less important: if Asian farmers could not have produced more food than they themselves ate, all Asians would have to produce food for themselves, and so full time priests and rulers could not have come into existence *for whatever reasons they did come into existence*. If the quote means the latter—simply that non-food producers depend on food producers for food in an already stratified society—why emphasize such an obvious point that priests and rulers have to eat? Why use the question-begging term "based"? And why not go on to consider what specific forces may have brought the roles of priests and rulers into existence, once there was food available for them to eat? If the quote means the former—that the priests and rulers came into being in direct consequence of the food surplus—then, I suggest, it is either very improbable, or it is an assertion incapable of proof. To show why, I shall paraphrase the quote above to make it strictly applicable to another society that has many non-food producers:

Around the fertile, irrigated, and technologically efficient farms of California, Iowa, Nebraska, and other states, were formed stable communities, and a surplus of food *was possible*—where land, water, tractors, land-grant colleges, bank credit, and hybrid seeds are plentiful *today,* a family using rather complicated tools can grow on the average more than twelve times as much food as it eats. On such a surplus have been *based* the federal and state courts, the presidency and both Houses of Congress, the Army, Navy, Marines, Air Force, and Space Agencies, the Greenwich Village and Provincetown Art Colonies, J. D. Salinger and Mickey Spillane, the Metropolitan Opera Company, the hundreds of universities and colleges, the thousands of professors, and the millions of students throughout the United States. Federal, state, and local tax collectors collected all they could of this food surplus (and automobile surplus, and submarine surplus)—indeed, in 1962, all the tax gatherers together (federal, state, and local) collected from the producers of surplus around 30 percent of everything produced. Generations of churchmen—Protestant, Catholic, and Jewish—have received their share.

For the United States, obviously, the notion of surplus becomes silly if it is meant as a direct cause of something, as a generative factor in creating the roles of non-food producers in the Army, Navy, the Metropolitan Opera Company, and all the rest "based" on the surplus.[7] Again, all surplus means here is that in an already stratified (specialized) society, some people must produce more food (or typewriters, or whiskey) than they use if there are to be non-food (and non-whiskey) producers who consume what they do not produce. It does not tell us how the non-food producers came into existence, why these and not others, or the special institutional arrangements which channel food to the non-food producers—that is, what kind of economic system exists.

It also becomes clear from applying the surplus notion to the United States that the complicated and lengthy sequence of change is glossed over: we start with the simple idea that more food *can be* produced than the producers eat and then jump to the present scene of a vast army of heterogeneous specialists who do not produce their own food. So, too, with the Asian sequence, which postulates the possibility of surplus food, from which are then deduced rulers, armies, art, philosophy, and religion. All the interesting questions remain unanswered: Is it certain a non-surplus situation (or a non-stratified situation) ever existed in fact? How about situations in which all produce food part-time, but some nevertheless are craftsmen, priests, or rulers? Which came first, the philosophy or the food? What determines which kinds of non-food producers come into existence? What causes surpluses? Are there societies in which food abundance exists, but not highly developed art, religion, and all the rest? Are there societies at relatively low consumption levels which nevertheless support non-food producers? What are the economic arrangements between food and non-food producers; do the food producers get services or goods in return? Those who think the concept of economic surplus important must show why it should have any more of a causal role for the Asian, Inca, or Trobriand non-food producers and institutional changes than it has for those of the United States.[8]

Moreover, one could easily reword my paraphrasing to make it apply to the Soviet Union, England, Japan, or the Dominican Republic. All produce surpluses by definition because all have non-food producers; but each has some markedly different economic and social institutions and some different kinds of non-food producers. Looking at a stratified society in being, one can say irrefutably that a necessary condition for non-food producers to exist in that society is that there be food producers who consume less than they produce. But it is not a very helpful statement in explaining how the non-food producers came to be. It belongs to that superficial level of causation which makes it true but trivial to know that all people die *because* their hearts stop beating, or that an automobile accident occurs *be-*

cause two cars occupy the same space simultaneously. It is a definition, not an explanation. Just so, surplus as a cause of something does not tell us how the surplus was caused, whether it preceded or followed the institutional change it is supposed to explain; and if the surplus created non-food producers, why priests in one case, artists in another, jet pilots in a third —and, in fact, all the experienced roles and events (Pearson 1957) which have been attributed to material surpluses?

In a word, in *some* circumstances a growth in food supply may be a necessary condition for social change to come about; *it is never a sufficient condition.* In *other* circumstances, as we are learning from economic development in Third World areas, just the opposite may be the case: social change may be a necessary condition for allowing an increase in the food supply to take place.[9]

II

Surplus is used in another way which deserves comment. It is sometimes used to mean that minor part of the produce of a subsistence farmer which he sells off in a local market. If four-fifths of a yam crop is consumed by the producer's family and he sells off the other fifth at market, it is not uncommon for anthropologists to identify the one-fifth sold as the yam surplus, without going on to say what they mean by surplus other than some amount sold.

The objection to calling surplus any amount which is sold is that the term implies the quantity sold was over and above what was needed, and so was sold off as a way of getting rid of it (as the U. S. government sells off its surplus rifles). It would never occur to anyone to label as surplus the 99 percent of the Iowa wheat farmer's crop that he sells, because what he sells obviously is not some amount left over after satisfying his family's need for bread. Rather, it is earmarked prenatally for sale. Here lies the difficulty in using the surplus label in the primitive situation. By calling surplus *anything* the subsistence farmer sells, the analytical point is left unanswered: Was it sold as an afterthought, because household needs were first filled, and the amount left over was simply available to be disposed of at market? Or was that portion sold deliberately produced for sale, whether the household was sated with the stuff or not?

The point is not lacking in empirical interest because a very common change in developing areas is just such a transition from subsistence production (meaning most gets eaten by the producer's family, or given away to kin, friends, or rulers rather than sold) to production for market or exchange—meaning most gets sold (Bohannan 1959:501; Gulliver 1962). To label both kinds of market sales as surplus does not tell us which of two very different situations is being described.

III

It may be of interest to point out that the same hypothetical assumption underlies the two usages of surplus described in this essay. By hypothetical is meant an assumption about an unobserved society whose existence is not known but postulated.

Surplus as the growth in food supply which explains the coming into being of priests, rulers, and other non-food producers in a stratified society known to exist (but whose origins are unknown) postulates an *unobserved,* prestratified stage of that society in which *all were food producers* (because, it is assumed, there were no priests, rulers, and the like before the surplus arose). The sequence of situations *assumed* is: (1) no surplus, all are food producers; (2) surplus arises; (3) it goes to priests and rulers. Note that only the last stage is known to exist; the first two are extrapolations backward to an unobserved past which is *deduced* from the last stage, the stratified society known to exist historically.

Surplus as that portion of the subsistence producer's output which is sold at market postulates an *unobserved* earlier condition when that producer was thought to consume *all he produced* and had no surplus for sale. The sequence of situations *assumed* is: (1) no surplus, all produce is consumed by the producer and his dependents; (2) surplus arises; (3) it is sold off at market. In some, but not all, cases where surplus is used in this meaning, the observer only observes the last stage, the first two being extrapolations backward to an unobserved past *deduced* from the last stage, the one in which market sales are known to exist.

Without, perhaps, fully realizing it, anthropologists use the presurplus, unobserved situation in which all are assumed to be food producers in exactly the same way that economists use Robinson Crusoe: to postulate special conditions in a hypothetical situation in order to make analytical points about a real-world situation known to exist. The anthropologist, however, is concerned with the emergence of the known society from the hypothetical one; the economist is not.

It seems fair to say also that the economist knows that Robinson Crusoe and his island never existed and is aware that he uses Robinson Crusoe, not because of any interest in the economics of desert islands, but to create a simple hypothetical example to make points of interest about real-world situations of complexity. It is not clear whether or not the anthropologist is aware that *his* Robinson Crusoe—hypothetical societies in which all were food producers—perhaps never actually existed.

NOTES

1. I am grateful to Karl Polanyi of Columbia and to Paul Bohannan of Northwestern for their very helpful suggestions and comments.

2. If material goods were measured by their effectiveness in fulfilling a specific purpose, we could then indicate which of two qualitatively different bundles of goods was larger. For example, if a bushel of rice contained three times the calories of a bushel of wheat, we could say that for food subsistence the bushel of rice was greater than the bushel of wheat.

3. A similar orientation is reflected in Harris (1959:198): "The decisive question now becomes: what force or incentive makes the food producers surrender a portion of their necessary food supply in order to support a class of non-food producers."

4. Herskovits himself points out that the attitudes of those who contribute to the material support of rulers and priests is far from that of hostility due to any feeling of exploitation: "It cannot be maintained on the basis of our existing knowledge that from either a psychological or an ethnological point of view, attitudes of blame are held by those who contribute to the support of their superiors. Rather we find far more frequently a lively pride in display, a drive toward emulation, a joy in following sanctioned leadership, and pleasure derived from the fact that adequate direction is being given political or religious matters by those whose competence is based on the divine order, or inherited position, or special training [1952:482, 483]."

5. It was the theoretical basis for Henry George's policy of the single tax. The "surplus" (economic rent) could be taxed without reducing the quantity of land. Another application was in rent-control policy during and after World War II. Housing already in existence is in fixed supply. Rental rates on such housing can be reduced (or prevented from rising) by law, without diminishing the quantity.

6. For extensive bibliographical references to the use of surplus as causal mechanism, see Pearson (1957) and Harris (1959).

7. In the United States, a food surplus (that is, non-food producers) existed, say, in 1912 as well as in 1962. Is one to attribute—in some causal sense—the institutional changes between 1912 and 1962, and the coming into being of new kinds of non-food producers (space vehicle drivers), to more food? Only, it seems, in the sense that space vehicle drivers also have to eat.

8. What meaning for the United States can be attributed to the following generalization: "But wherever we find a non-food producing elite [read President Kennedy, the United States Senate, J. D. Salinger] we may assume that they exist by virtue of their ability to control food supplies [Harris 1959:198]." Why not say the non-food producers exist because they perform political, religious, or artistic services regarded as valuable by the food producers?

9. Sekou Touré's government in Guinea has declared every seventh day a day of voluntary labor (work without pay) to create village public works, including extra farm work to increase food output. Here, the antecedent social changes—political independence, the drive for economic development, the official adoption of a socialist ethic—have preceded the increase in food supply. Moreover, as Rostow (1960) makes abundantly clear, a growth in output may have a wide variety of social, economic, and technological causes and a wide range of consequences. For a revealing case of a primitive social structure which inhibits economic growth, see Douglas (1962).

REFERENCES

BOHANNAN, PAUL
  1959   The impact of money on an African subsistence economy. *Journal of Economic History* 19:491–503.
DALTON, GEORGE
  1960   A note of clarification on economic surplus. *American Anthropologist* 62:483–490.
DOUGLAS, MARY
  1962   Lele economy compared with the Bushong: a study of economic backwardness. In *Markets in Africa,* Paul Bohannan and George Dalton ed. Evanston: Northwestern University Press.
ENGELS, FRIEDRICH
  1883   Speech at the graveside of Karl Marx. In *Karl Marx selected works,* V. Adoratsky ed. Moscow: Co-operative Publishing Society of Foreign Workers in the USSR.
GULLIVER, P. H.
  1962   The evolution of Arusha trade. In *Markets in Africa,* Paul Bohannan and George Dalton ed. Evanston: Northwestern University Press.
HARRIS, MARVIN
  1959   The economy has no surplus? *American Anthropologist* 61:185–199.
HERSKOVITS, M. J.
  1952   Economic anthropology, revised ed. New York: Knopf.
KEYFITZ, NATHAN
  1959   The interlocking of social and economic factors in Asian development. *Canadian Journal of Economics and Political Science* 25:34–46.
KLUCKHOHN, CLYDE
  1949   Mirror for man. New York: Whittlesey House.
KNIGHT, F. H.
  1941   Anthropology and economics. *Journal of Political Economy* 49:247–268.
PEARSON, HARRY W.
  1957   The economy has no surplus: critique of a theory of development. In *Trade and market in the early empires,* K. Polanyi, C. M. Arensberg, H. W. Pearson ed. Glencoe: The Free Press.
ROSTOW, W. W.
  1960   The stages of economic growth. Cambridge: Cambridge University Press.

9

Peasantries in Anthropology and History[1]

> . . . literature on peasant communities is not, at the moment, a very likely place to look for ideas, and certainly not for systems of ideas [Geertz 1962:18].

> Perhaps the single most challenging problem in peasant studies is still the conceptualization of the relationship of the villages to larger civilizational wholes [Anderson 1963:196].

> . . . I would like to make a plea for a careful typology of peasant economies [Ortiz 1967:197].

This essay originated in an attempt to solve several problems in the anthropological literature of peasantry. One is the problem of specifying a distinctive set of economic characteristics that would clearly mark off peasant from tribal economies. Another is the problem of accounting for the extraordinary range of variation among peasantries, what Clifford Geertz quite rightly calls the need for a systematic understanding of the complexities of peasantry. A third is the problem of resolving contentious issues such as "Are African cultivators to be called 'Peasants'? (Fallers 1961)"; contentious issues are always symptoms that some sort of conceptual difficulty exists.

This paper tries to solve the problems and explain the complexities by using a combination of historical, economic, and anthropological analysis. To understand the similarities and differences among peasantries currently studied by anthropologists in Latin America, the Caribbean, Asia, and the Middle East, it is useful to make very specific comparisons between their

Reprinted, with revision, from "Peasantries in Anthropology and History," *Current Anthropology* (forthcoming, 1971). Reprinted by permission of the publisher.

institutions and those of tribal communities before and after modernizing activities began, as well as those institutions prevailing in three sequential stages of West European peasantry: village communities and the larger cultures and societies of which they were a part before the modernization and industrialization of Western Europe (approximately 800–1300); the early centuries of modernization and industrialization (approximately 1300–1900); and late European development, during which the agricultural sector of national economies shrank, and many of the remaining farmers became "post-peasants" (approximately 1900 to the present, but especially since the end of World War II).

Such elaborate bases of comparison are necessary because any peasant village community studied by an anthropologist today is in a developing, independent nation—India, Peru—and is composed of some sort of special mixture of traditional and modern institutions and technology. Either it is a "hybrid" peasantry combining primitive and some type(s) of peasant institutions and technology (as in Latin America), or it is a "composite" peasantry combining institutions (and technology) equivalent to those found in two, or all three, stages of West European peasantry (feudal, early modern, late modern).

Peasantries: Complexity and Diversity

Even without the special difficulties that inhere in the study of peasantries, anthropology is an unusually complicated subject. Its universe comprises millions of small communities. India alone has half a million villages, and China (in 1949), a million. The rest of Asia, Africa, Latin America, the Middle East, and Oceania must contain at least another million. Anthropologists are interested in these millions of small communities as they were organized in all historical situations about which there is information. For those that were colonized, we can mark off the historical periods roughly as before colonization (aboriginal or traditional society), the period of European (or American) colonization, and post-colonial which, except for Latin America, is barely one generation old. Already the diversity is enormous. But there is much more.

Anthropologists are interested in all the principal activities, relationships, and institutions in these millions of small communities, past and present. They do the work of historians, political scientists, economists, psychologists, specialists in linguistics, law, religion—and, these days (see Vayda 1969)—they also study agronomy, technology, medicine, and ecology, to give an incomplete listing. Anthropologists, moreover, are interested in the attributes of persons, of village communities, and of the larger cultures and societies of which the persons and villages may be part.

Anthropologists must also have some expert knowledge about the counterpart activities, institutions, and relationships in their own European or

American society to those they study in the field. Because they must write about Tiv or Trobriands economy in their own European language, they must know precisely what meanings their readers will attach to the English or French words they use. This is particularly important in their usage of technical terms such as "capital," "market," or "money" (therefore, anthropologists must know how economists use words, as well). Finally, anthropologists studying African or Asian communities must know about American capitalism or European Christianity because they continually compare and contrast what they study in the field with their own society's economy or religion.

This preamble about anthropology in general was necessary because the subject of this essay, peasantries, contains all the diversity and complexity characteristic of anthropological inquiry in general and some special difficulties of its own. It is the extraordinary diversity among peasantries that makes necessary the special classifications and distinctions this essay will use.[2]

Once we point out that the large number of past and present peasantries comprise sets of characteristics with European types providing some sort of reference group, the existence of conceptual difficulties in the anthropological literature is not surprising, especially when we add one further complicating feature. Their existence over long periods of time in many parts of the world means that peasantries have experienced internal and external shocks such as war, revolution, famine, plague, emigration, colonization, and religious conversion. Yet we use the same designation— peasantry—before and after watershed changes. The French and Russian revolutions, the Irish famine, did change French, Russian, and Irish peasantries, and European industrialization affected them all.

The term "peasant," moreover, is sometimes used very loosely. It is being substituted for "primitive" and "tribal," which convey crudity and barbarity in English. Peasant is a less offensive term, apparently, and so it is sometimes used euphemistically to designate *all* the non-Western rural peoples or communities studied by anthropologists, without any specific social or economic institutions meant by the term: [3] "A trend to broaden the frame of reference by changing the classification of many from tribal to peasant is perceptible [Anderson 1963:178]."

A second way in which tribal and peasant are merged is by equating peasant with agriculturalist who produces some (unspecified) proportion of his own food (subsistence) requirements: "By a peasant economy one means a system of small-scale producers, with a simple technology and equipment often relying primarily for their subsistence on what they themselves produce. The primary means of livelihood of the peasant is cultivation of the soil [Firth 1951:87]."

By defining peasant in this simple fashion, the agriculturalists of New Guinea (Malinowski 1935) and Africa (Bohannan and Bohannan 1968) are merged with those of India (Epstein 1962) and Latin America (Holm-berg *et al.* 1965); the definition fits them all.

Redfield's and Kroeber's characterization of peasantries, adopted by the anthropologists who followed them, did not mark off peasant economy as a distinct type in contrast to tribal or primitive economy. They differentiated peasant from tribal in showing that peasant communities were parts of larger societies or civilizations: world religion (Christianity, Islam), in con-trast to the particularistic animisms and ancestor cults of tribal peoples; the presence of literacy in the larger culture; widely shared language in contrast to local languages; and that rank-and-file villagers are under the jurisdiction of superior political authority located outside the village (as in state systems), or political superiors who are not peasants (for example, feudal lords).

The anthropological literature marks off peasant from tribal by the characteristics of religion, language, and government, but not economy: re-liance on agriculture, the presence of markets, the use of some form of money, simple technology, a combination of production for self-use (sub-sistence production) together with production for sale, low output, a nar-row range of items produced, extreme ecological dependence (that is, the inability to control the vagaries of weather, plant disease, insects, and so on), the importance of family labor and the family as a production unit—all these characterize *some range* of tribal as well as *some range* of peasant economies.[4]

At the outset, then, we see how difficult it is to generalize about peas-antries, given the very many real differences among them and the absence of distinctive economic criteria marking off peasant from primitive. Yet the anthropological literature continually stresses what is true for some ideal type of peasantry-in-general, regardless of time, place, and specific institutions. This, we shall see, is the reason for the paucity of theoretical insights about peasantry the quotations heading this essay complain of.

EUROPEAN PEASANTRIES

I must explain why a systematic formulation of sequential types of Eu-ropean peasantry provides a useful base of comparison with Third World peasantries studied by anthropologists.

There is a rich literature because European social and economic history are old subjects and because some first-rate minds—Rostovsteff, Bloch, Pirenne, Maitland—have written analytically on European peasantries. But what makes this literature of special value to the anthropological study of peasantries is its depth, the long stretches of time it covers. Anthropol-ogy is a recent subject compared to history, and fieldwork studies of peas-antry more recent still (Geertz 1962); most have been done only within the last thirty years late in the colonial periods of the people studied (as in

India), when the forces of economic development and cultural modernization were already distinctly present (Firth and Yamey 1966). Anthropological field work is a microscope focused on a small community for a year or two. History is a telescope through which one can view the village and the larger society of which it is part over centuries (Hoskins 1957). Both are necessary to see peasantries properly.

For Europe we can study peasants from serfs to post-peasants, from the ninth to the twentieth centuries: [5] before and after the mercantilistic expansion of foreign trade accompanying the discovery and colonization of North and South America; before and after the French Revolution, industrialization, massive urbanization, widespread literacy, the formation of modern nation-states, and, indeed, welfare and communist states. The historical literature for Europe, moreover, includes peasant villages as well as the larger societies and non-peasant sectors for each of the three periods that interest us—before modernization, early, and then late modernization. For Europe we can see *how peasant villagers changed in relation to nonpeasants in each stage of modernization.* [6]

In short, we can analyze European peasantries in a way that we cannot yet do for any other (except for those in Japan): trace their changes from the traditional system of the Middle Ages, through early and then late modernization. In so doing we can determine which few of a larger set of defining characteristics are really central to peasantry by seeing what in fact changes and does not change over time, and then to what extent their counterparts change or do not change in non-European peasantries studied by anthropologists (Table 9–1).

Table 9–1 *Western Europe* [7]

Traditional Peasantries *(approx. 800–1300)*	*Early Modernization* *(approx. 1300–1900)*	*Late Modernization* *(post-peasant; approx.* *1900–present)*
Before Industrialization	By 1900:	By 1970:
> ¾ of population agricul.	Early Industrialization	Highly Industrialized
Weak Monarch / Feudalism	< half pop. agricultural	< ¼ of pop. agricul.
Petty rural / urban markets	Nation-State	Welfare State
Petty labor and land markets	Produce markets dominant	Integrated Nat'l. Resource
Subsistence / cash production	Factor markets dominant	Markets
Before mass literacy and ed.	Cash / subsistence prod.	Integrated Nat'l. Produce
Servile peasantry	> half population lit.	Markets
Dependent land tenure	Legally free peasantry	Cash production
Little urbanization	Market land tenure	Universal literacy and ed.
	dominant	Citizen-farmers
	Cities grow	Market land tenure
		Most of pop. is urban

Finally, we must distinguish between shared culture—what peasant villagers shared with non-peasants—and the specific kinds of material and political transactions and social relationships between peasants and their contemporary non-peasants in each of the three historical situations. These distinctions point up what I think is an essential characteristic of *peasant transformations:* in moving from traditional peasantry to early and then late modernization, the simple fact of shared culture between peasants and non-peasants (language, religion) remains intact,[8] but specific *transactions* and *social relationships* between peasant and non-peasant change utterly.

Table 9–2   *Distinctions between Peasants and*
                 Non-peasants in Traditional Peasantry,
                 Early Modernization, and
                 Late Modernization

Culture shared by peasants and non-peasants (Redfield-Kroeber)
Material transactions between peasants and non-peasants
Cultural and political transactions between peasants and non-peasants
Social relationships between peasants and non-peasants

For each kind of peasantry we now consider the structured modes of interaction between the peasant and the non-peasants in his universe. Peasants and their village communities remain identifiable as distinct entities as long as significant aspects of local village organization, activities, and peasant rights and obligations remain different from those of urban and elite persons within the same contemporary larger society, culture, and economy. When this is no longer so, peasants have become post-peasant citizen-farmers, different from their fellow citizens only in their agricultural mode of livelihood and rural residence (Table 9–2).

Medieval European Peasantries: Transactions and Social Relationships with Non-Peasants

We can explain at once why Redfield and Kroeber did not assign a distinctive set of economic characteristics to peasantries–in–general and why Firth's simple definition of peasant economy would include the Tiv and Trobrianders as well as village India: allocation of land, organization of work, and the disposition of ordinary produce in traditional (medieval) European peasantries differ only slightly from traditional (pre-colonial) primitive or tribal economies in Africa and Oceania (Table 9–3).

The principal economic difference between traditional peasant and tribal village economy in ordinary production of subsistence goods was in the *form* of dependent land tenure. This is a matter of importance.

Traditional band, tribal, and peasant economies share several negative characteristics (when contrasted with developed, industrial capitalism), two

Table 9–3 *Medieval European Village Economy (under Feudalism, 800–1300)*

Organization	*Performance*
1. Dependent land tenure feudalism: master-client	1. Narrow range of goods produced; bread grains as staple crops
2. Subsistence production dominant; cash and markets, petty; sales primarily in local markets	2. Low per capita real income
3. Absence of integrative land, labor, and produce markets	3. Threat of sporadic famine (material insecurity)
4. Primitive technology; ecological dependence	

of which are of immediate concern to us: the absence of industrial technology and applied science in production processes, and the absence of dominant, integrative networks of markets for land, labor, and produce. Markets and cash transactions most certainly existed in traditional European peasant (and some tribal) economies. But where they existed, as, for example, in towns and cities, they were most frequently controlled markets for small amounts of produce (foodstuffs); even less frequently were labor and land transacted by commercial purchase and sale.[9]

By dependent land tenure we mean non-market land tenure: land usage is acquired through social relationships—lineage affiliation, master-client relationships—that is, by means other than purchase or rental. The Tiv (Bohannan 1960; Bohannan and Bohannan 1968) and the Bantu, as well as medieval Europe, institutionalized forms of dependent land tenure:

> Every [Bantu] household-head has an exclusive right to land for building his home and for cultivation. Generally he can take up such land for himself within the area controlled by his sub-chief or headman, provided that he does not encroach upon land already occupied or cultivated by others. Failing this, it is the duty of his headman to provide him gratuitously with as much land as he needs. . . . He also has the right, subject to the approval of his headman, to give away part of it to a relative or friend, or to lend it to someone else. But he can never sell it or dispose of it in any other way in return for material considerations. Should he finally abandon the spot, his land reverts to the tribe as a whole and can subsequently be assigned to someone else. The only other way he can lose his right to the land is by confiscation, if he is found guilty of some serious crime [Schapera and Goodwin 1937:157; see also Sadie 1960:297].

We are told what sorts of obligatory payments are made to headmen by Bantu household-heads having such rights to land.

By virtue of his official status as head of the tribe he also played an important part in the economic organization. . . . He received tribute from his people, both in kind and in labor. He was given a portion of every animal slaughtered or killed in the chase; the *lobola* [bridewealth] for his chief wife was paid by the members of his tribe; he had the right to call upon his subjects to perform certain tasks for him, such as building his huts or clearing the land for his wives' gardens; above all, he received fees for hearing cases and fines for misdemeanors, and, in cases of homicide the culprit paid compensation not to the relatives of the deceased but to him [Schapera 1928:175].

Traditional Bantu shared with medieval European peasants two crucial characteristics of livelihood and land tenure: neither had alternative means of procuring livelihood for themselves other than the agricultural or pastoral production undertaken in their local communities; and neither could acquire the use of land with which to produce their subsistence needs in ways other than through social relationships with their socio-political superiors, who were the stewards of land allocation. Both lived in systems of dependent land tenure, the exact forms of which (the man-man relationship, and the man-land relationship, in Bohannan's phrase) differed; but both were non-market modes of acquisition, and both entailed the employment of a diffuse socio-economic relationship with social superiors as the mode of land acquisition, requiring return payments of material goods, labor, and socio-political services and clientage (such as military service and labor for road-building).

In short, medieval European peasants acquired the use of land through that variant of a patron-client relationship conventionally called feudal, which, in its classic form, appeared in Europe between the ninth and twelfth centuries.[10] In admirably succinct language, Bloch summarized the nature of the feudal patron-client relationship based on dependent land tenure and the absence of commercial and industrial alternatives to subsistence agriculture:

In the absence then of a strong state, of blood ties capable of dominating the whole life and of an economic system founded upon money payments there grew up in Carolingian and post-Carolingian society relations of man to man of a peculiar type. The superior individual granted his protection and divers material advantages that assured a subsistence to the dependent directly or indirectly; the inferior pledged various pretestations [obligatory payments] or various services and was under a general obligation to render aid [Bloch 1933:203].[11]

In medieval European society, the principal transactions between peasant and non-peasant were these:

PEASANT PAYMENTS TO FEUDAL LORD
annual specified material payments in produce and/or cash for use of
    land
annual specified labor services to work the lord's land and herds
annual specified obligation to attend lord's law court
contingency labor services such as boon days to harvest lord's crop
contingency non-economic duties such as military service under lord
contingency levies (special tax) such as tallage at will (for instance, to
    ransom lord captured during war)
obligatory payments to lord for use of lord's mill, fishpond, and so on
contingency payments such as fines and death duties

FEUDAL LORD'S SERVICES AND PAYMENTS TO PEASANTS [12]
granting peasant right to use land for his subsistence crops
military protection (for example, against invaders)
police protection (for example, against robbery)
juridical services to settle disputes
feasts to peasants at Christmas, Easter; also harvest gifts
food given to peasants on days when they work the lord's demesne

PEASANT PAYMENTS TO CHURCH AND PRIESTS
obligatory tithes of produce and/or cash
death duties (mortuary payments)
fines for religious offenses

CHURCH SERVICES TO PEASANTS
sacraments at life crises—birth, communion, marriage, death
ordinary (Sunday) services of mass
church holidays as rest days
charitable gifts to the needy [13]

PEASANT MARKET TRANSACTIONS WITH TOWNSMEN
peasants sell food and raw materials for cash
peasants buy goods fabricated in town or imported

Social and Economic Relationships between Peasant and Non-peasant

Peasants were legal, political, social, and economic inferiors in medieval
Europe. The structured subordination of peasants to non-peasants was expressed in many ways, *de jure* and *de facto,* from physical constraints on
their movement to sumptuary constraints on what kinds of weapons, clothing, and adornments they could wear and use, and foods they could legally
consume.[14]

The details regarding the servile status of peasants vary enormously between regions of a country, between countries, and between centuries. There were degrees of unfreedom (Finley 1964). Pronounced social and economic stratification within the peasant village was not uncommon. In England, the peasant's obligations and rights were in rough proportion to the land he held from his lord. But even in his market dealings with townsmen the European peasant was controlled and subordinate:

> Each of the [medieval] cities had its own trade area, which it kept in monopoly, partly even in a compulsory way: The rural population of the surrounding territory was obliged to buy and sell, and to pay corresponding duries [tolls] at the market of the city to which it was "attached" [Sorokin *et al.* 1930:vol. 1, 330].

We must use words carefully to describe the salient characteristics of medieval European peasant economy. To characterize it as "capitalist" or "communist," "cooperative" or "individualistic," "rational" or "irrational," is to confuse rather than illuminate.

The peasant's economic rights were carefully specified, and varied with his status (as did his economic obligations). He had a lifelong and heritable right to land and other natural resources under the stewardship of his lord, as long as he made specified and contingent payments to his lord of produce and labor services and fulfilled social and political obligations. The more important of these was his right to arable land to grow his subsistence staple of bread grains; his right to gather wood for fuel, farm implements, and house repairs; and his right to pasture animals. In return, he paid his lord in specified amounts of labor services (provided by himself and his nuclear family), including work days to farm the lord's demesne, payments of specified amounts of his own produce, and occasionally petty amounts of cash, and by specified and contingent services of a more strictly social and political sort, expressing in diffuse fashion his subordinate-client status. The peasant got labor principally from his own nuclear family and secondarily through reciprocal work arrangements with kin, friends, and neighbors, or by hiring occasional day laborers.[15]

His range of economic choice was very narrow. Even those who were not legally bound to their lord's service had no real alternatives outside of subsistence agriculture. Occupational mobility existed only for a few, late in the period when cities grew. Strip-farming in the two- or three-field system meant that the individual peasant had no autonomy in deciding his principal bread grain crops.[16] Nor, after the harvest, could he choose to prevent animals belonging to others from grazing on the stubble of the strips he farmed.

In its organization and performance, medieval peasant subsistence economy very closely resembled tribal economy: in some areas market sales of land, labor, and produce did not exist, and in others they were infrequent and petty transactions. Only a few items were produced, food staples being overwhelmingly important. Low-grade technology (tools and knowledge of production processes) meant low productivity, sporadic hunger, and extreme ecological dependence: the technology of farming could not compensate for or control the physical environment; as almost to the present day in Africa (Allan 1965:chapter 4) and India (Epstein 1967), flood, drought, plant or animal disease, meant widely fluctuating harvests and not infrequent hunger.

Although the similarities are more striking, there were also differences between medieval village peasant economy and tribal economy, and these, too, should be carefully specified: (1) Hunting, fishing, gathering, and slash and burn (swidden) agriculture were relatively more important sources of subsistence (compared to settled agriculture) in pre-colonial band and tribal economies than in medieval European peasant economy. (2) There were cities, markets, and cash transactions in the larger society of which the peasant village was a part, although most peasants in most of Europe from 800 to 1300 did not participate in these in a quantitatively important way.[17] The presence of cash and urban markets we may regard as the legacy of Rome, surviving the centuries of upheaval accompanying the Germanic, Islamic, and Scandinavian invasions, in much diminished form. (3) In both tribal and medieval peasant economy, non-market forms of land tenure dominated; but the master-client form of dependent land tenure so inseparably a part of European feudalism is less frequently found in pre-colonial Africa, Oceania, and the Americas than other forms of dependent tenure (Bohannan 1960; Hogbin and Lawrence 1967).

For a significant proportion of medieval European peasants—impossible to quantify—their dependent-client form of land tenure was the economic expression of an inferior, servile status, expressed in all the important aspects of social existence. They were legal, political, and social inferiors as well. As the lowest class in a sharply stratified society, they were less constrained (more rights, choices, and mobility) than low castes in traditional India, but almost certainly more constrained than, say, Negroes in the United States between 1880 and 1940.

West European Peasantries: Early Modernization (approximately 1300–1900)

We conventionally date the beginnings of "modernization" for several European countries with wars, revolutions, and other such upheavals: Britain since the Black Death (1350), France since its great revolution (1789), Western Europe since the Napoleonic wars (1815), Russia since the emancipation of its serfs (1861). From the viewpoint of our concerns with peasantry, these turning points initiated or accelerated two changes: they changed the *legal* status of peasants and with it the system of land tenure, from dependent tenure to market tenure, and they began to endow the peasant with civil, legal, and political rights which eventually equaled those of non-peasants. This legal freedom, together with the expansion of agricultural production for market sale and, later, the beginnings of industrialization, gave peasants new economic alternatives as well as the legal right to pursue them; in short, economic and social mobility.

What I shall loosely call the early period of European modernization, from around 1300 to 1900, in its radical restructuring of *national* political, religious, and economic life, changed the transactions and social relationships between peasants and non-peasants that existed under feudalism. But the several aspects of life being transformed changed very unevenly. These time lags in rates of change in different dimensions of life are very important, make generalization difficult, and—I might add—are currently the case once again for the presently developing countries of the Third World. Uneven change meant that differences between peasants and non-peasants were still considerable for hundreds of years after feudalism ended. But that which distinguished European peasant from non-peasant was for the most part different in 1900 compared to 900. The fact of continued differences allows one to identify peasantries as distinct entities until quite late, and, of course, in some parts of Europe, up to the present time (Franklin 1969).

It was not until the period of late modernization—since, say, 1900, and especially since 1950—with the coming of the welfare state in Western and northern Europe, Communism in Eastern Europe, accelerated industrialization and built-in economic growth in all of Europe, that peasants and their local economies, as distinct entities systematically different from non-peasants and urban economies, changed radically. In part the change was quantitative, that is, the proportion of national populations directly engaged in farming diminished to the point that today, in all but a few West European countries, farm households comprise fewer than one-fourth of the population. But it is the qualitative changes in transactions and social relationships that concern us in the transformation from peasant to post-peasant citizen farmer.

Political Modernization

In pouring old historical wine into new anthropological bottles, I shall inevitably destroy its flavor. Historians, quite rightly, are concerned with why and how these European transformations occurred. I am not. I must simply register the changes from the viewpoint of our anthropological interests in non-European peasantries of the present day.

European peasants and their village communities were changed by the momentous transformations that it is now fashionable to call "modernization," "development," and "national integration," which the historians have long called the end of feudalism, the Renaissance, the Reformation, the rise of nationalism, and the Industrial Revolution. Peasants changed and non-peasants changed. But for centuries yet peasantries neither shrank appreciably nor transmogrified into non-peasants or post-peasants; they remained agriculturalists different from townsmen in a variety of ways. In 900 peasants were legal inferiors with dependent land tenure. In 1900 they were legally free citizens with market land tenure, most of whom were still poor, semi-literate, backward farmers, using simple technology and living in semi-isolation from national cultural and political life.

Two features of the impact of early political modernization on European peasantries stand out. First, it is changes which affect the entire nation that are the important ones changing the peasants as well. Peasants along with non-peasants became nationalized. Second, the changes in the legal and constitutional position of peasants were for centuries greater than the actual changes in peasant economic and cultural life because the national economies of Europe remained undeveloped for centuries after feudalism ended. Both points apply to Latin American and Asian peasantries today, as well. If we were to survey village peasantries of Western (and Eastern) Europe even as late as, say, 1870, we would find incredible variety and mixtures of old and new economy, technology, political, social, and cultural life—the same sorts of mixtures and variations that anthropologists now find in Asia and the Middle East because they, too, are now in their early stage of political and economic modernization (see Hunter 1969).

The early political modernization of Western Europe consisted of abolishing feudalism, disestablishing religion, establishing centralized governments with effective national jurisdiction, conferring civil rights and equality before the (national) law on all citizens (including the peasantry), and the state's initiation of new public services such as elementary education, extended nationally.

It is startling to be reminded of how long so many European peasantries remained *de facto* inferiors despite the legal freedom and civil rights conferred on them. In parts of Eastern Europe up to World War I their position resembled that of American Negroes in the South between 1880 and 1950. Poverty, lack of education, and the taint of traditional social inferiority meant little change from their feudal status and their transactions with non-peasants.[18] Even in France, the fount of continental liberty, it is estimated that one-third of the peasants were still illiterate in 1880 (Wright 1964:10). And in England, the fount of parliamentary government, property qualifications for voting were not abolished until the 1870's (when free, universal elementary education was also introduced), and women not given the vote until after World War I.

In short, early political modernization meant national political unification and legal freedom for peasants, but *de facto* inferiority because of continued poverty and *very weak participation in national political life.*

Full-blooded democracy, education and the mobility it confers, and economic development widely shared were not yet in being anywhere in Europe; effective monarchies remained in political control; illiteracy, poverty, cultural isolation, and, in some areas, physical isolation continued. But, to be a peasant in 1900 meant to be a poor and backward farmer, culturally isolated; it no longer meant a low-class servile person politically and economically dependent on his aristocratic superiors.[19]

Economic and Technological Modernization

As in the political sphere, it was nation-wide changes that transformed the economic life of peasantries. The mercantilistic creation of national markets and their expansion internationally (Heckscher 1955) meant the ever-widening and deepening commercialization of agriculture. As subsistence production declined, farmers' incomes came increasingly to depend on market forces regionally, nationally, and internationally. The growth of industrialization and cities meant an increased demand for food and agricultural raw materials, reinforcing the commercialization of agriculture and giving peasants new occupational alternatives outside of agriculture. Improvements in agricultural technology meant increased productivity (and farm incomes) and increased control over the crop-reducing depredations of nature (flood, drought, insects, plant disease). Technological improvements also intensified the commercialization of agriculture by increasing the importance of purchased factors of production. Cash outlays for fertilizers and pesticides meant that farmers became forced to make cost-profit calculations, especially when expensive items such as farm machinery became available. With the bulk of income taking the form of cash receipts, farm households could buy an ever-widening range of manufactured consumption goods from the national (and international) economy, as well as improved producer's technology.

Early national development also affected the rural sector in its provision of those powerful instruments of social capital, canals, railroads, and finally electricity; and that most powerful of institutional engines of capitalist development, the commercial banking system (Table 9–4).

It is necessary to put the same questions about European peasantries in 1900 that we put to them in 900—Who are the non-peasants? What has happened to shared culture, transactions, and social relationships between peasants and non-peasants?—and then to gauge what has changed the most and the least in peasant life.

The basic attributes of shared culture that struck Redfield and Kroeber as that which differentiated peasant from tribal remain intact (with some very important qualifications). European peasants in 1900 still spoke the same language and shared the same religion as non-peasants in their larger culture as they did in 900 and were still parts of larger political systems. But they were now citizens of nation-states, and religion in some countries

Table 9—4   *Early Modernization of European Peasant Economy (1300–1900)*

Organization	Performance
1. Market land tenure: peasant land ownership; cash rental / share-cropping	1. Widening range of foodstuffs and crops for industrial processing; increased specialization of agricultural production; growth of agricultural exports
2. Production for cash sale dominant; subsistence production petty; sale to regional, national, and international markets	2. Growth in per capita real income
3. Presence of nationally integrative land, labor, and produce markets; growing price sensitivity	3. Dependence on fluctuating market prices
4. Beginnings of technological modernization of agriculture; rising productivity (and incomes); reduced ecological dependence	

had become disestablished. The Protestant religion had displaced Catholicism as the principal religion in England and northern Europe; and as we approach the twentieth century, agnosticism and atheism could be professed with legal impunity. What is important from the point of view of our anthropological interests in European peasantry is the heterogeneity —the variability—in *all* the principal aspects of life begun by modernizing institutions and activities and the specific ways in which changes in rural life lagged behind changes in urban life.

To say that peasants continue to share culture with non-peasants in the period of early European modernization is a weak—indeed, a misleading —generalization. It is, I think, an anthropological vice to attribute great importance to statements which are true regardless of time, place, and specific institutions. And it is not entirely true to say that peasantries-in-general are parts of larger systems and tribal groups are not, for two reasons: The statement is analytically important *only* in contrasting traditional, pre-modern peasantries with traditional band and tribal communities,[20] say, European peasantries in the feudal period and pre-colonial Tiv or Trobrianders. Once primitive groups begin to modernize—with cash, commerce, machines, literacy, national political independence—tribal village communities also become parts of national cultures, societies, and economies.[21]

To say that European peasantries are parts of larger cultures before and after modernization begins is a misleading truth because the larger economy, polity, society, and culture, of which the peasantries continue to be a part, change structurally. In our terms, the transactions and the social relationships between peasants and non-peasants change as modernization proceeds.

What is typical and true of European peasantries of, say, 1900, compared to their medieval condition under feudalism? The end of feudalism in England and Western Europe meant the substitution of market land tenure for the feudal variety of dependent land tenure. Peasants now either owned land outright and could themselves sell or lease it to others for a money rent or acquired its use by paying a money rent exclusively. The social and political dues, tributes, payments, and labor services attached to their servile status and land tenure as feudal subordinates are abolished.

The end of feudalism also meant that peasants became the political subjects of their king and/or central national government and not of their (former) local lord of the manor. This legal and political nationalization of peasantries had quite direct repercussions on local social life. It meant the enlargement of personal freedom. Physical mobility was to become legal and occupational mobility locally, regionally, and nationally an increasingly important alternative as modernization proceeded in agriculture and then industry.

By 1900, most peasantries had been radically changed from their feudal condition; a minority, particularly in Eastern and southern Europe, had not. The peasantries of northern and Western Europe sold most of their produce, crops were diversified, and their markets were wide: they sold foodstuffs to urban markets for direct consumption by urban households; they sold produce for processing and industrial usage (for example, sugar beets) in manufacturing; they sold produce destined for local, regional, national, and international markets. They were beginning to buy manufactured consumption goods and some improved technology (such as chemical fertilizers) from the national economy.

Economic life had changed in other ways as well. The growth of mining, transport, and manufacture brought urban occupations to the countryside and attracted peasants to the cities (Bendix 1956). In short, economic life became more and more commercialized; peasants as agriculturalists became increasingly dependent upon production for the national market; and the purchase of consumers' and producers' goods from the market with their cash income, and new occupational alternatives were available in the countryside and the cities.

By 1900, the larger political system(s) and therefore political transactions between peasant and non-peasant had also changed; but the political scene was even more variable in Europe than the economic. As citizens, peasants now paid impersonal taxes in cash to local and national governments and were liable for national military conscription. They received back only a few modern social services; elementary education for their children and improved transportation (railroads) were perhaps the most important. Traditional public services such as the maintenance of law and order, defense, and justice were now provided in large measure by central, not local, government. The extent of political *participation* (in 1900) by peasants in national government varied enormously, with England and Russia representing the extreme cases.

Here we touch on a matter of some importance to our anthropological concerns with peasantry and modernization. Peasants and peasant villages remain distinct entities as long as they differ in important aspects from non-peasants and urban groups *in their larger contemporary cultures,* in ways other than those inevitably associated with differences in rural compared to urban life. For the period of early European modernization, there are, I think, two such differences of primary importance because they account for several others as well: differences in income and in education between peasant and non-peasant.[22]

Most West European peasants by 1900 were citizen-farmers with low incomes and little or no education, living in nation-states having just begun to industrialize and develop.[23] There were two paths by which they were to become non-peasants, both of which were taken, especially after 1900. They could leave agriculture and rural life entirely by emigrating (to the United States, Canada, South Africa, Latin America) or by moving to towns and cities within their nations. But moving to urban areas within their nations required massive and sustained industrialization which, for most of Europe, was not to happen until after 1900.

Or they could become "post-peasants," citizen-farmers who remain in agriculture but with growing incomes and education which allow new cultural and economic achievements that diminish the differences between rural and urban life. This, too, required sustained industrialization, development, and income growth in the national economy in which they lived, in addition to welfare state (and communist state) policies and peasant participation in national political life; all these having the crucial consequences of reducing rural-urban income and educational inequalities (Myrdal 1960; Franklin 1969; Carr 1951) and therefore "styles of life."

Late European Modernization, 1900—

. . . one [Greek] farmer, at a time of unseasonable drought [in the 1950's] remarked as he looked at his tobacco fields, "I won't make the sign of the cross, I'll bring my pump over here and irrigate the field" [Friedl 1962:75].

The ideal case about to be described exists nowhere completely. What matters is that it is being approached by an ever-larger proportion of European (and Japanese) farmers and that it is again macro-changes in the national economy and culture that are the important levers changing rural life.

In twentieth-century Europe large numbers of villagers became non-peasants by moving to non-agricultural occupations in the cities and the countryside. What concerns us more are those who remain in agriculture but become post-peasant citizen-farmers. What was (and is) the process?

In the industrial capitalist countries of northern and Western Europe—Sweden, England, France—it is the combined workings of the welfare state, democratic political institutions, a developed economy, and a sustained rate of national income growth which create economic, political, and cultural integration nationally; by so doing, the systematic differences between peasant and non-peasant with regard to income, education, cultural expression, and political participation diminish. Our first question then, is, How were European peasantries affected by the welfare state policies of their governments in the twentieth century? [24]

Sustaining the Full Employment Level of National Output

Since World War II, all governments in the developed capitalist countries use fiscal and monetary policies to keep the level of gross national product from falling below the rate at which (near) full employment occurs. The point is to avoid a repetition of the disastrous decline in output and employment experienced in the 1930's, during which farm incomes and prices fell further than the average. Sustained full employment in non-agricultural sectors also affects farmers by giving them alternative employment opportunities outside of agriculture.

Market Controls

Farm price-support programs put a floor below which the prices of agricultural produce (and therefore farmers' incomes) cannot fall.

Regional Development

The depressed, less developed, rural hinterland sectors of national economies have been helped directly by governmental programs which subsidize the creation of expensive capital facilities providing public utilities—electricity, irrigation, flood control, roads—as well as agricultural extension services and loans to farmers.

Direct Welfare Services

The provision of modern medical facilities and services through socialized medicine and old-age pensions increases the real income and material security of farmers and enlarges the areas of common experience and activity farmers share with fellow citizens in cities and towns. National governments' recently expanded provision of free or subsidized higher education, open to all on criteria of ability, is a potentially powerful solvent of rural-urban differences (as it has long been in the United States).

These welfare state policies all work in the same direction to reduce differences in the quality of life between rural and urban residents. Many of them have multiplier effects of the sort Myrdal emphasizes in his analysis of "cumulative causation" (Myrdal 1957:chapters 1–3). Marked increases in income and widened access to higher education—obviously related to each other—are particularly powerful in eroding rural-urban differentials.

Welfare state policies integrate the nation economically: differences in income and material security among regions and producing sectors are reduced; differences in social overhead capital facilities and governmental services between regions within the nation are reduced; differences in the quality of technology employed in agriculture compared to industry are reduced. National cultural integration is also enhanced by policies which reduce regional isolation by enlarging the means of transport and communication and by late developments in technology, such as radio and television.

Perhaps one may sum up the economic changes that transform the peasantry during the late stage of development and modernization by saying that rural households and villages become more dependent on market forces and governmental services external to the village. The *Gemeinschaft* qualities of local life carried over from the feudal period and early modernization are further weakened as villagers and villages become less and less isolated from urban and national life and more and more dependent on their transactions with and participation in institutions outside the village.

APPLICATION

How Do Peasant Economies Differ from Tribal Economies?

By "primitive" or "tribal," one means aboriginal Africa and Oceania before acculturation, applied anthropology, or micro-development began; that is, before the changes brought by European colonial incursion (or post-colonial development). In short, one means the Trobrianders, the Nuer, and the Tiv as they are reported in the ethnographies of Malinowski, Evans-Pritchard, and Bohannan. These contain very specific descriptions of land tenure, technology, labor allocation, and the like. But unless these are compared to equally specific institutions of actual peasant economies of time and place, one is confined to pointing out only a few non-institutional similarities between tribal and peasant modes of livelihood. Traditional Trobriand and Tiv *economy* is made to appear similar to the *economy* of peasantry-in-general because the comparison is confined to both sorts being agricultural, producing some subsistence goods and some for market sale with simple technology. When it comes to culture and society, anthropologists stress the differences between tribal and peasant: that peasantry-in-general shares language, religion, and government with non-peasants within a larger society—those characteristics that remain true for peasantries before and after modernization begins.

To compare tribal and peasant economies in an analytically revealing fashion requires us to choose specific peasant groupings of time and place, because the conclusions we reach will be different if we choose the dependent feudal tenure of the French serf-peasant of 900 or the market tenure of the French citizen-peasant of 1900. As with land tenure, so, too, with the allocation of labor, the disposition of produce, the role of markets, the amounts of money used, and the quantities and types of foreign trade. We must compare the Tiv or Trobrianders not with peasantry-in-general or with a peasant community after modernization begins, but with a peasant community at the same stage of "traditional-ness": for our European peasants, this means after the Romans detribalized them and before modernization began. The appropriate comparison for aboriginal tribal economies is with European peasantries of the feudal period. We must also describe how economy for both was related to social organization. Otherwise, the differences between tribal and peasant economy remain invisible: "By a peasant economy one means a system of small-scale producers, with a simple technology and equipment often relying primarily for their subsistence on what they themselves produce. The primary means of livelihood of the peasant is cultivation of the soil [Firth 1951:87]."

Firth's definition applies equally well to the Trobrianders and to the French peasants of 900 and 1790 because it omits comparison of specific economic and social institutions and the way social organization expresses material transactions. Traditional tribal societies have the pig-tusk sort of primitive money, bloodwealth, bridewealth, and land tenure as an expression of lineage affiliation. They have idiosyncratic religions. The tribes without rulers subset has no centralized government. Medieval European peasantries differed on all these counts.

The tribes of Europe were transformed by Roman institutions—central government, coined money, markets, cities—and by Christianity, all of which the victorious German barbarian tribesmen also succumbed to. The differences between medieval European peasant economy and aboriginal Tiv are principally in the "prestige" sphere: the pig-tusk (actually, cows in Europe) sort of primitive money was displaced by Roman cash.[25] The bloodwealth kind of institution was displaced by courts of the king or the local lord.[26] Mortuary payments within lineage and affinal groupings were displaced by payments to the feudal lord and the Catholic church. The ability of "big men" to work their way up to positions of leadership through the (pre-Roman) tribal European equivalents of prowess in kula, potlatch, and primitive warfare was displaced by formal political roles and military organization and by formal social stratification into rigid classes. Reciprocal labor allocation and work parties based on lineage obligation were displaced by the nuclear family as the production unit and primary source of labor.

Our medieval European peasant lacked those socio-economic institutions and modes of cultural expression that are most peculiarly tribal— potlatch, kula, bridewealth, primitive monies. These, too (as well as agriculture, simple technology, and so on), are parts of tribal economy. The French peasant of 900 was a low-class dependent in a sharply stratified system. He was outside the prestige sphere of the elite and could not distinguish himself in battle or win eminence and reputation by success in kula or potlatch or win their primitive monies, the tangible means to make status payments and acquire power over clients in the community.[27]

In short, the French peasant of 900 was no longer a tribal person because he was part of a larger system containing the institutions of Catholicism, cash, cities, markets, kings and noble lords and their central and local governmental and military offices, and a kind of social stratification expressed in a master-client feudal land and feudal political tenure arrangement. Each of the cultural, social, and political differences that anthropologists emphasize as distinguishing peasant from tribal expresses economic differences between them as well.

Catholicism, cash, cities, markets, kings, and noble lords all represent external ties between peasant villagers on the one hand and institutions and people outside the village on the other. Each also represents looser and weaker ties and dependence within the village community, compared to traditional bands and tribes (see Sahlins 1965: 179–186).

Religion in band and tribal societies means beliefs and practices unique to the small group, idiosyncratic religions, as it were, which separate "us" from the rest of the world. Catholicism and Islam are universal religions. Where band and tribal languages are also idiosyncratic, they too intensify the special identification of the band or tribe, its social distance from outsiders.

Cash, cities, and markets mean sources of income *not* dependent on tribal social ties, such as those with extended kinsmen. So too with emergency support. In famine and war it is the church and the feudal lord who feed and protect. Some characteristic features of traditional peasantries (and some in early modernization) follow: weak extended kinship ties (although the nuclear family remains important); factions, rivalries, jealousies, and "the image of the limited good." These can persist without destroying the community because *mutual dependence* is structured differently in peasantries compared to bands and tribes: the persons from whom one gets land, labor, and emergency support are different. To put it briefly, cash, markets, kings, cities, and world religion kill reciprocity of the many sorts Sahlins (1965) so usefully delineates for bands and tribes.

The differences between traditional tribal and peasant institutions also tell us something about modernization. Despite the very real similarities between primitive and peasant food technology, subsistence production, and low output, traditional peasant communities are closer to being modern because cash, commerce, cities, literacy, and centralized polity were structured parts of the larger civilizations of which the peasant segments were part (see Hunter 1969:20–24).

Peasantry-in-General

Peasantry-in-general is a very misleading simplification and an illogical one for a profession which expresses a strong interest in modernization. Kroeber's definition applies to European peasantries under feudalism and after feudalism ended, but contrasts these only with aboriginal band and tribal societies. (When modernization begins, tribal groups also become part-societies with part-cultures.) Those who emphasize the concept of peasantry-in-general, moreover, cannot then specify institutional structures of land tenure and polity, the kinds, frequencies, and amounts of material and labor transactions between peasants and non-peasants, and the social relationships between them. Because these change after modernization begins, we have at least two structurally different kinds of peasant societies and economies to deal with, traditional and modernizing. (The same, of course, is true for primitive societies and economies.[28])

No ideal type of peasantry-in-general can be conceived which is equally informative about peasant economies under feudalism (or its traditional equivalent), early modernization, and late modernization. Dependent land tenure with client status versus market land tenure with citizenship status should not be packed into the same ideal type of general peasant, even though agriculture and the quality of being a part-society with a part-culture remains true for both.

In their dubious quest for general statements which are true regardless of time and place, anthropologists ignore some critical differences among peasantries: the nature of land tenure and the political relationships and material transactions peasants have with non-peasants. ". . . one sees a peasant as a man who is in effective control of a piece of land. . . . [This] does not require of the peasant that he own the land or that he have any particular form of tenure or any particular form of institutional relationship to the gentry or the townsmen [Redfield 1960:19]."

Fallers' brief article, "Are African Cultivators to Be Called 'Peasants'?" (1961:108–110), illustrates the difficulties that arise when one tries to fit actual societies existing in time and place into the general concept of peasantry which is timeless and placeless and lacks specific institutional criteria for types of land tenure and polity—criteria the present essay argues are essential to make analytical sense of the enormous variety of peasantries in anthropology and history.

Fallers asks, To what extent does the standard concept of peasantry-in-general fit sub-Saharan, non-Muslim, pagan Africa? He takes as the nub of peasantry their being part-societies with part-cultures, a feature which is expressed in peasant economic, political, and cultural life:

> . . . part-societies with part-cultures—we may take to be the heart of the matter. . . . Now this semi-autonomy of constituent local communities, which we may take to be the differentiating characteristic of the peasant society, may be decomposed into a number of aspects . . . (1) the economic, (2) the political, and (3) [less satisfactorily], the "cultural." . . . How far [do] they find counterparts in the more complex African societies [of sub-Saharan Africa, excluding Muslim areas and Ethiopia] [1961:108]?

The part-society, part-culture definition of peasantry is so general that Fallers has no difficulty deciding that the Africans he has in mind are peasants economically and politically.

> In economic terms, a peasant is presumably a man who produces—usually through cultivation—mainly for his own household's consumption, but who also produces something to exchange in a market for other goods and services. This is the economic aspect of the peasant community's semi-autonomy [Firth 1951:87]. In this sense, peasants abound in Africa. . . . Economically, most Africans were traditionally peasants . . . [1961:108–109].

If so, the concept of primitive or tribal economy disappears, and the detailed distinctions between types and consequences of land tenure arrangements (Bohannan 1960), and primitive as compared to commercial monies (Dalton 1965; 1970*a*), prestige sectors and spheres of exchange, and the extent of market participation (Bohannan and Dalton 1962) are seemingly of no distinguishing importance. To single out the simple criterion of production for both subsistence and market sale as that which defines peasant economy is to put the Trobrianders and the French peasant of 900 and 1790 in the same category.

Fallers suggests that the larger governments having jurisdiction over local peasant communities can be quite different; for example, the Roman Empire, medieval monarchies, colonial regimes, post-colonial independent states. The semi-autonomy of the village group—the aspect Fallers sees as pivotal in defining peasantry-in-general—occurs in all these larger polities. Since kingdoms structurally connected to village communities exist(ed) in Africa, the semiautonomy of the local group aspect fits parts of Africa politically, as well as economically. "These political peasant-like features, like the economic ones, are common enough in African states. . . . Thus, there would seem to be no reason why African villagers should not be called 'peasants' politically and economically [1961:109–110]."

But this quality of semi-autonomy of the village grouping vis-à-vis a larger polity of *any* sort is so general that it excludes only the "tribes with-out rulers" of indigenous Africa, Oceania, and North America. A village within the political orbit of the Roman Empire, the France of Louis XIV, Nazi Germany, Communist Russia, democratic Britain—monarchy, repub-lic, dictatorship, democracy—no matter what, where, and when the larger political system, there is semi-autonomy at the local level. A township in the rural United States arranges its own police force and elementary schools, but pays taxes to Washington as well; hence semi-autonomy. Surely such generality is not analytically interesting.[29] All the interesting questions require that the specific institutions be described, that is, an analysis of the exact ways a village is and is not autonomous; the exact ways it is a part-society with a part-culture, the exact political and mate-rial transactions with its larger polity and economy.

Wolf's book on peasantry (1966) is similarly afflicted with this disease of generality which cripples the ability to analyze how specific institutions change in the course of peasant modernization. He gives us an equally misleading restatement of Kroeber's theme.

> In primitive society, producers control the means of production, including their own labor, and exchange their own labor and its products for the cul-turally defined equivalent goods and services of others [1966:3].

> [in peasantries] . . . control of the means of production including the dis-position of human labor, passes from the hands of the primary producers into the hands of groups that do not carry on the productive process them-selves, but assume instead special executive and administrative functions, backed by the use of force [*ibid*.].

This is not really a distinction between all primitive societies on the one hand and all peasantries on the other; it distinguishes bands and traditional tribes without centralized polity from *all* other social systems, past and present, some primitive, some peasant, some in industrial capitalist na-tions, and some in industrial communist nations. His distinction lumps in one category the traditional Bantu (Schapera 1928; Schapera and Goodwin 1937), where chiefs allocate land and collect tribute, and primitive king-doms, such as those discussed by Fallers (1961). But in the same enor-mous residual category in which all but traditional tribes without rulers fit, one can also place American farmers today who rent land, and Soviet collective farmers as well, who also do not "control" the means of produc-tion.

The same criticisms hold for another attempt by Wolf to distinguish be-tween primitive and peasant-in-general, by using such unspecific terms as "control" and "surplus" (that is, terms which do not specify institutions). Wolf's peasants in the quotation immediately to follow would include any farmers who pay taxes to central government (for example, both U.S. and

Soviet farmers) or rent land from anyone who is part of a "dominant group of rulers," whatever that means. My insertions in square brackets show how his definition of peasant applies to U.S. farmers today, even those with university degrees whose farms yield them $50,000 a year. (It applies equally well to Russian farmers before and after the Revolution.)

In primitive societies, surpluses are exchanged directly among groups or members of groups; peasants, however, are rural cultivators whose surpluses [taxes] are transferred to a dominant group of rulers [local, state, and federal American governments] both to underwrite its own standard of living [President Nixon's salary] and to distribute the remainder to groups in society that do not farm but must be fed for their specific goods and services in turn [that is, everyone in the United States who is not a farmer regardless of his kind of employment is consuming the farmer's surplus] [1966:3–4].[30]

Finally, we come to Wolf's categorization of the components of peasant income, his employment of these categories to draw distinctions between primitive and peasant, and his analytical conclusions about peasantry-in-general.

In Wolf's terms, the income [31] of a peasant's household is allocated to four kinds of outlays, expenditures, or purposes: (1) Basic food requirements necessary to sustain life, which, if not met, means hunger and a shrinkage in population. (2) A replacement fund (actually, a household and farm depreciation allowance, in modern terms), that is, material and labor to repair broken and worn-out household and farming equipment, seed for next season's planting, and so forth. If the replacement fund is not provided for, either capacity to produce output shrinks or/and the cultivator's household welfare (real income) shrinks (for example, a leaky unrepaired roof, fewer pots to cook in). (3) A ceremonial fund, meaning outlays on family ritual (marriage) and religious institutions and events (tithes). (4) Finally, a fund of rent (which is so defined as to include taxes as well as rent). This fund of rent plays a pivotal role in Wolf's concept of peasantry-in-general, so it is best to quote his own words:

. . . there exist in more complex societies social relations which are not symmetrical, but are based, in some form, upon the exercise of power. In the case of the Mecklenburg farm [in Germany during the fourteenth and fifteenth centuries] . . . more than half the effective yield [in grain] went in payment of dues to a lord who maintained jurisdiction, or domain, over the land. . . . This peasant, then, was subject to asymmetrical power relations which made a permanent charge, paid out as the result of some superior claim to his labor on the land, we call rent, regardless of whether that rent is paid in labor, in produce, or in money. Where someone exercises an effective superior power, or domain, over a cultivator, the cultivator must produce a fund of rent.

It is this production of a fund of rent which critically distinguishes the peasant from the primitive cultivator [italics in original]. This production in turn is spurred by the existence of a social order in which some men can through power demand payments from others, resulting in the transfer of wealth from one section of the population to another. The peasant's loss is the powerholder's gain [1966:9–10].

Although the example in this quotation is from German peasantry under feudalism, the various funds, including the pivotal fund of rent—". . . *which critically distinguishes the peasant from the primitive cultivator"*— is meant as a general statement (although the paragraph that follows it, which I shall also consider, essentially negates all these general statements).

Wolf's general fund of rent actually applies to almost all agricultural societies, past and present. Any rural cultivator paying a tax (including present-day Soviet and American farmers) is paying it out of his fund of rent. This includes African cultivators in Bantu chiefdoms (Schapera 1928; Schapera and Goodwin 1937), as well as those in the African kingdoms described by Fallers (1961). Any rural cultivator today, in any part of the world, in any economic system, developed or underdeveloped, who rents land from a landowner, paying his rent in cash or kind, is paying it out of his fund of rent. But even in Malinowski's Trobriands, the kind of primitive economy which presumably is being contrasted with *the* peasant economy, a man pays over a large portion of his yam crop to his sister's husband in recognition of her matrilineal rights to land he is using. This obligatory *urigubu* payment also comes out of the Trobriander's fund of rent. There is simply no point in defining terms so generally as to put markedly different systems into one gigantic category.

In the quotation just given on the fund of rent, Wolf really has in mind traditional European feudalism and its nearly equivalent hacienda system in hybrid peasantries of Latin America (for instance, Holmberg *et al.* 1965). It is these he thinks of as entailing ". . . social relations which are not symmetrical . . . based, in some form, upon the exercise of power" (meaning that feudal peasants are low-class servile dependents of their lord). But instead of saying that he is characterizing feudal peasantries under conditions of dependent land tenure and inferior status expressed politically and socially as well as economically, he generalizes this special case by using words which suggest that what he says is true for all peasantries. It is not. The French peasant after the Revolution, owning his own land and paying taxes (fund of rent) to the French government as did other (non-peasant) citizens of France, is no longer in ". . . a social order in which some men can through power demand payments from others, resulting in the transfer of wealth from one section of the population to another. The peasant's loss is the powerholder's gain [Wolf 1966:10]." [32] He is still a peasant, but now is just another citizen paying taxes and receiving back social services from his central government.

Wolf's four funds, subsistence, replacement, ceremonial, and rent, are so general as to apply to all low-income farm households, whatever the economic system of the village (primitive, peasant) or the nation (capitalist, communist).

All these misinformed generalizations about *the* peasant are then vitiated by the paragraph which concludes the section on funds. My insertions in square brackets indicate why.

> It is important to note . . . that there are many different ways in which this fund of rent is produced [cash, labor services, produce], and many different ways in which it is siphoned from the peasant stratum into the hands of the controlling group [the French peasant of 900 pays feudal dues in labor services and produce to his lord; the French peasant of 1900 pays taxes in cash as a citizen of France to his government, just as non-peasants do]. Since the distinctions in the exercise of this power [feudalism, monarchy, republic, dictatorship, democracy, communism, fascism] have important structural effects on the way the peasantry is organized [medieval feudalism, early modernization], there are consequently many kinds of peasantry, not just one [amen]. So far, then, the term "peasant" denotes no more than an asymmetrical structural relationship between producers of surplus [all farmers, everywhere in the world] and controllers [all who rent land to others in any economic system together with all governments, everywhere, who tax farmers, and all kin who have a right to a portion of the cultivator's produce].

Hybrid-Composite Peasantries: Latin America and the Caribbean

> We distinguish nine significant Latin American subculture types. . . . Undoubtedly there are many other[s]. . . . everywhere [in Latin America] Peasant-type subcultures are characterized by a predominance of archaic European patterns which survive alongside the American Indian or African patterns and which are slowly giving way to new national patterns and institutions . . . [which] play a larger role in Peasant than in Modern Indian subcultures. Peasant subculture economies are closely tied with regional and national economies [Wagley and Harris 1955:429, 431–432].

> The trauma of the Conquest remains an open wound upon the body of Middle American society to this day [Wolf 1959:214].

Latin America and the Caribbean are of particular importance in the anthropological literature of peasantry, and especially in the writings of North American anthropologists. Many of the concepts, generalizations, and shorthand expressions one immediately associates with peasantry originated with them: "folk-urban continuum" and "great and little traditions"

(Redfield); "penny capitalism" (Tax); "open and closed corporate peasant communities" (Wolf); "levelling devices" (Nash); "the image of the limited good" (Foster); "the culture of poverty" (Lewis). Other anthropologists, such as Erasmus, Harris, Mintz, and Wagley, have written deeply and widely on Latin American and Caribbean peasantries.

Yet the peasantries of Latin America differ from all others in profound ways and differ very widely among themselves. The purpose of considering them here is to suggest that they are best regarded apart from the peasantries of long settlement in Europe and Asia because they have only recently been fabricated from primitive and several sorts of peasant components. We must explain the underlying reasons for the extraordinary variation among them.

Latin American peasantries are special mixtures in two senses: some are "hybrid," combining both primitive (pre-conquest) and peasant aspects of culture, economy, and society. Some are "composite" peasantries, combining institutions equivalent to those from feudal Europe (for example, dependent land tenure) and postfeudal Europe (for example, market land tenure). And yet others are both hybrid and composite simultaneously. Finally, Latin American peasantries are different from all others because there has been no colonial episode equivalent to the Spanish conquest.[33]

The peasantries of Latin America and the Caribbean were created since the sixteenth century in the aftermath of African slavery and Spanish conquest. They differ from European and Japanese peasantries of long settlement in the recency of their creation: they were quite literally fabricated out of several peoples and several sets of institutions four hundred years ago; their creation entailed unusually severe coercion and transplantation, either enslavement and overseas resettlement (of individuals, not communities), as with Africans in the Caribbean plantations, or military conquest and enforced conversion, as with Central and South American Indians made into Catholics and colonial subject-inferiors (most of whom died or also were physically resettled in the process).[34]

The Spanish conquest was an unparalleled event for reasons both obvious and not so obvious. The sources say that one hundred and forty years after the Spanish arrived, the Indian population had declined by something like two-thirds (Wolf 1959:30,195): disease, famine, and warfare killed two out of every three Indians descended from those who were alive when Cortés arrived. Indeed, within only twenty years of the earlier arrival of the Spanish in Hispaniola (Haiti and Santo Domingo), the Carib Indians were so reduced in numbers that the Spanish had to import Indian laborers from the Bahamas (Simpson 1950:18). The Indians who survived were able to transmit only bits of their indigenous culture and practically none of their social organization to future generations. Their elite transmogrified themselves into Spaniards or themselves suffered the same afflictions as the rank and file (Chevalier 1963:209–214). Their scribes and craftsmen became extinct. What got transmitted to the cultural hybrids of the present day was language, slash and burn agriculture, some simple tools and household equipment, and maize, squash, and beans as the principal items of diet. Latin America was repeopled by transformed Indians and by foreign ethnic groups rather different from the pre-conquest Indians: Spanish, Africans, and a smaller number of Asians.[35]

There are other reasons why Latin American peasantries are both different from those of long settlement and differ markedly from one another (nine subcultures, closed and open communities, and so on). The Spanish introduced two sets of European institutions simultaneously, both of which survive to the present day. They used feudal institutions (*encomienda, hacienda*) to organize the Indian labor force (Chevalier 1963:36) and mercantilism to sell the cash crops abroad that were produced with the dependent Indian labor. This is an illustration of the composite structure of Latin American peasantries, built in right from the beginning. Finally, the Latin American peasantries differ from others studied today by anthropologists because their Spanish and Portuguese conquerors remain among the least developed, least industrialized, and least modern in Western Europe, and as the Latin American colonies achieved political independence almost a century and a half earlier than other Third World ex-colonies of Africa and Asia we conventionally lump them with as underdeveloped.

In summary, there are three related reasons for the extraordinary diver-

Table 9–5 *Hybrid / Composite Peasantries of Present-Day Latin America and the Caribbean: Variability and Diversity*

Indigenous Cultures	:	Inca, Maya, Aztec, hunting and gathering bands
Colonizing Powers and Settlers	:	Spanish, Portuguese, English, French, Africans, Asians
Village Language	:	Indian only; Indian and Spanish; Spanish and Indian; Spanish only
Extent of Literacy	:	from overwhelmingly illiterate to overwhelmingly literate
Religion	:	Catholicism only; Catholicism with pagan survivals
Legal Status	:	from full citizenship to *de facto* serfdom (hacienda)
Social Stratification	:	Indian as rural inferior to mestizo
Technology	:	Primitive; early modernization; late modernization
Land Tenure	:	Dependent; controlled market; free market
Labor Allocation	:	family labor exclusively; family plus market (hired) labor, with or without occasional reciprocity
Production	:	Subsistence dominant with petty cash sales; production for market sale dominant, with petty amounts for subsistence; production exclusively for market sale
Extent of Development of the National Economy	:	Great diversity (see Adelman and Morris 1967)

sity among Latin American peasantries: the deep and wide impacts of the Spanish conquest (physical decimation, Spanish and African settlement, Catholicism, feudal and mercantile institutions without sustained development and industrialization),[36] their hybrid aspects, and their composite aspects. The peasantries of Latin America, moreover, are today in nation-states in the early stage of development and modernization, which itself—as we have seen for Europe—means unusual diversity as national economy, society, and culture change unevenly. When we add to these the usual complexities and diversities which stem from the conventionally broad interests of anthropologists in the peasant attributes of persons, villages, polities, economies, technologies, ecologies, cultures, and societies —and their mutual interaction—the diversity is simply enormous (Table 9–5).

Conclusion

The game of comparing primitive and peasant societies in general produces a cupful of spurious generalizations that cannot survive critical scrutiny. It is also a serious impediment to the formulation of theory in economic anthropology and micro-development.

Anyone who attempts to make generalizations which are true for all peasants, past and present, in Europe, Asia, Latin America, the Caribbean, and the Middle East is necessarily confined to Kroeber's definition: agriculture,[37] a mixture of subsistence production and production for market sale, and the general statement that villages are partly autonomous and partly related to cities of some sort and to larger cultural and political groupings. One cannot go further and still make generally true statements. To specify type of land tenure, legal and political rights and obligations of peasants compared to those of non-peasants, material transactions between them, level of income, kinds of non-peasants in the village, region, or larger society, extent of education provided, quality of technology—in short, specific institutions, activities, performance, and peasant/non-peasant relationships—is inevitably to single out one of several structurally different peasant types.

The words chosen to characterize peasantry-in-general (which, according to the game, have to fit French peasants of both 900 and 1900) are therefore "part-society," "part-culture," "great and little traditions," and "surplus" (tax? rent? tithe? paid in cash? paid in labor? paid in produce?). Words such as "surplus" are chosen in order to find common denominators between different institutions, so that structural differences among peasantries may be turned into amorphous similarities.[38] The French peasant's feudal dues paid to his lord in labor services and produce in 900 are "surplus"; and his taxes paid to the French government in cash as a citizen in 1900 are also "surplus." The differences between feudal status with dependent land tenure compared to citizenship status with market land tenure become glossed over. Although a thousand years and several kinds of revolution separate them, what gets registered is that both kinds of French peasant are cultivators paying over their surplus.

All that peasantry-in-general tells us is that dualism of *some sort* exists: that the rural villagers and villages are in some ways systematically different from some of the non-peasants and cities in their larger contemporary cultures, societies, and economies. This is certainly true for French villagers and villages of 900 and 1900. But all the interesting questions have to do with the specific forms these differences take and their consequences.

The concept of peasantry-in-general, moreover, impedes the anthropological analysis of peasantries in the course of modernization—analysis that requires specification of sequential changes in economy, technology, polity, and culture: What changes, what does not, why, and with what consequences? To answer these questions, one must reverse the concern with peasantry-in-general. It is not what the French peasant of 900, 1900, and 1970 have in common that is important, but how and why they differ.

The quest for general statements about peasantries of all times and places has its counterpart in "cultural" or "social" change in general, with equally unfortunate results. Here, too, differences in historical circumstances and external shocks, in basic institutions, and in sequential process are too important to be left out of the analysis and too variable to permit definitions and generalizations of grand historical scope. What is being changed, how, by whom, over what period of time, for what purpose—these vary enormously.

The literatures of acculturation, applied anthropology, and micro-development put different questions about processes of change, and each is really addressed to real-world circumstances—institutional structures and historical situations of specific time and place—which differ markedly from one another. It is this latter point particularly which must be made clear. As with peasantry, much anthropological theorizing on social change is also stated in general terms unwarranted by the quite special historical and institutional circumstances that underlie it and that differentiate one sort from another.

The literature of acculturation refers to specific situations of European and American colonial presence and political control of conquered peoples in the four and a half centuries that lie between the Spanish conquest of Central and South America and World War II.[39] The "colonial impact" made by the colonizing powers on their subject peoples varied enormously: in ferocity of initial conquest, according to the extent of economic development of the mother country at the time it colonized the natives, in the numbers of Europeans settling, the types of natural resources present in the colonies, and so on. Those were centuries when slavery existed in the world and when differences in physiognomy were equated with differences in mental and moral capacity. The God of the Christians was the only true God, and they used both guns and butter to prove it to the natives. The colonial powers had an unquestioned sense of their total superiority. These specific conditions rooted in time and place underlay studies of acculturation. They no longer exist.

In such circumstances anthropologists asked, Which features of the dominating culture of the colonizing power got transmitted to the natives and with what consequences? Since culture included everything, anthropologists excluded nothing. They seemed not to feel the need to distinguish between big and little acculturation.[40] One African learning to smoke French cigarettes and another learning French engineering are both "acculturating." But the social consequences are obviously of a different order of importance.

Applied anthropology, also born under colonialism, is also addressed to very special conditions and asks very special questions: how the visiting expert, in temporary residence, can succeed in inducing the hinterland villagers to adopt one or a few "innovations." Innovations is in quotation marks to point up the general nature of the term. Smoking cigarettes for the first time is an innovation, and using irrigation equipment for the first time is also an innovation; anything new is an innovation.

During the colonial period (see, for instance, Spicer 1952), applied anthropologists were severely limited in the kinds of innovations they could introduce because macro-development and modernization were not going on outside the village the visiting expert was teaching to use vitamin pills and sewing machines. "Steel Axes for Stone-Age Australians" (Sharp 1952), of course, is an extreme example of such piecemeal innovation in utter isolation from regional and national change. In such circumstances, applied anthropologists stressed the need to know the past experience and present community structure of the villagers, so as to enlist their cooperation in introducing innovations piecemeal. Anthropologists stressed the people's cultural predisposition to accept innovations rather than the need to provide them with external facilities (roads, agricultural credit, electricity) and new opportunities, to which the villagers could respond and which could provide the economic and technological bases for sustained growth in village income and diversification of production (for example, as in Epstein 1962).

We reserve the term "micro-development" for the post-colonial period during which village transformation becomes part of national modernization and development: the long-run process of continual interaction and growing mutual dependence between villages and the rest of the country; in short, the process that European peasantries have been through in the course of their national development politically, economically, and culturally (see Franklin 1969).

To create a theoretical framework for peasantry, one must see that national institutions and development policies vitally affect peasant village transformation. Turning points in the historical sequence transforming peasants and their village societies were (and are) macro-changes originating outside the village. These changed the larger society and polity, its peasant segment, and the previously existing relationships and transactions between peasant and non-peasant. The transformation came earlier in Europe (Polanyi 1944) than in the parts of the world most anthropologists study. But the essential processes—the formation of the modern nation-state with a citizenry who are legally and politically equal, ever-widening commercialization of production, and industrialization—are the same. The new activities, institutions, and equipment that we lump together as "modernization" [41] all work to displace local with national ties, activities, and dependence (Smelser 1963).

Peasantries remain identifiable entities for so long because national economic development and cultural modernization take centuries to transform all sectors of the nation, once begun, and are continually shunted in new directions by external shocks such as war and new technologies.[42] Except for countries like the United States and Australia, which had no traditional peasantries,[43] development and modernization of the agricultural sector typically lag behind the industrial-urban sector (for instance, as in Italy).

The structural changes begun when market land tenure displaces dependent tenures, the modern nation-state displaces feudalism (or its traditional monarchical equivalent), the independent nation-state displaces colonial rule, and the growth of industrial employment begins to reduce the size of the agricultural sector, are watershed changes for tribal as well as traditional peasant societies. For both, markets, cash, and modern technology change village economy. New and diversified economic, political, and cultural transactions make the village an interacting part of its larger society, with ever-diminishing differences between rural and urban life.

NOTES

1. This essay tries to disentangle some rather complicated matters relating to a large number of societies over long periods of time. I therefore adopt several expedients to enhance clarity. One is to use footnotes frequently to cite supporting evidence and to make necessary qualifications and side remarks, in order to keep the text as unencumbered as possible. Another is to use boxes, charts, and diagrams to point up the conceptual classifications and distinctions crucial for the points I want to make. I am grateful to Donald Brown, Paula Felt, George Foster, Ilona Polanyi, James Sheehan, and Conrad Totman for giving me their critical comments on an earlier draft. I regret that several books relevant to the topics of this essay came to my attention too late for me to make extensive use of them, particularly Hunter (1969) and Franklin (1969).

2. A statement by Fallers applies equally well to this essay: "The point of

this [paper] is not, of course, merely to play with definitions but rather to ex-
plore some of the implications of the fact—of which we are all aware—that
the concept peasant society refers to a bundle of features which do not always
go together [Fallers 1961:108].ʺ

3. Although ʺpeasant,ʺ too, has unlovely associations of the Good Soldier
Schweik sort, ʺIn describing the people of Vasilika [in Greece] I have avoided
using the term 'peasant' for two reasons. First, the layman's concept of the
peasant often includes the traits of stupidity and stubborn resistance to change
that are by no means characteristic of the people of Vasilika. And second, social scientists have not yet arrived at a definition of the term that is generally
accepted among them [Friedl 1962:6].ʺ

4. Kroeber's celebrated characterization of peasantries includes economic
characteristics, but not of a sort which differentiate primitive from peasant
economies: ʺPeasants are definitely rural—yet live in relation to market towns;
they form a class segment of a larger population which usually contains urban
centers, sometimes metropolitan capitals. They constitute part-societies with
part-cultures [Kroeber 1948:284].ʺ Being rural and having some (unspecified)
connection with markets is true for some range of tribal as well as peasant
economies.

5. Before the ninth century, the literature on European village communities
is too fragmentary for my purposes.

6. There is one further reason to study European peasantries in historical
sequence in order to get insights of use to anthropology. Colonial policies of
the Spanish in Central and South America, and, to a lesser extent, the English
and French in Asia, transplanted Spanish, English, and French institutions into
those societies now called peasant that are studied by anthropologists, the most
obvious example being the hacienda system instituted by the Spanish (Holmberg *et al.* 1965). Economic policies in their overseas colonies, moreover, reflected the needs of the European home countries at the time, European countries which themselves were changing with industrialization. The European
powers who established overseas colonies before industrialization was importantly begun in their home countries (like Spain) viewed the potential economic benefits to themselves differently from those who colonized after industrialization had burgeoned at home. Geertz contrasts the economic policies of
the Dutch in the Outer Islands of Indonesia after 1863 with their earlier policies in Java: ʺ. . . rather than being focused on condiments [like pepper],
confections [such as sugar], and stimulants [for example, coffee, tobacco], the
[colonial] development centered on the production of industrial raw materials
—a reflex . . . of the alteration in world market conditions attendant upon the
spectacular growth of large-scale manufacturing in the West after the middle of
the nineteenth century [1963:105].ʺ

7. Each of the designations ʺtraditional peasantries,ʺ ʺearly modernization,ʺ ʺlate modernizationʺ is a broad category, within which there is much diversity on the principal defining characteristics. It could hardly be otherwise,
considering the large number of peasantries and the long periods of historical
time over which they exist(ed). The definitions and characterizations used in
this essay are to be regarded as ideal types, underscoring what is typical and
true for most peasantries in each category. The first and third categories, tradi-

tional peasants and late modernization (post-peasants), are less heterogeneous than the middle category, for an obvious reason. Once modernization is under-way (India, at present, for example), clusters of peasant villages undergo differ-ent rates and sequences of transformation in each of the several defining characteristics—economic, social, cultural, and others. So we find within the same country in the same year individual villages of each of the three sorts de-marcated, although the preponderant number fit the second category best. "Dualism" increases in the early stage of modernization (Adelman and Morris 1967; Adelman and Dalton 1971; Hunter 1969:48).

8. Although, of course, the culture they share with non-peasants changes in early and late modernization; for example, the growth of literacy and education comes to be shared by peasants and non-peasants (in late modernization), as does the extent and quality of rural participation in national political and cul-tural life. If, with Redfield and Kroeber, one wants to stress the differences be-tween traditional primitive and traditional peasant societies, the fact of shared culture—that peasants are part of wider language, religious, and political groupings—is important. If one wants to differentiate among peasantries be-fore, during, and after modern institutions and activities have been instituted, the nature of transactions and social relationships between peasants and non-peasants is important.

9. See Schultz (1969) and Slicher Van Bath (1963). Quantitative informa-tion is lacking to allow fine estimates of relative amounts of produced goods, labor, and land transacted via market sale compared to subsistence production and the amounts transacted otherwise (as corvée, tithe, and such) in traditional European peasantries. It is almost certain that between 800 and 1300, the bulk of land, labor, and produce transactions was of non-market sorts: "The large number of markets might seem at first sight to contradict the commercial pa-ralysis of the age for from the beginning of the ninth century they increased rapidly and new ones were continually being founded. But their number is it-self proof of their insignificance. Only the fair of St. Denys, near Paris (the Fair of Lendit), attracted once a year, among its pilgrims, occasional sellers and buyers from a distance. Apart from it there were only innumerable small weekly markets, where the peasants of the district offered for sale a few eggs, chickens, pounds of wool, or ells of coarse cloth woven at home. The nature of the business transacted appears quite clearly from the fact that people sold per *denaratas,* that is to say, by quantities not exceeding a few pence in value. In short, the utility of these small assemblies was limited to satisfying the house-hold needs of the surrounding population, and also, no doubt, as among the Kabyles today, to satisfying that instinct of sociability which is inherent in all men. They constituted the sole distraction offered by a society settled in work on the land. Charlemagne's order to the serfs on his estates not to 'run about to markets' shows that they were attracted much more by the desire to enjoy themselves than by considerations of trade [Pirenne 1936:10–11]." Latouche (1966:235ff.) attributes much greater importance to markets, especially in Ger-many. Marc Bloch makes a very important point in stressing that, although medieval documents frequently specify obligations to be paid in amount of coin (money), produce or labor could be the form of actual payment: ". . . far fewer payments in fact took the form of specie . . . than one would be in-

clined to infer from a casual and incautious reading of the documents. A particularly instructive example is found in the payment of the personal due(s), ordinarily known in France as *'chevage.'* Originally the sign of a protective relationship between lord and man, it became—at any rate in France—one of the symptoms of servitude in the new sense of the term; and under a variety of names it certainly constituted one of the most widespread of the seignorial dues in the Europe of the first feudal age. It is to be found commonly fixed at an annual rate of a few *deniers* per head. A literal interpretation of these requirements would make it appear that innumerable persons of both sexes and generally belonging to the humblest classes were in a position to make a payment each year of a number of small silver pieces. But the true situation was something quite different. Certain chargers, or other documents which happen to be less guarded in language, explain clearly how the *deniers* required for the *chevage* might be replaced by goods—the nature and quantity of which was sometimes specified and sometimes passed over in silence. Sometimes they could even be replaced by a few days' work. Among the great majority of texts which do not indicate the possibility of such substitution, most do not, it seems, assert that such a procedure was ruled out; they simply deemed it superfluous to allude to a universally known custom, and one that was often imposed by inescapable necessity. Everyone knew that to pay in *deniers* [meant *deniers*] or their equivalent . . . [Bloch 1967:236]." Bloch also mentions that swidden agriculture (shifting cultivation using slash and burn techniques) survived in Europe up to the eighteenth century.

10. "The bankruptcy of the state represents the most potent fact during this period. . . . Men . . . lost the habit of expecting protection from a too distant sovereign. They sought it elsewhere and supplanted their obedience to the more remote ruler by other ties of dependence. . . . The social environment in which the feudal relations developed was characterized by an economic system in which [commercial] exchange although not entirely absent was comparatively rare and in which the not very abundant specie [cash] played but a restricted role. . . . the paucity of commercial relations caused the very existence of every man to depend narrowly upon his possibility of disposing in some way of the resources furnished by a portion of the soil placed under his control. But an important fraction of the population drew its revenue [livelihood] from the land only indirectly under the form of personal service in money or in kind for the use of the land. Moreover, the possession of superior rights to the land was for the possessor in many respects but a means of exercising an effective power of command over the men to whom he conceded or permitted the direct enjoyment of the fields. One of the essential characteristics of feudalism is that prestige and social worth sprang less from the free disposal of property than from the free disposal of human forces. But the difficulty of commercial exchange had a considerable effect upon the structure of society. The absence of an easy flow of sales and purchases such as exists in present-day societies prevented the formation of agricultural or industrial salaried classes and of any body of functionaries remunerated periodically in money [Bloch 1933:203–204]."

11. For our purposes it is useful to point out that there were two kinds of master-client relationships in feudalism: that between the king and his land-

holding noble-warriors (barons and counts), and that between the landholding noble-warriors and their rank-and-file peasants.

12. Marxists suffer from a certain myopia with regard to these return services from lords to peasants, for several reasons. One is that they strongly disapprove of such systems and simply do not attribute any worth (value, importance) to community services provided by overlords, such as military protection. Another is their unequal regard for tangible goods and economic services compared to non-economic services. The peasant-serfs paid upward to their lords tangible goods such as grain, chickens, eggs, and cash and economic services such as days of work on the lord's land; they received back mostly non-economic services of a public sort, such as defense, law, and the like. That the lord also granted his peasant-serfs the right to use land to produce their own subsistence is, of course, simply dismissed by Marxists, who disapprove of the lord's legal right to do so in the first place. For these reasons, the Marxists call the material transactions between lord and peasant "exploitation," taking for granted that the peasant paid out to the lord much more than he received back. But it is impossible to make such a judgment objectively because of the *incommensurability* of what is paid out and received back by peasants. All this, of course, would apply to the Bantu and to the Soviet Union and the United States as well, where military defense and law enforcement are also obligatorily paid for by the rank and file. Are present-day Americans (and Russians) "exploited" because we are forced under threat of legal penalty to pay one-third of our income to federal, state, and local governments? I suggest that whether or not "exploitation" exists in such situations should be made to depend on the rank and file's subjective reactions to such obligatory payments upward; when U.S. (or, presumably, Soviet) citizens approve of the quantity and quality of public services they receive back for their tax money, they do not feel exploited. For a clear example of such subjectively-felt exploitation in Africa, see Jaspan (1953).

13. On the Catholic Church providing emergency support and community services in seventeenth-century Mexico: "We also catch a glimpse in travelers' accounts of more unassuming bishops, devoted to their studies and spending more than their incomes on alms and good works. In 1639, His Majesty took the trouble of congratulating the Archbishop of Mexico City on his having sold his silver and books to aid the poor during a serious maize shortage. Many episcopal palaces seem to have had a special dining hall where the poor were fed and at the same time were edified with pious readings.

"The Jesuits distributed alms generously; the different convents gave free meals to anyone knocking at their doors between specified hours. Orders like the Brothers of St. João de Deus and St. Hippolytus maintained numerous hospitals. Bishops' palaces were always filled with travelers and visitors; while, for village monasteries, hospitality was a sacred duty that has persisted to this day in remote pueblos. The many brotherhoods fulfilled the function of modern mutual-aid societies.

"A natural balance, somewhat medieval in flavor, was thus struck between what society gave the Church and what it received in return. Revenues from rich haciendas, dwellings, rents, and alms did flow into the Church's coffers;

but they were returned in the form of charity, education, advancement of knowledge, and literary and artistic works [Chevalier 1963:261]."

14. "But when the peasant had performed all the plowings and carryings demanded of him, and had sown and mown, and threshed and garnered for the lord, he was still under many obligations. His lack of freedom showed itself in a host of ways: he could neither brew nor bake where he would; he was not allowed to grind his own corn, to sell his own beasts, to give his own daughter in marriage . . . without his lord's permission 'prayed and obtained.' The lord's power was about him on all sides: not only did he fear the occasional visit of the [lord's] steward—armed with powers of life and death as it seemed— . . . or the bailiff, whose authoritative commands everyone learned to respect, but he also came under the supervision of the local village officials—reeve, messor, beadle, etc. All these were constantly influencing his actions, and to some extent infringing on his freedoms [Bennett 1937:129]."

I realize that there were peasants in medieval Europe who were free and who owned their own land. But no source I read suggests that they comprised a large proportion of the peasantry between 800 and 1300 in any country except Scandinavia. Several sources emphasize that even free peasants paid dues and services to lords, which is not surprising because feudal dues were an amalgam of taxes and rents, the feudal lord himself being both landowner and public official endowed with political power:

"Nothing could be more misleading than to dwell exclusively on the economic aspects of the relationship between a lord and his men, however important they may seem. For the lord was not merely the director of an undertaking [farming estate]; he was also a leader. He had power of command over his tenants, levied his armed forces from them as occasion demanded, and in return gave them his protection. . . . [From] the Frankish period onward the seigneurial court was the recognized place for hearing most of the pleas affecting the lord's dependents. . . . Many a Frankish and French baron, if asked what his land brought in for him, would have answered like the Highlander who said '500 men.' In economic terms the tenant owed his lord two types of obligation, the payment of rents and the performance of services [agricultural labor and craft-work].

"The complex of rents was so intricate that it is not always easy to grasp the primary significance of each separate strand. Some payments represented a kind of ground rent, at once a recognition of the lord's proprietary right over the soil and a recompense for the tenant's enjoyment of it. Other rents, which were assessed like a poll tax, were a mark of personal servitude, and only affected certain categories of tenants; others again were payable in respect of auxiliary benefits made available to small-holders, pasturage, for example. Finally, there were the archaic charges formerly levied by the State which the lords had managed to usurp for their own profit. Sometimes, though this was rare, a proportion of the harvest was taken as payment. The majority of rents were fixed, sometimes in money, more often in kind. All in all they must have been a considerable burden—but the services were more oppressive still. The tenant of the Carolingian period owed more by way of [labor] service than he did in rent . . . the services were just as variegated as the rents; but leaving aside minor activities such as cartage, two major categories can be distinguished, agricultural labor and craft-work [Bloch 1966:71–72]." On page 76 Bloch tells us that "Frankish Gaul was not wholly manorialized. There were probably still small holders unencumbered by any dues or services—save what they owed the king and his representatives. . . ."

The medieval system I am describing, then, is meant to portray the dominant organization, transactions, and relationships, not the only ones.

15. For the equivalent organization in traditional village Japan, see the excellent account by Smith (1959).

16. He could choose what to plant on enclosed vegetable gardens near the house and on assarts (land newly brought under cultivation isolated from other arable land).

17. I can only mention in passing here and elaborate a bit later in this essay a matter that is important in economic anthropology and deserves detailed analysis. If one reads early European economic and social history after reading the descriptive literature on "primitive money" (such as Einzig 1948; Quiggin 1949), an interesting point emerges: that the "tribes without rulers" of traditional Africa and Oceania have characteristic valuables (the pig-tusk kind of primitive money) and transactions (like kula trade) that disappeared in tribal Europe once the Roman Empire, with its sophisticated *state apparatus* and *coined money,* was established. It seems almost certain from the *analytical* literature of primitive money (Douglas 1958; 1967; Bohannan 1959; Polanyi 1968a; 1968b; Dalton 1965; 1970a) that the highly ranked valuables (raffia cloth, brass rods, cows, kula bracelets, Rossel Island shells) are used by the elders and the powerful as devices of social control—to control access to status positions and to direct and initiate community activities—through the big men's control of the non-commercial sort of primitive valuables or "money." If so, the prestige sector (sphere) in that subset of primitive societies lacking centralized government and money used in commercial (market) exchange contrasts directly with all peasantries. Peasantries are always parts of larger political systems (although, as under European feudalism, the monarchy may be weak), in which cash transactions and the use of cash as a unit of account in non-commercial transactions (such as fines for religious transgression and for not serving on juries) are present. In short, kula trade and the potlach copper and pig-tusk sorts of primitive money do not appear in peasantries because government, cash, and world religion perform the social control functions that the prestige sector performs in tribes without rulers. Displacement of traditional primitive monies by cash and the transformation of the traditional prestige sphere of which they were a part (and also the powerful social control by big men) have been reported in the anthropological literature frequently. Cases in point are what happens when cash displaces cows as bridewealth and ordinary people get access to purchased steel axes.

18. That dependent peasants comprised a "class" in medieval feudalism is a very clear and meaningful statement because the lowly position of peasants was expressed *de jure* and *de facto* and ramified into *all* sectors of life, economic, political, religious, and so on. The social distance between peasant and lord was great, and the allowable interaction between them, little. All of this was reinforced by sumptuary laws prohibiting certain foods to peasants and by differences in modes of dress, speech, deference, and respect. The differences be-

tween servile peasant and lord were as palpable and general as those between traditional Brahmin and low-caste Indian. With the end of feudalism and the beginnings of political and economic modernization (say, by the time Marx wrote), "class" becomes an ambiguous concept. There is now a discrepancy between *de jure* and *de facto* status: rich and poor, peasant and non-peasant, lowborn and highborn are equal before the law and the government, *de jure;* but the status of each, *de facto,* depends on a combination of income, education, and lineage, and the channels of upward mobility widen and diversify.

19. Friedl (1962), writing on a village in Greece, Wright (1964), writing on rural France, and Franklin (1969), writing on Western and Eastern Europe, all show how much technological and cultural modernization took place only after World War II. Wright emphasizes as an important component of rural French transformation the effective national political participation by rural leaders.

20. Kroeber was probably aware of this. Both Foster (1961) and Geertz (1962) point out that Kroeber had in mind European peasantries of the nineteenth century. Unfortunately, Kroeber's point seems to be regarded as important for all peasantries, regardless of time and place, by the anthropologists who followed him.

21. Again we see the need for historical demarcations in anthropology: precolonial/colonial/post-colonial; before modernization/early modernization/late modernization. To say that peasantries at all times and places are parts of larger systems while primitives are not is to generalize about peasantries before, during, and after serious modernization begins, but to confine the comparison with band and tribal societies only to their traditional, pre-modernization forms.

22. In 900 peasants were low-class subordinates, politically and legally inferior to all non-peasants. A crucial aspect of their inferiority was structured in their client position within the feudal system of dependent land tenure. By 1900 their political and legal inferiority to non-peasants had disappeared, and dependent land tenure had been displaced by market or commercial tenure. In 1900 there are two groups of non-peasants to contrast them with: the urban working "class," also citizens, but quite like the peasants in their poverty and lack of education, and the rural and urban upper "classes" (also citizens), legally equal to peasants and urban workers, but superior in lineage, or income, or education, and in *de facto* political participation.

23. In many ways, the non-agricultural urbanized working classes, sharing the rural peasants' poverty and lack of education (and therefore their occupational and social immobility), resembled the rural peasants. See Mayhew (1851).

24. Welfare state policies, of course, began much earlier than 1900. Legislation controlling the conditions of employment of children (minimum age, maximum hours) and safety requirements for hazardous occupations were initiated in England in the 1820's. See Roberts (1960); Polanyi (1944:chapter 17); Carr (1951).

25. "Money began to depreciate after the Great [Germanic] Invasions. . . . When the barbarian monarchies took root in the West, they made no innovations, and were content to keep the Byzantine *solidus.* Most of their kings were incapable of a monetary policy; the newcomers followed the example of the

local inhabitants and used the imperial gold *solidus,* which was in circulation throughout the whole of Europe and was everywhere accepted [Latouche 1966:126] ."

26. The same is true for the Inca's governing of conquered peoples: "Thus the central government [of the Inca] jealously reserved for itself the exclusive right to punish homicide. Neither the *ayllu* [endogamous lineage group] nor family of the murdered man had any right to take the law into its own hands. The immediate governing official had to obtain permission from above. The central government alone had the authority to act independently.

"This is an extremely important indicator of the development of Inca [imperial] government. One has only to compare it with more primitive arrangements where self-help, clan feuds, and retaliatory killings are the order of the day to realize what the state had become by Inca times [Moore 1958:79–80; see also p. 119] ."

So, too, for England: "Dependence on a lord was not the only check on the individual freedom of a freeborn man. Anglo-Saxon polity preserved, even down to the Norman Conquest, many traces of a time when kinship was the strongest of all bonds. . . . when [there is] strife between hostile kindreds, it is shown in the war of tribal factions, and more specifically in the blood-feud. A man's kindred are his avengers; and, as it is their right and honor to avenge him, so it is their duty to make amends for his misdeeds, or else maintain his cause in fight. Step by step, as the power of the State waxes, the self-centered and self-helping autonomy of the kindred wanes. Private feud is controlled, regulated, put, one may say, into legal harness. . . . There is a constant tendency to conflict between the old customs of the family and the newer laws of the State. . . . In the England of the tenth century, we find that a powerful kindred may still be a danger to public order. . . . [Pollock and Maitland 1968, I:31–32] ."

27. Malinowski never explained satisfactorily why the kula was so important to his Trobrianders. He said that possession of the kula valuables was important for its own sake (although some sort of unexplained "inland" kula also went on) and that the kula trade had taken on a heightened intensity since warfare had been curtailed by colonial authorities and dancing frowned on by the missionaries. Uberoi (1962) gives part of the answer in his persuasive analysis of the political implications of success in the kula. But there is more than this involved. Possession of kula valuables, as with possession of raffia cloth among the Lele (Douglas 1958; 1967) and traditional primitive monies of several sorts among the Tiv (Bohannan 1959), enabled one to make important (non-commercial) payments, command the services of ritual and other specialists, initiate community activities, and thereby enhance one's position and power. The primitive monies are devices of social control over juniors and clients. But they do not survive the arrival of central government and cash. See Dalton (1965; 1970*a*).

28. It is not at all clear why anthropologists have accepted Kroeber's definition of a timeless, placeless, and institutionless peasantry as in some sense a good thing. "Even as late as 1948, Kroeber, in his monumental survey of the state of the discipline, could dispose of peasantry in a single paragraph [p. 284] .

". . . Kroeber managed to formulate most clearly and exactly what has turned out to be the recurrent theme in subsequent anthropological studies of peasants: namely, that they constitute part-societies with part-cultures. Peasants, he said, are definitely rural, yet they live in relation to market towns. They form a class segment of a larger stratifactory system, within which they are far from being the dominant group. They lack the isolation, political autonomy, and self-sufficiency of tribal populations. Yet their local units nevertheless retain much of their old identity, integration, and attachment to the soil and cult, to parochial custom and folk art. It was mainly the European peasantry of the nineteenth century and the early twentieth that was in Kroeber's mind as he wrote; but his stress on the fractional, incomplete quality of peasant society and culture has reappeared in virtually every anthropological study of peasant life from Mexico to India as well as in every theoretical treatise on the subject, that has since appeared [Geertz 1962:1–2]."

Summary phrases used to characterize peasantries-in-general are merely variations on Kroeber's theme. To call peasantries "intermediate" societies is to say they are different from traditional tribes and from the modern United States. To say that there is a "continuum" of peasantries is to say that they vary from one another without saying what the *analytically revealing* structural differences are. To differentiate between "open" and "closed" peasantries is something of an improvement, especially if the writer goes on to specify the exact ways they are open (to the larger economy, society, and polity) and what difference this openness makes compared to life in closed systems. All modernizing activities and institutions—economic, political, and cultural—create "openness."

29. The principal point of Fallers' article is that it is mainly in the cultural realm that the African kingdoms do not fit the "classical" (i.e. ideal) concept of peasantry because African kingdoms do not have the gap between folk and elite high culture, so stressed by Redfield: "Now it would seem to be just the relative absence of this differentiation into high and folk cultures which principally distinguishes the African kingdoms from the societies which have commonly been called 'peasant.' . . . Dahomean and Yoruba villagers were not separated from their urban cousins by a cultural gap of the same magnitude as that which divided medieval European and Asian countrymen from city folk. . . . In large part this difference is due simply to the absence in traditional Africa of the literary religious traditions which formed the bases for the European and Asian high cultures [1961:110]."

30. To no avail, apparently, I pointed out ten years ago the morass of nonsense one lets himself in for if he uses this treacherous notion of an undefined "surplus" (Dalton 1960; 1963, Essay 8 in this volume). The critical points are these: anything any farmer pays over in money, labor services, or produce—as tax or rent—is "surplus." But taxes and rents are paid in all kinds of past and present societies. It is also necessary to be told what the farmer gets back from those to whom he pays taxes and/or rents. These return services also vary enormously in past and present societies. The peasant, moreover, sells some portion of his "surplus" and receives back (buys) goods and services from non-farmers. This, too, goes on in all sorts of societies, communistic and capitalistic, old and new. One simply cannot say anything analytically interesting with-

out examining the specific forms these "surplus" transactions take in any given society. See also Pearson (1957).

31. Wolf's concern to make general statements about peasantry is so pronounced that he wants his statements about the four funds to apply equally well whether the peasant's income is all (or mostly) in cash, partly in cash, or all in produce. But obviously it makes a real difference to the peasant's range of choice which form his income takes. The greater the proportion of his income that takes the form of cash receipts, the greater his options in purchasing consumer and producer goods.

32. Even for the medieval feudal system, Wolf is distorting the situation by using language which suggests that the lord is simply extorting payments from the dependent serfs because of his superior power position—"Social relations which are not symmetrical, based . . . upon the exercise of power . . . some men through power demand payments from others . . . the peasant's loss is the powerholder's gain." Wolf does not mention the return services the lord was providing in the form of military and police protection and perhaps, as well, as emergency provider in times of hunger—services sufficiently important for some peasants to have voluntarily infeudated themselves.

In another of his writings, Wolf does point out the material security got by the serf-peon in the Mexican hacienda system of the sixteenth century: "Each man [peon] was given a house, and—if he proved faithful and obedient—a plot of land on which he could raise crops for himself. If a man proved properly submissive, moreover, the owner would finance his wedding or a baptism or a religious devotion, or aid him in other times of financial need. To repay these advances, such a worker would then bind himself to work for the owner until the debt was paid, an occurrence not marked by its frequency.

"From 1540 on, growing numbers of Indians accepted the liabilities of peonage. Often they welcomed the system [*nota bene*] as a way of freeing themselves from the increasingly onerous bondage to Indian communities ravaged by death and disease, threatened with loss of land and water, yet all too often required to bear burdens of tribute and labor services assessed on the basis of their past number of inhabitants. Many of the newcomers were attracted also by the novel goods of Spanish manufacture, more accessible through hacienda channels than in the impoverished Indian villages. . . . Thus the system had advantages for both owner and worker: the owner was guaranteed labor, the worker a measure of novelty, together with security. . . . The owner's person became the governor of their lives, their relation with this person the major guarantee of the security and stability on which depended their daily bread and a roof over their heads [Wolf 1959:206–208]." In assessing Bolivia's agrarian reform of the 1950's, which abolished the feudalistic "fund of rent," Erasmus reports that ". . . a few [peasant households] felt they were worse off because there was no longer a patron to help them when in need . . . [Erasmus 1967:357]."

33. Certainly there has been nothing on the scale of the Spanish conquest which at the same time so deeply disrupted—indeed decimated and then transmogrified—aboriginal peoples. Much smaller groups, particularly those on islands in the Pacific and some North American Indians, did experience equivalent subjugation, traumatic disruption, and decimation of population through

disease, and more or less apathetic acculturation. See Colson (1949) and Worsley (1957).

34. We touch here on another complicated point. The history of European peasantries is not without its traumatic incursions. The German barbarians invading and settling in parts of the Roman Empire, the Viking forays and settlements in France and England, and the Norman conquest of England are cases in point. But the last mentioned of these occurred 900 years ago, and, unlike the Africans transplanted to the Caribbean and the Central and South American Indians, it was the German, Scandinavian, and Norman conquerors who "acculturated," (for example, in language) not the peasant rank-and-file they subjugated (as in Latin America).

35. "The total number of Spaniards who migrated to Middle America [Mexico and Guatemala] has been estimated at 300,000.

"With the Spaniards came . . . the African slaves. Roughly 250,000 were imported into Mexico during the three centuries of the slave trade. . . . Negroes were not the only slaves imported into Middle America. Small numbers of [Asian] Indians, Burmese, Siamese, Indonesians, and Filipinos were also brought to serve in a similar capacity [Wolf 1959:29–30]."

36. For an excellent account of the failure of Mexico to develop economically when silver production declined, see Chevalier (1963:291–292).

37. Agriculture is the predominant but not the only production line peasants engage in. On peasant fishermen, see Firth (1946).

38. To adduce an analogy that illustrates the point: It is perfectly true and general to say that from 1619 to 1970 Negroes as a group have occupied an *inferior position* to whites in America (this is equivalent to saying that peasantries are part-societies with part-cultures). But surely all the interesting questions about the position of Negroes require the sort of disaggregation and subclassification I attempt in this essay for peasantry, so as to isolate turning points and sequential change, that is, to analyze *the nature of* the inferior position under slavery; in the early decades of emancipation; between 1880 and the massive emigration out of the South during World War II; and the drive toward "post-inferiority," so to speak, since 1954.

Another analogy would be the game of comparing all industrial with all non-industrial societies, confining oneself only to statements which hold true in general. Soviet Russia and capitalist United States would then be put in the same category. So, too, the differences between French peasants of 900 and 1900 are ignored (when one concentrates on what is true for all peasantries regardless of time and place), and questions about how they developed over time, not raised.

39. Acculturation studies also include overseas ethnic minorities different from both the natives and the colonial power (for example, Asians in East Africa under British rule) and immigrant streams to such countries as the United States.

40. The most likely reason for their not distinguishing between major and minor acculturation is the absence of theoretical goals or perceived ends to the process, such as exist in today's analysis of economic development. We know that villages, say, in India, are underdeveloped because their present incomes,

technology, educational attainments, and so on, *compared to the farming sectors of developed nations,* are much lower. Since the colonized people who were the subject of acculturation studies were neither members of politically independent states nor citizens of the colonizing power, today's criteria for economic development and cultural modernization were not perceived by anthropologists as relevant ones. Rather, in studying acculturation, they were studying a process of piecemeal permeation, an amalgam of European activities (mining, plantation agriculture) and institutions (Christianity, modern education). Perhaps some of the acculturation studies did assume that the end of the process was a sort of total assimilation to the colonizer's culture, in the sense that descendants of European immigrants to the United States assimilate to American "culture." If so, they guessed wrong.

41. "Modernization" is a very mixed bag: industrialization, the creation of national market networks for natural resources, labor, and products, a national banking system, railroads, expanded literacy and education, and so forth.

42. To simplify, national development and cultural modernization take so long for at least three disparate reasons (and hence all the social sciences are interested in "modernization"): One is capital formation, the enormously expensive process of accumulating public utilities (systems of transport, communication, education, power supply, and the like), urban construction, and a manufacturing establishment. A second reason, much more difficult to analyze than the first (see Hagen 1962), is personality formation: the inculcation of values, attitudes, and capacities necessary to undertake modern activities. Finally, it requires a relatively uncorrupt and efficient governmental organization and civil service devoted to national development and welfare policies (see Adelman and Morris 1967; Myrdal 1960; Carr 1951; Clower *et al.* 1966).

Peasantries remain identifiable entities so long for a less obvious reason. Until recently, anthropologists have concentrated their attention on rural villages rather than cities, and they contrasted *actual* peasant villagers with hypothetical urbanites (or elite townsmen). When they come to study rank-and-file townsmen, the uneducated poor, and the urban working classes (Mayhew 1851; Lewis 1964), they find personalities, ethnic enclaves, and neighborhood networks which are not so different from those of their rural peasant cousins, except in mode of employment and urban residence. On such "worker-peasants" in Germany, see Franklin (1969).

43. "The United States did not face the problem of dismounting a complex and well-established agrarian society of either the feudal or the bureaucratic forms. From the very beginning commercial agriculture was important, as in the Virginian tobacco plantations, and rapidly became dominant as the country was settled. The political struggles between a precommercial landed aristocracy and a monarch were not part of American history. Nor has American society ever had a massive class of peasants comparable to those in Europe and Asia. . . . Like many such terms it is impossible to define the word peasantry with absolute precision because distinctions are blurred at the edges in social reality itself. A previous history of subordination to a landed upper class recognized and enforced in the laws, which, however, need not always prohibit movement out of this class, sharp cultural distinctions, and a considerable degree of *de*

facto possession of the land, constitute the main distinguishing features of a peasantry. Hence Negro sharecroppers in the present-day South could be legitimately regarded as a class of peasants in American society [Moore 1966:111]."

White American farmers were never like traditional European peasants under feudalism: they never had dependent land tenure nor were they ever political inferiors. Markets, cash, and citizenship characterize them throughout American history.

American farmers were unlike European peasants in the early stage of modernization: their education and income, extent of political participation, style of life, social and economic mobility, the use of modern technology, did not mark off white farmer from non-farmer systematically. Nor did American farmers carry with them the stigma of class inferiority from a traditional system in which they were servile.

REFERENCES

ADELMAN, IRMA, and GEORGE DALTON
    1971   A factor analysis of modernization in village India. In *Economic development and social change,* George Dalton ed. New York: Natural History Press.
ADELMAN, IRMA, and CYNTHIA TAFT MORRIS
    1967   *Society, politics, and economic development.* Baltimore: Johns Hopkins Press.
ALLAN, W.
    1965   *The African husbandman.* London and Edinburgh: Oliver and Boyd.
ANDERSON, ROBERT T.
    1963   Studies in peasant life. In *Biennial review of anthropology,* B. J. Siegel ed. Stanford: Stanford University Press.
BENDIX, REINHARD
    1956   *Work and authority in industry.* New York: Wiley.
BENNETT, H. S.
    1937   *Life on the English manor, 1150–1400.* Cambridge: University Press.
BLOCH, MARC
    1933   Feudalism, European. In *The encyclopaedia of the social sciences.* New York: Macmillan.
    1966   *French rural history.* London: Routledge and Kegan Paul.
    1967   *Land and work in medieval Europe.* London: Routledge and Kegan Paul.
BOHANNAN, PAUL
    1959   The impact of money on an African subsistence economy. *Journal of Economic History* 19:491–503.
    1960   Africa's land. *Centennial Review,* vol. 4.
BOHANNAN, PAUL, and LAURA BOHANNAN
    1968   *Tiv economy.* Evanston: Northwestern University Press.
BOHANNAN, PAUL, and GEORGE DALTON
    1962   Introduction. In *Markets in Africa,* Paul Bohannan and George Dalton ed. Evanston: Northwestern University Press.

CARR, E. H.
  1951   *The new society.* London: Macmillan.
CHEVALIER, FRANÇOIS
  1963   *Land and society in colonial Mexico.* Berkeley: University of Califor-
         nia Press.
CLOWER, ROBERT W., GEORGE DALTON, MITCHELL HARWITZ, and A. A. WAL-
      TERS
  1966   *Growth without development: an economic survey of Liberia.*
         Evanston: Northwestern University Press.
COLSON, ELIZABETH
  1949   Assimilation of an American Indian group. *Human Problems in Brit-
         ish Central Africa (Rhodes-Livingstone Journal)* 5:1–13.
DALTON, GEORGE
  1960   A note of clarification on economic surplus. *American Anthropolo-
         gist* 62:483–490.
  1963   Economic surplus, once again. *American Anthropologist* 65:389–394.
  1965   Primitive money. *American Anthropologist* 67:44–65.
  1970*a* Currency, primitive, in *Encyclopaedia Britannica,* 14th ed.
  1970*b* *Economic development and social change.* New York: Natural His-
         tory Press.
DOUGLAS, MARY
  1958   Raffia cloth distribution in the Lele economy. *Africa* 28:109–122.
  1967   Primitive rationing: a study in controlled exchange. In *Themes in
         economic anthropology,* Raymond Firth ed. London: Tavistock.
EINZIG, PAUL
  1948   *Primitive money.* London: Eyre and Spottiswoode.
EPSTEIN, T. SCARLETT
  1962   *Economic development and social change in South India.* Manches-
         ter: Manchester University Press.
  1967   Customary systems of rewards in rural South India. In *Themes in
         economic anthropology,* Raymond Firth ed. London : Tavistock.
ERASMUS, CHARLES
  1967   Upper limits of peasantry and agrarian reform: Bolivia, Venezuela,
         and Mexico compared. *Ethnology* 6:349–380.
FALLERS, LLOYD A.
  1961   Are African cultivators to be called "peasants"? *Current Anthropol-
         ogy* 2:108–110.
FINLEY, M. I.
  1965   Between slavery and freedom. *Comparative Studies in Society and
         History* 6:233–49.
FIRTH, RAYMOND
  1946   *Malay fishermen: their peasant economy.* London: Routledge and
         Kegan Paul.
  1951   *The elements of social organisation.* London: Watts.
FIRTH, RAYMOND, and BASIL YAMEY
  1966   *Capital, saving, and credit in peasant societies.* Chicago: Aldine.
FRANKLIN, S. H.
  1969   *The European peasantry.* London: Methuen and Co.

FRIEDL, ERNESTINE
   1962   *Vasilika: a village in modern Greece.* New York: Holt, Rinehart, and Winston.

GEERTZ, CLIFFORD
   1962   Studies in peasant life: community and society. In *Biennial review of anthropology,* B. J. Siegel ed. Stanford: Stanford University Press.
   1963   *Agricultural involution.* Berkeley: University of California Press.

HAGEN, E. E.
   1962   *On the theory of social change.* Homewood, Ill.: Dorsey Press.

HECKSCHER, ELI F.
   1955   *Mercantilism,* 2 vols. London: G. Allen and Unwin.

HOGBIN, IAN, and PETER LAWRENCE
   1967   *Studies in New Guinea land tenure.* Sydney: Sydney University Press.

HOLMBERG, ALLAN, *et al.*
   1965   The Vicos case: peasant society in transition. *American Behavioral Scientist* 8:3–33.

HOSKINS, W. G.
   1957   *The midland peasant: the economic and social history of a Leicestershire village.* London: Macmillan.

JASPAN, M. A.
   1953   A sociological case study: communal hostility to imposed social changes in South Africa. In *Approaches to community development,* Phillips Ruopp ed. The Hague: W. Van Hoeve.

KROEBER, A. L.
   1948   *Anthropology.* New York: Harcourt, Brace.

LATOUCHE, ROBERT
   1966   *The birth of western economy: economic aspects of the Dark Ages.* New York: Harper Torchbooks.

LEWIS, OSCAR
   1964   *The children of Sanchez.* Harmondsworth: Penguin Book Co.

MALINOWSKI, BRONISLAW
   1935   *Coral gardens and their magic,* vol. 1. New York: American Book.

MAYHEW, HENRY
   1851   *London labor and the London poor,* 4 vols. London: Griffin, Bohn, and Company. (Reprinted by Dover Publications, Inc., New York, in 1968.)

MOORE, BARRINGTON, JR.
   1966   *Social origins of dictatorship and democracy: lord and peasant in the making of the modern world.* Boston: Beacon.

MOORE, SALLY FALK
   1958   Power and property in Inca Peru. New York: Columbia University Press.

MYRDAL, GUNNAR
   1957   *Rich lands and poor.* New York: Harper.
   1960   *Beyond the welfare state.* New Haven: Yale University Press.

ORTIZ, SUTTI
   1967   The structure of decision-making among Indians of Colombia. In

Themes in economic anthropology, Raymond Firth ed. London: Tavistock.

PEARSON, HARRY
1957   The economy has no surplus: critique of a theory of development. In *Trade and market in the early empires*, K. Polanyi, C. M. Arensberg, H. W. Pearson ed. Glencoe: The Free Press.

PIRENNE, HENRI
1936   *Economic and social history of medieval Europe*. London: Routledge and Kegan Paul.

POLANYI, KARL
1944   *The great transformation*. New York: Rinehart.
1968a   The semantics of money uses. In *Primitive, archaic, and modern economies: essays of Karl Polanyi*, George Dalton ed. New York: Doubleday Anchor Books.
1968b   Archaic economic institutions: cowrie money. In *Primitive, archaic, and modern economies: essays of Karl Polanyi*, George Dalton ed. New York: Doubleday Anchor Books.

POLLOCK, FREDERICK, FREDERIC WILLIAM MAITLAND
1968   *The history of English law*, 2 vols. Cambridge: Cambridge University Press. (First edition, 1895.)

QUIGGIN, A. H.
1949   *A survey of primitive money*. London: Methuen.

REDFIELD, ROBERT
1960   *Peasant society and culture*. Chicago: University of Chicago Press.

ROBERTS, DAVID
1960   *Victorian origins of the British welfare state*. New Haven: Yale University Press.

SADIE, J. L.
1960   The social anthropology of economic development. *Economic Journal* 70:294–303.

SCHAPERA, I.
1928   Economic changes in South African native life. *Africa* 1:170–188.

SCHAPERA, I., and A. J. H. GOODWIN
1937   Work and wealth. In *The Bantu-speaking tribes of South Africa*, I. Schapera London: Routledge and Kegan Paul.

SCHULTZ, T. W.
1969   New evidence on farmer responses to economic opportunities from the early agrarian history of western Europe. In *Subsistence agriculture and economic development*, Clifton R. Wharton, Jr. ed. Chicago: Aldine.

SHARP, R. L.
1952   Steel axes for stone-age Australians. *Human organization* 11:17–22.

SIMPSON, LESLEY BYRD
1950   *The encomienda in New Spain*. Berkeley: University of California Press.

SLICHER VAN BATH, B. H.
1963   *The agrarian history of western Europe, A.D. 500 to 1850*. New York: St. Martin's.

SMELSER, NEIL J.
  1963   Mechanisms of change and adjustment to change. In *Industrializa-tion and society*, B. F. Hoselitz and W. E. Moore ed. The Hague: UNESCO-Mouton.
SMITH, THOMAS C.
  1959   *The agrarian origins of modern Japan*. Stanford: Stanford University Press.
SOROKIN, P. A., *et al.*
  1930   *A systematic sourcebook in rural sociology*. Minneapolis: University of Minnesota Press.
SPICER, EDWARD H.
  1952   *Human problems in technological change*. New York: Russell Sage Foundation.
UBEROI, J. P. SINGH
  1962   *The politics of the Kula ring*. Manchester: The University Press.
VAYDA, ANDREW P.
  1969   *Environment and cultural behavior*. New York: Natural History Press.
WAGLEY, CHARLES, and MARVIN HARRIS
  1955   A typology of Latin American subcultures. *American Anthropologist* 57:428–451.
WHARTON, CLIFTON R., Jr.
  1969   *Subsistence agriculture and economic development*. Chicago: Aldine.
WOLF, ERIC R.
  1959   *Sons of the shaking earth*. Chicago: University of Chicago Press.
  1966   *Peasants*. Englewood Cliffs: Prentice-Hall.
WORSLEY, PETER
  1957   Millenarian movements in Melanesia. *Rhodes-Livingstone Institute Journal*, pp. 18–31.
WRIGHT, GORDON
  1964   *Rural revolution in France*. Stanford: Stanford University Press.

III

DEVELOPMENT AND MODERNIZATION

Institutions are embodiments of human meaning and purpose.

KARL POLANYI

. . . we must assign to the technical and socio-cultural variables the role of prime movers in the *initiation* of economic development.

IRMA ADELMAN

In the long-lasting earliest stages, while man, almost as part of the animal kingdom, is gaining his food and life from the soil, institutions have long to grow, gain great power, provide a metaphysical comfort for unchanging poverty or sudden catastrophe, yield with great difficulty to social pressure, perhaps even delay the growth of technical or commercial change. A food surplus (probably technically induced) and a market provide the first essential break in this circle. . . . As the market grows, technology responds; technology in turn increases the market by lowering unit costs. . . . Eventually, growing differentiation and economic pressure first break through the outdated hierarchy [of social stratification], and, as Marx points out, in secularizing it destroys its metaphysical pretensions. Finally, it mobilizes—and here a wide extension of education becomes essential—more and more of those under-employed (perhaps in subsistence) and those employed in superseded forms of production, until it has mustered the entire labor force to its aid. Then, and only then, is something like the full human potential harnessed to the process of growth. . . . This process is controlled by the rate of invention, by the organization of the market and specialization, and by the conservatism of the hierarchy.

GUY HUNTER

10

Economic Development
and Social Change [1]

THE SCOPE OF ECONOMIC ANTHROPOLOGY

Economic anthropology has only recently become a field of special interest within social and cultural anthropology, with which it shares much. Its subject is thousands of small-scale communities in Africa, Asia, Latin America, Oceania, and the Middle East.[2] Its principal method of research is personal observation during field work. The anthropologist, usually working alone, lives in the small community he studies for a year or two and supplements the data he himself collects by reading whatever literature exists on the social group and the cultural area he is studying. Anthropologists are professionally sensitive to the mutual interaction of cultural, social, and economic forces. Indeed, anthropologists differ from other social scientists in their overwhelming reliance on the field-work technique of face-to-face immersion in the community life of the people studied, their focus on village-level communities in the non-Western world, and their wide interests in all the principal activities, institutions, and relationships in the small communities studied. It is rare for an anthropologist to concentrate exclusively on economic matters because the *Gemeinschaft* structure of the small societies anthropologists study requires them to analyze kinship, religion, technology, ecology, and polity, in order to say interesting things about economy.

The economic anthropologist's world, then, is composed of thousands of small economies on all the continents for whose analysis detailed knowledge of non-economic aspects of society is required. The economic anthropologist is also interested in two different dimensions of economy—organization and performance—and in economies under three sets of conditions, each of which itself varies greatly: their aboriginal condition before European contact and colonization; their changed condition during the colonial period of European presence and control; and their presently changing condition in the post-colonial period, which, for Africa

269

and much of Asia, is barely one generation old.[3] Anthropology is a complicated subject, not because it has developed a body of abstract theory—as with physics and economics—but because its subject matter is so varied. If the topics of interest to economic anthropologists were translated into the counterpart interests of economists (as fields in economics are demarcated in the study of industrial capitalism), the list would be formidable: economic history, comparative economic systems, industrial organization, agricultural economics, national income accounting, industrial sociology, and economic development.

Anthropologists, moreover, use two approaches, two professional emphases, in portraying real-world societies. One is an artistic approach which shares much with psychological and sociological fiction (for example, Alan Sillitoe's *The Loneliness of the Long Distance Runner;* Eugene O'Neill's *Long Day's Journey into Night*). The aim here is to convey the inward meaning of events, actions, and relationships in the small tribal or village community—folk views, attitudes, values, and individual behavior. The anthropologist, like the playwright and novelist, becomes a sensitive translator of personality, world views, and social events (compare Colin Turnbull, *The Forest People,* and his *The Lonely African* with Laura Bohannan, *Return to Laughter,* and Isak Dinesen, *Out of Africa*). There is much to be learned from such portrayals of personal views and community life in other cultures. All the great ethnographers convey such artistic essence in some of their writings.

The social science approach, however, now dominates. Here, the emphasis is on concepts, analytical conclusions, generalizations, and comparisons: to show how a given economic system works, how it compares with other economic systems, and how it relates to culture and society. But until recently, little was done to create an analytical framework for economic anthropology. Malinowski's pioneer—and, indeed, brilliant—work remained the dominating format: rich ethnographic description of activities and organization; sensitive portrayals of the perceptions of the people and the inward meaning they attributed to land, work, and valuables. The themes stressed were the interpenetration of economic and social organization and the special regard people had for the prestige sectors of economy (kula, pig tusks, potlatch, bridewealth). Works such as these continue to supply us with factual raw materials necessary for analysis. But rather little was done from the more technical social science viewpoint: to contrive conceptual categories, to draw analytical conclusions, to make systematic comparisons, to quantify, and to prescribe policy.

In the last ten years the social science emphasis in economic anthropology has been influenced from three directions. A group of economists and anthropologists, associated with the economic historian Karl Polanyi, have argued the need for a special analytical framework and conceptual vocabulary to study the socio-economic organization of pre-industrial systems and have begun to construct some useful theory.[4] Another group of economists and anthropologists have argued the need to incorporate the conceptual vocabulary, leading ideas, and methodology of conventional economic analysis and to measure the economic performance of primitive and peasant economies.[5]

The third happening which has affected economic anthropology, its theory and its direction, consists of two sets of related events. One is the Colonial Revolution, begun with India's achievement of political independence in 1947, and followed by nation-statehood for some fifty or more countries, principally in Africa and Asia, accompanied by policies to initiate national economic development and modernization. The related event is the rapid establishment of sub-fields in all the social sciences concerned with the new nations. For the first time ever, I believe, large groups of professionals from all the social sciences came to have a common focus of interest in the same set of processes and problems—structural transformation in the developing world.

ECONOMICS AND DEVELOPMENT

Of all the social sciences concerned with development and modernization, economics has achieved the most in generating theory and policy prescriptions. The reasons are worth examining. We may be able to see why other social sciences (including cultural and economic anthropology) have a more difficult task than economics when they consider modernization. It is the quantifiable nature of the segment of social reality that economists deal with and their ability to contrive theoretical models that accounts for their performance.

The glaring fact of the underdeveloped world is its material poverty. The fact is glaring to the leaders and an increasing number of ordinary people in Africa, Asia, and Latin America; to the governments and people of the developed countries; to the international civil service of the UN; to the social scientists in the universities on all the continents; and to the great private philanthropies of the United States. Poverty means not only insufficient food but also eradicable disease, early death, and a life sentence of ignorance, immobility, and meanness for hundreds of millions of people. The overriding priority, therefore, is to increase incomes of persons, village communities, and nations. So it is economic analysis, economic planning, economic policy, and economic aid that appear paramount.

But it is not only the pressing need for material improvement that accounts for the prominence of economists in the subject of modernization. There are reinforcing reasons attributable to the kinds of theory and measurement used in economics and ultimately to the quantifiable nature of that special sphere of social reality economists deal with. The extent of success each social science has in analyzing development and modernization probably reflects its ability to employ its conventional methods and theories—the theoretical and policy achievements of the subject *before* development came to be a focus of interest. Economists who turn to development studies are able to employ much of their ordinary analyses and measurements. Herein lies one of their strengths.

Economists bring to their work on development a strong conviction that they must create theory in order to derive policy prescriptions. The tradition is deeply imbedded in economics. Adam Smith, David Ricardo, Karl Marx, and Maynard Keynes were theoreticians as well as policymakers. Good theory makes clear the strategic relationships determining real-world processes of importance and suggests policy levers to direct the processes toward desired goals. Good theory is an essential tool to transform what *is* into what *ought to be*. One reason, then, for the effectiveness of economics in development studies is the ability of economists to create persuasive theory as a rationale for policy guidelines. Another is their ability to quantify. Economic theory and policy are most powerful when economists can establish the numerical dimensions of economic structure, performance, processes, and transactions from hard data series.

Other social sciences consider spheres of human activity and social organization which are not as amenable to statistical specification. Anthropology and political science have very few quantified factual bases equivalent to national income accounts, input-output tables, and balance of payments components. It is the quantifiable nature of the portion of social reality economists deal with and their ability to build theoretical models depicting strategic functional relationships that make them effective analyzers of development. The economist is more fortunate than the anthropologist for the same reason that the surgeon is more fortunate than the psychiatrist: the symptoms of illness can be more exactly ascertained; the essential causes can be more assuredly established; and therefore the alleviation of pain can be more confidently prescribed and implemented.[6]

Economists spoke development from 1776 to 1870, from Adam Smith to Karl Marx; forgot it for the next seventy years, but resumed speaking a mandarin dialect called "growth theory" just before the Colonial Revolution made economists remember their childhood tongue. In the late 1930's, Keynes answered the questions, What makes the size of the aggregate national income for a developed capitalist country what it is for any one year? And what accounts for its short-run fluctuations? In the late 1940's, Harrod and Domar asked, What determines the long-run growth of aggregate national income for such countries? And Schumpeter stressed the strategic roles in the process played by entrepreneurs and innovations. The econometricians measured national economic structure and performance.

They filled in the theoretical skeleton with the flesh of numbers and trans-actional facts. Macro-economic theory, inter-industry analysis, and the use of national income statistics to measure performance were established be-fore economists turned to the development of Africa and Asia.

Economists were equipped in other ways as well to undertake develop-ment studies. The economic historians and specialists in Soviet economy quickly discovered that they, too, had been speaking development all their lives. Rostow and Gerschenkron, among others, pointed out that we could learn things of interest about the current transformation of India and Ni-geria by reexamining the historical transformation of England and Ger-many and the deliberate development efforts of Soviet Russia and Japan.[7]

We have always had with us, moreover, our Veblens and Galbraiths—semi-pariahs within the profession, heroes to the rest of the world—lecturing us on the social implications of economic organization and performance and the need to study institutions and the cultural frame-work within which the economy functions. The lesson was remembered by a few economists, who set out to investigate the interpenetration of socio-political institutions, or personality and culture, with economic activity in the process of development.[8] It seems easier for economists to cross over into politics, sociology, and anthropology than for the other social scien-tists to incorporate economics in their formal analyses. Almost certainly it is because economics is less easily self-taught than the other social sci-ences. In part, perhaps, it is also due to an older tradition in economics of pragmatic engagement. Some economists have always chosen real problems to investigate and used whatever methods produce interesting results, even, as with Everett Hagen, if it required them to put down their surgeon's tools and take up the psychiatrist's.

Finally, real-world events in Europe and America prepared the econo-mists to undertake modern development analysis and planning. The Great Depression of the 1930's killed laissez faire in practice and in ideology, and Keynesian economics killed its theoretical rationale. Central govern-ment was to "intervene" in the private market economy to assure some-thing close to full employment. Government was to be not only the spo-radic compensator in emergency but the institutionalized governor and regulator. Central planning in capitalist countries during World War II proved that Keynes was right and also that governmental policies could in-crease the national growth rate. (We also came to understand what the Russians had been doing since 1928. During the war, Britain and the United States also displaced market autonomy with central planning in order to produce quickly a narrow range of high-priority goods.) We emerged from the war with knowledge and experience in economic plan-ning and perhaps, as well, with a fresh appreciation of the developmental power of technological innovation. Radar was converted to television, jet propulsion to commercial aviation, and military rocketry to space research. The Marshall Plan to help European reconstruction was the last of these preparations for development planning and analysis.[9]

ANTHROPOLOGY AND MODERNIZATION

Anthropology has catalogued and described many strange societies always with scrupulous care not to disturb them, with its focus of interest on culture rather than on social change, its powerful instrument the notion of the validity of all cultures. More than any other social science it has seen institutions in context; it has striven always to penetrate the mode of thought of the group under study.

Economics on the other hand has sought out the mechanism of change. It has been very close to business and government; economic thinking everywhere influences major decisions [Keyfitz 1959:46].

Just as the economist's approach to development was in large measure shaped by the working methods of economics and the problems and processes it addressed before the Colonial Revolution, so, too, with anthropology and modernization. But the circumstances here were entirely different. Anthropologists were not well prepared to undertake post-colonial studies of micro-development.

Anthropology has many fewer practicing professionals than does economics and was established as a university subject much later. As an international subject, it is much less uniform than economics. Swedish, Italian, and American economists have in common not only a large base of economic theory and techniques of statistical measurement but also a common focus of empirical interest: the organization and performance of the industrial capitalism of their own national economies. National traditions in anthropology, however, were shaped principally by colonial experience. In those European nations which were not important colonial powers, archaeology and physical anthropology, rather than social anthropology, were likely to be stressed. Britain had tribal societies intact and functioning in its colonies in Africa, Oceania, and Asia; social anthropologists studied these societies as living social systems. In the United States, where American Indian bands and tribes were already radically changed from their aboriginal condition by 1875, cultural anthropology became established with different emphases.

Until quite recently, moreover, social and cultural anthropologists concentrated their studies on tribal rather than the Latin American and Asian peasant societies which comprise the bulk of today's underdeveloped world (Geertz 1962a). Classic ethnographies, such as Boas on Eskimos and northwest coast Indians, Malinowski on the Trobriands, and Evans-Pritchard on the Nuer, were on small, stateless, relatively isolated groups, whose language and religion were not widely shared. The village communities of India and Latin America received much less attention.

When anthropologists studied social and economic change, they frequently studied situations which were different from those typifying today's modernization. Aside from grand theories of evolution concerned with unobserved early change in archaic and ancient societies, anthropologists studied acculturation of American Indians, or the early generations of culture contact under colonial conditions (Broom *et al.* 1954). Many of those engaged in applied anthropology tried to introduce innovations piecemeal in village communities before national development programs came to be established with political independence (Spicer 1952).

APPLIED ANTHROPOLOGY AND AGRICULTURAL ECONOMICS

If the economist's model of behavior tends to be the prizefight, the sociologist's model tends to be the quilting bee [Moore 1955:158].

Economists and anthropologists also have somewhat different conceptions of what the process of development consists of. When economists turn to the problem of inducing rural peoples to undertake new economic activities (like planting new cash crops) and using new technology (such as chemical fertilizers), they think in terms of providing sufficient material incentives (profitable prices for cash crops), needed skills, resources, and equipment to undertake the activities (agricultural extension services, farm-to-market roads and transport, and credit). The economist, moreover, views development as a long-run continuing process of new, improved, and diversified activities and technology, so that community income rises continually.

The conception of micro-development contained in many studies of applied anthropology is both different and a special case. Many of the studies consider problems of introducing one or two specific innovations— improved seed, mosquito control—into a village community.[10] Overwhelmingly, the case studies of applied anthropology entail the special situation of the visiting expert ("change agent") in temporary residence as the initiator of the one or few innovations to be introduced. The literature describes cases of success and failure in introducing innovations piecemeal and draws analytical and policy conclusions from them (Spicer 1952; Erasmus 1961). It stresses the need for the visiting expert to know the history and the present organization of the community. Above all, it stresses the *cultural* complexity of innovations—the many resistances to innovation stemming from the people's values, attitudes, social relationships, and past experiences—and the *social* consequences of innovations: that the adoption of a steel axe can induce a train of unforeseen social consequences, changed relationships, and even new conflict situations (Sharp 1952).

The literature of applied anthropology is useful to agricultural extension agents, public health field workers, Peace Corps volunteers, and other visiting experts charged with introducing specific innovations in their short-run visits. But its relevance to the study of modernization is limited. It is insufficient for both theoretical and policy reasons and should be supplemented in several ways. To study present-day development, we must include the new social and economic conditions and policies accompanying the end of colonialism and the new knowledge being brought forth by the several subjects now analyzing development processes.

One supplementary field is agricultural economics. Agronomists and economists show the *ecological, economic,* and *technological* complexity of agricultural innovation: the monetary costs, new skills, soil and water conditions, and enlarged labor requirements entailed in successful innovation. It is almost certainly so nowadays that developmental projects fail more frequently because of faulty ecological, economic, and technical analysis than because of cultural resistances: that the soil or rainfall conditions are unsuitable to the innovation; that the profitable use of chemical fertilizer requires more labor than is physically available in the community.

> Difficulties were encountered in harvesting groundnuts because the soil becomes incredibly hard when it dries. Sugar cane suffered from lack of irrigation facilities . . . the herbicides presently in use are ineffective in controlling the local weeds; techniques for irrigating wheat are scarcely understood; insecticides are misused. . . . In 1909 cultivators reportedly gave three reasons for not transplanting their paddy [rice]: insufficient irrigation, poor soils, and scattered holdings. Farmers contacted during the 1963–64 farm survey claimed they did not transplant because their draft animals were too weak for puddling, labor was insufficient, and grazing was not controlled [Weaver 1968:194, 199].

The applied anthropologists teach us about the cultural and social interdependence of innovations. What deserves at least as much emphasis in studying today's rural modernization is the technical, ecological, and economic complementarity and interdependence of agricultural (and industrial) innovations: that the profitable use of irrigation equipment also requires chemical fertilizers, pesticides, and additional labor—a package of innovations simultaneously introduced as a condition for success.

It should also be understood that much socio-economic change currently goes on without the entrepreneurial presence of visiting experts transmitting innovative skills (see, for example, Epstein 1962). Nowadays, new opportunities for income growth, new modes of production, and new cultural achievement are frequently provided by *impersonal* agencies and facilities which link the village to the region and nation by creating whole new sets of economic and cultural transactions: all-weather roads and regular bus service, electricity, radios and newspapers, postal savings facilities. The applied anthropologists who were in the field before 1950 studied village economies at a time when the regions and nations of which they were a part were relatively static economically. They are no longer so. With an end to semi-isolation come mobility, new alternatives, and new activities —development from above. It is this movement of people, goods, and ideas in the post-colonial framework of new regional and national institutions, policies, and capital facilities which is central to modernization.

DIFFICULTIES IN STUDYING MICRO-DEVELOPMENT AND MODERNIZATION

The empirical data and analyses of micro-development are spread over several branches of social science. Anyone who attempts to create a theoretical framework has to read deeply in several subjects other than his own. Consider the relevant sources one would turn to in constructing models of change, development, and modernization of village communities.

The anthropological literature is very large, indeed, and appears under the headings of evolution, adaptation to ecology, culture contact, acculturation, applied anthropology, culture change, and, recently, the anthropology of modernization. The common focus of interest is change at the village community level, but the underlying conditions, the historical periods, and the kinds of change studied vary enormously (see the survey articles by Spindler 1959; Rubin 1962; Voget 1963).

Several fields within economics contribute to the study of micro-development. The agricultural economists have long been interested in measuring and analyzing rural development (Jones 1961; Miracle 1962; Allan 1965; Mellor *et al.* 1968). Several national income statisticians have measured the performance of village economies in the hinterland of developing nations (Deane 1953; Samuels 1963). The literature of the economic and social history of already developed nations in Europe and Asia contains much that is relevant to current experiences, particularly, as with Japan and Eastern Europe, where traditional economy and society—peasantries, pronounced social stratification—bore striking similarities to structures of the nations developing today (Smith 1959; Polanyi 1944; Coulborn and Strayer 1956; Duby 1968). The industrial sociologists also have made some notable contributions in their studies of social change accompanying European industrialization (Bendix 1956; Smelser 1958).

Finally, there is the institutional literature of economic development concerned with the interaction of economic, social, and political forces in the processes of modernization. I shall have more to say later in this essay about the insights into micro-development to be got from the work of Myrdal, Hagen, Smelser, and Adelman and Morris.

Anthropologists and others who work on the theoretical and policy aspects of micro-development are handicapped by the absence of hard data series relating to village economies (Hill 1966). There are very few village or tribal economies for which comparable data series exist of the sort economists find essential to analyze national economic development: the composition and totals of community income and output; balance of payments figures; the data to construct input-output matrices; productivity measurements for various lines of production; price series, figures on investment, and so on (Fogg 1965; Lewis 1953; Stolper 1966).[11]

There is insufficient theory of socio-economic change and development at the village level. There are some leading ideas, insights, and the beginnings of a conceptual vocabulary, but little in the way of verbal or mathematical models depicting strategic relationships. We are only beginning to discern the important regularities that underlie the transformation sequence for village communities and to understand what are the prime inducers of modernization. And we now look for the general lessons to be learned from the empirical studies of unusual success or unusual failure and to expect that it is *both* cultural heredity and economic and physical environment which induce success or failure.

NEW METHODS OF INVESTIGATION

The circumstances under which economic development and cultural modernization of village communities now proceed require new techniques of investigation in addition to the traditional field excursion of one man studying one village for one year. The changes we call modernization occur as sequential processes which take place over generations; they are not once-and-for-all changes. Enlarged commercialization, the use of new technology, the growth of literacy and its consequences, the transactional and institutional links created between hinterland communities and the new central governments and cities since the former colonies became independent nation-states, are very long-run changes.

These complicated changes never occur evenly. Some are always lagged and occur piecemeal over several generations, for at least three disparate reasons. One is personality formation, which conditions the ability of different age groups during any one time period to absorb new skills and values and undertake new activities (Hagen 1962). Another is capital formation, that lengthy and expensive process of building private and public investment goods (Singer 1952). To equip a nation with machine-using factories, roads, power facilities, and schools requires the work and savings of generations. A third is the inevitable lags in reforming political and social institutions—political corruption, caste discrimination—to enable government to undertake its tasks of development and provision of social services (Myrdal 1960). We in industrialized, modernized, developed America should learn from our national strife over Vietnam and the restructuring of Negro life in our society that the reform of political and social institutions is neither simple nor painless. The tenacity, the inertia, the resistance to deep reform, seem shakable—lamentably—only when shocked by undeniable signs of malaise, expressed forcibly. We in America who are seeing years of strife in Berkeley, Watts, and Chicago in pursuit of social and political reform should not be surprised at African and Latin American coups. Nor should the Russians be surprised after Prague. One of the least understood aspects of modernization is what determines time rates of change, especially change in political and social institutions.

The new technology, and the new economic and cultural activities that comprise modernization, mutually interact and displace the old, thereby affecting individuals and networks of social groupings. Not only are traditional economies changing but also cultures and social relationships; not only are social and economic organization changing but also economic and cultural performance. Individual persons are changing, their relationships in and to social groupings are changing, and the local community's transactions—economic, cultural, political—with the region, the nation, and the rest of the world are changing. To measure and analyze these changes requires more than one man working one year in one community. The processes at work are altogether more complicated than a single innovation working itself out within a traditional culture otherwise intact. Modernization is not the same as the introduction of the horse among the Plains Indians or the steel axe among aboriginal Australians.[12]

Modernization at the village level now takes place within the larger settings of regional and national development. Frequently we are dealing with local communities being vitally affected by new taxes, new goods, new experts, new roads, new political parties, all originating outside the local community. If anthropologists are to understand the causes and consequences of change in the rural community, they must enlarge their studies these days to include the region and the nation whose policies, activities, and personnel now impinge on the local community in unprecedented ways and with unprecedented frequency.

In recent years anthropologists have developed new methods to study change in reaction to the more complicated circumstances and longer time horizon which characterize economic development and cultural modernization. A few older anthropologists have restudied communities they first visited twenty or thirty years earlier in order to record and analyze the intervening change. Raymond Firth's excellent restudies of Tikopia and Malay fishermen are works of this sort (Firth 1959; 1966b).

T. Scarlett Epstein's work (1962) deserves wide reading for both its substance and its methods. She used the traditional field-work approach, but chose a strategic field situation: two agricultural village communities in

India within six miles of each other, only one of which got irrigation facilities (some twenty-five years earlier). She analyzed the social and economic changes occurring in both villages. Enough time had elapsed so that important changes were discernible. Her training in economics allowed her to measure productivity, income, and expenditure, so as to buttress her qualitative analysis of socio-economic organization with statistical data on comparative economic performance. Her work should be recognized as a model of how the traditional field-work approach of anthropologists can be adapted to study the social and cultural consequences of modern technological and economic change.[13]

Clifford Geertz's work in Indonesia on entrepreneurs (1962*b;* 1963*a*), and on agricultural change (1963*b*) is noteworthy for his fruitful combination of historical, ecological, and anthropological analysis and for his study of the economic growth of towns. (His more recent field work in Morocco is designed to study change in depth by frequent residence over a ten-year period.)

Collaborative field work is another method of coping with the complicated processes of social and economic change. Several kinds of teams of researchers have done useful work in the field. A group of anthropologists from Cornell (Holmberg *et al.* 1965), in residence over several years, studied minutely the transformation of Vicos, a peasant hacienda community in Peru. Their work is unusual because of the quick success the group had in initiating technological, economic, and socio-cultural innovations. The theoretical sophistication brought to bear, moreover, together with the depth and breadth of description and analysis, allows the reader to learn some important lessons from Vicos.

A different kind of collaborative effort is a recent piece of work sponsored by the World Bank (deWilde *et al.* 1967). A group of economists and anthropologists studied problems of transforming agriculture in tropical Africa. They did brief field investigations in thirteen areas of varying ecological, cultural, economic, and technological conditions.

MICRO-DEVELOPMENT AND HISTORICAL SEQUENCE

> Any planned growth is embedded in a set of institutions and attitudes
> which come from the past [Keyfitz 1959:34].

The study of modernization at the village community level should begin with two leading ideas: that the communities we observe undergoing social and economic change today were importantly shaped by their social and economic organization, physical environment, and contact experiences with Europeans and others in the pre-colonial and colonial periods. Anthropological analysis therefore should be done within a conscious framework of historical time periods. Second, that the characteristic forces of change were different in the pre-colonial, colonial, and post-colonial periods.

Pre-colonial Africa, Asia, and Latin America (like pre-industrial Europe) were not static, but the characteristic changes which moved people and restructured social, political, and economic life were principally ravages of nature and ravages of man: famine, pestilence, war, and conquest. These brought change, but not the sorts of modern structural change induced by industrialization and mass literacy. The changes were like those caused by the external shocks of the bubonic plague in fourteenth-century Europe, the Viking raids on Britain and France in the tenth century, and the Norman conquest of England in the eleventh. Frequently, the culture and polity of the conquerors were not of a different order of complexity or achievement from those of the conquered. (Roman civilization confronting barbarians was a rare thing.) As with Christianity in Europe, the spread of new religions, such as Islam in Africa, also brought important change. Occasionally, foreign trade—and most dramatically, although much later, the slave trade—brought important change. But here, too, frequently, the cultural contacts it entailed were confined to trade goods, the goods few and the trade sporadic, and the trading parties represented economic systems at roughly the same level of technology and economic performance (Hogbin 1958; Polanyi, Arensberg, and Pearson 1957).

With European colonization from the sixteenth through the nineteenth centuries (when the European powers themselves began and then intensified their industrialization and economic growth) came new kinds of change with irreversible consequences for what we now call the developing areas. It is, perhaps, a commonplace among historians of colonialism that one must know what was happening in the European home country to understand its policies and actions in its colonies (Simpson 1950). Europeans who established overseas colonies before industrialization was importantly begun in their home countries (for example, the Spanish) viewed the potential economic benefits to themselves differently from those who colonized after industrialization had burgeoned at home. Geertz contrasts the economic policies of the Dutch in the Outer Islands of Indonesia after 1863 with their earlier policies in Java:

> . . . rather than being focused on condiments [like pepper], confections [such as sugar], and stimulants [for example, coffee and tobacco], the development centered on the production of industrial raw materials—a reflex, as Wertheim [1956:67,97] has pointed out, of the alteration in world market conditions attendant upon the spectacular growth of large-scale manufacturing in the West after the middle of the nineteenth century. In 1900, rubber, tin, and petroleum—almost entirely Outer Island products—accounted for about 17 percent of Indonesia's export value . . . in 1930 about 37 percent; in 1940, after the collapse of sugar in the depression, about 66 percent [see Geertz 1963b:105; Furnivall 1944:36–37].

The colonial powers moved and resettled peoples. Slaves were taken out of Africa and resettled in utterly different circumstances in the Caribbean and in North and South America. The Indians in Latin America were moved to haciendas and settled as serfs under Spanish overlords. Some American Indians and Africans were moved to reservations. Chinese and Asian Indian laborers formed overseas enclaves in societies as radically different from their own as Hawaii, the Fiji Islands, East Africa, and British Guiana. White Europeans settled everywhere, either as colonial administrators or missionaries doing tours of duty, or, as with merchants and farmers, as permanent settlers with families.

Colonial policies and decrees forbade traditional religious and warfare activities and practices, thereby disrupting indigenous culture and social organization. Public health measures and the curtailment of tribal warfare set in motion long-run changes such as population growth and land shortages. Colonial administration and European commerce and industry brought new political institutions and the beginnings of new economic activities. Colonialism created dual economies by establishing European commercial enclaves of mining and agricultural production for export alongside traditional societies producing subsistence goods with homemade technology. What Geertz says about the social and psychological changes which accompanied the rapid commercialization of agricultural production in the Outer Islands of Indonesia around 1910 holds widely:

> This [economic, or market-capitalist] mentality has had its customary socio-cultural accompaniments: increasing flexibility of land tenure; growth of individualism and slackening of extended family ties; greater class differentiation and conflict, intensified opposition between young and old, modern and conservative; weakening of traditional authority and wavering of traditional social standards; and even the growth of "Protestant ethic" religious ideologies (see Schrieke 1955:107ff.). What changed here (as in Java though in a different way) was not just a pattern of land use or a set of productive techniques but a system of functionally interrelated adaptively relevant institutions, practices and ideas—a "cultural core" [Geertz 1963*b*:120].

The post-colonial period (except in Latin America) is a scant generation old, but it is already clear that the changes begun with political independence are in part qualitatively and in part quantitatively different from the changes experienced in the pre-colonial and colonial periods. What is new is not the general fact of "change," but the particular, radical changes: the beginnings of national political integration, national market integration, industrialization and the application of science to agricultural production, and mass literacy and education. The governments of India and the Ivory Coast are now able to mobilize their nation's resources through national plans and budgets and to participate as sovereign nations in international economic institutions. The small communities on which anthropologists have traditionally focused their interest can no longer be studied in isolation from the national institutions and activities in which they now participate.

THEORETICAL GUIDELINES

Which are the promising ideas or lines of analysis in the study of socio-economic change, development, and modernization at the village level? Which concepts and generalizations contribute to the formulation of theory? Which published works on micro-development should be read for the theoretical guidelines they provide? What are the interesting questions to be answered about processes and problems of social and economic change?

In a subject as vast and complex as the causes and consequences of social and economic change in village communities in Africa, Asia, Latin America, Oceania, and the Middle East, in the pre-colonial, colonial, and post-colonial periods, it is well to specify which of a large set of questions are most worth answering. Indeed, it is essential to do so. What we call theory in the social sciences—leading ideas, concepts, specification of functional relationships, and analytical conclusions and generalizations— can always be regarded as addressed to specific questions. If we want to invent good theory in order to understand and direct processes of modernization, it is sensible to specify the questions such theory should be able to answer.

1. Are there typical sequences of socio-economic change at the village level? Are there underlying regularities in the transformation sequence?

2. Which features of traditional economy, society, and culture make for receptivity or resistance to innovations of a modernizing sort? How are receptivity and resistance to modernizing innovations related to earlier experiences of intrusion (for example, by missionaries, colonial government, the slave trade)?

3. Once modernizing activities have begun, such as producing export crops, using improved technology, establishing modern schools, how and why do traditional social organization and culture change? What do such changes tell us about traditional society?

4. What comprises "successful" village development? Can we define it? Can we construct models of successful village development from case studies of real-world experience? What analytical lessons are to be learned from case studies of unusual success and definite failure in development projects? Does success or failure depend on the sequence in which economic as compared to non-economic innovations are introduced? What analytical time dimension is most useful in studying socio-economic change?

5. To what extent are processes of social and economic change at the village level related to economic development and cultural modernization at the national level? What theoretical benefits would accrue to anthropological analysis by considering the work of economists, political scientists, and sociologists on national modernization?

I turn now to a few of the theoretical guidelines, concepts, analytical insights, and lines of research that I think most fruitful.

THE MUTUAL INTERACTION OF ECONOMIC AND CULTURAL FORCES

Modernization is a sequential process of cumulative change over time, generated by the interaction of technological, economic, and cultural innovations impinging on traditional economy, polity, and society, with feedback effects on the innovating activities. To put it this way is to point up the problem of inventing analytical categories which reveal the strategic workings of such a complicated process in the real world of developing areas. The conceptual categories must include both economic and non-economic attributes; they must show how the attributes mutually affect one another in changing traditional society, and in what sequence, over what period of time, and with what consequences.

Gunnar Myrdal's *Rich Lands and Poor* (especially chapters 1–3) [14] speaks to all the social sciences in his insistence on the need to include all relevant variables regardless of which social science jurisdiction they traditionally have been under. His points are additionally persuasive because they illuminate development processes and problems of several sorts characterized by the mutual interaction of diverse forces. We learn from Myrdal, moreover, some useful language with which to talk about modernization—cumulative causation, spread effects, backwash effects—and why piecemeal change (the attempt to introduce a single innovation into traditional societies) frequently fails to generate more comprehensive structural change: ". . . the principle of interlocking circular interdependence within a process of cumulative causation has validity over the entire field of social relations. It should be the main hypothesis when studying economic underdevelopment and development [1957:23]."

Myrdal argues that complicated social situations, such as the position of Negroes in America, and underdevelopment share crucial characteristics of a sort which require a special kind of analysis. The social reality underlying these situations consists of interlocking, mutually dependent, and mutually reinforcing economic, social, political, historical, and cultural forces. There is no single cause of underdevelopment; there are many, and they are not independent of each other; they are integral, not additive. The essential idea is of a vicious circle of numerous and different causes mutually reinforcing one another, working in the same direction to produce the same result.

Several analytical and policy conclusions follow from Myrdal's work: (1) Underdevelopment does not mean simply a shortage of capital or an absence of entrepreneurial initiative. Whole sets of disparate forces are determining the outcome we perceive as underdevelopment. (2) No single social science provides all the data or conceptual apparatus necessary to analyze underdevelopment. Rather than identify "economic" or "cultural" forces, the analyst must identify all relevant forces at work, regardless of which sector of social reality they come from. (3) Development is a dynamic and complicated process which takes place over generations of time. If sufficient improvement in the several spheres of activity that comprise development can be successfully initiated, they, too, will be mutually reinforcing. Development is a cumulative process upward: improvements in income make improvements in health, education, and technology easier, and vice versa.

Myrdal recognizes that there is a great deal we do not know about these processes. From the large set of potential development improvements—income, health, education, new lines of production—can we identify a smaller set of strategic factors and specific policies, which, if successful, produce large multiplier effects; or policies which work more quickly than others? [15] What are the most powerful levers of change that are available to policymakers; how, why, and how long do they take to work, and with what induced effects?

The writings of Boeke (1942), Furnivall (1948), Lewis (1954), and Singer (1950) on dual economies analyze the mutual interaction of economic and non-economic forces under the special conditions of colonialism: the transactional flows between the European, commercial-industrial sector and the traditional tribal or peasant hinterland. Much of this sort of analysis remains relevant for the post-colonial period in those least developed nations where there remains a sharp dichotomy between the urban-commercial-export sector and traditional village subsistence economies.[16]

In extremely clear terms, Smelser (1963) describes the typical kinds of social change that accompany economic and technological development: from subsistence farming to production of agricultural commodities for markets; from the use of simple tools and traditional techniques to the application of scientific knowledge and advanced technology; from the use of human and animal power to the kinds of inanimate power and mechanized techniques entailed in industrialization; from farm and village life toward increased urbanization; from apprentice training within the family and farm to formal schooling.[17]

His point is that all important modernizing activities induce similar changes away from the base of traditional society. Smelser addresses himself particularly to two questions: How exactly do development activities and values change traditional society and economy? What are the new forms of social organization created in the course of economic, technological, and cultural modernization?

The process of change in traditional economy and society induced by modern activities is what Smelser (following Parsons) calls "structural differentiation."

> The concept of structural differentiation can be employed to analyze what is frequently termed the "marked break in established patterns of social and economic life" in periods of development. . . . "differentiation" is the evolution from a multi-functional role structure to several more specialized structures [1963:35].

Agricultural production for sale, the use of modern technology, factory work, urbanism, modern education, all involve activities carried on with persons outside the family household or local village and create what might be called new dependency relationships, external to the family and village. A more familiar way to put these points is to say that impersonal market forces and contractual relationships displace local dependence on kin and status. And, indeed, people come to move physically and occupationally in new orbits of economic and cultural activity. Production and education are no longer carried on exclusively within the family; new specialized agencies carry on activities in the modern sector:

> During a society's transition from domestic to factory industry the division of labor increases and the economic activities previously lodged in the family move to the firm. As a formal educational system emerges, the functions previously performed by the family and church are established in a more specialized unit, the school. The modern political party has a more complex structure than do tribal factions, and the former is less likely to be fettered with kinship loyalties, competition for religious leadership, etc. . . . structural differentiation is a process whereby one social role or organization . . . differentiates into *two or more* roles or organizations which function more effectively in the new historical circumstances. The new social units are structurally distinct from each other, but taken together are functionally equivalent to the original unit [Smelser 1965:35].

Differentiation characterizes the changes in traditional economy and society induced by modernizing activities. Following Durkheim (*The Division of Labor in Society,* Chs. 3–8), Smelser calls "integration" the institutions and mechanisms ". . . for coordinating and solidifying the interaction among individuals whose interests are becoming progressively more diversified [Smelser 1963:41]." Durkheim emphasizes the role of the legal system as an integrative or coordinating device. Smelser points to many such devices and institutions that accompany development and modernization, such as ". . . trade unions, associations, political parties, and a mushrooming state apparatus [1963:41]."

The work of Irma Adelman and Cynthia Taft Morris (1965; 1967; 1968a and b) is pathbreaking in its use of statistical techniques to investigate how social and political organizations interact with economic and technological performance in the transformation sequences of development. They draw their data from seventy-four developing nations.[18] The work is noteworthy for its methodology, its analytical conclusions, and the policy guidelines its conclusions suggest. It draws widely on comparable data, so that its conclusions are of general significance. Its statistical techniques cluster inter-correlated variables and show the importance of different clusters as the process of development advances.

Aside from their statistical methods, which are most certainly applicable to micro-analysis of village development (see the essay by Adelman and Dalton in this volume), the Adelman-Morris work shows that cultural, political, and economic components of development vary sharply in their importance, depending on the level of modernization achieved: the lower the level of achieved development, the more powerfully do non-economic characteristics of traditional society, polity, and culture act as obstacles to economic development. But it is nevertheless economic and technological innovations, such as the enlargement of production for sale, the use of improved technology, and the establishment of modern financial institutions, that are the most powerful levers that change traditional society. For its methods and its substance, the work is important to all social scientists interested in national and village development and modernization.

DIFFERENTIATION AND INTEGRATION: CHANGING THE TRADITIONAL VILLAGE COMMUNITY AND LINKING IT WITH NEW NATIONAL ECONOMY AND SOCIETY

The transformation sequence we call modernization is an interaction process in two senses. Not only do economic and socio-cultural activities and relationships interact but also *old* economic activities, social relationships, and cultural practices change in reaction to *new* ones becoming instituted. We described how Smelser characterized the process of changing the old as "differentiation" and instituting the new as "integration." These are central ideas, and I should like to show their power in an anthropological context.

Case studies of colonial and post-colonial development teach us a good deal about traditional societies that was not obvious before they began to modernize.[19] For example, a rather common characteristic of tribal and peasant agricultural communities was their material insecurity, the experience of sporadic famine or months of hunger due to the failure of the principal food staple relied upon. The simple technology employed had two chief consequences. One was low average productivity; the other was its inability to compensate for or control plant disease, insects, soil deficiencies, or adverse weather. Too little rain, too many insects, a blighting plant disease, or a decimating animal disease meant hunger.[20] The village or tribal segment was relatively isolated economically, that is, frequently it had no access to markets. In pre-colonial times, there was often physical isolation as well due to tribal enmities and the consequent risks of travel (see Douglas 1962). It is important to note that the condition of material insecurity—the sporadic threat of famine—was the combined result of different forces working in the same direction: poor technology, physical isolation, absence of market organization, and the absence of real alternatives to secure material livelihood aside from the few agricultural production lines or hunting and gathering activities in the home community.

The traditional practices employed to mitigate the ever-present threat of starvation are also several and of very different sorts. One is the people's minute knowledge of its natural environment (which plants are edible, the habits of game animals, and the like). Another is the practice of planting too much of the preferred staple crop in the hope that if bad weather or insects decimate the crop a sufficient amount will be harvestable to stave off hunger. Another is to plant a less preferred crop which is eaten only if the preferred crop fails. But social relationships and cultural practices are also used to cope with material uncertainty: the use of magic and ritual to induce agricultural success (Malinowski 1935); and, of course, several sharing devices based on reciprocal social relationships. If a single household suffers disaster while the local community is not similarly afflicted, it receives gifts from kin, friends, neighbors, lineage heads, chiefs. If the local community is similarly afflicted, it calls upon distant kin, allies, and gift-friends for emergency support; if these fail or are unavailable, it resorts to money-lenders, debt-bondage, infanticide, abortion, or migration.

To say that traditional primitive and peasant economies were economically self-sufficient is to say they were not integrated into any larger economy outside the local community. There were external trade transactions, but, with rare exceptions, they were sporadic and not relied on for basic livelihood. Subsistence producers depend for livelihood on *local* ecology, *local* technology, and *local* social organization.

Economic development and cultural modernization radically change local dependence and local self-sufficiency. The interlocking characteristics of traditional band, tribal, and peasant economies produce local social security systems, turned inward, so to speak. Commercialization and cash-earning, literacy and education, and new technology turn them outward. Material income and security come to depend on transactions and institutions outside the village. Above all, modern activities create new income alternatives, and modern technology allows control over the physical environment. Irrigation equipment creates its own rainy season.

At primitive levels, man has to struggle for subsistence. With great drudgery he succeeds in wresting from the soil barely enough to keep himself alive. Every year he passes through a starvation period for several months, because the year's crop barely lasts out until the next harvest. Regularly he is visited by famine, plague or pestilence. Half his children die before reaching the age of ten, and at forty his wife is wrinkled and old. Economic growth enables him to escape from this servitude. Improved techniques yield more abundant and more varied food for less labor. Famine is banished, the infant mortality rate falls . . . the death rate [falls]. . . . Cholera, smallpox, malaria, hookworm, yellow fever, plague, leprosy, and tuberculosis disappear altogether. Thus life itself is freed from some of nature's menaces [Lewis 1955:420, 421].

Modernization consists of new activities which displace local dependence with external dependence on markets and governmental services, and by so doing integrates the village community into the region, the nation, and, through foreign trade transactions, the rest of the world. Almost all the important innovations that comprise modernization reduce household dependence on the local village community, its physical environment and network of social relationships, and increase household dependence on local, national, and international market networks. From the viewpoint of individual persons, real alternatives and mobility, as well as real income, are increased with the new and diversified transactions and opportunities.

What distinguishes post-colonial modernization from the changes which occurred in the pre-colonial and colonial periods is the establishment of the sovereign nation-state and its initiation of nation-wide development activities and institutions: principally, widespread commercialization of production processes, industrialization and the use of improved technology, and the inculcation of mass education and vocational training. These are watershed changes for Africa and Asia, as, indeed, they were in the eighteenth and nineteenth centuries for Europe and Japan. They are also mutually reinforcing changes that work in the same direction to change more or less self-sufficient village economies and societies into interacting sectors of national economy, culture, and polity. Integration means two-way transactional flows which create mutual dependence between villages, their regions, and national markets and government.[21] The structure of traditional village society becomes undermined because its traditional functions of mutual aid, security, and protection become displaced, once superior economic and technological alternatives become available.

SUMMARY AND CONCLUSION

The systematic study of national economic development came into being after the former colonies in Asia and Africa achieved their political independence, beginning with India in 1947.[22] The geographical scope of the subject is extraordinarily wide. It includes some eighty countries, containing most of the world's population. The range of processes and problems entailed in the structural transformation of these countries is also very great. To say that all the social sciences have an interest in the subject is an understatement. Economics, for example, contains a dozen or more sub-fields, many of which now have counterpart interests in the study of developing countries: economic history (Rostow 1960; Gerschenkron 1962), international trade (Chenery 1965; Levin 1960), national income accounting, statistics, and econometrics (Deane 1954; Samuels 1965; Adelman and Morris 1967), agricultural economics (deWilde *et al.* 1967; Mellor *et al.* 1968), are some examples. Others could be added in economics and in other social sciences. The common focus of interest in Africa or Asia has also generated interdisciplinary research and the establishment of programs of area studies.

The profound impact of development studies is felt beyond the social science subjects in the universities on all the continents. An international civil service of development research, planning, and project implementation is now also in being. The Ford and Rockefeller foundations, governments of the industrialized developed nations, agencies of the United Nations and the World Bank, are very much engaged. The wide and deep concern with development comes from the pragmatic urgency for income growth, which, in turn, requires the theoretical understanding of the transformation processes and sequences that comprise modernization. The developing countries need good policies and planning. To formulate them, they need good theory and measurement.

Most social scientists, and economists in particular, are concerned with development from above—national, macro-development—or with impersonal problems and sectors, such as capital formation and foreign trade. These are necessary and important concerns. Many fewer social scientists study development from below—village community, or micro-development; traditionally, only anthropologists, agricultural economists, and rural sociologists. Yet, some of the most intractable problems of development exist at the rural community level: how to increase agricultural productivity, village literacy, and vocational skills.

We know from European and Japanese history that pre-industrial economic structure and the early decades of modernization importantly influenced the sequential path and therefore the structure and performance of today's developed national economies (Rostow 1960; Smith 1959). So, too, for developing village economies. Hacienda communities in Peru still reflect the Spanish conquest of four hundred years ago, and African communities the coming of the Dutch and English three hundred years ago (see Schapera 1928; Hunter 1961).

Modernization is an historical subject because sequential events in precolonial and colonial times shaped the present. And it is a subject for all the social sciences—and some of the physical sciences (see Vayda 1969)—because economic, political, and social forces interact in the course of development and modernization (Adelman and Morris 1967; Dalton 1965c). What used to be almost the exclusive preserve of anthropologists a generation ago is now a field of wide professional interest to economists, sociologists, psychologists, and others, all over the world, in universities, governments, and research institutes. Recent anthropological studies of community change and development reflect the changes brought by the Colonial Revolution in their use of new field-work methods and new techniques of analysis. Anthropology will continue to figure prominently, but theories of village development as well as policy formulation must now draw on all the social sciences.

A number of economists have written works bearing directly on development at the local community level (and on the cultural and social aspects of national economic development). The work of Myrdal (1957:chapters 1–3), Hagen (1962), and Adelman and Morris (1967), in particular, is of wide application because it is concerned with the mutual interaction of economic and non-economic forces over long periods of time—the essence of development. In what must be the most imaginative departure from conventional economics ever attempted by an economist, Hagen employs psychoanalytical theory to trace out the inter-generational changes in personality formation necessary to produce persons of entrepreneurial initiative. With an utterly different approach, Adelman and Morris use the statistical technique of factor analysis to show the varying influence of social, cultural, and economic forces at different levels of national development.

Several economists have written on the problems of transforming subsistence agriculture and increasing agricultural productivity in underdeveloped areas (Yudelman 1964a; 1964b; Schultz 1964; Jones 1961; Fogg 1965). Others consider the important question of how to widen the scope of conventional economics so as to bring formal analysis to bear on the special problems and processes of development (Seers 1963; Myint 1965; Hill 1966; Martin and Knapp 1967). Boeke (1953), of course, in his analysis of "dualism" was one of the first to point out how traditional peasant societies existed side by side with colonially implanted commercial production for export. Lewis (1954), in an important article, showed how development proceeded in dualistic economies.

As with the anthropologists and economists, the sociologists, psychologists, and political scientists perceive the processes of transformation from their special viewpoints: Smelser (1958) has written on the social changes that accompanied the British Industrial Revolution and the similar changes in the present-day transformations of underdeveloped areas (Smelser 1963). The rural sociologists have extended their interests from Europe and America to the underdeveloped world (Rogers 1960; see especially his bibliography). The psychologist McClelland (1961) has started a special line of investigation with his work on achievement motivation. Apter (1960), one of the most perceptive political scientists, has written on the connections between traditional and modern political leadership in the new context of politically independent African states.

Economic anthropology considers the organization and performance of small band, tribal, and peasant economies under pre-colonial, colonial, and post-colonial conditions. It differs from counterpart subjects in other social sciences, such as comparative economic systems, economic development, and industrial sociology, in several ways. Its principal focus of interest is the small economy of village or tribal segment; its predominant concern is with such communities outside of Western Europe and the United States (today's developing areas). The bulk of its literature consists of field-work studies of traditional systems or their changing condition under European colonialism and post-colonial development. Economic anthropologists have analyzed economic organization more extensively than quantifiable economic performance, and they emphasize the systematic relationships between economy, ecology, culture, and society. Applied anthropology—action programs to initiate and implement community development projects —is an old subject which is attracting younger anthropologists.

All these topics in economic anthropology—organization, performance, primitive, peasant, traditional, modernizing, theory, policy—have received relatively little systematic formulation. But the prospects for more intensive and extensive theoretical treatment are good because of the rapidly burgeoning interest in the subject, due primarily to the social science concern with development and modernization. The two branches of the subject, traditional and modernizing economies, are complementary: the more we learn about either, the more we can learn about the other.

Anthropologists in training who intend to specialize in economic anthropology would do well to do a great deal of library research, particularly to read deeply in European and Asian economic history (for example, Smith 1959), economic development (Adelman and Morris 1967), and comparative economic systems (Carr 1951; Myrdal 1960; Nove 1962). If economic anthropologists are to pursue comparative analysis, the systematic study of European economies before they industrialized, as well as today's developed economies, becomes important. The importance of comparative studies becomes obvious when one considers topics such as slavery, feudalism, or peasantry. But so too for the analysis of money, markets, external trade, land tenure, and, indeed, many others in both branches of economic anthropology.

India alone has a half-million village communities, and Africa probably another several hundred thousand. They vary enormously with regard to size of population, physical resource endowment, quality of technology, extent of commercialization, access to transport and to urban areas, access to education and health facilities, in basic social organization and culture, and in historical experiences shaping their present structures. There are people in New Guinea who had their first contact with Europeans only 30 years ago (Salisbury 1962), while others in India felt the impact of English commerce, culture, and administration 300 years ago. A good deal of useful work is yet to be done in formulating analytical classifications and historical demarcations to cope with such diversity.

The more anthropologists are concerned with economic development, the more important measurement of economic performance becomes. Indeed, as commercial production, cash income, and modern technology displace subsistence production and traditional techniques, the more scope is there for using ordinary economic terms, concepts of measurement, and conventional economic analysis. One branch of economic anthropology will move toward the economist's fields of economic development and agricultural economics (Joy 1968). Such analysis would be facilitated if anthropologists in the field collected hard data series—statistical information on village structure and performance.

Tribal and village communities have special and tenacious problems of development which stem from their traditional condition of material insecurity: the sporadic threat of hunger due to reliance on one or two staple foodstuffs produced with technology of low quality under circumstances of relative economic isolation and uncontrolled physical environment. Much of traditional social organization may be regarded as a social security system to assure access to labor, land, and emergency support.

What an older generation of anthropologists called the tenacity of custom was in part due to the cultural and physical isolation of the communities studied. Many had no firsthand knowledge of alternative ways of producing, especially when the larger regions of which they were a part were economically stagnant (see Foster 1965). But it was also due to the high risk of adopting innovations which might fail and cause hunger. To innovate, moreover, might require new activities, new skills, new outlays of time and effort, movement outside the community, which made it impossible to fulfill traditional obligations to kin, neighbors, community, or chief, those on whom one traditionally relied for material security and emergency support.

Modernization and development inevitably restructure the economy and society of village communities because the principal innovations that comprise modernization are new economic, cultural, and political transactions, activities, and institutions which connect the village to the outside world, thereby undoing local dependence, autonomy, and isolation. What anthropologists sometimes call the increase in scale that accompanies modernization means new mobility and alternatives, new activities and occupations, new transactional flows. These integrate local communities with the nation, economically, and eventually create a new common cultural identity—shared values and attitudes—as well as new equipment and diversified lines of production.

Village development involves complex processes of world-wide scope taking place over long periods of time. The need for anthropologists and other social scientists to confront these special difficulties has brought forth new approaches, interdisciplinary sophistication, and some fruitful results. It is to be hoped that an increasing number of the young social scientists emerging from university training with a specialist's interest in the subject will be New Men, combining the several talents necessary. They should be field workers and historians, anthropological economists and economic anthropologists, theoreticians and practitioners.

NOTES

1. This essay is a revised and expanded version of a paper given at Syracuse University in April, 1969. I am grateful to David Brokensha, Walter Neale, Frederick Pryor, and Manfred Stanley for their critical comments on an earlier draft.

2. A relatively small number of anthropologists study communities in Japan and Europe, principally the less developed rural parts (like Yugoslavia and Spain), or special sorts of communities such as kibbutzim in Israel.

3. For the study of communities in Europe, like those of Pitt-Rivers in Spain (1954) and Arensberg in Ireland (1937), an appropriate distinction is before and since the beginnings of industrialization and the modern nation-state.

4. Polanyi (1944:chapters 4, 5, 6); Polanyi, Arensberg, and Pearson (1957); Polanyi (1966). Bohannan (1959); Bohannan and Bohannan (1968); Bohannan and Dalton (1962). Sahlins (1965; 1968). Dalton (1961; 1962; 1965a; 1969d). The most extensive evaluation of Polanyi's work yet to appear is Humphreys (1969).

5. Firth (1968; 1964a); LeClair (1962); Burling (1962); Salisbury (1962); Hill (1963a; 1965); Epstein (1962); Deane (1953). On the very important topic of physical environment (ecology) as it relates to traditional and changing primitive and peasant communities, see Vayda (1969).

6. I do not mean to overstate the case. For many problems and processes of national development, conventional economic analysis is necessary but certainly not sufficient. There is a growing literature of contention on the relevance and adequacy of conventional economics to studies of modernization and development. See Myrdal (1957); Seers (1963); Martin and Knapp (1967); Adelman and Morris (1967); and Dalton (1968b). On the need for development

economists to engage in wider social analyses, see the essays by Myrdal and Sawyer in Dalton (1971); also Dalton (1965c).

7. Japan should be of special interest to all the social sciences because it is the most successful non-European country in its economic and technological development. The extent to which Japan retained its traditional culture while undergoing its industrial revolution should make it of very special interest to anthropology (see Smith 1959).

8. Lewis (1954; 1955); Myrdal (1957); Hagen (1962); Adelman and Morris (1967); Seers (1963); Singer (1950); Clower, Dalton, Harwitz, Walters (1966).

9. The quick and dramatic success of the Marshall Plan probably had the unfortunate consequence of creating over-optimism about the potential effectiveness of economic aid for developing nations. Europe and Japan needed only short-run aid, principally food and capital equipment, to repair the devastation of war and the overworking of physical plants during the war. They were already industrialized and developed. Africa and Asia require much more than food and capital transfers. The problems of structural transformation they now confront had no real counterpart in the countries receiving Marshall aid.

10. The case of Vicos, described by Holmberg and Vázquez in Dalton (1971), is an unusual example of applied anthropology for several reasons, including the comprehensiveness of the innovations introduced and the extent of departure from traditional ways in a short period of time.

11. There seems to be no equivalent in the conventional subjects of anthropological inquiry, such as kinship, religion, and polity, to what is here meant by the quantifiable performance of an economy. The closest one comes is simple enumeration: for example, the frequency of murder, theft, or divorce.

12. One of several ways in which agricultural economics supplements applied anthropology is in showing how more complicated modern innovations in agricultural technology are compared to the famous case of the steel axe displacing the stone axe. Note that the steel axe is a simple innovation because it requires no complementary resources in order to be used effectively. Chemical fertilizer is a complicated innovation because its effective usage requires several associated resources and labor redeployment: more water, more labor in weeding, and sometimes different methods in preparing the soil. See Mellor *et al.* (1968).

13. See her two essays (Epstein 1962:chapter 10; 1967) reprinted in Dalton (1971).

14. Chapters 2 and 3 are reprinted in Dalton (1971).

15. See Adelman and Morris (1968a).

16. See Dalton (1965c). There is a rich anthropological literature of ethnographic description and analysis which properly belongs under the heading of dualism, particularly empirical works such as Watson (1958) and Gulliver (1962), on the response of tribal groups to the penetration of European commercial economy.

17. Smelser (1963) is reprinted in Dalton (1971). A succinct summary of the secular changes entailed in the national transformation toward greater development, from the viewpoint of an economist, is the following: "Countries which have attained high levels of per capita income have experienced rather drastic changes in the relative importance of different industrial sectors—a sharp de-

cline in agriculture, a growth in the manufacturing sector, and a later, more pronounced expansion of transportation, communication, and the service sectors generally (retailing, finance, government, and so on). Associated with this have been declines in numbers of unskilled workers, proprietors, and managers (largely in the farm sector) and increases in numbers of clerical, professional, and technical workers. These [labor] input changes in large part reflect the differential impact of technical change and the changing composition of output associated with rising incomes, such as the rising proportion of government expenditures in total output and the major compositional changes in consumer expenditures—growth in the relative importance of durable goods and in the provision of services, such as education, medical care, and recreation. Superimposed on these changes are the decline of the household as a nucleus of productive activity and the increasing importance of the market nexus, an increase in leisure time, and a massive shift of the population from a primarily rural to a primarily urban environment [Rosenberg 1964:660]."

18. Adelman and Morris are presently engaged in a complementary study of historical development using the same kinds of statistical techniques. They attempt to answer the question, Considering the structure of society, polity, and economy of some twenty-five nations in 1870 (most of which have since become highly developed), could one—on the bases of these structures and performances in 1870—have predicted their development paths and rates?

19. There are many examples from our own social and economic history of how a changed situation brings to light features of the earlier condition which were insufficiently appreciated. The structure of nineteenth-century capitalism appeared different to us when it changed in the 1930's and 1940's with increasing government participation in response to depression, Keynesian analysis, and economic planning during World War II. The traditional position of Negroes in U.S. life has been made very clear to us in the fifteen years since the Supreme Court decision on school integration and the momentous episodes of civil strife, agitation for reform, and growing integration of Negroes into all areas of national life.

20. We see immediately that aside from yielding greater productivity, modern technology and applied science also confer much greater material *security and certainty* in their ability to counteract fluctuations in weather and the depredation of insects and plant disease.

21. "Integration" means several things, all of which occur in the course of successful development. Its *economic* meaning is best stated in terms of the growth and diversification of purchase, sale, financial and capital transactions between village-based households and firms and those based outside the village, in cities, the region, and the nation. Social overhead capital, such as roads, power facilities, and regional irrigation works, play an important implemental role in increasing and diversifying such transactions. So, too, do new institutional facilities, such as banks and agricultural experiment stations. "Integration" also has socio-political expressions, which consist of new political transactions, such as village participation in national elections and growth in common cultural identity, as when regional and ethnic differences diminish with the national use of a common language and national access to the same school system, newspapers, and radio programs.

22. For theories of growth and development in the literature of classical and neoclassical economics, see Adelman (1961) and Robbins (1968).

REFERENCES

ADELMAN, IRMA
1961 *Theories of growth and development*. Stanford: Stanford University Press.
ADELMAN, IRMA, and GEORGE DALTON
1971 A factor analysis of modernization in village India. In *Economic development and social change*, George Dalton ed. New York: Natural History Press.
ADELMAN, IRMA, and CYNTHIA TAFT MORRIS
1965 Factor analysis of the interrelationship between social and political variables and per capita gross national product. *Quarterly Journal of Economics* 89:555–578.
1967 *Society, politics, and economic development*. Baltimore: Johns Hopkins Press.
1968a Performance criteria for evaluating economic development potential: an operational approach. *Quarterly Journal of Economics* vol. 82.
1968b An econometric model of socioeconomic and political change in underdeveloped countries. *American Economic Review* (December).
ALLAN, W.
1965 *The African husbandman*. London and Edinburgh: Oliver and Boyd.
APTER, DAVID E.
1960 The role of traditionalism in the political modernization of Ghana and Uganda. *World Politics* 13:45–68.
ARENSBERG, CONRAD M.
1937 *The Irish countryman*. Cambridge: Harvard University Press.
BENDIX, R.
1956 *Work and authority in industry: ideologies of management in the course of industrialization*. New York: Harper.
BOEKE, J. H.
1942 *The structure of Netherlands Indian economy*. New York: Institute of Pacific Relations.
1953 *Economics and economic policy of dual societies*. Haarlem: H. D. Tjeenk Willink. New York: Institute of Pacific Relations.
BOHANNAN, PAUL
1959 The impact of money on an African subsistence economy. *Journal of Economic History* 19:491–503.
BOHANNAN, PAUL, and LAURA BOHANNAN
1968 *Tiv economy*. Evanston: Northwestern University Press.
BOHANNAN, PAUL, and GEORGE DALTON
1962 *Markets in Africa*. Evanston: Northwestern University Press.
BROOM, LEONARD, B. J. SIEGEL, E. Z. VOGT, and J. B. WATSON
1954 Acculturation: an exploratory formulation. *American Anthropologist* 56:973–1000.

BURLING, ROBBINS
1962   Maximization theories and the study of economic anthropology. *American Anthropologist* 64:802–821.
CARR, E. H.
1951   *The new society*. London: Macmillan.
CHENERY, HOLLIS
1965   Comparative advantage and development policy. In *Surveys of economic theory*, E. A. G. Robinson, ed., vol. 2, *Growth and development*. New York: St. Martin's Press.
CLOWER, R. W. *et al.*
1966   *Growth without development: an economic survey of Liberia*. Evanston: Northwestern University Press.
COULBORN, R., and J. R. STRAYER
1956   *Feudalism in history*. Princeton: Princeton University Press.
DALTON, GEORGE
1961   Economic theory and primitive society. *American Anthropologist*, 63:1–25.
1962   Traditional production in primitive African economies. *Quarterly Journal of Economics* 76:360–378.
1965a   Primitive money. *American Anthropologist* 67:44–65.
1965b   Primitive, archaic, and modern economies: Karl Polanyi's contribution to economic anthropology and comparative economy. *Proceedings of the 1965 Annual Spring Symposium of the American Ethnological Society*. Seattle: University of Washington Press.
1965c   History, politics, and economic development in Liberia. *Journal of Economic History* 25:568–591.
1967   *Tribal and peasant economies: readings in economic anthropology*. New York: Natural History Press.
1968a   Ed. *Primitive, archaic, and modern economies: essays of Karl Polanyi*. New York: Anchor Books.
1968b   Economics, economic development, and economic anthropology. *Journal of Economic Issues* (June).
1968c   Review of *Primitive and peasant economic systems*, by Manning Nash (San Francisco: Chandler, 1966). *American Anthropologist* 70:368–369.
1969a   Economics, anthropology, and economic anthropology. In *Anthropology and related disciplines*, Otto von Mering ed. Pittsburgh: University of Pittsburgh Press.
1969b   Traditional economic systems. In *The African experience*, John Paden and Edward Soja ed. Evanston: Northwestern University Press.
1969c   The economic system. In *A handbook of method in cultural anthropology*, R. Naroll and R. Cohen ed. New York: Doubleday.
1969d   Theoretical issues in economic anthropology. *Current Anthropology* 10:63–102.
1971   *Economic development and social change*. New York: Natural History Press.

DEANE, PHYLLIS
1953   *Colonial social accounting.* Cambridge: Cambridge University Press.
DEWILDE, JOHN C., *et al.*
1967   *Experiences with agricultural development in tropical Africa,* 2 vols. Baltimore: Johns Hopkins Press.
DOUGLAS, MARY
1962   Lele economy compared with the Bushong: a study of economic backwardness. In *Markets in Africa,* P. Bohannan and G. Dalton ed. Evanston: Northwestern University Press.
DUBY, GEORGES
1968   *Rural economy and country life in the medieval west.* London: Edward Arnold Publishers.
DURKHEIM, E.
1949   *The division of labor in society.* Glencoe: The Free Press.
EPSTEIN, T. SCARLETT
1962   *Economic development and social change in South India.* Manchester: Manchester University Press.
1967   Productive efficiency and customary systems of rewards in rural south India. In *Themes in economic anthropology,* R. Firth ed. London: Tavistock Publications.
ERASMUS, CHARLES J.
1961   *Man takes control.* Minneapolis: University of Minnesota Press.
FIRTH, RAYMOND
1959   *Social change in Tikopia.* London: George Allen and Unwin.
1964a Capital, saving, and credit in peasant societies: a viewpoint from economic anthropology. In *Capital, saving, and credit in peasant societies,* R. Firth and B. Yamey ed. Chicago: Aldine.
1964b *Essays on social organization and values.* London: Athlone.
1966a *Primitive polynesian economy,* revised ed. London: Routledge and Kegan Paul.
1966b *Malay fishermen: their peasant economy,* 2d ed. London: Routledge and Kegan Paul.
1967   *Themes in economic anthropology.* London: Tavistock Publications.
FOGG, C. DAVIS
1965   Economic and social factors affecting the development of smallholder agriculture in eastern Nigeria. *Economic development and cultural change* 13:278–292.
FOSTER, G. M.
1965   Peasant society and the image of the limited good. *American Anthropologist* 67:293–315.
FURNIVALL, J. S.
1944   *Netherlands India.* Cambridge: Cambridge University Press.
1948   *Colonial policy and practice.* Cambridge: Cambridge University Press.
GEERTZ, CLIFFORD
1962a Studies in peasant life: community and society. In *Biennial review of*

anthropology for 1961, Bernard J. Siegel ed. Stanford: Stanford University Press.

1962*b* Social change and economic modernization in two Indonesian towns: a case in point. In *On the theory of social change,* Everett E. Hagen Homewood: Dorsey.

1963*a* *Peddlers and princes.* Chicago: University of Chicago Press.

1963*b* *Agricultural involution.* Berkeley: University of California Press.

GERSCHENKRON, ALEXANDER

1962   *Economic backwardness in historical perspective.* Cambridge: The Belknap Press of Harvard University Press.

GULLIVER, P. H.

1962   The evolution of Arusha trade. In *Markets in Africa,* P. Bohannan and G. Dalton eds. Evanston: Northwestern University Press.

HAGEN, EVERETT E.

1962   *On the theory of social change: how economic growth begins.* Homewood: Dorsey.

HILL, POLLY

1963*a* *Migrant cocoa-farmers of southern Ghana.* Cambridge: Cambridge University Press.

1963*b* Review of *Markets in Africa. Journal of Modern Africa Studies* vol. 1, no. 4.

1965   *A plea for indigenous economics: the West African example.* Working Papers of the Economic Development Institute 5. Ibadan: Economic Development Institute, University of Ibadan.

1966   A plea for indigenous economics. *Economic Development and Cultural Change* 15:10–20.

HOGBIN, IAN H.

1958   *Social change.* London: Watts.

HOLMBERG, ALLAN R., *et al.*

1965   The changing values and institutions of Vicos in the context of national development. *American Behavioral Scientist* 8:3–8.

HUMPHREYS, S. C.

1969   History, economics, and anthropology: the work of Karl Polanyi. *History and theory,* VIII, no. 2.

HUNTER, MONICA

1961   *Reaction to conquest,* 2d ed. London: Oxford University Press.

JONES, WILLIAM O.

1961   Food and agricultural economies of tropical Africa: a summary view. *Food Research Institute Studies* 2:3–20 (Stanford University).

JOY, LEONARD

1968   One economist's view of the relationship between economics and anthropology. In *Themes in economic anthropology,* R. Firth ed. London: Tavistock Publications.

KEYFITZ, NATHAN

1959   The interlocking of social and economic factors in Asian development. *Canadian Journal of Economics and Political Science* 25:34–46.

LeClair, E. E., Jr.
1962 Economic theory and economic anthropology. *American Anthropologist* 64:1179–1203.
Levin, Jonathan V.
1960 *The export economies.* Cambridge: Harvard University Press.
Lewis, W. Arthur
1953 *Report on the industrialization of the Gold Coast.* Accra: Government Printing Department.
1954 Economic development with unlimited supplies of labour. *Manchester School of Economic and Social Studies* 22:139–191.
1955 *The theory of economic growth.* London: Allen and Unwin.
McClelland, David C.
1961 *The achieving society.* Princeton: Van Nostrand.
Malinowski, Bronislaw
1935 *Coral gardens and their magic,* vol. 1. New York: American Book.
Martin, K., and J. Knapp
1967 *The teaching of development economics.* Chicago: Aldine.
Mellor, John W., *et al.*
1968 *Developing rural India.* Ithaca: Cornell University Press.
Miracle, Marvin
1962 African markets and trade in the copperbelt. In *Markets in Africa,* P. Bohannan and G. Dalton ed. Evanston: Northwestern University Press.
Moore, Wilbert E.
1955 Labor attitudes toward industrialization in underdeveloped countries. *American Economic Review* 45:156–165.
Myint, Hla
1965 Economic theory and the underdeveloped countries. *Journal of Political Economy* 62:477–491.
Myrdal, Gunnar
1957 *Rich lands and poor.* New York: Harper.
1960 *Beyond the welfare state.* New Haven: Yale University Press.
Nove, Alec
1962 *The Soviet economy.* New York: Praeger.
Pitt-Rivers, J. A.
1954 *The people of the Sierra.* London: Weidenfeld and Nicolson.
Polanyi, Karl
1944 *The great transformation.* New York: Rinehart.
1966 *Dahomey and the slave trade.* Seattle: University of Washington Press.
Polanyi, K., C. M. Arensberg, H. W. Pearson ed.
1957 *Trade and market in the early empires.* Glencoe: The Free Press.
Robbins, Lionel
1968 *The theory of economic development in the history of economic thought.* New York: St. Martin's Press.
Rogers, Everett
1960 *Diffusion of innovations.* Glencoe: The Free Press.

ROSENBERG, NATHAN
   1964   Neglected dimensions in the analysis of economic change. In *Explorations in social change,* G. K. Zollschan and W. Hirsch eds. New York: Houghton Mifflin.
ROSTOW, W. W.
   1960   *The stages of economic growth.* Cambridge: Cambridge University Press.
RUBIN, VERA
   1962   Cultural change. In *Biennial review of anthropology for 1961,* Bernard J. Siegel ed. Stanford: Stanford University Press.
SAHLINS, MARSHALL
   1965   On the sociology of primitive exchange. In *The relevance of models for social anthropology,* M. Banton ed. London: Tavistock.
   1968   Tribal economics. In *Tribesmen.* Englewood Cliffs: Prentice-Hall.
SALISBURY, RICHARD
   1962   *From stone to steel.* London: Cambridge University Press.
SAMUELS, L. H. ed.
   1963   *African studies in income and wealth.* Chicago: Quadrangle Books.
SCHAPERA, I.
   1928   Economic changes in South African native life. *Africa* 1:170–188.
SCHRIEKE, B.
   1955   *Indonesian sociological studies, Part I.* The Hague: van Hoeve.
SCHULTZ, T. W.
   1964   *Transforming traditional agriculture.* New Haven: Yale University Press.
SEERS, DUDLEY
   1963   The limitations of the special case. *Institute of Economics and Statistics Bulletin* 25:77–98 (Oxford).
SHARP, R. L.
   1952   Steel axes for stone-age Australians. *Human Organization* 11:17–22.
SIMPSON, LESLEY BYRD
   1950   *The encomienda in New Spain.* Berkeley and Los Angeles: University of California Press.
SINGER, HANS
   1950   The distribution of gains between investing and lending countries. *American Economic Review* (May).
   1952   The mechanics of economic development. *The Indian Economic Review* (August).
SMELSER, NEIL J.
   1958   *Social change in the industrial revolution.* London: Routledge and Kegan Paul.
   1963   Mechanisms of change and adjustment to change. In *Industrialization and society,* B. F. Hoselitz and W. E. Moore ed. The Hague: UNESCO-Mouton.
   1965   *Readings on economic sociology.* Englewood Cliffs: Prentice-Hall.
SMITH, THOMAS C.
   1959   *The agrarian origins of modern Japan.* Stanford: Stanford University Press.

SPICER, EDWARD
  1952 *Human problems in technological change.* New York: Russell Sage
        Foundation.
SPINDLER, LOUISE S., and GEORGE SPINDLER
  1959 Culture change. In *Biennial Review of Anthropology for 1959*, Ber-
        nard J. Siegel ed. Stanford: Stanford University Press.
STOLPER, WOLFGANG
  1966 *Planning without facts.* Cambridge: Harvard University Press.
VAYDA, ANDREW
  1969 *Environment and cultural behavior: ecological studies in cultural an-
        thropology.* New York: Natural History Press.
VOGET, FRED
  1963 Cultural change. In *Biennial Review of Anthropology for 1963*, Ber-
        nard J. Siegel ed. Stanford: Stanford University Press.
WATSON, WILLIAM
  1958 *Tribal cohesion in a money economy.* Manchester: The University
        Press.
WEAVER, THOMAS F.
  1968 The farmers of Raipur. In *Developing rural India*, by John W. Mallor
        et al. Ithaca: Cornell University Press.
YUDELMAN, MONTAGUE
  1964a *Africans on the land.* Cambridge: Harvard University Press.
  1964b Some aspects of African agricultural development. In *Economic de-
        velopment for Africa south of the Sahara*, E. A. G. Robinson ed.
        London: Macmillan.

11

A Factor Analysis of
Modernization in
Village India

Irma Adelman and George Dalton

INTRODUCTION

There does not now exist a field of study which analyzes the economic and social processes that are transforming village communities in the developing world and relates village to national development. Yet policies to increase agricultural productivity and inculcate attitudes and skills favorable to new economic and cultural achievements at the village level are important in developing countries.

There are three basic obstacles which must be surmounted in studying micro-development. First, the communities undergoing change are many and widely different. Studies of individual villages based on sustained field work can provide us with insights into the process for specific communities (for example, Epstein 1962; Bailey 1962; Mellor *et al.* 1968), but the conclusions reached cannot readily be generalized to other villages because of the extraordinary range of variation among them. Second, statistical information on village economic organization and performance is scarce and often of dubious accuracy. Third, there are no theories generating models of sequential change and development at the village level which are theoretically persuasive and amenable to policy implementation. Agricultural economists, anthropologists, and rural sociologists usually concern themselves with the introduction of innovations piecemeal and emphasize different aspects of the transformation process, even though they recognize that the effectiveness of modernization policies is influenced by many disparate, mutually interacting forces. Unlike planners working on macroeconomic development, development planners who must devise policies to apply at the village level therefore have little knowledge of the functional relationships among variables.

In this essay we attempt to overcome some of these difficulties in analyzing village development in India. Of the many forces at work, we try, by statistical means, to isolate the few that are most important, explain their operation, and indicate their policy uses.

DATA

The data for the research described in this essay are taken from village surveys carried out by the Indian government in representative villages in each of the fifteen states between 1960 and 1962 as part of the national Census of India for 1961 (India 1961). The purpose of the village surveys was to obtain comparable information on the structure and performance of village communities. The published results contain statistics on income, landholdings, educational and transport facilities, and so on, as well as verbal descriptions of village history, caste composition, and styles of life.

Of the 300 village surveys available in the summer of 1967, we chose a representative sample of 108. The number of villages included from each state is proportional to the rural population of that state. We also chose our sample so as to reflect the full range of variation in village development contained in the original studies.

We were able to include in our analysis only those variables for which data were given in the published surveys. We had to leave out an index of ecological conditions, for example, because information on rainfall, soil quality, sub-soil, water, and the like was not reported. An index of household wealth had to be excluded because it would have required data on savings, consumer durables, holdings of jewelry and other real assets which were not consistently reported. Nor were we able to include data on family planning programs or data which would enable us to evaluate the effectiveness of land reform legislation.

Several variables were discarded from the study because they lacked systematic association with any other included variable. Among these were indicators of peasant indebtedness (the amount of household debt, the ratio of debt to income, and the proportion of debt incurred for productive purposes) and of the quality of health facilities. Finally, we omitted a variable describing the type of religion because it proved impossible to define it in a manner which is both conceptually appropriate and capable of implementation with our data sources.

Definition of Variables and
Method of Classification

We ranked the 108 villages with regard to each of 17 variables. Where the information or concept was not specifiable in numerical terms, we grouped the villages into three, four, or five ranked categories, depending on the fineness of the survey data. In those cases, numerical scores were assigned to the ranked groups according to the scale described in I. Adelman and C. T. Morris, *Society, Politics and Economic Development* (pp. 14–15). Experiments with alternative scales (logarithmic and squared) indicated that the results were insensitive to the scale chosen.

1. *Population*. Villages were ranked according to the number of households, which ranges from 932 to 8, with a mean of 158 households.

2. *Number of Castes*. This indicator ranks villages into five categories according to the number of named caste groups resident in the village. The top group consisted of villages having more than 15 castes (the highest number being 26 castes). The second, third, and fourth groups contained villages with 12–14, 8–11, and 1–7 castes, respectively. The lowest group was composed of villages with predominantly tribal organization in which castes are unimportant.

3. *Extent of Commercialization*. This indicator groups villages into one of three sets (high, medium, and low), depending on the proportion of yearly village produce which is sold to markets. The top group contains villages which sold over 50 percent of production; villages in the lowest group sold less than 25 percent of their output. The proportion of total output sold ranged from 100 percent to 0.

4. *Quality of Agricultural Technology*. This composite index ranks villages according to the proportion of arable land which is irrigated and the proportion of farm households which use chemical fertilizer or pesticides. The percentage of cultivated land under irrigation ranged from 0 to 100 percent, with a mean of 24.3 percent and a mode of 0 percent. Villages were also divided into three groups according to the percentage of their households using improved tools, chemical fertilizers, and pesticides. The composite index was formed by factor analysis.

5. *Location and Access to Transport*. This indicator also is a composite of several data series: quantity and quality of village access to transport facilities (all-weather roads, bus service, railway service), and the distance of the village from towns and cities. Villages were divided into four groups according to the following criteria: in the first group villages were six miles or less from a town, had access to an all-year motorable road and to frequent bus services, and were within six miles of a railroad. In the second group, villages were ten miles or less from the nearest town with access to an all-year motorable road, or within five miles of a railroad. Villages in the third group were fifteen miles or less from a town and had no access to an all-year motorable road and no railroad within five miles. In the fourth group the villages were more than fifteen miles from a town and ten miles from a railroad and had no access to an all-year motorable road.

6. *Awareness of Social Legislation*. One of the very few indicators of social attitudes we could contrive from the survey information was the ex-

tent of awareness in the village of legislation on social issues. This index was based on the percentage of villagers who were aware of legislation introduced since independence prohibiting untouchability. The range was from 100 percent to 3 percent, with a mean of 38.1 percent and median and mode of 25.0 percent.

7. *Education.* This variable is a composite (determined by factor analysis) of four "primary" variables: (1) the percentage of children aged 5 to 14 who attended school, which ranged from 0 to 89 percent with a mean of 32.5 percent; (2) the percentage of female children aged 5 to 14 in school, which had a mean of 18.3 percent and a mode of 5 percent and ranged from 0 to 75 percent; (3) the number of literate males over 14 expressed as a percentage of all males over 14 (mean 30.6 percent and range 0 to 81 percent); and (4) the educational facilities available in and near the village. The type of school (primary or secondary) and proximity to the village were taken into account when dividing villages into four groups for this last indicator.

8. *Family Household Type.* This variable ranks villages according to the proportion of simple households (that is, containing one married couple with their unmarried children) in the village. This percentage had a mean value of 48 percent and ranged from 92 percent to 6 percent.

9. *Female Child Marriage.* This variable ranks villages by the number of married females who are less than 14 years old, expressed as a percentage of the total number of females under 14 in the village. The percentage ranged from 0 to 37 percent, with a mean of 3.8 percent.

10. *Percent of Low-Caste Households.* The number of people belonging to low castes expressed as a percentage of the total village population ranged from 0 to 100 percent, with a mean of 29 percent and median and mode of 11 percent.

11. *Cooperative Membership.* The number of village households which were members of multipurpose cooperative societies was expressed as a percentage of all the village households. The range was 0 to 78 percent, with a mean, median, and mode of 20.5, 2.5, and 0.

12. *Income.* This variable combines two aspects of village income: the average monthly income per household and a measure of extent of inequality in income distribution. The latter was indicated by the percentage of households in the village with average monthly incomes below 50 rupees.

Average monthly incomes range from 20 to 213 rupees, with a mean of 80.9 and median of 72. The percentage of households in each village earning less than 50 rupees per month had a mean of 40.7 and ranged from 0 to 95.

13. *Land per Capita.* This indicator classifies villages according to the quantity of arable land per capita (the total amount of land used for farming divided by the village population). The arable land per capita ranged

from 0.1 acre to 9.2 acres. The distribution of landholdings has two modes —1.2 and 3.7 acres, and a mean and median of 1.85 and 1.2, respectively.

14. *Community Development Activity.* Villages were divided into four groups according to the number and size of development projects undertaken by the community. These ranged from villages which had undertaken more than four substantial projects (like building new roads or schools) to villages where no community projects had been undertaken.

15. *Employment in Agriculture.* For each village, the number of people aged 15 to 59 who were employed in agriculture was expressed as a percentage of all people in that age group. The percentage ranged from 0 to 99, with a mean and a mode of 56.0 percent.

16. *Percentage of Households Owning Land.* Villages were classified according to the percentage of households owning some farm land. The percentage varies from 14 to 100, with mean, median, and mode of 71.9, 80.0, and 100. (The data were not available to calculate a frequency distribution of landownership by amounts of land held.)

17. *Percent of Tenant Farmers.* This variable classifies villages according to the percentage of households who lease land from owners or who work land they do not own, on a share-cropping arrangement. The mean percentage was 20 percent and ranged from 0 to 100.

THE STATISTICAL TECHNIQUE

Factor analysis [2] requires no pre-existing theory of functional relationships, can handle masses of diverse data relating to a large number of social and economic characteristics and communities, and is not sensitive to the scale chosen for the quantitative specification of the variables. Factor analysis therefore helps circumvent many of the difficulties inherent in the study of micro-development.

This technique uses an analysis of variance to group variables into a few clusters (Factors) according to the closeness of the linear relationship between the variables. The mathematical principles by which each cluster or "Factor" is formed from the observable variables are as follows: (1) Those variables that are most closely intercorrelated are combined within a single Factor. (2) The variables assigned to a given Factor are those that are most nearly independent of the variables assigned to the other Factors. (3) The Factor sets are derived so as to maximize the percentage of the total variance attributable to each successive Factor (given the inclusion of the preceding Factors). (4) The Factors are independent (uncorrelated with each other). The number of Factors is determined by the criterion that the last Factor extracted explain at least 5 percent of the over-all inter-village variance.

Factor analysis does not allow us to attribute cause and effect. It does, however, permit us to delineate the *underlying regularities* in a complex mass of data by extracting from a larger set of variables the *mutual interdependence* among the subsets of characteristics comprising each Factor.

The results of the Factor analysis are summarized in Table 10–1. Each entry in the table (or matrix) shows the importance of the influence of the Factors (or columns) on the variables (rows). More specifically, each entry, or "Factor loading," is the net correlation between a Factor (set) and a single observed variable.

The Factor loadings may be interpreted more familiarly in terms of the squares of the entries in the Factor matrix. Excluding the last column, which will be explained later, the square of each entry in the matrix represents the proportion (percentage) of the total unit variance of each variable which is explained by each Factor, after allowing for the contributions of the other Factors. The first row of the table, for example, shows that 49 percent ($=.702^2$) of the variation in population among villages is explained by Factor 1, and an additional 9 percent each ($=.290^2$ and $.290^2$) by Factors 3 and 4, while the net contribution of Factors 2 and 5 is less than 1 percent.

The right-hand column of the table gives the sum of the squared Factor loadings, or the "communality" of each variable. The communality indicates the proportion of the total unit variance explained by all the common Factors taken together and is therefore analogous to R^2 in regression analysis. The communality of village population for example is

$$(.702)^2 + (.044)^2 + (-.290)^2 + (.290)^2 + (-.045)^2 = .664$$

That is, 66 percent of the variation in population size among villages is associated with the six common Factors extracted from the seventeen variables included in our analysis. The six influences associated with population in Factor 1 account for roughly 70 percent ($=49/66$) of the "explained" intervillage variation in population.

In addition to indicating the weight of each Factor in explaining the observed variables, the matrix of loadings provides the basis for grouping the variables into common Factors. It is this power to extract statistically cohesive sets of social and economic forces which vary together systematically that makes the technique of Factor analysis of interest to social scientists analyzing development and modernization. Each variable may reasonably be assigned to that Factor with which it has the closest linear relationship, that is, where it has the highest loading. Once variables have been assigned to Factors, each Factor may be "identified" by giving a reasonable explanation of the underlying economic and social forces which it represents.

Table 11–1 is arranged so that variables with their highest loadings in Factor 1 are listed first, followed by variables with their highest loadings in Factors 2 through 5 consecutively. The boxes mark off the Factor sets to which each indicator is assigned.

Table 11–1 *Rotated Factor Matrix for 17 Economic and Social Variables*

Economic and Social Indicators	Rotated Factor Loadings					
	F_1	F_2	F_3	F_4	F_5	R^2
1. Population	**.702**	.044	−.290	.290	−.045	.664
2. Number of Castes	**.820**	−.199	−.113	.026	−.061	.730
3. Commercialization	**.665**	.124	.149	−.337	.000	.593
4. Level of Agricultural Technology	**.706**	.048	.247	.047	.039	.566
5. Transport and Location	**.608**	.116	.171	−.043	−.338	.528
6. Awareness of National Social Legislation	**.540**	.383	.096	−.310	−.079	.550
7. Education	**.522**	.413	.143	.157	−.105	.499
8. Family Type	−.231	**.666**	−.225	−.053	−.250	.613
9. % Female Children Married	−.193	**−.797**	−.060	−.079	.028	.682
10. % Low Caste	.012	−.043	**.815**	.076	.053	.676
11. Cooperative Membership	.118	.009	**.825**	−.107	−.155	.731
12. Income	.402	−.084	.037	**−.577**	.023	.503
13. Land per Capita	−.148	.049	.073	**−.689**	.410	.672
14. Community Development Activities	.326	.123	.280	**.474**	.244	.484
15. % Employment in Agriculture	−.154	−.242	−.096	.054	**.742**	.645
16. % Landowners	−.203	−.358	−.075	−.145	**.668**	.643
17. % Tenant Farmers	−.084	−.111	−.053	.086	**−.773**	.627

THE RESULTS OF THE ANALYSIS

The First Factor

The economic characteristics which have their highest loadings in Factor 1 are the population of the village, the extent of commercialization of productive output, the quality of agricultural technology, and the nearness of villages to towns and transport facilities. The cultural and social characteristics included are the number of castes, the extent of awareness of social legislation, and the level of educational attainment of the village.

Villages which score high on Factor 1 have relatively large populations stratified into many castes. They use more modern agricultural techniques and sell a high proportion of their output to nearby, easily accessible towns. They are also more aware of national legislation concerning untouchability and have better educational facilities, more school-age children in school, and a higher incidence of literacy. By contrast, the villages which score low on Factor 1 have small populations and few castes, use traditional agricultural techniques, produce principally for their own consumption rather than for market sale, are distant from towns and cities, and have poor access (or none at all) to modern means of transport. They are also less aware of national social legislation, have fewer educational facilities, and are less educated. Theirs is a profile of traditional economic and cultural isolation and self-sufficiency and reflects the absence of integrative interactions with the larger economy and society.

The composition of Factor 1, therefore, suggests that it represents the extent of economic and social modernization at the village level. Two of the characteristics in Factor 1, population and number of castes, indicate the scope for economic specialization and division of labor. The larger the village population and the number of castes, the greater the local supply of labor and the capacity for occupational specialization. A large population, moreover, means greater effective demand in the local market. The extent of commercialization, the quality of agricultural technology, and the quality of access to towns and transport facilities (the other three economic characteristics which cluster in Factor 1) indicate the extent to which local communities are economically integrated with the regional and national economy. Greater commercialization means that a larger proportion of village producers are selling to markets outside the village. A higher level of agricultural technology involves greater use of purchased inputs (such as fertilizer). Nearness to towns and transport facilities gives superior access to markets external to the village in which to sell produce and buy consumers' and producers' goods, as well as wider occupational alternatives. Villages that rank high on commercialization, agricultural technology, and nearness to transport facilities and towns are facing outward economically;

they are coming to depend on impersonal market forces and on economic opportunities and facilities external to the village.

Extent of awareness of social legislation and extent of educational achievement also appear in Factor 1, which suggests that close economic linkages with the external world induce more cultural contact. The larger, more commercialized, and better located villages tend also to receive relatively more educational facilities and to make fuller use of the facilities provided.

Our measure of income and its distribution has an important secondary loading (16 percent of variance) in Factor 1. That higher, more evenly distributed income associates with higher village scores on Factor 1 probably reflects the fact that three of the component variables of Factor 1 are the usual targets of agricultural extension and regional development activities: to provide social overhead capital, to enlarge production for sale, and to provide better transport facilities to link villages to cities and to market towns. But the association is not very strong, an indication that as of 1961, the base line of our data, differences among villages in technology, commercialization, and transport still largely reflected historical conditions long in existence in India rather than recently initiated agricultural policies. Irrigation had been started as long as a century back; fertilizer use was still low and, for technical reasons, could be intensively used only where irrigation assured abundant and certain supply of water. Irrigated, more productive land was also settled more densely, leading to larger villages and more castes. The economic and social characteristics which associate in this Factor therefore represent mostly a slowly changing, low-level, static equilibrium.[3]

The Second Factor

Factor 2 indicates the extent to which traditional social arrangements in the village are retained. Villages with high scores on Factor 2 have a *large* proportion of nuclear (as compared to extended) family households and a *small* proportion of girls under the age of 14 who are married. The more traditional villages have a larger proportion of joint family households and a higher frequency of child marriage.

We note that awareness of national social legislation (5 percent of variance), extent of education (16 percent of variance), and percent of landowners (13 percent of variance) have secondary associations with Factor 2. Traditional villages have not only a higher proportion of joint family households and more frequent child marriages but also a higher percentage of landownership and little education and awareness of national social legislation.

It appears that ownership of land tends to keep extended families together in order to avoid uneconomical fragmentation of plots. This socially retarding influence is reinforced by the land-reform legislation, which sets ceilings on legally permissible amounts of land owned according to family size. Material incentives therefore tend to encourage landowners to retain the joint family (a point stressed by Epstein 1962).

Factor 1 explains 24 percent of over-all variance among villages in the extent of economic and cultural modernization. Factor 2 accounts for only 12 percent. This, together with the low average levels of social development represented in our data (the average village in the sample still had 52 percent of joint families and 5.3 percent child brides), implies that actual social change in Indian villages has lagged behind economic change.

The Third Factor

The variables which appear in Factor 3 are the proportion of all village households which are low caste and the proportion of households which belong to cooperatives. Villages that score high on this Factor have a high proportion of low-caste households and a large percentage of households who are members of cooperatives. This Factor explains 10 percent of the over-all variance in all characteristics among villages.

There are several possible explanations for the association shown in Factor 3. Governmental authorities may have deliberately established cooperatives in areas densely populated by low-caste villages. Alternatively, the high-caste, landowning minorities, who dominate villages politically, may have induced their low-caste dependent clients to form cooperatives in order that the village receive some material benefits that the government provides through the cooperatives. The material benefits received in these paper cooperatives then accrue largely to the high-caste persons.[4]

The Fourth Factor

Income, land per capita, and (with a negative correlation) the extent of community development activities undertaken cluster in Factor 4. That income has its highest loading in the fourth rather than the first Factor suggests that (as of 1961) income differences between villages were not as great as other differences and were neither as strongly nor as systematically related to the other economic indicators of development as were the characteristics which cluster in Factor 1. The principal reason for income differences among Indian villages in our analysis is differences in the amount of land cultivated. Since our data are for 1961, technology had been largely static for a long time. Both the quality of technology and land tenure arrangements had therefore adjusted to the inherent productivity of land, with the result that income differentials are more the consequence of differences in relative abundance of land than of technological or economic improvements.

It is reassuring that income has its second highest loading in the economic modernization Factor (1) and that the extent of commercialization and awareness of social legislation have high secondary loadings in Factor 4, the income Factor. This suggests that village income is responsive to the policy programs to improve agriculture: commercialization of production, improvements in irrigation and in the use of fertilizer, and the provision of farm-to-market roads. As of 1961, these programs were not the primary influences on income differences between villages because there was little improved technology to be disseminated and much of it required an expensive package of complementary resources. (This point is stressed by Mellor, Hopper, and Weisblat.)

In a country as agricultural as India, it is not surprising to find income and land per capita strongly related. What is in part puzzling is that community development activity is most strongly associated with the variables in Factor 4, in a negative way, and has its second highest loading in Factor 1, with which it is positively correlated. This suggests to us that villages scoring high on community development activities undertake them under two markedly different sets of circumstances. In villages with lower than average incomes and less than the average amount of land per capita, community development projects may have been initiated from above as an attempt to alleviate unusual poverty. This would explain the high negative correlation with income and land. Its high secondary loading in Factor 1 suggests that more developed villages—better than average commercialization, technology, access to transport—also undertake community development projects more frequently than the average village. If so, community development projects would have a bimodal distribution with unusual community development activity clustering both in villages poor in income and land and in villages more developed than most. (See footnote 6.)

The Fifth Factor

Factor 5, which accounts for 8 percent of the over-all variance between villages, indicates the type of land tenure and the extent to which land resources allow agricultural specialization. Villages that have a high proportion of households owning land (and therefore relatively few tenant farmers) have many people employed full time in agriculture as well as a relatively large amount of land per capita. By contrast, the low-scoring villages have little land per capita, a smaller proportion of landowners, a higher proportion of tenant farmers, and a greater than average percentage of households supplementing their agricultural income with non-agricultural employment.

Professor Mellor suggests that the positive association of larger plots, more frequent land ownership, and greater reliance on agricultural employment probably arise because where the soil is highly productive as in the alluvial deltaic areas, there is a tendency for sharply rising production functions relating labor input and output. This provides a basis for labor productivity way beyond the subsistence requirements of the labor force which, in turn, provides a basis for a landlord class living off of the land and labor of others. Such landlordism will be associated with high population density and small farms, both tracing from the high productivity of the land base. Where there is a prosperous landlord class of this type one would expect them to demand a number of services beyond those in agriculture and, hence, to have a substantial amount of nonagricultural employment.

When the land base is adequate, moreover, fewer households need to supplement their agricultural incomes with secondary and tertiary employments outside of agriculture.

It is not surprising that the four characteristics which portray the nature of the agricultural base of the villages should associate together in a single Factor. But given the overwhelmingly agricultural character of village India, it is surprising that this Factor is the weakest of the five: it explains less variance among villages than any one of the first four Factors. It is also surprising that forces of agricultural dynamism such as better agricultural technology, greater commercialization, and higher incomes should have relatively small associations with the characteristics of land. (Their loadings in Factor 5 are only .039, .000, and .023, implying negligible correlations with this Factor.) These findings support the contention of Neale (1962) that the nature of agrarian tenure has not been a primary obstacle to increasing agricultural productivity and income in the past. The absence of a strong association between land tenure, income, and technology might also mean that tenant farming tends to occur where ecological conditions favor the use of advanced technology, the latter factor more or less balancing the former.

FACTOR ROWS

The Factors that affect each variable and the extent of their influence are shown in the rows of Table 10–1. We comment here only on those rows which yield additional information on the relationships between the variables.

Income

A profile of high-income villages would include the following characteristics in order of importance: a relatively large amount of land per capita (in Factor 4), a high degree of commercialization (Factors 1 and 4), better than average performance in adopting improved agricultural technology

(Factor 1), a relatively large number of castes (Factor 1), more awareness of national social legislation (Factors 4 and 1), and a higher than average level of educational achievement (Factor 1).

As of 1961, programs to commercialize production and to improve technology and access roads, while responsible for 16 percent of intervillage variance in income, were not the most important influences on income differences among villages for two major reasons: (1) the differing qualities of technology reflected in our data were largely historical differences, long in existence, and were all within the framework of traditional (rather than modern) agriculture (Hopper 1965; Schultz 1964), and (2) the available spectrum of technology required an expensive package of complementary innovations and was not very profitable.

Agricultural Technology

The quality of agricultural technology bears no systematic relationship to the agricultural characteristics included in Factor 4, but relates instead to commercialization, size of village, and nearness to transport facilities and towns (Factor 1, 55 percent of variance). These associations indicate that by 1961, reforms in land tenure had had considerably less impact on technical innovations in Indian agriculture than had commercialization and the creation of farm-to-market roads. However, as pointed out by Professor Mellor (in correspondence),

> Your data show that improvements in agricultural incomes and agricultural methods are not associated with the tenure system when studied on a cross-sectional basis. However there may be a number of other factors such as the profitability of new methods and the basic productivity of land which are associated with the tenure system. Thus it may well be that where the land reforms were effective in India they brought about tenure changes which did bring about income increases greater than would otherwise have occurred and improvements in agricultural methods greater than would otherwise have occurred.

Extent of Commercialization

The extent of commercialization has considerable weight in three of the five Factors, confirming findings elsewhere that growth in market activities is a particularly powerful solvent of traditional society (Bohannan and Dalton 1962: Introduction; Smith 1959:297–338). Increased commercialization means greater dependence on market sales, a corresponding reduction in production for self-use, and a resulting increase in the proportion of cash receipts to total real income. Increased dependence on market sale for livelihood enhances the sensitivity of production decisions to market prices; farms thereby become integrated into the larger regional and national economy. The receipt of cash income enables producers to purchase technologically superior inputs, such as pesticides and chemical fertilizers, from the national economy. In addition, farmers are able to make economic decisions on the basis of cost accounting and to hire seasonal wage-labor on short-run, cash-wage terms, instead of through traditional long-run master-client dependency relationships. On the household budget side, cash income widens the range of choice of consumption goods, allows modern forms of savings to take place, and makes possible the purchase of services such as education, which enable people to move out of the traditional village-bound culture and economy.

Several of these effects are captured in Factor 1 (45 percent of variation in extent of commercialization), which reflects interrelatedness among increased commercialization, more economic specialization, enlarged use of modern (purchased) agricultural technology, superior access to transport facilities and towns, higher village income, and more awareness of events external to the village. In addition, 10 percent of the variance in extent of commercialization is associated directly with the income Factor (4).

On the other hand, we find that the extent of commercialization does not vary with the amount of land per capita and the nature of land tenure (Factor 5). With the low-grade technology employed in 1961, differences in size of landholdings and in type of land tenure largely compensated for variations in ecological conditions, so that larger landholdings did not tend to generate a greater proportion of marketable produce.

Transport and Location

Access to transport facilities and to towns is recognized in the literature on development as a powerful force for inducing modernization. Better transport facilities allow goods and people to become outwardly mobile. Opportunities are created for new occupational choices, for new earnings from market sale, and for imports of producer and consumer goods into the hinterland. The economic integration of villages into the national economy leads to the diversification and enlargement of commercial and cultural transactions between the village and the outside world.

The force of these remarks is shown in our Factor analysis, which indicates that 36 percent of the total variance in transport and locational advantages is associated with the economic and social modernization Factor (1). The effects of transport and location are also evident from the association in Factor 5 of relative isolation with higher dependence on agriculture. This association, which accounts for only 10 percent of variance, is probably best explained by the relatively limited employment opportunities outside of agriculture in inaccessible villages.

Employment in Agriculture

Fifty-five percent of the variance in agricultural employment is associated with the components of Factor 5, which indicate the nature of the agricultural base. It is not surprising that villages tend to specialize according to comparative advantage; those with better conditions for agriculture have more people engaged in agriculture.

The low statistical correlation between agricultural employment and Factor 1 is noteworthy. Apparently, the better located, highly commercialized, more technologically advanced villages do not differ significantly from their opposites with regard to the proportion of households engaged in agriculture. This lack of significant correlation between agricultural and other aspects of modernization is probably due to the relative infrequency of livelihood alternatives outside of agriculture. Although it is common for village households to supplement their agricultural income with subordinate occupations, these are usually not sufficiently remunerative to allow villagers to move out of agriculture completely.

Land per Capita

The amount of land worked per capita depends on the quality of land. With low-level technology and a massive population, Indian villages are in a Malthusian and a Ricardian universe: population density varies directly with the capacity of land to produce subsistence requirements, and the more inherently productive land is cultivated more intensively.

Land per capita has its greatest secondary loading in Factor 5 (16 percent of variance), indicating a relationship between the amount of land available, the extent of employment in agriculture, and the prevailing system of land tenure. These associations probably capture the results of a historical adjustment to subsistence production and to the absence of real economic alternatives, a salient characteristic of traditional systems: economic and institutional arrangements in agriculture have adjusted to ecological and technological differences in the productivity of land.

Awareness of National Social Legislation

The extent of awareness of national social legislation on untouchability is the only attitudinal characteristic we were able to include in our analysis. It is probably a proxy for other changes in attitudes which we were unable to capture with our data sources.

Twenty-six percent of the variance in awareness of national social legislation is associated with variance in the economic development indicators of Factor 1. This interaction may arise either because the wider horizons represented in the attitudinal changes induce greater economic integration or because the transformations in activities and technology represented in Factor 1, which tend to integrate the village into the larger economy, also tend to expand the desire for, and the sources of, outside information and contacts.

Fifteen percent of the variance in awareness of national social legislation among villages is associated with the social change indicators of Factor 2. To some extent, therefore, changes in attitudes and in family practices vary together. The limited interaction between the two in our data suggests that change in family practices lags significantly behind changes in attitudes or awareness of external events.

Another 9 percent of the variance in awareness of national social legislation (regarding untouchability) is associated directly with income change in Factor 4. Caste restrictions are a socio-religious mechanism for sharing unemployment and underemployment; prosperity permits a relaxation of these arrangements. Alternatively, causality may work in the opposite direction. The restrictions on occupation imposed by caste lead to a suboptimal distribution of factors of production, which is reflected in somewhat lower incomes. The weakness of the association between income and strength of caste restrictions suggests the existence of long time lags in the mutual feedback process, or of little actual change in whichever is the potentially causal variable, or some combination of the two.

Education

Our variable indicating the number, type, and nearness of educational facilities and their effectiveness (as measured by adult literacy and percentage of school-age children in school) associates most closely with economic and attitudinal modernization as indicated in Factor 1. An examination of the simple correlations of education with the variables in Factor 1 suggests, however, that this association arises primarily because large villages also tend to be better endowed with educational facilities rather than because of the association of education with the more dynamic economic and social variables.

There are also discernible associations between educational achievement and Factors other than the one to which it is assigned. The strongest (16 percent) is a positive relationship with Factor 2, which suggests that where educational attainment markedly improves there is also a greater tendency to depart from traditional family practices (such as the joint family household and early female marriage).

Family Household Type

The literature on kinship stresses that the joint family household (three generations with or without collateral relatives living together) is an economic unit of peasants working cooperatively for subsistence and that the joint household tends to give way to the nuclear family household, once cash earnings grow and alternative modes of employment emerge. Our analysis supports these views (see Factor 2). Where there are many nuclear households and infrequent child marriages, there is less landownership and greater awareness of national social legislation.

Number of Castes

The fact that the number of castes has its highest loading in the economic modernization Factor is one indication of the influence of the caste system on economic progress in India. Since different castes are associated with different occupations, a larger number of castes permits a greater division of labor and more occupational specialization. Because all castes are permitted to engage in agriculture, and the number of castes is correlated with the size of the village, a larger number of castes also indicates the availability of a greater locally mobile pool of labor. This is important because improved agricultural technology requires much greater labor inputs.

Proportion of Low-Caste Households

The absence of systematic relationships between density of low-caste households and Factors other than 3 implies that villages with a relatively large proportion of low-caste households are neither better nor worse off than other villages with regard to income and other positive attributes of welfare and modernization. The probable reason for this is the greater geographic and occupational mobility of low-caste households.

Membership in Cooperatives

The frequency of membership in cooperatives is associated only with Factor 3, indicating that as of 1961 cooperatives had not yet contributed significantly to economic development and to social modernization. There are several possible explanations. The cooperative movement may have been too recent for its effects to be evident by 1961. Moreover, rural cooperatives may not in themselves be sufficient to generate conditions for an agricultural transformation without strong supporting technical agricultural services and without accessible markets for the product.[5] Most agricultural innovations require a set of several innovations introduced simultaneously: to use chemical fertilizer profitably requires more water and more labor per acre. Therefore, "threshold effects" are likely, with sharp and discrete improvements in productivity following the introduction of a package of innovations, rather than a slow growth in productivity following the introduction of a single innovation. We cannot tell from our analysis whether the institution of cooperatives is inappropriate to conditions in India or whether there simply was not available in 1961 any significant quantity of improved seeds, chemical fertilizer, rural credit, and the like for cooperatives to acquire and distribute to members.[6]

Community Development Activities

The negative association between community development activity and income in Factor 4, which reflects the compensatory character of the program, also suggests that, as of 1961, community development efforts had not been very successful in raising village incomes. Many reasons could account for the ineffectiveness of this program. (1) The institution of community development may be inherently unsuited to inducing rural economic modernization in India; or (2) while the institution is, in principle, suitable, its implementation had been defective (the quality of extension agents was below par, the nature of technical support services was defective, the emphasis of the programs on physical accomplishments was misguided, and so forth); or (3) the community development programs were operating below the threshold level of effectiveness (too few agents per farmer, too short a span of time for the effectiveness of their programs to manifest itself, too little credit to disburse at too high a cost, and so on); or (4) community development programs, to be effective, require complementary resources or activities which at the time were not available (profitable technologies, rural education, and the like).[7] Intensive micro-research is required to decide which combination of these explanations is correct.

CONCLUSION

India

Our data refer to rural India as of 1961, when deliberate policies of agricultural development and cultural modernization had just begun to have discernible effects. The differences between economically progressive and backward villages were largely the result of a historical adjustment to superior growing conditions and access to urban markets, rather than the result of recently initiated development programs.

Our Factor analysis points up the importance of various economic forces to village modernization. Factor 1, which explains most of the variance between villages, includes the extent of commercialization, the quality of agricultural technology, and nearness to transport and cities. The importance of economic forces is shown also in the relationships (in Factors 4 and 1) between higher income and commercialization and improvements in agricultural technology. These economic associations suggest that rural development policy in India can profitably be concerned with conventional economic programs: the creation of farm-to-market roads, agricultural extension services, profitable technologies, and the fostering of commercial crops.

Giving up traditional social practices in village India seems to lag behind economic improvement and changes in social attitudes. Our indicators of social change (movement to nuclear households and decline in female child marriage) appeared in the second Factor and accounted for only half as much variation among villages as the indicators of economic and cultural modernization in Factor 1. Economic improvement had not yet induced much social change in village India. Indeed, economic incentives worked to keep the extended family together.

The influence of caste in our study appears in the awareness of social legislation prohibiting untouchability, in the number of castes per village, and in the percentage of village population composed of low castes. The Factor analysis suggests that the weaker the caste system, the higher the level of income and development, and that the income and modernization status of the untouchables is equivalent to that of other rural Indians: the simple correlation between percentage of low-caste persons in a village and village income is .09!

There is evidence in our study that cooperatives and community development efforts had little positive effect on the rural economy as of 1961. These programs had very weak associations with rural economic modernization, commercialization, agricultural technology, and rural incomes. (However, see footnote 6 for a necessary qualification.)

The evidence on land reform is mixed. Types of land tenure do not appear to influence agricultural incomes or agricultural technology. There is, however, a significant association between larger farms and higher than average incomes per head.

In summary, our study suggests that future prospects for rural development in India are mixed. On the one hand, there is evidence that rural modernization is responsive to economic policies such as improvements in farm-to-market roads, the dissemination of agricultural technology, and greater commercialization. On the other hand, such rural development policies encouraging cooperatives, community development blocks, and land reform seem ineffective. There is also evidence that the social transformation of rural India has barely begun and that the caste system and traditional attitudes continue to exercise a retarding influence on economic modernization.

Micro-Development

Although traditional peasantries have a head-start on tribal societies, their problems and processes of village transformation have much in common. The constraints imposed by simple technology, ecological dependence, and physical and economic isolation (and therefore smallness of scale) are similar. The self-sufficiency of their subsistence economies represents a long-run adjustment to the severe conditions of life; villagers depend on local ecology, technology, and social organization for material survival.

In India, population density, land tenure arrangements, agricultural technology, and family and caste have all adjusted to superior ecological and locational advantages. Disparities among villages in per capita income are not very large and are explained primarily by differences in natural resource endowments. The family and caste relationships evolved are risk-sharing devices designed to distribute the proceeds of uncertain, low-income agricultural activities in a way which assures survival through a system of mutual dependence in securing livelihood. In Africa, similar ecological, technological, and economic conditions were coped with principally through kinship arrangements or chieftainship. Mutual dependence for survival there, too, ramified into all village institutions; everyday life as well as ceremony reinforced it.

Such adjustment of economy to society remains intact only as long as agricultural technology remains static and opportunities to earn livelihood outside of agriculture are few.

The redirection of village communities away from activities and institutions designed for survival to those which make for income growth and cultural modernization poses a "dilemma of transition." The old systems of local mutual dependence worked for untold centuries to keep people alive in conditions of harsh uncertainty, when drought or flood or the ravages of war meant hunger or worse. The activities and institutions which bring economic development require and reward an entirely different underlying principle: dependence on impersonal transactions and institutions outside the village (regional, national, and international markets for village sales and purchases, and regional or national governments for the provision of technical and social services). The dilemma of the transition is how to contrive institutional devices to assure material security to peasants willing to undertake risky and expensive innovations, so that failure will not starve or impoverish them.

Our work suggests that the interactions between economic and social change during the process of transition occur in the following fashion. First, economic and technological improvement tends to erode the material security rationale underlying the traditional social institutions such as caste and the joint family household. Economic modernization also tends to induce changes in social awareness and attitudes. Together, these create a new perception of traditional social institutions, whose costs are now felt to outweigh their benefits. The eventual result is to modify the social institutions themselves. The beginnings of such a sequence of change in India are discernible.

NOTES

1. We are grateful to the National Science Foundation for supporting this research under grant GS1235 and to the Council of Intersocietal Studies of Northwestern University for financing a trip to India to check out the results of the statistical analysis. We are indebted to Robert Edminster, Clarence Gulick, David Hopper, Wolf Ladijinsky, John Mellor, Ronald Ridker, Abraham Weisblat, and Clifton Wharton, Jr., for their constructive comments, and to Dylis Rennie and Joyce Nussbaum for their research assistance. Professor Mellor has kindly allowed us to quote some of his comments on this paper as plausible alternative or supplementary interpretations.

2. For full explanations of the technique see Adelman and Morris (1967); Harman (1961); and Thurstone (1961).

3. We are indebted to Hopper and Weisblat for this point.

4. Professor Mellor comments: "It was my impression, although I have not seen statistical evidence to support it, that this is particularly true of the credit cooperatives which are the most numerous types of cooperatives. The higher caste people dominate them and pull what is in effect, subsidized credit for their own purposes. Perhaps high caste people are more likely to organize, join and dominate cooperatives if there are a lot of low-caste people in the community." See footnote 6 for another explanation.

5. Mellor *et al.* (1968) suggest that many cooperatives in India are ineffective.

6. The present authors are preparing another essay using a stepwise analysis of variance applied to the same data. It shows that the situation with regard to cooperatives is more complicated than the Factor analysis shows. Briefly, there is a small group of a dozen villages largely composed of low-caste households with extremely high membership in cooperatives. It is this association which swamped the Factor analysis and yielded Factor 3. In removing this association between low caste and membership in cooperatives, the stepwise analysis of variance does show positive correlation of some strength between cooperative membership and other indicators of development and modernization. See Adelman and Dalton (1971).

7. This point is stressed by Mellor, who writes: "I would state that the most important feature of rural development policy should be policy concerned with generating highly profitable new technologies. One of the great problems with rural development in the periods to which your data refer is the lack of profitable technology available to villagers. In the late sixties we have begun to see some highly profitable new technologies coming out of research programs which were generated in an earlier period."

REFERENCES

ADELMAN, I., and C. T. MORRIS
    1967   *Society, politics, and economic development.* Baltimore: Johns Hopkins Press.

ADELMAN, I., and G. DALTON
  1971   A statistical analysis of modernization in village India. In *Studies in economic anthropology,* G. Dalton ed., American Anthropological Assn.
BAILEY, F.
  1962   *Caste and the economic frontier.* Manchester: Manchester University Press.
BOHANNAN, P., and G. DALTON ed.
  1962   *Markets in Africa.* Evanston: Northwestern University Press.
EPSTEIN, T. S.
  1962   *Economic development and social change in South India.* Manchester: Manchester University Press.
HARMAN, H. H.
  1961   *Modern factor analysis.* Chicago: University of Chicago Press.
HOPPER, W. D.
  1965   The mainsprings of agricultural growth. Dr. Rajendra Prasad Memorial Lecture to the 18th Annual Conference of the Indian Society of Agricultural Statistics, 1965.
INDIA, GOVERNMENT OF
  1961   *Census of India.* Part VI: Village survey monographs (Monographs on selected villages) and District census handbooks.
MELLOR, JOHN W., *et al.*
  1968   *Developing rural India.* Ithaca: Cornell University Press.
NEALE, W. C.
  1962   *Economic change in rural India: land tenure and reform in Uttar Pradesh 1800–1955.* New Haven: Yale University Press.
SCHULTZ, T. W.
  1964   *Transforming traditional agriculture.* New Haven: Yale University Press.
SMITH, THOMAS C.
  1959   *The agrarian origins of modern Japan.* Stanford: Stanford University Press.
THURSTONE, L. L.
  1961   *Multiple factor analysis.* Chicago: University of Chicago Press.

12

History, Politics, and Economic Development in Liberia [1]

> We are insisting only on the direct relevance of the total social structure to economic activity, and on the need of its further analysis in relation to economic processes if we are to get at the big questions of economic progress.
>
> JOHN E. SAWYER

> There is a deep-seated yearning in social science to discover one general approach, one general law valid for all time and all climes. But these primitive attitudes must be outgrown.
>
> ALEXANDER GERSCHENKRON

> It is of the nature of the social sciences that the more rigorous the demonstration, the less interesting or important the point demonstrated.
>
> PETER WILES

I

American and European economists who work in the least developed countries of Africa, Asia, or the Middle East sometimes come away with the feeling of having learned more than they imparted. Nor is this surprising: the minds of economists are often more receptive to development than are the exotic economies in which they now work. In considering problems of underdevelopment and processes of development we learn—inadvertently, as it were—new things about conventional fields of economics and about the developed economies of Europe and America. These

Reprinted, with revision, from "History, Politics, and Economic Development in Liberia," *Journal of Economic History,* 25 (December 1965):569–591. Reprinted by permission of the publisher.

feedbacks have been particularly valuable to economic historians who have given us fresh insights into European, Russian, Japanese, and American development as a direct consequence of the present concern with developing Africa and Asia (Rostow 1960; Gerschenkron 1962; Supple 1963; Nove 1961). Economic history is now wedded to economic development.

Concern with economic development has also brought about a shotgun wedding of economics and the other social sciences. No longer are Africa, Asia, and Latin America the exclusive preserve of anthropologists, nor is development the concern only of economists. Anthropologists, economists, historians, sociologists, political scientists—we are all developers now (for example, Bohannan 1959; Moore 1955). Indeed, economists now venture not only into the African bush but into the thickets of sociology and psychiatry as well (Hagen 1962).

Two kinds of analytical treatment of economic development now exist. (1) The adaptation of conventional fields of economics to the novel circumstances of underdevelopment has produced growth models, national income accounts, and foreign trade analysis for African, Asian, and Latin American countries (for example, Samuels 1963; Chenery 1961). Actually, each of the conventional fields of economics—public finance, money, labor—now has its counterpart in the development literature. (2) Economists are also creating special socio-economic analyses of development processes which have no counterparts in conventional fields of economics: Myrdal's analysis of cumulative causation (Myrdal 1957), Hagen's analysis of institutional change (Hagen 1962), and Lewis' analysis of dualism (Lewis 1954) are cases in point. The reasons for these Veblenesque excursions into social organization, culture, and politics arc clear. Economists want to say useful things about development processes and policy. To do so requires them to scrutinize the idiosyncratic structures of underdevelopment. And for the least developed parts of the world, development entails institutional change as well as change in production lines, and explicit concern with calendar time and practicable policy; it also demands what is new in economics—the need to do field work. Economists contrive unconventional analysis where they are faced with unconventional structures, processes, and problems.

It is difficult to estimate how many of the hundred or so underdeveloped nations of the world are still "traditional societies" or are still acquiring what Rostow calls the pre-conditions for growth and development. Perhaps one-half would be a conservative guess. These are countries in which the principal impediments to development lie in traditional social organization, culture, and politics—institutional arrangements unreceptive to development policies suggested by economists. It is these refractory institutional arrangements that have inspired the socio-economic analyses of Myrdal, Hagen, and Lewis.

II

Liberia is an extreme example of underdevelopment which persists because of traditional social organization, culture, and politics. It is a dual economy and an enclave economy. Fewer than 15 percent of its population are literate, and two-thirds of its people still derive the bulk of their livelihood from subsistence activities. The few new production lines initiated by foreigners since World War II make for short-run income growth but not long-run development: they do not induce complementary activities so as progressively to enmesh wider sectors of the economy in new skills, new technology, and higher productivity. Liberia is not appreciably more developed in 1970 than it was in 1960.

Despite its smallness—it is about the size of Indiana, with a population of about one million—Liberia is of special interest from several points of view. It has rich resource endowments relative to population. There is no land shortage. Its rainfall and soil make it highly suitable for growing tree crops. It has extremely large deposits of high-grade iron ore which are presently being mined on a large scale. Since 1950, four foreign firms have invested more than $300 million in iron-ore mining alone. There are known deposits of other minerals as yet largely untapped. Liberia's iron ore and rubber are like oil and gold elsewhere: valuable export commodities, the initial exploitation of which could be made to serve as the income source for long-term private and public development outlays.

Liberia is of special interest to the U.S. government and to those concerned with the politics of underdeveloped nations. It is the only country in Africa with which the United States has had an historical affiliation. Americo-Liberians (descendants of the freed slaves) regard the United States as friend, ally, and relative. English is the national language, the U.S. flag (with one star only) is the national emblem, and the U.S. dollar is the national currency. A professor from Harvard drew up its constitution on the American model in 1838, and professors from Cornell codified its laws in the 1950's. Liberia declared war on Germany after Pearl Harbor and allowed the United States to station five thousand troops at a base to ferry airplanes to the war zones. The "Voice of America" has its largest African installation in Liberia. On a per capita basis, the U.S. government gives more aid to Liberia than to any other African country. The Firestone Rubber Company of Akron, Ohio, was the first foreign firm to establish large-scale plantation agriculture (1926), and it still employs almost one-fourth of the wage-earning labor force.

With the partial exception of Ethiopia, Liberia is the only country in Africa which was never the colony of a European power. It has been a sovereign republic since 1847. For those who are impressed by the favorite myth of African political leaders—that before European colonization Africa must have enjoyed some sort of golden age, because its present economic and social problems are the evil legacy of wicked European colonialism—an examination of Liberia is instructive.

III

The salient characteristics of Liberia's economy are the recent start of private and governmental development activities, the unusual extent to which new lines of production are undertaken by foreign firms, the extreme extent of concentration of commercial activities in primary production for export (iron ore and rubber), and the absence of systematic national planning to transform traditional sectors of the economy and to initiate other long-term structural changes. From 1950 to 1962 Liberia had a high growth rate due to heavy foreign investment in iron ore and rubber, but it remains largely undeveloped otherwise. American and European investments affect Liberian development in two principal ways. (1) The wage bill grows absolutely as the number of Liberian wage laborers grows. The wage-earning labor force more than doubled between 1950 and 1960. But the increased effective demand due to higher wage incomes has not induced enlarged domestic production of goods bought by wage earn-

Table 12–1 *Liberia: Gross Domestic Product at Market Price by Industry of Origin* * (MILLIONS OF U.S. DOLLARS)

Industry	1950	1960
Agriculture, forestry, fishing, hunting		
Subsistence	22.2	18.1
Peasant money	1.8	7.3
Large-scale commercial	21.0	31.4
Mining and quarrying	0.1	31.1
Construction		28.0[a]
Electricity, gas, and water	7.4	2.4
Ownership of dwellings		12.1
Others not elsewhere specified (distribution, transport, manufacture, etc.)		19.3
Public administration and defense	3.0	18.1[b]
Services (including banking and insurance)	2.6	5.0
Gross domestic product at market prices	58.1	172.8

SOURCE: *Growth without Development* (cited in footnote to title). Clower *et al.* (1966).

* Indirect taxes were $15.7 million (1960) and $2.8 million (1950).

[a] A very rough estimate only.

[b] Includes interest ($1.5 million) on productive government debt.

Table 12-2 *Liberia: Domestic Income Components, 1950–1960* *

(MILLIONS OF U.S. DOLLARS)

Section A	1950	1951	1952	1953	1954	1955	1956	1957	1958	1959	1960
Wages, salaries, plus pay of the armed forces	11.5	14.0	16.5	19.0	22.0	25.6	30.2	31.6	35.6	41.2	46.9
Net money income of tribal households (other than wages)	1.8	2.2	2.7	3.0	3.4	3.9	4.5	4.8	5.5	6.3	7.3
Gross business surplus (including interest, rent, depreciation) Concessions	16.2	18.3	19.6	21.7	19.1	30.5	32.9	29.1	27.4	44.6	53.3
Other (including government but *excluding* interest on government debt)	3.5	5.1	8.1	8.2	9.8	12.1	14.2	16.1	18.7	22.5	29.8
Indirect taxes	2.8	6.1	5.7	6.5	6.2	7.0	7.9	9.3	9.9	15.5	15.7
Section B											
Gross domestic money income at market prices (excluding interest on government debt)	35.8	45.7	52.6	58.4	60.5	79.1	89.7	90.9	97.1	130.1	153.0
Plus subsistence agriculture not entering money sector	22.2	21.7	20.9	20.0	18.8	18.4	18.0	17.0	17.5	17.8	18.1
Gross domestic income at market prices	58.0	67.4	73.5	78.4	79.3	97.5	107.7	107.9	114.6	147.9	171.1
Less net property income paid overseas	9.8	11.1	13.2	14.2	10.6	17.1	19.0	16.3	16.6	28.9	34.6
Gross national income at market prices	48.2	56.3	60.3	64.2	68.7	80.4	88.7	91.6	98.0	119.0	136.5
Less indirect taxes	2.8	6.1	5.7	6.5	6.2	7.0	7.9	9.3	9.9	15.5	15.7
Gross national income at factor cost	45.4	50.2	54.6	57.7	62.5	73.4	80.8	82.3	88.1	103.5	120.8

ers; it has increased imports. (2) Government revenue grew eightfold between 1950 and 1960, and the total of external borrowing by the government grew from almost zero to $100 million. But for the most part the government spends its revenues and borrowings in ways that do not create enlarged productive capacity (nor, indeed, provide welfare services to any but a few Liberians). The bulk of government spending goes for wages and salaries of employees, and, on capital account, to public buildings, roads, and facilities to provide public utility services to the capital city of Monrovia. Cost-benefit analyses are unknown in Liberian public finance.

Table 12–3 *Key Indicators of Liberian Economic Growth* *

1. G.D.P. at factor cost per capita	$150–170 (1960)
2. Rate of growth of real G.D.P. per capita	1955–60 annual, 11.0 percent per annum
3. Rate of population growth over 1955–60 (latest five years)	about 1.0 percent per annum
4. Imports/G.D.P.	49.0 percent (1960)
5. Exports and reexports/G.D.P.	49.0 percent (1960)
6. Government tax revenue/G.D.P.	17.4 percent (1960)
7. Government capital expenditure/Government recurrent expenditure	22.5 percent (1960)
8. Capital formation/G.D.P.	33.6 percent[a]
9. Government capital formation/Private capital formation	9.0 percent

SOURCE: *Growth without Development*. Dalton *et al.* (1966).

* With the exception of 1 and 2, all calculations of G.D.P. and capital formation are at market prices and not at factory cost.

[a] High value partly due to extensive mining investment. It is expected to decline to 20-25 percent in mid-1960's.

Whether one looks at national income accounts, at a functional classification of government expenditures, or at more qualitative indicators of structure and performance, the same picture emerges: labor's share of national income is among the lowest on record for any country, which reflects the unusual proportion of unskilled labor to total labor supply; the low wage rates prevailing in the money sector are set by the low opportunity income available in the subsistence sector. But institutional arrangements also work to reduce wage rates: one-fourth of the wage-earning labor force is supplied involuntarily—labor recruitment is the euphemism for forced labor—and unions are kept ineffective by government. An unusual proportion of governmental expenditure is what Adam Smith quite rightly would have regarded as unproductive: spending on public buildings and public employees. Government employs 15 percent of all wage earners. In 1960 almost as much was spent on diplomacy as on education.

Roughly, about 65 percent of the Liberian work force are engaged in subsistence agriculture and to a minor extent in growing cash crops; about 30 percent are wage earners, most of whom are unskilled workers on rubber farms who earned in 1962 about seventy-five cents per day (in cash and wage supplements); under 5 percent comprise the professional, managerial, and entrepreneurial labor force, who work for government, are absentee owners (for the most part) of rubber farms, of transport facilities, and of buildings,[2] or who provide legal services and to a small extent medical and commercial services. (Almost all staff positions in iron ore and rubber are occupied by foreigners. Where Liberians are employed in staff positions by foreign firms, they most frequently act as "consultants" on legal matters, public relations, and advertising.)

The only clearly successful growth activity undertaken by Liberians is rubber production. However, the conditions are very special. Aside from high prices during World War II and the Korean war, the growth is largely

Table 12–4   *Liberia: Government Economic Accounts: 1960*
(MILLIONS OF U.S. DOLLARS)

Government Current Revenue and Expenditure Account			
Receipts		*Expenditures*	
Direct taxes on income:		Current expenditure:	
Rubber concessions	7.0		
Iron-ore concessions	6.4	Wages and salaries	8.8
Other	1.9	Travel and transport	1.3
Customs and external trade taxes	14.5	Other goods and services	8.3
Public utility revenues	0.8	Transfers	2.0
Other revenues and fees:		Depreciation	0.8
Hut, health, and development taxes	0.7		
Other taxes and fees	1.0	Surplus on current account	11.0
	32.3		32.3

Government Savings—Investment Account			
Receipts		*Expenditures*	
Surplus on current account	11.0	Gross fixed capital formation	4.9
Sales of government property	0.1	Transfers to local government	0.9
		Transfers to business sector	4.9
		Balance	0.4
	11.1		11.1

SOURCE: Dalton *et al.* (1966).

Table 12–5 *Liberia: Functional Classification*
of Government Expenditures, 1960
(MILLIONS OF U.S. DOLLARS)

Function	Current Expenditure	Capital Expenditure	Total Expenditure	Percentage of Total Expenditure
General services:				
General administration	5.7	0.7	6.4	19
Foreign affairs	2.7		2.7	8
Defense	1.4	0.1	1.5	5
Justice and police	1.1		1.1	4
General services, subtotal	10.9	0.8	11.7	36
Community services:				
Roads, waterways, and fire protection	2.0	3.0	5.0	15
Water supply	0.2	0.3	0.5	1
Other	0.3	0.1	0.4	1
Community services, subtotal	2.5	3.4	5.9	17
Social services:				
Education	2.9	0.6	3.5	10
Health and welfare	2.7	0.3	3.0	9
Other	0.1	0.1	0.2	1
Social services, subtotal	5.7	1.0	6.7	20
Economic services:				
Agriculture	0.6	0.1	0.7	2
Fuel and power	0.2	0.3	0.5	1
Mineral resources, manufacturing		4.8	4.8	14
Transport and communication	0.6		0.6	2
Other	0.1	0.1	0.2	1
Economic services, subtotal	1.5	5.3	6.8	20
Unallocable:				
Transfers and subsidies	0.8	0.2	1.0	3
Misc. contingencies	1.1		1.1	4
Unallocable subtotal	1.9	0.2	2.1	7
Total, all functions	22.5	10.7	33.2	100

SOURCE: Dalton *et al.* (1966).

Table 12–6   *Liberia: Annual Production of Independent*
Rubber Farms

Year[a]	Production (thousand lbs.)	Number of Farms
1941	475	150
1950	2,716	477
1955	7,805	991
1960	13,926	2,312

SOURCE: Firestone Plantation, Liberia.

[a] Year is from November 1 of previous year to October 31 of current year.

attributable to the extension services and demonstration effect provided by Firestone and to the fact that most of the rubber produced by independents is on farms owned by highly-placed Americo-Liberians rather than by tribal persons. Of some 2,300 rubber farms owned by Liberians, the seventy largest accounted for 60 percent of the rubber grown by independents in 1960. Firestone's extension services to private growers have been effective because practical advice is given to Liberian producers on all aspects of rubber-farm management, and many of the farmers assisted are literate and commercially minded. As the sole buyer of rubber in Liberia, Fire-

Table 12–7   *Average Full-Time Employment in Money*
Sector of Liberian Economy
by Principal Activity of Employer
(NUMBER OF EQUIVALENT MAN-YEARS)

	1955[a]	1958[a]	1960[b]
Agriculture:			
Concessions	22,000	23,500	24,500
Independent farms	5,000	6,500	8,400
Forestry and fishing	200	400	600
Construction	5,000	6,300	9,100
Mining	2,900	4,200	8,000
Trade	2,500	3,000	4,000
Manufacturing	300	500	1,100
Services	7,000	8,000	11,200
Transport and communication	2,100	3,200	3,500
Government	9,500	10,400	11,600
Total:	56,500	66,000	82,000

[a] Based on U.S. Foreign Service Report No. 71, Monrovia, 1958.

[b] Based on a sample census of employment conducted in 1960 by the Bureau of Economic Research and Statistics, Republic of Liberia. The statistics were processed for Dalton *et al.* (1966).

stone was able to impose quality standards on Liberian producers by using price differentials for different grades of rubber.[3] Aside from its interest in contributing to Liberia's development and introducing politically important Liberians to a profitable plantation crop, Firestone has a financial stake in knowing exactly how much rubber is produced by Liberians (to ensure that the rubber it buys does not come from its own trees).

If conditions of the kind that characterize rubber production could be created for other cash crops, the success of Firestone's program of extension services might be duplicated and departure from subsistence agriculture become more frequent. However, unlike rice, palm kernels, sugar cane, and most other cash crops grown in Liberia, rubber has no domestic use and only one domestic market outlet. If rubber could be eaten, demanded as tribute, or stolen and sold with impunity, it is unlikely that its growth rate would have been so high.

In sum, the foreign enclave sector is growing, but Liberia is not developing. Rapid growth in primary commodities for export produced by foreign firms has meant a higher wage bill paid to Liberian workers and higher taxes paid to the Liberian government, neither of which has induced significant output expansion in production lines undertaken by Liberians, except for the special case of rubber. The question is, why?

IV

What is disturbing to economists who work in Liberia is not so much its present state of underdevelopment—given the fact that most growth activities have begun only since 1950, it could hardly be otherwise; rather, it is the absence of those beginnings of a development program which would allow one to believe that the economy will be structurally different in ten or twenty years. One may peel off the layers of causation in this fashion: in an extremely backward country such as Liberia, government must bear an unusually large burden of initiative to begin those long-range changes in economy, technology, and culture that we call economic development (Myrdal 1957:chapter 2). It must plan to transform subsistence agriculture to commercial farming (Yudelman 1964; Fogg 1965), to educate and train young people to acquire skills in accordance with development needs (Myers 1963; Fogg 1963), and to specify the conditions under which foreign firms in residence are to operate which will yield developmental effects (Lewis 1953). In a word, it must have some conscious strategy for development based on knowledge of present economic structure and performance and knowledge of economic processes (Hirschman 1958; Tinbergen 1958; Stolper 1962). To contrive and implement development policies, the upper echelons of government must be sufficiently honest, sufficiently competent, and sufficiently concerned with national economic development. These conditions are absent in Liberia. There is neither sufficient honesty, competence, nor concern with national development. To understand why and how this is so, one must understand the present political and social organization of Liberia, which, in turn, requires understanding Liberian history. The present structures and policies which prevent development are the unreformed, traditional, pre-World War II structures and policies carried into the new economic environment of massive iron-ore mines and rubber plantations.

The dominant characteristics of Liberian political and social organization were embedded by the last quarter of the nineteenth century, after the first fifty years of settlement by the freed Negroes. The economic backwardness of Liberia is not attributable to lack of resources or to domination by foreign financial and political interests. The underlying difficulty is rather that the traditional Americo-Liberian rulers, for fear of losing political control to tribal people, have not allowed those changes to take place which are necessary to develop the national society and economy.

Like the Portuguese in Angola and the Africaners in the Republic of South Africa, the rulers of Liberia are descendants of an alien minority of colonial settlers. Americo-Liberian families, who comprise 3 to 5 percent of the population, control the country and govern the tribes on a colonial pattern of indirect rule. District Commissioners appointed by central government are local governers in the tribal hinterland. Paramount chiefs, who serve at the pleasure of the president, have local jurisdiction over everyday matters. With regard to taxation, land tenure, residence and movement, marriage and divorce, legal jurisdiction, access to education and medical services, obligatory (no pay) labor service to local authorities, labor recruitment (forced labor with pay), and extralegal exactions of money, rice, and services, tribal Liberians in the hinterland are subject to a socio-legal system different from that of Americo-Liberians. Economic development requires the elimination of these distinctions to permit tribal Liberians to become increasingly enmeshed in new economic activities, skills, and values. But this would lead inevitably to demands by the tribal people for a voice in the political management of Liberia. At present, only those changes in economic and social structure are allowed that do not threaten the political control of the Americo-Liberians, and these changes alone are simply insufficient to transform the economy. The foreign enclave sector grows, but the country does not develop. The overriding goal of Liberian authority is what it has been for the past one hundred fifty years: to retain political control among the families of settler descent and to share out any material benefits of economic growth among its own members. It is the politics and society, not the economics, of Liberia that are arcane and problematical.

V

From the earliest days of settlement in 1821–1822 to the present, the Americo-Liberians have acted like Portuguese, British, and South African colonists in other parts of Africa. They maintain an identity distinct from tribal persons in speech, dress, source and level of income, style of life, and culture. Indeed, in their preference for politics, law, and plantations, and in their disdain for commerce, the descendants of the freed slaves are an aristocracy. Like European colonizers in other parts of Africa, the Americo-Liberians subdued the tribes with force and fraud for high-sounding purposes. The large land purchases (paid for with beads, muskets, tobacco, and umbrellas) were negotiated with chiefs to whom the practice of permanent alienation of land was unfamiliar. Americo-Liberian leaders said they had a manifest destiny to bring civilization to the tribal heathen; slavery was to be suppressed, and the colony was to be a beach-head for Christianity in Africa.

From 1821 to 1839, several Americo-Liberian settlements, independent from one another, were established along the coast on the initiative of the American Colonization Society (to repatriate free Negroes) and similar organizations set up on its model in several American states. The first move toward consolidation into a central polity—the isolated coastal settlements joining together as a "commonwealth"—occurred in 1839 in response to tribal hostility. It was imperative that the isolated settlements band to-gether for mutual defense. The Americo-Liberians learned early that the survival of their community depended on cohesion within. They learned also to defeat tribal uprisings with cannon and guns. As late as 1915 the U.S. government provided the settler community with military advisers and weapons to put down an uprising among the Kru (an energetic people who rebelled again in 1931–1932).

The second and final move toward consolidation into a central polity—the formation of a nation-state claiming sovereignty over a hinterland of tribes—occurred in 1847, again in response to external threat. This crisis was precipitated by British claims to territory on the Sierra Leone frontier and by a British challenge to the legality of the tax powers of the Liberian Commonwealth. The Americo-Liberians met this crisis by declaring Liberia an independent republic and calling upon the United States for aid and protection. The threat of European incursion, like the threat of tribal hostility, continued well into the twentieth century. As late as 1931, in response to a League of Nations inquiry into slavery and forced labor in Liberia, Britain wanted the League to set up a governing commission to displace Americo-Liberian rule.[4]

By the last quarter of the nineteenth century, after fifty years of Americo-Liberian settlement, much of the present structure of Liberian political and social organization was fixed. The leading families of the Americo-Liberian community (probably between ten and fifteen thousand persons in 1875) occupied the coastal strip and ruled a hinterland of tribes they had learned to subdue and treat harshly. Special taxes and coercive sanctions were imposed on tribal people, special regulations were in force to control tribal residence and migration, compulsory recruitment to work on private farms and public projects was imposed on tribal men, and extra-legal exactions of tribute were imposed on hinterland communities. The inferior status of tribal people hardened into policy. In law as well as practice, Americo-Liberians and Natives were distinct social classes with markedly different rights and obligations. The Americo-Liberians had also learned to retain their independence against British and French encroachment with the reluctant protection of the United States (which carefully avoided making Liberia an official appendage of itself).

Like the newer African nations, Liberia is a one-party state. The True Whig Party has been in office continuously since 1877. Unlike most African political leaders, the Americo-Liberians are not reformist intellectuals with ethnic roots in the tribes who fashioned their political movement in response to colonial domination and the urge to modernize their nation. Neither the Sorbonne nor the London School of Economics is the spiritual homeland of Liberian leaders. When Americo-Liberians speak of the "nation," they mean themselves. There is no nationalist mystique in Liberia. The Americo-Liberians do not yearn to transform tribal society. Ironically, it is the ethic of Mississippi that most nearly characterizes their outlook: to retain power in traditional fashion and to keep the Natives in their place.

In Liberia, political form differs radically from political substance, and official pronouncement differs radically from actual practice. Liberia had a compulsory elementary education law as early as 1912, but fifty years later less than 15 percent of the population was literate. It has a constitution and governmental forms—executive, legislative, and judicial—modeled carefully on those of the United States, but without the remotest resemblance in actual operation. It has a declared policy of national unification, but—in 1962—the rights and obligations of tribal persons were utterly different from those of Americo-Liberians, and one-fourth of the wage-earning labor force was recruited involuntarily, as in the harsh days of early African colonialism. It had two trade unions in 1962, but the president's son was the head of one and the president's social secretary was the head of the other, strikes were illegal, and there were no collective bargaining contracts. It had a minimum wage law (four cents an hour), but the law did not cover agricultural and domestic workers who comprised more than 80 percent of all non-governmental wage workers.

Since his assumption of office in 1944, President Tubman has initiated two new policies, but has controlled the changes forthcoming to prevent any essential reform of the traditional political and social structure, thus preventing from happening what the Americo-Liberian leadership has always feared: losing control to Europeans or to tribal persons.

The most dramatic change has been President Tubman's "open-door policy": inviting European and American firms to extract iron ore, engage in plantation agriculture, and undertake a variety of other commercial ventures, and, concomitantly, seeking external loans, economic aid, and technical assistance. The result has been growth in primary production and the accumulation of new buildings, roads, and other social capital reflected in the national income accounts. But Europeans cannot become citizens or own land in Liberia. They are contractual guests—resident aliens who take no part in political life.[5] The few Negro immigrants from America and the West Indies who become citizens are almost never permitted to enter the higher echelons of government.

The second break with the past is President Tubman's "unification policy," reflected mainly in a noticeable decline in harshness of treatment of tribal persons. President Tubman himself visits hinterland areas, listens to grievances and petitions, and has been known to remove district commissioners guilty of brutality or theft. Compulsory labor has been made less onerous, and the appropriation of tribal land without compensation is less frequent under the Tubman administration. And since so many countries in Africa have become independent, it is no longer acceptable in Liberia publicly to make distinctions between civilized and uncivilized elements of the population or, indeed, to use the traditional designations of Americo-Liberians and Natives. The fiction of equality receives official sanction; but in matters of structure and substance, it remains fiction.

Before 1944, the three hinterland provinces (in which most of the tribespeople reside) had no representation in the legislature. By paying $100 a tribe could send someone to sit in the House of Representatives, but without a vote. Since 1944 the provinces have been allowed to elect six of the thirty-nine members of the House (but no senators). Similarly, universal suffrage has been introduced in presidential elections. But elections are so rigged that it makes no difference to the result.[6] The electoral reforms may give the tribes an illusion of participation and may improve Liberia's "image" abroad, but they are a change in appearance with no change in reality.

Educated men of tribal background have attained high political office, but only at the price of succumbing to the aristocratic embrace—of acting in all ways like Americo-Liberians.[7] Insofar as there can be said to exist any unification or assimilation policy at all, it consists of transmogrifying tribal people into Americo-Liberians, one at a time, so to speak. There is no person in high office whose actions can be judged as representing the special interests of the tribes.

The governing authorities do not have a policy of denying material improvement to tribal persons and areas. There have long been educational and medical missionaries in the hinterland and medical and educational facilities provided by foreign firms. And, especially since 1955, some minor portion of educational outlay from public funds has been allocated to the three hinterland provinces (although never as much as is spent in Montserrado County, the home base of America-Liberian settlement). But neither is there anything that can be called national development policy—to transform subsistence agriculture, to choose the most gifted Liberians (regardless of status and family connection) for training and education abroad, to analyze various sectors of the economy in order to project the requirements for structural improvement.

VI

Liberia enjoyed none of the benefits of European colonization which in some measure were conferred on most other African countries. It received neither the tangible benefits of roads and schools nor the more important but less tangible benefits of trained administrators and a civil service ethic of efficient and honest performance. Instead, the traditional practices and values of America-Liberian society were carried into the postwar period. The traditional rulers of Liberia sustain their absolute political control by dispensing patronage to the loyal and punishment to the restive and by preventing political opposition from being expressed at all. In 1960 approximately one out of seven wage and salary earners (11,600 out of 82,000) worked for the government, but there were only fifty elected officials in all (the president, ten senators, and thirty-nine representatives). The governing authorities reward loyalty and conformity with jobs, many of which are sinecures requiring not even the physical presence of the incumbent. To each level of governmental employment there is attached a special set of fringe benefits. The highest echelons and their kin obtain the most lucrative material prerogatives: purchases of shares of stock in iron-ore concessions at bargain prices; purchases of tribal land along new roads; sales of phantom services (public relations, advertising) to foreign concessions; sales of real economic services to concessions (for example, trucking), but at higher cost than the buyers would incur in providing their own services; acquiring compulsory labor for their rubber farms; the right to impose private levies in rice on tribal groups; the use of government vehicles and other equipment for private gain; extraordinarily large expense accounts; free housing and trips abroad; government scholarships for education abroad, regardless of merit. Lower-echelon civil servants have a narrower but still impressive array of prerogatives.

Both the carrot and the stick are used to encourage loyalty to the governing authorities and to prevent the expression of opposition. The material rewards of faithfulness grow as governmental revenue and private economic activity grow. A person who expresses opposition to the authorities is denied access to good jobs and valuable perquisites of office, and his kin are made to suffer such deprivation as well. Collective punishment for individual disloyalty is visited upon Americo-Liberian families and tribal groups alike.

As with one-party states elsewhere, so also in Liberia there is no tradition, no concept, no practice of "loyal opposition." Criticism of the president, or of the government and its policies, is interpreted as disloyalty, sedition, subversion, and is punished severely. Democracy as we know it in the West requires the institutionalization of loyal opposition; endowing political parties out of office but in the legislature with real functions, power, and the possibility of achieving office without revolution; and allowing newspapers, radio, unions, and university professors to express criticism of government and its works without calling down retribution.

The legislature has never been known to initiate legislation not previously approved by the president, nor—with one or two showpiece exceptions—to veto a bill or a budget proposed by the president. The judiciary is not independent. Supreme Court justices can be (and are) removed by a declaration of the legislature. Several times, court rulings have simply been ignored. The officer corps of the Army (Liberian Frontier Force) consists largely of sons of Americo-Liberians whose values and actions are no different from those of other government employees. The enlisted soldiers are unskilled young men recruited for the most part from the few Liberian tribes with a warrior tradition. The Frontier Force was formed in 1868 to punish hostile tribes and to collect taxes. When stationed in the interior, they still live off the land and are allowed license to requisition and pillage.

Voluntary associations and channels of public expression are either ineffective, silent, or adoring. The trade unions are allowed to exist on condition that they do not turn political or, indeed, press economic demands too hard. The Liberian churches (as distinct from the European and American missionaries) are adaptations of low Protestant sects whose governing authorities are highly-placed Americo-Liberians. There are two newspapers in Liberia, one owned wholly by government, the other subsidized. Neither has been known to criticize the government and its works. (There have been elections in which the names of opposition candidates have not been mentioned in the papers.) There are two radio stations in Liberia. One is operated by the government; the other is owned by a Protestant mission, and its broadcasts are concerned exclusively with matters relating to the next world.

A president elected for the first time has an initial term of office of

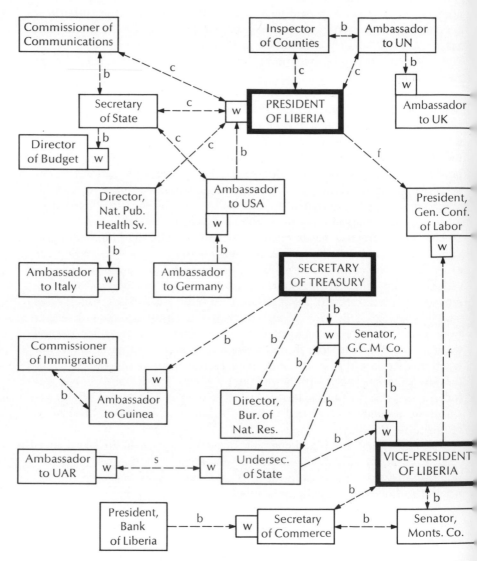

Key: b = brother; f = father; c = cousin; s = sister; w = wife.
Source: Liebenow (1962:369).

Figure 12–1 *Family and Politics in the Republic of Liberia, 1960–1961*

eight years, after which elections are held every four years. The legally-minded Americo-Liberians go through a solemn minuet of conventions, speeches, and votes, without there being the slightest possibility that opposition can gain political power through elections. Indeed, it is a difficult task—as in Alabama in the United States elections of 1964—for opposition candidates to get placed on the ballot. Serious opposition will have been squashed long before the appointees of the True Whig Party count ballots. There is no organized opposition party between elections.

To understand Liberian politics, knowledge of kinship connections among high government officials is more useful than knowledge of the Liberian constitution. Marriage and divorce make and break family alliances with important political repercussions. One manifestation of the historical cohesion within the Americo-Liberian community of families is shown in Figure 12–1.

President Tubman is not a dictator, but rather a dedicated and—compared with former presidents—benevolent managing director of Americo-Liberian interests. For thirty years he has succeeded in keeping political control within the Americo-Liberian establishment and enriching it beyond precedent out of the revenues and economic opportunities provided by foreign firms. This golden harvest, combined, perhaps, with the pressure of foreign aid and advisers, has induced some amelioration in the tribesman's lot. But no political power has accrued to the tribes. Neither factions from within the country nor African nationalism from outside—neither Liberian tribes and dissidents nor its leftist neighbors—have threatened the political dominance of the traditional rulers. Potential sources of internal opposition are brought into the True Whig fold by jobs and money. Students returning from abroad are embraced by the patronage system, and their skins quickly thicken. And where the carrot will not work, the stick is applied.

Foreign economists who work in countries like Liberia confront a dilemma: if they confine themselves to conventional measurement, economic analysis, and policy prescriptions for development, they are wasting their effort. The governing authorities of Liberia have no intention of developing the national economy and the Liberian people. Under present political and social arrangements, offering economic advice to Liberian leaders is futile. What is the point of showing them how to increase tax revenues by $5 million, if the revenue would be frittered away on objects and activities that had little if any effect on national welfare or development? Economic development is the proper concern of economists; but in Liberia political and social reform are the most important of all "preconditions" for development, and so economists are forced into political and social as well as economic analysis.

Table 12–8   *The Social Hierarchy* [*in Monrovia*]

Class	Characteristics	Occupation
A. The elite	Dress suits; Dior fashions; children schooled overseas; own rubber plantations; own large houses and lease out others. Large motorcars. Members of Masonic lodges and crowds, Protestant, Episcopalian, Methodist, or Baptist churches.	Senior officers of the three branches of government, and their families.
B. Honorables		Other government officials from head of bureau up; certain doctors, lawyers, clergymen.
C. Civilized	Suit and tie to work; children sent to school and usually speak English first; some starting rubber farms. Walk or on long distances hire taxis. Members of lodges, United Brothers of Friendship, and church associations. Own their houses and may rent out others. Intertribal marriage frequent.	Minor officials, clerks, schoolteachers, nurses.
		Electricians, mechanics and drivers, craftsmen.
D. Indeterminate		Domestics.
E. Tribal or Uncivilized	Women wear lappas, men shirt and trousers; illiterate but majority speak some English. Pay hut tax. Walk long distances. Pentecostal, Methodist and Baptist churches and associations based on membership of specific tribes. Legal redress from urban tribal courts. Intertribal marriage rare.	Laborers, stevedores, fishermen, petty traders.

SOURCE: Fraenkel (1964).

NOTES

1. The author resided in Liberia in 1961–1962. With R. W. Clower, M. Harwitz, and A. A. Walters, he is coauthor of *Growth without Development: An Economic Survey of Liberia* (Evanston: Northwestern University Press, 1966), which is the source for most of the statistical tables and some of the text of this chapter. On politics and history he has drawn from conventional published sources and his own observations. He is especially indebted to the work of J. Gus Liebenow (1962; 1964). The author is grateful to Edward Budd for his critical comments.

2. Under Liberian law, only citizens may own land or commercial transport facilities, and only people of African descent may become citizens.

3. It is almost certain that Firestone does not exercise its monopsonistic power for several reasons, the most important of which is that the largest Liberian producers Firestone buys rubber from are the president, vice-president, cabinet members, and some others. Firestone pays the price prevailing in New York the previous month, minus several cents per pound for processing and transportation costs. In 1960, Liberians produced 15 percent and Firestone 85 percent of all rubber exported.

4. Two persistent themes in Liberian history are carried into the present scheme of things. The one we have emphasized is the Americo-Liberian community's defense of its autonomy in the face of tribal and European hostility. The other theme is fiscal irresponsibility. European loans in 1871 and 1906 were defaulted, as was an American loan in 1912. A $5 million loan made by Firestone to the government of Liberia in 1927 as part of its original concession agreement was finally repaid in 1952 but left a history of bitterness and recrimination toward Firestone. As recently as 1963, the government of Liberia had to get emergency loans from the United States because of its inability to meet external debt.

5. As far as one can judge in these amorphous matters, the notion commonly believed in Africa and Europe that the U.S. government and large American firms such as Firestone have real political control in Liberia is utterly unfounded. The government of Liberia is at least as jealous of its political autonomy as are its newly independent African neighbors. The ironic result—and, as with Batista's Cuba, the potentially costly result to the United States—is that while neither the U.S. government nor American business controls the country, the United States is held responsible for events in Liberia.

6. For example, election returns for the presidency in 1955 and 1959 were as follows:

	Wm. V. S. Tubman	*Wm. O. Davies-Bright*
1955	244,937	16
1959	530,566	55

See Liebenow (1962; 1964).

7. In Liberia, the phrase "a man of tribal background" applies to two very different kinds of persons. Children born out of wedlock to tribal women and Americo-Liberian men are frequently reared in the man's "official household"

in Monrovia and so grow up speaking English and acquiring the cultural attributes of Americo-Liberians. Such children have no connection with tribal life other than the accident of their mother. They are Americo-Liberians without any cultural or psychological roots in the tribes. Charles Sherman, the urbane former Secretary of Treasury, is such a person. Persons born of tribal parents, reared in a tribal milieu, and without Americo-Liberian connections, very rarely rise to high office. (Three cabinet members "of tribal background" were fired from office between 1959 and 1963.)

REFERENCES

BOHANNAN, PAUL
    1959   The impact of money on an African subsistence economy. *Journal of Economic History* 19:491–503.

CHENERY, H. B.
    1961   Comparative advantage and development policy. *American Economic Review* vol. 51.

CLOWER, ROBERT, GEORGE DALTON, and A. A. WALTERS
    1962   Statistics and development policy decisions. *Development Research Review* vol. 1 no. 1 (currently *Development Digest*).

CLOWER, ROBERT, *et al.*
    1966   *Growth without development: an economic survey of Liberia.* Evanston: Northwestern University Press.

FOGG, C. DAVIS
    1963   Manpower planning. In *Managing economic development in Africa,* W. H. Hausman ed. Cambridge: M.I.T. Press.
    1965   Economic and social factors affecting the development of smallholder agriculture in eastern Nigeria. *Economic Development and Cultural Change* 13:278–292.

FRAENKEL, MERRAN
    1964   *Tribe and class in Monrovia.* London: Oxford University Press.

GERSCHENKRON, ALEXANDER
    1954   Social attitudes, entrepreneurship, and economic development. *International Social Science Journal* 6:252–258.
    1962   *Economic backwardness in historical perspective.* Cambridge: The Belknap Press of Harvard University Press.

HAGEN, EVERETT E.
    1962   *On the theory of social change.* Homewood: Dorsey.

HIRSCHMAN, A. O.
    1958   *The strategy of economic development.* New Haven: Yale University Press.

LEWIS, W. ARTHUR
    1953   *Report on the industrialization of the Gold Coast.* Accra: Government Printer's Office.
    1954   Economic development with unlimited supplies of labour. *Manchester School* 22:139–191.

LIEBENOW, J. GUS
  1962   The republic of Liberia. In *African one-party states,* Gwendolen M. Carter ed. Ithaca: Cornell University Press.
  1964   Liberia. In *Political parties and national integration in Tropical Africa,* James S. Coleman and Carl G. Rosberg, Jr., ed. Berkeley: University of California Press.
MOORE, WILBERT E.
  1955   Labor attitudes toward industrialization in underdeveloped countries. *American Economic Review* 45:156–165.
MYERS, CHARLES A.
  1963   Human resources for economic development. In *Managing economic development in Africa,* W. H. Hausman ed. Cambridge: M.I.T. Press.
MYRDAL, GUNNAR
  1957   *Rich lands and poor.* New York: Harper.
NOVE, ALEC
  1961   Assessment. In *The Soviet economy,* by Alec Nove. New York: Praeger.
ROSTOW, W. W.
  1960   *The stages of economic growth.* Cambridge: Cambridge University Press.
SAMUELS, L. H., ed.
  1963   *African studies in income and wealth.* Chicago: Quadrangle Books.
SAWYER, JOHN E.
  1951   Social structure and economic progress. *American Economic Review* 41:321–329.
STOLPER, W.
  1962   The contribution of economic research to African development. In *Economic development for Africa south of the Sahara,* E. A. G. Robinson ed. New York: St. Martin's Press.
SUPPLE, BARRY E., ed.
  1963   *The experience of economic growth.* New York: Random House.
TINBERGEN, JAN
  1958   *The design of development.* Baltimore: Johns Hopkins Press.
WILES, PETER
  1963   Pilkington and the theory of value. *Economic Journal* 73:195.
YUDELMAN, M.
  1964   Some aspects of African agricultural development. In *Economic development for Africa south of the Sahara,* E. A. G. Robinson ed. New York: St. Martin's Press.

13

Economic Development
and Economic Anthropology

Little else is requisite to carry a state to the highest degree of opulence from the lowest barbarism, but peace, easy taxes, and a tolerable administration of justice.

ADAM SMITH

I should like to address the question, "Is economic theory culture-bound?" in two contexts: as the question relates to the economist's field, economic development, and as it relates to the anthropologist's field, economic anthropology.

ECONOMIC DEVELOPMENT AND ECONOMICS

In the last ten years several prominent economists have questioned the relevance of conventional economics (for example, price, aggregate income, and growth theory) for dealing with the processes and problems of economic development.[1] This is an old theme stated in a new context. Similar examples are the German *methodenstreit* debate; von Mises and von Hayek versus Taylor, Lange, and Lerner on planning without market prices under socialism; and the marginalist controversy after World War II. In all these, the same question was debated: the extent of realism, relevance, and adequacy of formal economics in dealing with real-world processes and problems of importance.

In order to answer the question as it relates to economic development, one must first answer two other questions: What are the special characteristics of the structure and performance of underdeveloped countries which

Reprinted, with revision, from "Economics, Economic Development, and Economic Anthropology," *Journal of Economic Issues* (June 1968):173–186. Reprinted by permission of the publisher.

lead some economists to question the relevance of economics? What are the special characteristics of conventional economics which seem to these economists to be misleading or irrelevant in the context of underdevelopment? We turn first to the special characteristics of underdeveloped countries.

1. The basic fact of the underdeveloped world is the existence of some one hundred underdeveloped nation-states, principally in Africa, Asia, Latin America, and the Middle East. The economic, political, and social differences among them are much greater than are the differences among the few developed capitalist nations of Western Europe and North America for which economic theory was invented. The fact of extreme diversity in the underdeveloped world—that it includes tiny Liberia as well as massive India—means that nothing like a single analytical model of underdevelopment is feasible: the structures, processes, and problems are too different.

2. Half or more of these countries are developing their polities and societies as well as their economies. They are in the process of structural transformation politically and culturally as well as economically and technologically. They are combining their Industrial Revolutions with their French Revolutions and their nation-building Mercantilist periods. They are creating nationwide political and social institutions as well as national systems of banking, taxation, and transportation.

One reflection of this simultaneity of structural change is that all the other social sciences now have interests in Asia, Africa, and Latin America which are counterparts to the interests of economists. What economists call development, political scientists call "modernization" (Apter 1965), sociologists, "role differentiation" (Smelser 1966), and anthropologists, "culture change" (Epstein 1962; Douglas 1965). These accompanying political and social changes make economic development processes even more complicated. Indeed, from a Western economist's viewpoint, a sort of non-Euclidean universe is sometimes created: if building roads and radio transmitters, in order to connect hitherto isolated regions in African countries, is thought to provide valuable integrating devices for increasing the political interaction among ethnically different citizens of what is now one nation and for spreading the usage of English or French, cost-benefit analysts must guess at the worth of these amorphous political and linguistic benefits of roads and radios.

3. These countries are not only underdeveloped; they are also overexposed. By this I mean two things: they are pursuing development deliberately, consciously, and quickly; and they are following policies which, except for Japan and Soviet Russia, are outside the experience of the already developed nations. The United States and Britain developed less consciously, less as a matter of deliberate national effort, less as an urgent responsibility of governmental initiative. One consequence of current de-

velopment as an effort of conscious purpose is that the economic policy of governments is pressing. Whatever one means by the economics of development, it is not a field of pure theory, but an applied field. Neither Marshall nor Keynes invented economic theory with civil servants waiting in the next room to put it into practice. A second consequence of this overexposure—this pressing public need to formulate development policy in the quick pursuit of higher income—is the creation of impossible expectations and therefore inevitable disappointments. Satisfaction or disappointment with development progress is a fraction, the numerator being realized results, the denominator, expectations. Rarely in the underdeveloped world does the fraction approach one.

There are other reasons, moreover, for built-in disappointment with realized results. Not only is development policy conscious, deliberate, and pressing; too often, as Wolfgang Stolper (1966) reminds us, it is made on the basis of fragmentary data. In primary producing countries, it should be remembered, economic policy is very much less autonomous than it is in developed economies. Underdeveloped countries depend on externally set export prices and financial aid to an unusual extent.

4. Finally, the least-developed one-third or more of the underdeveloped countries have what I shall call micro-development problems of a sort which are unfamiliar to Western economists (Hill 1966; also 1963) but which in part are familiar to Western agricultural economists and rural sociologists: problems of how to transform subsistence agriculture (deWilde *et al.* 1967; Yudelman 1964) and how to create more persons of entrepreneurial initiative (Hagen 1962).

To sum up: The reality of underdevelopment—the set of real-world circumstances to which economists address their theory—entails the following: wide diversity because of the large number of countries included; social, cultural, political, and economic complexity because of the simultaneous changes toward modernization being experienced; and the pressing need to make policy decisions within constraints set by inadequate information and exaggerated expectations.

We turn now to the second set of components which bear on our problem: those characteristics of economics which make some economists argue that conventional economics is irrelevant or downright misleading for the analysis of the processes and problems of development. Here I need only summarize what has been so clearly spelled out by Myrdal, Seers, Hagen, and others. It is useful, I think, to put these characteristics into three sets that are by no means mutually exclusive.

1. Many economic concepts, such as the multiplier, and much economic analysis, such as the Keynesian theory of aggregate income determination, were contrived in response to the special problems (for example, chronic unemployment) of already industrialized, already developed, nationally-integrated, large-scale market economies; underdeveloped countries have

other problems for which neither the concepts nor the analysis is relevant.

2. Many economic concepts, such as the accelerator, and much economic analysis, such as growth theory, are interesting, useful, applicable —indeed, even operational—because of the special structure of already industrialized, already developed, nationally-integrated, large-scale market economies; underdeveloped economies have different structures, and neither the concepts nor the analysis is relevant.

3. The leading ideas of economics, such as equilibrium analysis, and the inherited policy preferences of economists, such as laissez faire, reflect the special ethic of Anglo-America—a sort of Marshallian mentality— and the special political, social, and even religious institutions and traditions of Anglo-America. Africans, Asians, and Latin Americans have markedly different histories, social structures, and political experiences and therefore find the leading ideas and policy preferences of conventional economics uncongenial.

Among the development economists, two utterly different things are meant by "applying economic theory." It means a general method of approach used to identify problems, to measure sectoral relationships, and to put important questions to an economy. Here, the economist as diagnostician of structure and measurer of performance is useful in all underdeveloped countries. The second meaning is quite narrow: it is that the micro- and macro-market processes which economists analyze in developed economies somehow have functional equivalents in underdeveloped economies, and so the analyses and the policy conclusions drawn from them somehow can be directly "applied" in underdeveloped economies. This second meaning of "applying economic theory" is the one that rightly has been criticized.

One of the sad ironies of underdevelopment is that the less developed economically a country is, the less able it is to apply economic analysis and policy because of its social and political structures. Those countries needing economic improvement the most are the least capable of making effective use of both economic analysis and economic aid.

The interesting question is not: "Is economics relevant or irrelevant for underdeveloped countries?" This is not a good question because there is so much economics and so many underdeveloped countries. A better question is: "For which underdeveloped countries is what portion of economics directly relevant; and how must economics, where it is not relevant, be supplemented with socio-economic analysis, and of what sort?"

The work of Irma Adelman and Cynthia Taft Morris (1967) serves as a point of departure. They have shown that the large set of underdeveloped countries can be divided into three groups, low, intermediate, and high, and that such a separation into subsets is analytically useful because the socio-economic structures and the socio-economic problems of development for each subset are markedly different.

At the lowest level of development are countries most of which are in sub-Saharan Africa and are overwhelmingly agricultural, having large subsistence sectors, a few primary commodities for export, little social capital, and few developed market institutions.[2] In economic terms, these are not yet national economies, but rather congeries of primitive and peasant villages only weakly linked to the national society, polity, or economy. Direct taxation and banking do not reach the bulk of the village communities, and markets transact considerably less than half of what is produced. There is no national integration culturally or politically; rather, there is ethnic and linguistic diversity. (The small West African country Liberia is in the middle of this lowest group [Clower *et al.* 1966]. It is a "dual" economy and an "enclave" economy. Foreign firms producing iron ore and rubber for export account for most of the commodities produced for sale.)

To this least developed subset of countries, whose economies, polities, and societies are least like those of developed nations, we can put the question: "How relevant is conventional economics to analyze their processes and problems?" The answer, I think, is that economics is necessary but not sufficient and that only a relatively small portion of that large set of concepts, theories, and measurements which we call economics is applicable.

The most directly applicable economics in such countries is statistical measurement to establish quantitatively the nature of each one's structure and performance. The first job of the economist in such countries is to create or improve national income accounts and other hard-data series—to establish the factual base necessary to avoid costly mistakes (Clower, Dalton, and Walters 1962).

The second job of the economist is that which former Secretary of Defense McNamara is reputed to have accomplished so successfully in the overdeveloped (and underexposed) Pentagon: to establish cost-benefit criteria for making policy decisions. Here the economist is very much at home, whether he is at the Pentagon or in agricultural Nigeria (Fogg 1965). Economics is a gigantic machine to compare costs with benefits.

In the subset of least developed countries there are other important jobs of analysis for economists to do, but these jobs are socio-economic analyses, which require the economist (alone, or in collaboration with other social scientists) to analyze and make policy within the special institutional constraints of each country: how to transform subsistence agriculture, how to increase agricultural productivity, what kind of educational system to establish and with what priority of budgetary outlay.

If someone should tell me that conventional economics was not designed to answer such questions, I would agree; but I would also reply that neither does conventional sociology, anthropology, political science, or psychology answer such questions. And I would argue further that economists

—from Marx and Veblen to Lewis and Hagen—have been notably more successful in doing socio-economic analysis than the other social scientists have been in crossing over from their special subjects.

To sum up: for that subset of underdeveloped economies which is least developed, only a narrow range of economics is directly applicable, and the most formidable problems encountered are socio-economic and purely political and social problems entailed in creating modern nationwide institutions.

Economics is culture-bound, but economists are not. The tradition in economics of valuing highly pure theory and elegant theory is not the only tradition. There is an equally strong tradition of pragmatic engagement: from Adam Smith to John Maynard Keynes, economists confronted real problems and invented whatever methods and analyses were necessary to find answers to them. It is true that economics abhors indeterminacy and that the social and political universes are notoriously indeterminate. However, it is an economist, Everett Hagen, who learned anthropology and psychoanalytical theory in order to say interesting things about the problem of the emergence of entrepreneurs in traditional societies. And it is the economists Irma Adelman and Cynthia Taft Morris who borrowed factor analysis, a statistical technique invented by psychologists, to say interesting things about the mutual interaction of cultural, political, and economic variables at different levels of economic development. And it is the economist Arthur Lewis who invented a beautifully Ricardian model to show us that in the non-Euclidean situation of dual economies one gets non-Euclidean paths to development.[3] And it is the economist Gunnar Myrdal who showed us, in his analysis of cumulative causation, how social and economic forces mutually affect each other in all situations of underdevelopment.

None of this should surprise us. We know from looking at our own economy that economics systematically ignores much that impinges on the economy. Why else do business administration and industrial sociology exist as fields of study? We know from looking at the Soviet economy and the writings of specialists in Soviet economy that (*a*) our statistical measurements of performance and process, such as national income accounts and input-output matrices, are important and applicable to national economies rather differently organized from our own; (*b*) cost-benefit analyses, such as linear programming models provide, are useful in institutional contexts different from our own; and (*c*) where political decisions extensively control economic process (as contrasted to situations of market autonomy), only socio-economic analysis is possible. Why else is there only a political economy of the Soviet system rather than a body of formal theory comparable to conventional economic analysis? And we know from the work of economic historians on the already developed economies that England,

Germany, and Japan developed in ways rather different from one another. It should not surprise us that Liberia, India, and Mexico—or neighboring Israel and Egypt—are also developing differently.

There are other lessons to be learned from the work of Adelman and Morris which bear on the questions posed in this paper. As one moves his focus from the least developed subset, to the intermediate one, to the highest subset of underdeveloped economies, one can say the following: The more developed they become, the more relevant and useful does economic analysis become and the more effective are purely economic policies. Indeed, for the highest subset, development economics merges into growth economics.

ECONOMIC ANTHROPOLOGY AND ECONOMICS

The economist who studies the non-market economy has to abandon most of what he has learnt, and adopts the techniques of the anthropologist [W. Arthur Lewis].

Of all the fields labeled social science, economics and anthropology are the least alike in their traditions, methods, and content. The mainstream of economics relates almost exclusively to our own kind of economy since it achieved its present industrialized, developed form. Price theory, income theory, growth theory, money and banking, public finance, and so forth analyze the processes of large-scale, nationally-integrated, industrialized, capitalist economies. With the occasional exception of writers such as Veblen and Galbraith, economists exclude institutional matters relating to social organization and culture from their analytical interests. These are relegated to sociology and psychology. Even the relatively few economists who specialize in economic history and comparative economic systems usually focus on the post-industrial period in Europe and America. In economics, there is no tradition of detailed field work, area studies (except for Soviet economy), or concern with small-scale, village-level economies. Neither is there concern with what anthropologists mean by folk views and what psychologists mean by human behavior. (Economists study the "behavior" of price and investment figures, not of people.) Economists almost never have occasion to incorporate the work done in sociology or psychology, except for the quite recent work by economists on the institutional aspects of economic development.

There are two positive traditions in economics. The first is formal theory of an abstract sort, which increasingly is stated in mathematical terms. The second is pragmatic concern for policy-making, a sensitivity to current problems of importance, such as depression or balance-of-payments problems. Keynes's work, of course, is a very clear example of formal analysis consciously designed to make policy.

In all these ways anthropology has a radically different tradition. Theory in anthropology is not highly abstract and only rarely is stated in mathematical terms. The empirical knowledge of anthropologists centers on societies and cultures other than our own. Detailed field work in face-to-face proximity with the peoples studied is an important part of training and research. Almost invariably the unit of observation and analysis is a small, village-level community (not, as with economists, a national economy). Anthropologists are concerned with human behavior and have broad interests in culture and society—language, kinship, religion, polity—all of which make anthropology much closer to sociology and psychology than is economics. Above all, anthropologists analyze the mutual interaction of social, cultural, and economic activities, institutions, roles, and relationships within the same small society. Finally, there is only a slight pragmatic tradition in anthropology (applied anthropology). Making policy has not been an important reason to create theory.

Anthropologists have been debating the same issues that have recently exercised the development economists: How relevant is conventional economics to economic anthropology? Should anthropologists make use of the conceptual language of economics in analyzing primitive and peasant economies, or are different concepts and theories necessary which have no counterpart in conventional economics? Indeed, these have been contentious issues for thirty years, going back to Raymond Firth's survey of economic anthropology in 1939 (chapter 1; also Goodfellow 1939:chapter 1; Herskovits 1940:chapter 2). The issues raised were never resolved, and they remained dormant until 1957 when Karl Polanyi's symposium volume (Polanyi, Arensberg, and Pearson 1957) touched off the second round of disputes which continue to the present.[4]

In this section I shall point out the underlying reasons why these theoretical disputes in economic anthropology persist.

1. It is not sufficiently realized how complex economic anthropology is, how wide and diverse is the scope of its subject matter. Economic anthropology is concerned with the organization and the performance of thousands of primitive and peasant economies—studied at different points of time, in all parts of the world—under static and dynamic conditions.

By structure I mean the organization of the economy: the transactional modes used to allocate land and labor, to arrange work, and to dispose of produce—in short, processes of production and marketing, external trade activities, and money uses. Structure also refers to the connections between economic and social organization, what Polanyi calls "the place of the economy in society." In this connection, Raymond Firth states, "Economic anthropology deals primarily with the economic aspects of social relations of persons [1951:138]."

By performance I mean the quantifiable results of economic processes: How much of what kinds of subsistence and prestige goods get produced? How equal or unequal is the distribution of income? Performance also relates to the productivity of labor, land, and other resources.[5]

By primitive economies, I mean the Trobriand and Tiv types, hunting and gathering bands and agricultural tribes whose principal modes of transacting labor, land, tools, and produce are socially obligatory gift-giving (Mauss's and Thurnwald's reciprocity) and redistribution through political or religious leaders. These are economies in which the bulk of resources and produce are transacted in non-market spheres.

By peasant economies I mean those in Latin America described by Tax (1963) and Wolf (1955) and in Asia by Firth (1946) where commercial (market) transactions for resources and produce are quantitatively important, and so cash transactions, the pricing of land and tools, and wage labor are common.

But this is not all. There are two basically different sets of conditions under which anthropologists analyze primitive and peasant economic structure and performance. The first is under relatively static conditions, by which I mean the situation before modernizing activities take place—what anthropologists sometimes refer to as traditional economy. (With the exception of very few economic historians, economists have no counterpart interest in traditional economies, that is, the economic organization and performance of pre-industrial Europe or Asia. Anthropologists, however, are concerned with many aspects of pre-industrial societies, including their economic organization.)

The second focus of analytical interest is community change, growth, and development: the enlargement of production for sale, the adoption of modern technology and applied science, and other modernizing activities. This interest is in micro-development; in studying community change and development, the anthropologist's unit of analysis remains the small-group economy and society.[6]

Analytical writings in economic anthropology are even more recent than those in the economist's field of development, and there are many fewer anthropologists working in economic anthropology than there are economists working in development. There is an old and large literature of descriptive ethnography in economic anthropology. But for the most part we are only at the beginning of systematic analysis of these several aspects of primitive and peasant communities: organization, performance, band, tribal, and peasant economy, traditional forms, change and development.

2. Despite the complexity and diversity of the subject matter, several writers search for a universally applicable theory of economic anthropology as though it were a Holy Grail which, once found, would shed the grace of understanding on all economies, those thousands studied by anthropologists as well as the dozens of developed, industrialized capitalist

and communist economies studied by economists. LeClair, for instance, asserts: "What is required . . . is a search for the general theory of economic process and structure of which contemporary economic theory is but a special case [1962:1185]." Such views betray not only insufficient appreciation of the complexity of the subject matter of economic anthropology but also gross misunderstanding of conventional economics, which until recently was concerned exclusively with our own type of economy. Economics contains no such notion of a general or universal theory which in any sense is addressed to widely different processes and problems. Price theory is concerned with the determinants of price under different market conditions. Aggregate income theory considers an utterly different process. The concepts employed are different, even though they relate to the same economy. And when economies different from our own are analyzed—the Soviet economy, the underdeveloped economies of Nigeria or India— additional theoretical concepts are invented to deal with what is special to their structures or performance.

3. Much of the recent literature of theoretical contention in economic anthropology describes what anthropologists think conventional economic theory is and does, and it urges anthropologists to base their analytical approach on the concepts of conventional economics. When anthropologists argue that conventional economics is applicable in economic anthropology, they have three things in mind. The first concerns peasant economies in which market dependence for livelihood is important, cash transactions frequent, and commercial activities familiar. Where there are wage labor and purchase and sale of land and produce, the conceptual categories of price theory are obviously applicable, and its generalizations about price and income formation relevant. The same is not true for traditional band and tribal economies (the Tiv and the Trobriand Islanders), whose main sectors of economy are not organized by market transactions.

Conventional statistics are adaptable to measuring economic performance. In the case of peasant economies, one can measure the money value of income generated in the commercial sectors of production (Firth 1946; Epstein 1962) and arrive at the local community equivalents of national income and gross national product and their components. For subsistence economies, measurement of community output is possible in terms of quantities of each sort of good produced, but not in terms of national income accounting (because of the absence of cash transactions). Attempts to measure productivity of resources, such as output per acre or per man-labor-day, are also feasible (Salisbury 1962).

A third way anthropologists "apply" conventional economics is much more dubious: it is simply to use the terminology of economics, such as "maximize," "economize," "scarcity," and "rational choice," to describe whatever economic processes and activities they find in primitive and peasant societies. As expressed by Herskovits, "Our primary concern in these pages is to understand the cross-cultural implications of the process of economizing [1952:4]."

To assume that what economists mean by "scarcity," "choice," and "economizing" in our own industrialized market economy are universally present in all economies is simply to misunderstand these terms. To apply these concepts to primitive economies lacking market organization of land, labor, and production is to equate all purposeful activity with "economizing" and then to conclude that the apparatus of economic theory is applicable because economizing activities have been identified. Burling elaborates this notion as follows:

> From this point of view, we are "economizing" in everything we do. We are always trying to maximize our satisfactions somehow, and so we are led back to the notion that economics deals not with a type but rather with an aspect of behavior. This economic view of society becomes . . . one model for looking at society. It is a model which sees the individuals of a society busily engaged in maximizing their own satisfactions—desire for power, sex, food independence . . . [1962:817–818].

However, this is to distort the meaning of economic activities in primitive societies. Priests become stockbrokers maximizing piety instead of profit. Bridewealth becomes the price one pays for sexual and domestic services. (To use market language to describe complicated socio-economic relationships such as marriage is to obliterate the distinction between marriage and prostitution: both become regarded as ways of purchasing services for a price [Dalton 1966].)

Theory in economic anthropology is in its infancy despite the fact that its literature of case studies is enormous, rich, and diverse. Even the obvious connections between economies studied by anthropologists and those studied by historians of pre-industrial Europe and Asia have scarcely been touched. Only in the last few years have we begun to construct a theoretical framework which, when used in systematically comparing traditional economies with each other and with our own, yields insights of the sort gained in analyzing traditional kinship, polity, and religion. Moreover, the second large branch of the subject, the processes of socio-economic change, growth, and development as small communities "modernize" and become integral parts of nation-states, is even less developed.

Like economics, economic anthropology borders at one end on historical description of economies that have long since been transformed, and at the other on quantitative measurement and dynamic processes of present-day change and development. As in economics, there is ample room for different theoretical approaches because of the different structures, processes, and problems that fall within the scope of economic anthropology.

CONCLUSION

Economic theory is culture-bound in the sense that its main lines of analysis relate to the special structures and problems of large-scale, industrialized, developed capitalist economies. Economic development, as done by economists, and economic anthropology, as done by anthropologists, are recent fields of specialization whose subject matter is a hundred or more national economies, on the one hand, and thousands of small-scale village economies, on the other, in Africa, Asia, Latin America, Oceania, and the Middle East. A large proportion of both sets of economies have economic and socio-political structures and problems markedly different from those of the already developed economies. Except for the most advanced subset of the underdeveloped national economies, institutional processes and problems of a sort unfamiliar to economic analysis are pervasive, and they make necessary socio-economic analyses of a novel sort. A number of economists—Myrdal, Lewis, Hagen, Adelman and Morris, and Polanyi—have already made important contributions to the socio-economic analysis of underdeveloped national and village economies.

There is a lesson to be learned from these literatures of contention in economic development and economic anthropology. The fact that intelligent men can disagree—and disagree rather heatedly—over long periods of time almost certainly means there are ingrained semantic difficulties underlying their disagreement. They are attaching different meanings to the same words. In both disciplines, the crucial words are "applying economic theory." The anthropologists think they are applying economic theory when they use the vocabulary of price theory to describe whatever transactions they observe in primitive economies. Instead of saying that a Trobriand Islander gives yams to his sister's husband partly to fulfill an obligation to his closest female relative and partly in recognition of her rights to land he is using, they say the Trobriander is "maximizing prestige." This is to use the terminology of economics as a fig leaf to cover their theoretical nakedness.

The development economists who are critical of conventional economics are really saying that many underdeveloped countries have social and political processes and problems which impede economic development and have economic structures of a sort for which aggregative concepts like "gross investment" are not operational. They are right. However, the conclusion should be not to discard economics, but to learn about social and political processes, and to disaggregate.

NOTES

1. Myrdal (1957); Hagen (1962); Seers (1963); see also Sawyer (1951) and Singer (1950). Seers's provocative article induced a symposium to consider the relevance of economics to economic development and problems involved in teaching development economics: Martin and Knapp (1967).

2. For example, four principal categories of less developed countries were distinguished with respect to the size of their traditional subsistence sectors as of about 1960. Two of the categories are relevant here: (*a*) countries with 80 percent or more of their population in traditional subsistence agriculture with the marketing of crops being of relatively minor importance: Afghanistan, Cameroun, Chad, Dahomey, Ethiopia, Gabon, Guinea, Laos, Liberia, Malagasy, Nepal, Niger, Malawi, Sudan, Tanganyika, Uganda, Yemen; (*b*) countries with from 55 to 79 percent of their population in traditional subsistence agriculture, with the marketing of crops being of relatively minor importance: Algeria, Bolivia, Burma, Cambodia, Indonesia, Iran, Iraq, Ivory Coast, Kenya, Libya, Morocco, South Korea, South Vietnam, Thailand, Tunisia, Zambia. Adelman and Morris (1967:21–22).

3. Singer (1950) is an illuminating companion piece to Lewis' model of development under dualism.

4. LeClair (1962); Burling (1962); Cook (1966). For views opposing these, see Dalton (1961; 1969; 1967).

5. There seems to be no equivalent in the conventional subjects of anthropological inquiry, such as kinship, religion, and polity, to what is here meant by the quantifiable performance of the economy. The closest one comes is simple enumeration: for example, the frequency of murder, theft, or divorce. The distinction between economic organization and the quantifiable performance of the economy applies to all economies, those studied by anthropologists, economists, and historians.

6. One of the best such studies is Epstein (1962).

REFERENCES

ADELMAN, IRMA, and CYNTHIA TAFT MORRIS
    1967   *Society, politics, and economic development.* Baltimore: Johns Hopkins Press.
APTER, DAVID
    1965   *The politics of modernization.* Chicago: University of Chicago Press.
BEATTIE, J. H. M.
    1964   Bunyoro: an African feudality? *Journal of African History* 5:25–36.
BURLING, ROBBINS
    1962   Maximization theories and the study of economic anthropology. *American Anthropologist* 64:802–821.
CLOWER, R. W., GEORGE DALTON, MITCHELL HARWITZ, and A. A. WALTERS
    1966   *Growth without development: an economic survey of Liberia.* Evanston: Northwestern University Press.

CLOWER, R. W., GEORGE DALTON, and A. A. WALTERS
  1962   Statistics and development policy decisions. *Development Research Review* vol. 1 no. 1 (currently *Development Digest*).
COOK, SCOTT
  1966   The obsolete "antimarket" mentality. *American Anthropologist* 68:323–345.
DALTON, GEORGE
  1961   Economic theory and primitive society. *American Anthropologist* 63:1–25.
  1966   Bridewealth versus brideprice. *American Anthropologist* 68:732–737.
  1967   Bibliographical essay. In *Tribal and peasant economies: readings in economic anthropology*, George Dalton ed. New York: Natural History Press.
  1969   Theoretical issues in economic anthropology. *Current Anthropology* 10:63–102.
DEWILDE, JOHN, *et al.*
  1967   *Experiences with agricultural development in tropical Africa*, 2 vols. Baltimore: Johns Hopkins Press.
DOUGLAS, MARY
  1965   The Lele—resistance to change. In *Markets in Africa,* Paul Bohannan and George Dalton ed. New York: Natural History Press.
EPSTEIN, T. S.
  1962   *Economic development and social change in South India*. Manchester: Manchester University Press.
FIRTH, RAYMOND
  1939   *Primitive Polynesian economy*. London: Routledge and Kegan Paul.
  1946   *Malay fishermen: their peasant economy*. London: Routledge and Kegan Paul (2d ed. 1966).
  1951   *The elements of social organisation*. London: Watts.
FOGG, C. DAVIS
  1965   Economic and social factors affecting the development of smallholder agriculture in eastern Nigeria. *Economic Development and Cultural Change* 13:278–292.
GOODFELLOW, D. M.
  1939   *Principles of economic sociology*. London: Routledge.
GOODY, JACK
  1963   Feudalism in Africa? *Journal of African History* 4:1–18.
HAGEN, EVERETT E. ed.
  1962   *On the theory of social change*. Homewood: Dorsey.
HERSKOVITS, M. J.
  1940   *The economic life of primitive peoples*. New York: Knopf.
  1952   *Economic anthropology*, revised ed. New York: Knopf.
HILL, POLLY
  1963   *Migrant cocoa-farmers of southern Ghana*. Cambridge: Cambridge University Press.
  1966   A plea for indigenous economics. *Economic Development and Cultural Change* 15:10–20.

LeClair, Edward E., Jr.
   1962   Economic theory and economic anthropology. *American Anthropologist* 64:1179–1203.
Martin, Kurt, and John Knapp ed.
   1967   *The teaching of development economics.* Chicago: Aldine.
Myrdal, Gunnar
   1957   *Rich lands and poor.* New York: Harper.
Polanyi, Karl, Conrad M. Arensberg, Harry W. Pearson ed.
   1957   *Trade and market in the early empires.* Glencoe: The Free Press.
Salisbury, R. F.
   1962   *From stone to steel.* London: Cambridge University Press.
Sawyer, John E.
   1951   Social structure and economic progress. *American Economic Review* 41:321–329.
Seers, Dudley
   1963   The limitations of the special case. *Oxford University, Institute of Statistics Bulletin* 25:77–98.
Singer, Hans W.
   1950   The distribution of gains between investing and borrowing countries. *American Economic Review* vol. 40 no. 2.
Smelser, Neil J.
   1966   Mechanisms of change and adjustment to change. In *Industrialization and society,* B. F. Hoselitz and W. E. Moore ed. The Hague: UNESCO-Mouton.
Stolper, Wolfgang
   1966   *Planning without facts.* Cambridge: Harvard University Press.
Tax, Sol
   1963   *Penny capitalism.* Chicago: University of Chicago Press. (First published in 1953.)
Wolf, Eric R.
   1955   Types of Latin American peasantry. *American Anthropologist* vol. 57 no. 3.
Yudelman, Montague
   1964   *Africans on the land.* Cambridge: Harvard University Press.

BIBLIOGRAPHICAL NOTES

GENERAL

Economic anthropology is now well served by reference works in the form of books of readings, symposium volumes, and other collections of essays on its various topics. All the volumes to be mentioned in this general section include both theoretical analyses and works of empirical description. R. Firth, *Themes in Economic Anthropology*, Tavistock, 1967. R. Firth and B. Yamey, *Capital, Credit and Saving in Peasant Societies*, Aldine, 1964. K. Polanyi, C. M. Arensberg, and H. W. Pearson, *Trade and Market in the Early Empires*, Free Press, 1957. K. Polanyi, *Primitive, Archaic, and Modern Economies*, Doubleday, 1968. P. Bohannan and G. Dalton, *Markets in Africa*, Northwestern University Press, 1962. M. Sahlins, *Essays in Stone-Age Economics*, Random House, 1971. E. E. LeClair and H. S. Schneider, *Economic Anthropology*, Holt, Rinehart, 1968. R. F. Gray and P. H. Gulliver, *The Family Estate in Africa*, Boston University Press, 1964. G. Dalton, *Tribal and Peasant Economies*, Doubleday, 1967. *Economic Development and Social Change*, Doubleday, 1971. *Studies in Economic Anthropology* (*American Anthropologist*, 1971). An older volume of essays is M. Mead, *Cooperation and Competition Among Primitive Peoples*, McGraw-Hill, 1937.

There is an excellent and comprehensive three volume set of readings in economic anthropology in French, edited by M. Godelier, containing essays translated from English and German, as well, of course, as essays originally published in French. (It is to be published in 1971.) There is also to be published in 1971 a volume of readings in economic anthropology in Italian, edited by T. Tentori, containing essays translated from English, French, and German.

Several other books of readings exist which include some writings on topics in economic anthropology. J. Potter, M. Diaz, and G. Foster, *Peasant Society*, Little, Brown, 1967. A. Vayda, *Environment and Cultural Behavior*, Doubleday, 1969. Also a forthcoming volume of readings on technology edited by P. Hammond. There are collections of essays on geographical areas of the world which include writings on traditional and modernizing economies. See the books edited by A. Vayda, *Cultures of the Pacific*, NHP, 1969, and T. Harding, *Peoples and Cultures of the Pacific*, Free Press, 1970, P. Van den Berghe, *Africa: Social Problems of Change and Conflict*, Chandler, 1965; and L. Sweet, *Peoples and Cultures of the Middle East*, Doubleday, 1970.

TEXTBOOKS

Two recent brief textbook surveys are C. Belshaw, *Traditional Exchange and Modern Markets*, Prentice-Hall, 1965, and M. Nash, *Primitive and Peasant*

363

Economic Systems, Chandler, 1966. Two older and longer books are R. Thurn-wald, *Economics in Primitive Communities,* Oxford University Press, 1932, and M. J. Herskovits, *Economic Anthropology,* Knopf, 1952. Thurnwald's bibliography refers to many early works in German, Herskovits', to many in English. Several related works are D. Forde, *Habitat, Economy, and Society,* Methuen, 1934, E. Service, *The Hunters,* Prentice-Hall, 1966. M. Sahlins, *Tribesmen,* Prentice-Hall, 1968. S. Udy, *Work in Traditional and Modern Society,* Prentice-Hall, 1970. C. Gabel, *Analysis of Prehistoric Economic Patterns.*

SURVEY CHAPTERS

There are some very good single articles and chapters which either survey economic anthropology as a subject or describe the economic characteristics of traditional bands, tribes, and peasantries, or do both. D. Forde and M. Douglas, "Primitive Economics," in *Man, Culture, and Society,* Oxford University Press, 1956. M. Nash, "The Organization of Economic Life" in *Horizons of Anthropology,* Aldine, 1964. M. Sahlins, "Tribal Economics," in *Tribesmen,* Prentice-Hall, 1968. P. Cohen, "Economic Analysis and Economic Man," in *Themes in Economic Anthropology* (R. Firth ed.), Tavistock, 1967. There are several by Firth: "The Social Framework of Economic Organization," in *Elements of Social Organization,* Watts and Co., 1951. "Work and Wealth of Primitive Communities," in *Human Types,* Mentor Books, 1958. "Problems of Economic Anthropology," in *Primitive Polynesian Economy,* Routledge and Kegan Paul, 1939; revised extensively for 1966 edition. "Themes in Economic Anthropology: A General Comment," in *Themes in Economic Anthropology,* Tavistock, 1967. J. Beattie, "Economic and Property Relations," in *Other Cultures,* Free Press, 1964. M. Godelier, "The Goals and Methods of Economic Anthropology," in *Studies in Economic Anthropology* (*American Anthropologist,* 1971). The new *International Encyclopaedia of the Social Sciences* has many brief survey articles on topics in economic anthropology, each containing bibliography. E.g., the articles on "Economic Anthropology," "Peasants," "Manorial Economy," "Modernization."

SCOPE AND CONTENT OF ECONOMIC ANTHROPOLOGY

There has been much contention—regrettably, rather heated—over the best theoretical framework for analyzing tribal and peasant economies. Much of it has centered around the question of the relevance of conventional economics to the analysis of the small traditional economies anthropologists study. This literature is linked chronologically in the sense that later writers were reacting to the positions put forth by earlier writers. There are four sets of writings. (Undergraduates should be warned off some of these as being rather esoteric.)

1. Early writings

R. Firth, "Problems of Primitive Economics," in *Primitive Polynesian Economy*, Routledge and Kegan Paul, 1939, rev. ed. 1966. D. M. Goodfellow, "The Applicability of Economic Theory to So-called Primitive Communities," in *Principles of Economic Sociology*, Routledge, 1939. C. DuBois, "The Wealth Concept as an Integrative Factor in Tolowa-Tututni Culture," in *Essays in Anthropology Presented to A. L. Kroeber* (R. H. Lowie ed.), 1936. M. J. Herskovits, "Anthropology and Economics," in *The Economic Life of Primitive Peoples*, Knopf, 1940; "Economizing and Rational Behavior," "Before the Machine," and "Anthropology and Economics," in *Economic Anthropology*, Knopf, 1952. Also, M. J. Herskovits and F. Knight, "Deduction and Induction in Economics," in *Economic Anthropology* (1952). R. Firth, "The Place of Malinowski in the History of Economic Anthropology," in *Man and Culture*, Harper Torchbooks, 1957. G. C. Homans, "Social Behavior as Exchange," in *The American Journal of Sociology*, 1958.

2. The Polanyi group (substantivists)

K. Polanyi, "Societies and Economic Systems," "The Self-regulating Market and the Fictitious Commodities: Land, Labor, and Money," in *The Great Transformation*, 1944. "Our Obsolete Market Mentality," *Commentary*, 1947. "Aristotle Discovers the Economy," "The Economy as Instituted Process" in *Trade and Market in the Early Empires*, Free Press, 1957. *Dahomey and the Slave Trade*, University of Washington Press, 1966. D. Fusfeld, "Economic Theory Misplaced: Livelihood in Primitive Society," in *Trade and Market in the Early Empires* (1957). W. Neale, "The Market in Theory and History," in *Trade and Market in the Early Empires* (1957). P. Bohannan, "Some Principles of Exchange and Investment Among the Tiv," *American Anthropologist*, (1955). M. Sahlins, "Political Power and the Economy in Primitive Society," in *Essays in the Science of Culture in Honor of Leslie White*, Crowell, 1960. "On the Sociology of Primitive Exchange," in *The Relevance of Models for Social Anthropology*, Tavistock, 1965. G. Dalton, "Economic Theory and Primitive Society," *American Anthropologist*, 1961. "Traditional Production in Primitive African Economies," *Quarterly Journal of Economics* (1962). "Primitive Money" *American Anthropologist*, 1965. All three are reprinted in this volume. Additional essays by Polanyi appear in his *Primitive, Archaic, and Modern Economies;* and in Dalton, *Economic Development and Social Change*, Doubleday, 1971. Also, *Studies in Economic Anthropology* (*American Anthropological Assn.*, 1971).

3. The Anti-Polanyi group (formalists)

E. LeClair, "Economic Theory and Economic Anthropology" (*American Anthropologist*, 1962). R. Burling, "Maximization Theories and the Study of Economic Anthropology," (*American Anthropologist*, 1962). S. Cook, "The Obsolete Anti-Market Mentality: A Critique," (*American Anthropologist*,

1966). All three are reprinted in a book of readings edited by E. LeClair and H. Schneider, *Economic Anthropology*, Holt, Rinehart, 1968, a book largely devoted to the formalist-substantivist controversey. L. Robbins, *Nature and Significance of Economic Science*, Macmillan, 1935, contains an elementary account of neo-classical economic theory (on "scarcity," "maximizing," and "economizing") that is important to the formalists. Two ethnographies which apply the market approach of the formalists are L. Pospisil, *Kapauku Papuan Economy*, Yale University Publications in Anthropology No. 67, 1963, and R. Salisbury, *From Stone to Steel*, Cambridge University Press, 1962.

4. Clarifications and recent assessments

N. Smelser, "A Comparative View of Exchange Systems," *Economic Development and Cultural Change*, 1959. R. Firth, "Problems of Economic Anthropology," *Primitive Polynesian Economy*, revised ed. 1966. "Themes in Economic Anthropology," in *Themes in Economic Anthropology* (1967). P. Cohen, "Economic Analysis and Economic Man," in *Themes in Economic Anthropology* (R. Firth ed.) (1967). G. Dalton, "Introduction," in *Primitive, Archaic, and Modern Economies* (1968). "Economics, Economic Development and Economic Anthropology," *Journal of Economic Issues* (1968). "Theoretical Issues in Economic Anthropology," *Current Anthropology* (1969). Further comments on this article are to be found in *Current Anthropology* (1970 and 1971) by A. Frank, D. Hymes, and H. Dobyns. Polanyi, "A Note on Menger's Two Meanings of 'Economic,' " in *Studies in Economic Anthropology* (1971). S. C. Humphreys, "History, Economics, and Anthropology: The Work of Karl Polanyi" *History and Theory* (1969). M. Godelier, "The Goals and Methods of Economic Anthropology," in *Studies in Economic Anthropology* (1971). R. Frankenberg, "Economic Anthropology: One Anthropologist's View," in *Themes in Economic Anthropology* (R. Firth ed.), Tavistock, 1967. L. Joy, "One Economist's View of the Relationship between Economics and Anthropology," in *Themes in Economic Anthropology* (R. Firth, ed.), Tavistock, 1967. F. Cancian, "Maximization as Norm, Strategy, and Theory," *American Anthropologist* (1966). D. Kaplan, "The Formal Substantive Controversy in Economic Anthropology," *Southwestern Journal of Anthropology* (1968). M. Edel, "Economic Analysis in an Anthropological Setting," *American Anthropologist* (1969). R. Salisbury, "Anthropology and Economics," (and comments by Dalton, Belshaw, and Kasden) in *Anthropology and the Behavioral and Health Sciences* (von Mering and Kasden eds), University of Pittsburgh Press, 1970.

TRADITIONAL TRIBAL ECONOMIES

There are several important books and articles that should be read by any serious student of economic anthropology. M. Mauss, *The Gift*, Cohen and West, 1954. B. Malinowski, *Argonauts of the Western Pacific*, Routledge, 1922. *Coral Gardens and Their Magic* (vol. 1), American Book Co., 1935. *Crime and Custom in Savage Society*, Littlefield, Adams and Co., 1959. (See also the excellent book on Malinowski's work by J. P. Singh Uberoi, *Politics of the Kula Ring*, Manchester University Press, 1962.) R. Firth, *Economics of the New Zealand Maori*, 2d ed. (revised), R. E. Owen, Government Printer, Wellington, New Zealand, 1959. *Primitive Polynesian Economy*, Routledge and Kegan Paul, rev. ed. 1966. P. Bohannan and L. Bohannan, *Tiv Economy*, Northwestern University Press, 1968. Some short essays of unusually high quality are P. Bohannan, "Africa's Land," in *Tribal and Peasant Economies*, Doubleday, 1967. M. Douglas, "Lele Economy Compared with the Bushong: A Study of Economic Backwardness," in *Markets in Africa*, Northwestern University Press, 1962. M. Sahlins, "The Sociology of Primitive Exchange," in *The Relevance of Models for Social Anthropology* (M. Banton ed.), Tavistock, 1965. P. Worsley, "The Kinship System of the Tallensi," *Journal of the Royal Anthropological Institute*, 1956.

TRADITIONAL LAND TENURE AND AGRICULTURE

These are very important topics. I can mention only a few works from what is a very large literature. C. K. Meek, *Land, Law and Custom in the Colonies*, Frank Cass, 1968. I. Hogbin and P. Lawrence, *Studies in New Guinea Land Tenure*, Sydney University Press, 1967. S. Van Bath, *The Agrarian History of Western Europe, A.D. 500–1850*, Arnold, 1963. R. Dumont, *Types of Rural Economy*, Methuen, 1957. D. Biebuyck, *African Agrarian Systems*, Oxford University Press, 1963. C. Geertz, *Agricultural Involution*, University of California Press, 1963. W. Allan, *The African Husbandman*, Oliver and Boyd, 1965. P. Lloyd, *Yoruba Land Law*, Oxford University Press, 1962. H. H. Mann, *The Social Framework of Agriculture*, Frank Cass, 1968.

EARLY EXTERNAL TRADE

As is true for several other topics within economic anthropology, there are writings on early external trade by archeologists, historians, and anthropologists. C. Renfrew, "Trade and Culture Process in European Prehistory," in *Current Anthropology*, 1969. C. Gabel, *Analysis of Prehistoric Economic Patterns*, Holt, Rinehart, 1967. B. Malinowski, *Argonauts of the Western Pacific*, Routledge, 1922. E. E. Hoyt, *Primitive Trade*, Augustus M. Kelley, 1968. P. J. H. Grierson, *The Silent Trade*, publ. William Green & Sons, Edinburgh, 1903. A. Vayda, "Pomo Trade Feasts," in *Tribal and Peasant Economies* (G. Dalton ed.), Doubleday, 1967. E. W. Bovill, *The Golden Trade of the Moors*, Oxford University Press, 1958. R. Gray and D. Birmingham, *Pre-Colonial African Trade*, Oxford University Press, 1970. On "ports of trade," see the following: K. Polanyi, "Ports of Trade in Early Societies," in his *Primitive, Archaic and Modern Economies*, Doubleday, 1968. *Dahomey and the Slave Trade*, University of Washington Press, 1966. "Sortings and the 'Ounce Trade' in the West African Slave Trade," in his *Primitive, Archaic, and Modern Economies*, Doubleday, 1968. R. Arnold, "A Port of Trade: Whydah on the Guinea Coast," in *Trade and Market in the Early Empires* (Polanyi, Arensberg and Pearson eds.), Free Press, 1957. A. Chapman, "Port of Trade Enclaves in Aztec and Maya Civilizations," in *Trade and Market in the Early Empires* (Polanyi, Arensberg and Pearson, eds.), The Free Press, 1957. A. Leeds, "The Port of Trade in Pre-European India and as an Ecological and Evolutionary Type," paper presented at the American Ethnological Society meetings, 1961.

MARKETS AND MARKET PLACES

W. Neale, "The Market in Theory and History," in *Trade and Market in the Early Empires* (Polanyi, Arensberg and Pearson, eds.), Free Press, 1957. P. Bohannan and G. Dalton, *Markets in Africa,* Northwestern University Press, 1962. A. Dewey, *Peasant Marketing in Java,* Free Press, 1962. C. Geertz, *Peddlers and Princes,* University of Chicago Press, 1963. F. Benet, "Explosive Markets: The Berber Highlands." R. Arnold, "Separation of [External] Trade and [Local] Market [place]: Great Market of Whydah," both in *Trade and Market in the Early Empires* (Polanyi, Arensberg and Pearson, eds.), Free Press, 1957. G. W. Skinner, "Marketing and Social Structure in Rural China," in *Peasant Society* (Potter, Diaz and Foster, eds.), Little, Brown, 1967. M. Bloch, "Natural Economy or Money Economy: A Pseudo-Dilemma," in his *Land and Work in Medieval Europe,* Routledge and Kegan Paul, 1967. On markets in the Caribbean, see the extensive work of Sidney Mintz, including "The Role of Middleman in the Internal Distribution System of a Caribbean Peasant Economy," *Human Organization,* 1956, 15:18–23; *"Internal Market Systems as Mechanisms of Social Articulation,"* Proceedings of the 1959 Annual Spring Meeting of the American Ethnological Society, 1959, pp. 20–30; Peasant Markets, "Scientific American," 1960, 203:112–122.

PRESTIGE ECONOMY, INCLUDING BRIDEWEALTH AND PRIMITIVE MONEY

General

C. DuBois, "The Wealth Concept as an Integrative Factor in Tolowa-Tututni Culture," in *Essays in Anthropology Presented to A. L. Kroeber,* University of California Press, 1936. M. Mauss, *The Gift,* Cohen and West, 1954. K. Polanyi, "The Economy as Instituted Process," in *Trade and Market in the Early Empires,* Free Press.

Kula

B. Malinowski, *Argonauts of the Western Pacific,* Routledge, 1922.

Potlatch

H. Codere, *Fighting with Property,* J. J. Augustin, 1951. P. Drucker, "The Potlatch," in his *Cultures of the North Pacific Coast,* Chandler, 1965. "Rank,

Wealth, and Kinship in Northwest Coast Society," in *American Anthropologist* (1939). S. Piddocke, "The Potlatch System of the Southern Kwakiutl: A New Perspective," in *Southwestern Journal of Anthropology* (1966).

Primitive money

P. Bohannan, "The Impact of Money on an African Subsistence Economy," *Journal of Economic History* (1959). G. Dalton, "Primitive Money," in *Tribal and Peasant Economies*, Doubleday, 1967. K. Polanyi, "The Semantics of Money-Uses," "Archaic Economic Institutions: Cowrie Money," both in his *Primitive, Archaic and Modern Economies*. M. Douglas, "Raffia Cloth Distribution in the Lele Economy," *Africa*, 1958. "Primitive Rationing: A Study in Controlled Exchange," in *Themes in Economic Anthropology*, Tavistock, 1967. H. Codere, "Money-Exchange Systems and a Theory of Money," *Man*, 1969. L. Sharp, "Steel Axes for Stone-Age Australians," in E. H. Spicer, *Human Problems in Technological Change*, Russell Sage, 1952. P. Einzig, *Primitive Money*, Eyre and Spottiswoode, 1948. A. H. Quiggin, *A Survey of Primitive Money*, Methuen, 1949.

Bridewealth

A. R. Radcliffe-Brown, "Bride-price, Earnest or Indemnity?" in *Man*, 1929. E. E. Evans-Pritchard, "An Alternative Term for 'Bride-Price,' " in *Man*, 1931. "Social Character of Bridewealth with Special Reference to the Azande," *Man*, 1934. "Zande Bridewealth," *Africa*, 1969. R. Gray, "Sonjo Brideprice and the Question of African 'Wife Purchase,' " *American Anthropologist*, 1960. P. H. Gulliver, "Bridewealth: The Economic vs. the Non-Economic Interpretation," *American Anthropologist*, 1961. G. Dalton, "Bridewealth vs. Brideprice," *American Anthropologist*, 1966. R. M. Glasse and M. J. Meggitt, *Pigs, Pearlshells and Women*, Prentice-Hall, 1969.

STATE SYSTEMS, KINGDOMS, AND EMPIRES

A good deal more analytical work needs to be done on the economic sectors of pre-industrial state systems. Some good source material is: S. F. Nadel, *A Black Byzantium: The Kingdom of Nupe in Nigeria*, Oxford University Press, 1942. S. F. Moore, *Power and Property in Inca Peru*, Columbia University Press, 1958. J. Maquet, *The Premise of Inequality in Ruanda*, Oxford University Press, 1961. K. Polanyi, *Dahomey and the Slave Trade*, University of Washington Press, 1966. M. J. Herskovits, *Dahomey*, Northwestern University Press, 1967. A. Richards, *East African Chiefs*, Faber and Faber, 1960. J. Vansina, *Kingdoms of the Savanna*, University of Wisconsin Press, 1966. D. Forde and P. M. Kaberry, *West African Kingdoms in the Nineteenth Century*, Oxford University Press, 1967. G. Balandier, *Daily Life in the Kingdom of the Kongo*, Meridian Books, 1969.

TRADITIONAL PEASANTRIES OF LONG SETTLEMENT

Bearing in mind that the literature on traditional peasantries includes Europe, China, Japan, India, the rest of Asia, and the Middle East, and, moreover, is an old subject in history as well as a recent one in anthropology, there is indeed a great deal in print. A useful general source (which translates into English old works in several languages) is P. Sorokin *et al., A Systematic Sourcebook in Rural Sociology,* University of Minnesota Press, 1930. Another is J. Potter, M. Diaz, and G. Foster, *Peasant Society,* Little, Brown, 1967. A third is B. Moore, *Social Origins of Dictatorship and Democracy,* Beacon Press, 1967. Two survey articles are C. Geertz, "Studies in Peasant Life," in *Biennial Review of Anthropology* for 1961, Stanford University Press, 1962. G. Dalton, "Peasantries in Anthropology and History," (in the present volume).

Western Europe

M. Bloch, *French Rural History,* Routledge and Kegan Paul, 1966. H. S. Van Bath, *The Agrarian History of Western Europe,* Arnold, 1963. R. Latouche, *The Birth of Western Economy,* Harper Torchbooks, 1966. M. M. Postan, *The Agrarian Life of the Middle Ages (The Cambridge Economic History of Europe,* vol. 1), second edition, Cambridge University Press, 1966. G. Duby, *Rural Economy and Country Life in the Medieval West,* Edward Arnold, 1968.

England

F. W. Maitland, *Domesday Book and Beyond,* The Fontana Library, 1960. G. C. Homans, *English Villagers in the Thirteenth Century,* Harper Torchbooks, 1970.

Eastern Europe

G. T. Robinson, *Rural Russia under the Old Regime,* University of California Press, 1969. A. V. Chayanov, *The Theory of Peasant Economy,* Irwin, 1966. D. Warriner, *Contrasts in Emerging Societies,* Indiana U Press, 1965.

China and Japan

H. Fei, *Peasant Life in China,* Routledge and Kegan Paul, 1939. T. C. Smith, *The Agrarian Origins of Modern Japan,* Stanford University Press, 1959.

India

W. C. Neale, "Reciprocity and Redistribution in the Indian Village," in *Trade and Market in the Early Empires,* Free Press, 1957. P. M. Kolenda,

"Toward a Model of the Hindu Jajmani System," *Human Organization,* 1963. T. S. Epstein, "Productive Efficiency and Customary Systems of Rewards in Rural South India," in *Themes in Economic Anthropology* (R. Firth ed.), Tavistock, 1967. T. O. Beidelman, *A Comparative Analysis of the Jajmani System,* J. J. Augustin, 1959. W. H. Wiser, *The Hindu Jajmani System,* Lucknow Publishing House, 1958. An excellent work on post-World War II modernization of European peasantry is S. H. Franklin, *The European Peasantry,* Methuen, 1969.

LATIN AMERICAN PEASANTRIES

It is particularly important to read about Latin American peasantries in historical sequence, that is, (1) The pre-conquest civilizations of Aztec, Maya, and Inca, as well as aboriginal hunting and gathering bands. (2) The three hundred years of Spanish (and Portuguese) conquest and colonization. (3) The post-colonial period of the last one hundred and fifty years, bearing in mind that field work studies by anthropologists have been undertaken only within the last forty years. Again, there is a very large literature, particularly for the period of the Spanish conquest and since. S. F. Moore, *Power and Property in Inca Peru,* Columbia University Press, 1958. (See also the several works of J. Murra on the Inca.) "The Economic Organization of the Inca State," Unpublished Ph.D. Dissertation, University of Chicago, 1956. "On Inca Political Structure," in V. F. Ray ed., *Systems of Political Control and Bureaucracy in Human Societies* (Seattle: University of Washington Press, 1958). L. B. Simpson, *The Encomienda in New Spain,* University of California Press, 1950. F. Chevalier, *Land and Society in Colonial Mexico,* University of California Press, 1963. G. Foster, *Culture and Conquest,* Wenner-Gren Foundation, 1960. L. Hanke, *History of Latin American Civilization,* vol. 1, *The Colonial Experience,* Little, Brown, 1967. C. Gibson, *Spain in America,* Harper Torchbooks, 1966. There are now a dozen or more English translations of early works about the Spanish conquest: A. de Zarate, *The Discovery and Conquest of Peru,* Penguin Books, 1968. B. Diaz, *The Conquest of New Spain,* Penguin Books, 1963. F. L. de Gómara, *Córtes,* University of California Press, 1966.

The ideas of R. Redfield have been very influential; see his *Peasant Society and Culture,* University of Chicago Press, 1956 (and his empirical works). A good general summary of the period since the conquest is E. Wolf, *Sons of the Shaking Earth,* University of Chicago Press, 1959, ch. 8–11. Some ethnographic works concentrating on economy are C. Wagley, *Economics of a Guatemalan Village,* American Anthropological Association Memoir No. 58, 1941. S. Tax, *Penny Capitalism,* University of Chicago Press, 1953. M. Nash, *Machine Age Maya,* University of Chicago Press, 1958. G. Foster, *A Primitive Mexican Economy,* University of Washington Press, 1942. Some excellent journal articles are E. Wolf, "Types of Latin American Peasantry," *American Anthropologist,* 1955. C. Wagley and M. Harris, "A Typology of Latin American Subcultures," *American Anthropologist,* 1955. C. Erasmus, "Culture Structure and Process: The Occurrence and Disappearance of Reciprocal Farm Labor," *Southwestern Journal of Anthropology,* 1956. "Upper Limits of Peasantry and

Agrarian Reform: Bolivia, Venezuela, and Mexico Compared," *Ethnology,* 1967.

RELATED WORKS

Graduate students in particular who have a specialist's interest in economic anthropology should read a number of works written in the nineteenth and early twentieth centuries that have greatly influenced our ideas about economy and society. K. Marx, *Pre-Capitalist Economic Formations,* Lawrence and Wishart, 1964. H. Maine, *Ancient Law,* John Murray, 1906 (especially Ch. 5, "Law in Primitive Society," on the movement from status to contract; and Ch. 8, "The Early History of Property"); *Village Communities in the East and West,* Henry Holt and Co., 1889 (especially his Rede Lecture, "The Effects of Observation of India on Modern European Thought"). M. Weber, *The Theory of Social and Economic Organization,* Free Press, 1948. *General Economic History,* Free Press, 1950. E. Durkheim, *The Division of Labor in Society,* Free Press, 1949. F. Tonnies, *Community and Association* (on Gemeinschaft and Gesellschaft), Routledge and Kegan Paul, 1955. C. Bücher, *Industrial Evolution,* Burt Franklin, 1967. Also, the eminent historians of Greece, Rome, and feudal Europe: M. Rostovsteff, F. De Coulanges, F. W. Maitland, H. Pirenne, M. Bloch and M. I. Finley.

Works on comparative economic systems (written by economists) tell us about the structure of nineteenth century capitalism, its transformation into welfare states, and about Soviet-type economies: K. Polanyi, *The Great Transformation,* Rinehart, 1944. A. Sievers, *Has Market Capitalism Collapsed?,* Columbia University Press, 1949, is a detailed critique of Polanyi's book. E. H. Carr, *The New Society,* Macmillan, 1951. G. Myrdal, *Beyond the Welfare State,* Yale University Press, 1960. A. Nove, *Soviet Economy,* Praeger, 1962. For the views of two eminent economic theorists on pre-industrial economies, see J. Robinson, *Freedom and Necessity,* Allen and Unwin, 1970. J. Hicks, *A Theory of Economic History,* Oxford University Press, 1969.

Aside from modernization, there are at least two other sets of topics of common interest to anthropologists and economic and social historians. One is economic institutions existing widely in both pre-industrial and post-industrial economies, such as money, markets, and external trade. The second consists of socio-economic institutions widely existing over long periods of time which do not survive into advanced industrialization, economic development, and cultural modernization: slavery, feudalism, and peasantry. I have already referred to peasantry. On slavery, see M. I. Finley, *Slavery in Antiquity,* W. Heffer, 1960. S. Elkins, *Slavery,* University of Chicago Press, 1959. Feudalism is a particularly interesting subject, and one about which there is (as with slavery and peasantry) a massive amount of literature. For works of historians, see R. Coulborn, *Feudalism in History,* Princeton University Press, 1956. M. Bloch, *Feudal Society,* Routledge and Kegan Paul, 1961 (and his chapter in vol. 1 of the *Cambridge Economic History of Europe*). For works of anthropologists, see J. Maquet, *The Premise of Inequality in Ruanda,* Oxford University Press, 1961. J. Goody, "Feudalism in Africa?," *Journal of African History,* 1963.

"Economy and Feudalism in Africa," *Economic History Review,* 1970. J. Beattie, "Bunyoro: An African Feudality?" *Journal of African History,* 1964. S. F. Nadel, *A Black Byzantium, the Kingdom of Nupe in Nigeria,* Oxford University Press, 1942. An interesting note by K. Polanyi attempts to combine an historical and an anthropological perspective: "Primitive Feudalism and the Feudalism of Decay," in *Economic Development and Social Change* (G. Dalton ed.) Doubleday, 1971.

Finally, literature on utopian communities reveals a great deal about the larger systems the utopians were escaping from, as well as the difficulties in deliberately fabricating a Gemeinschaft, to be organized on radically different principles from the contemporary larger society of the utopians. A closely related topic, which also has affinities with economic anthropology, is the very interesting literature on "meaningfulness in work." See D. Bell, *Work and Its Discontents,* 1956, and "Meaning in Work," *Dissent,* 1956. Both are reprinted in his *The End of Ideology.*

CHANGE, DEVELOPMENT, AND MODERNIZATION

The literature on socio-economic change in the Third World has exploded in the last ten years. I shall have to be very selective. Two bibliographical sources are J. Brode, *The Process of Modernization: An Annotated Bibliography on the Sociocultural Aspects of Development,* Harvard University Press, 1969. The Agricultural Development Council (630 Fifth Avenue, New York) publishes a useful series of bibliographies on agricultural development research in various parts of the developing world.

ACCULTURATION AND THE IMPACT OF COLONIZATION

An excellent collection of readings is P. Bohannan and F. Plog, *Beyond the Frontier,* Doubleday, 1967. Another is E. Wallerstein, *Social Change: The Colonial Situation,* Wiley, 1966. For anthropological accounts of acculturation, see B. J. Siegel, *Acculturation: Critical Abstracts, North America,* Stanford University Press, 1955. G. Foster, *Culture and Conquest, America's Spanish Heritage,* Wenner-Gren Foundation, 1960. Good works on English-speaking Africa are M. Hunter, *Reaction to Conquest,* Oxford University Press, 1961. I. Schapera, *Western Civilization and the Natives of South Africa,* Routledge, 1937. For a sensitive account of everyday life of a European in the East Africa of the 1920's, see Isak Dinesen, *Out of Africa,* Random House, 1937. Also, her *Shadows in the Grass,* Random House, 1958. (Other sensitive evocations are C. Laye, *An African Child,* Fontana Books, 1959. C. Turnbull, *The Forest People,* Simon and Schuster, 1961. L. Bohannan, *Return to Laughter,* Doubleday, 1966.) Psychological approaches to the impact of colonialism are E. E. Hagen, *On the Theory of Social Change,* Dorsey Press, 1962. O. Mannoni, *Prospero and Caliban: The Psychology of Colonization,* Praeger, 1964. Also the celebrated works of F. Fanon, e.g., *The Wretched of the Earth,* Grove Press, 1966.

C. Geertz, *Agricultural Involution,* University of California Press, 1963, is an excellent account of colonial impact in Indonesia. On Occania, see W. Rivers, *Essays on the Depopulation of Melanesia,* Cambridge University Press, 1922. The literature on cargo cults is now very large: see P. Worsley, *The Trumpet Shall Sound,* MacGibbon and Kee, 1957. On that kind of colonial impact called "growth without development," see W. Watson, *Tribal Cohesion in a Money Economy,* Manchester University Press, 1958. P. Bohannan and L. Bohannan, *Tiv Economy,* Northwestern University Press, 1968. L. Mair, *Studies in Applied Anthropology,* Athlone Press, 1957. Unesco, *Social Implications of Industrialization and Urbanization South of the Sahara,* 1956. P. Bohannan and G. Dalton, *Markets in Africa,* Northwestern University Press, 1962.

INTRODUCTORY SURVEYS ON MODERNIZATION

G. Hunter, *Modernizing Peasant Societies,* Oxford University Press, 1969, is an excellent book. There are also several written by anthropologists: I. Hogbin, *Social Change,* Watts, 1958. P. Worsley, *The Third World,* Weidenfeld and Nicolson, 1964. P. Lloyd, *Africa in Social Change,* Penguin Books, 1967. L. Mair, *The New Nations,* Weidenfeld and Nicolson, 1963. A book of readings is G. Dalton, *Economic Development and Social Change,* Doubleday, 1971. See also the symposium volumes, R. Firth and B. Yamey, *Capital, Saving, and Credit in Peasant Societies,* Aldine, 1964. M. J. Herskovits, *Economic Transition in Africa,* Northwestern University Press, 1964.

INTRODUCTORY WORKS ON
MACRO-ECONOMIC DEVELOPMENT

Economists who write on national economic development in such a way as to illuminate matters of interest to other social scientists are: G. Myrdal, *Rich Lands and Poor,* Harper, 1957. Myrdal, G., *Asian Drama,* Pantheon, 1968. W. A. Lewis, *The Theory of Economic Growth,* Allen and Unwin, 1955. H. Singer, *International Development,* McGraw-Hill, 1964. (See especially the essays, "The Distribution of Gains between Borrowing and Lending Countries," and "The Mechanics of Development.") A. Hirschman, *The Strategy of Economic Development,* Yale University Press, 1958. E. E. Hagen, *On the Theory of Social Change,* Dorsey Press, 1962. I. Adelman and C. T. Morris, *Society, Politics, and Economic Development,* Johns Hopkins Press, 1967. See K. Martin and J. Knapp, *The Teaching of Development Economics,* Aldine, 1967, for a symposium discussion of the relevance and adequacy of formal economics to the processes and problems of economic development in the Third World; this discussion is quite similar to the debate between formalists and substantivists in economic anthropology. A good book of readings in economic development is by G. Meier, *Leading Issues in Economic Development,* Oxford University Press, 1970. Some good textbooks are those of H. Myint, *The Economics of Developing Countries,* Hutchinson, 1964, and E. E. Hagen, *The Economics of Development,* Irwin, 1968. An excellent collection of essays on African development is P. Robson and D. A. Lury, *The Economies of Africa,* Allen and Unwin, 1969. An older collection is E. A. G. Robinson, *Economic Development for Africa South of the Sahara,* Macmillan, 1956. Some good books on problems and methods of quantification and statistical measurement are P. Deane, *Colonial Social Accounting,* Cambridge University Press, 1953. L. H. Samuels, *African Studies in Income and Wealth,* Quadrangle, 1963. B. Van Arkadie and C. Frank, *Economic Accounting and Development Planning,* Oxford University Press, 1966.

APPLIED ANTHROPOLOGY

The journal *Human Organization* is almost entirely devoted to applied anthropology. Some good general works are those of G. Foster, *Applied Anthropology,* Little, Brown, 1969; *Traditional Cultures: and the Impact of Technological Change,* Harper & Row, 1962; C. Erasmus, *Man Takes Control,* University of Minnesota Press, 1961; and W. Goodenough, *Cooperation in Change,* Russell Sage Foundation, 1963. Symposium volumes and books of case studies are those by E. Spicer, *Human Problems in Technological Change,* Russell Sage Foundation, 1952, and A. Niehoff, *A Casebook of Social Change,* Aldine, 1966. A book that should be better known (it is in English but was published in Holland) is P. Ruopp, *Approaches to Community Development,* Van Heuve, 1953. The literature on Vicos is very good indeed. See the six articles, "The Vicos Case" in *The American Behavioral Scientist,* March 1965, which also gives an extensive bibliography on Vicos.

MICRO-DEVELOPMENT

These are works on post-colonial village development and modernization written from an anthropological perspective, but are not descriptions of visiting experts transmitting innovations. The best of these is T. S. Epstein, *Economic Development and Social Change in South India,* Manchester University Press, 1962. See also her *Capitalism, Primitive and Modern,* Michigan State University Press, 1968. R. Firth, *Social Change in Tikopia,* Allen and Unwin, 1959. *Malay Fishermen,* Routledge and Kegan Paul, 2nd ed. 1966. S. C. Dube, *India's Changing Villages,* Routledge and Kegan Paul, 1958. There is a growing number of informative works on agricultural development: C. Wharton, *Subsistence Agriculture and Economic Development,* Aldine, 1970. L. R. Brown, *Seeds of Change: The Green Revolution and Development,* Praeger, 1970. J. Mellor *et al., Developing Rural India,* Cornell University Press, 1968. P. McLoughlin, *African Food Production Systems,* Johns Hopkins University Press, 1970.

Index

377